Pearl Pink Vol. 1
Created by Meca Tanaka

Translation - Adrienne Beck
English Adaption - Jamie Rich
Layout and Lettering - Gavin Hignight
Cover Layout - Jason Milligan

Editor - Katherine Schilling
Digital Imaging Manager - Chris Buford
Pre-Production Supervisor - Erika Terriquez
Art Director - Anne Marie Horne
Production Manager - Elisabeth Brizzi
VP of Production - Ron Klamert
Editor-in-Chief - Rob Tokar
Publisher - Mike Kiley
President and C.O.O. - John Parker
C.E.O. and Chief Creative Officer - Stuart Levy

A **TOKYOPOP** Manga

TOKYOPOP Inc.
5900 Wilshire Blvd. Suite 2000
Los Angeles, CA 90036

E-mail: info@TOKYOPOP.com
Come visit us online at www.TOKYOPOP.com

TENNEN PEARL PINK by Meca Tanaka
© 2002 Meca Tanaka All rights reserved.
First published in Japan in 2002 by HAKUSENSHA, INC., Tokyo
English language translation rights in the United States of
America and Canada arranged with HAKUSENSHA, INC., Tokyo
through Tuttle-Mori Agency Inc., Tokyo
English text copyright © 2007 TOKYOPOP Inc.

ISBN: 978-1-59816-775-7

First TOKYOPOP printing: January 2007
10 9 8 7 6 5 4 3 2 1
Printed in the USA

Pearl Pink™

Volume 1

Meca Tanaka

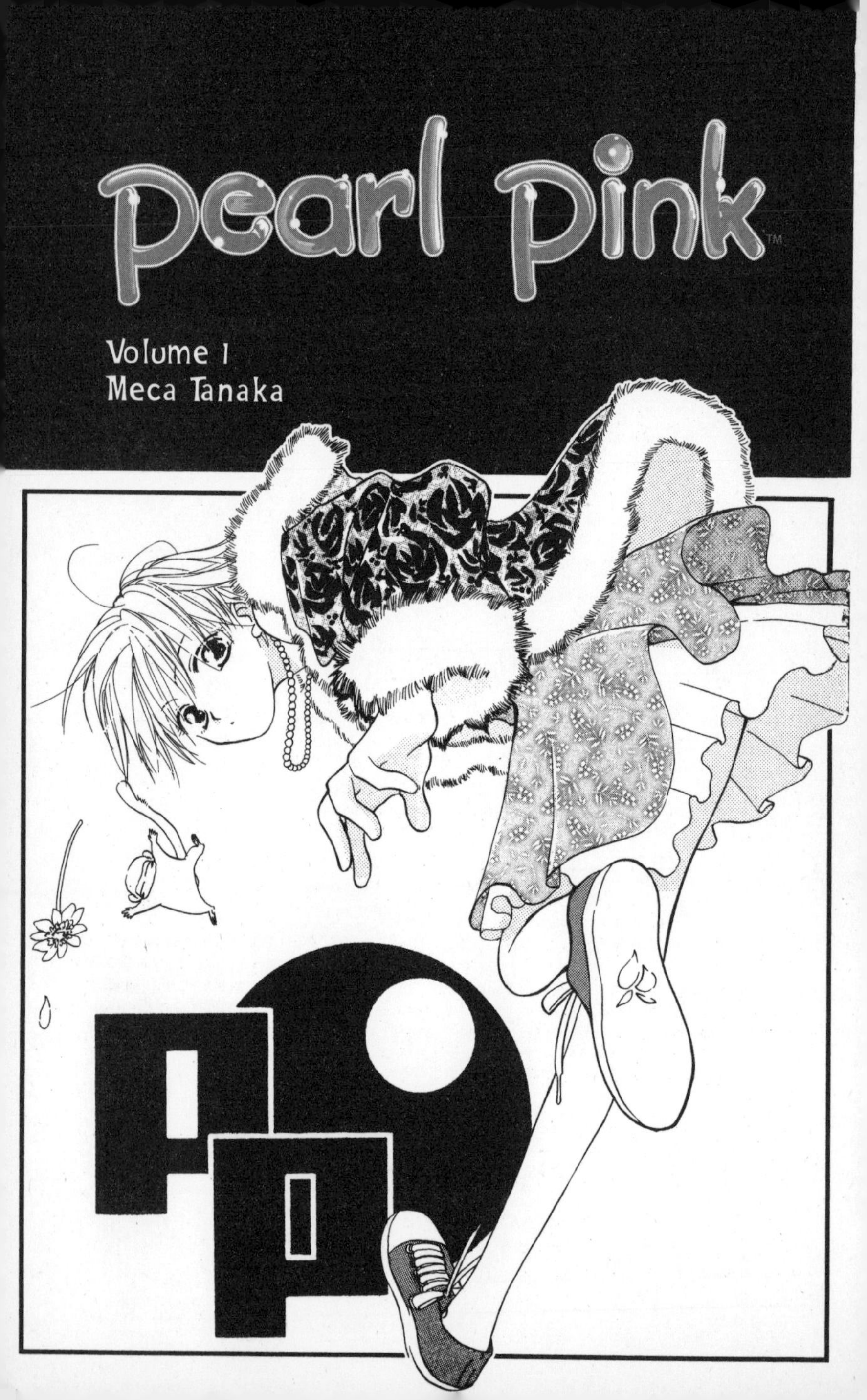

Contents

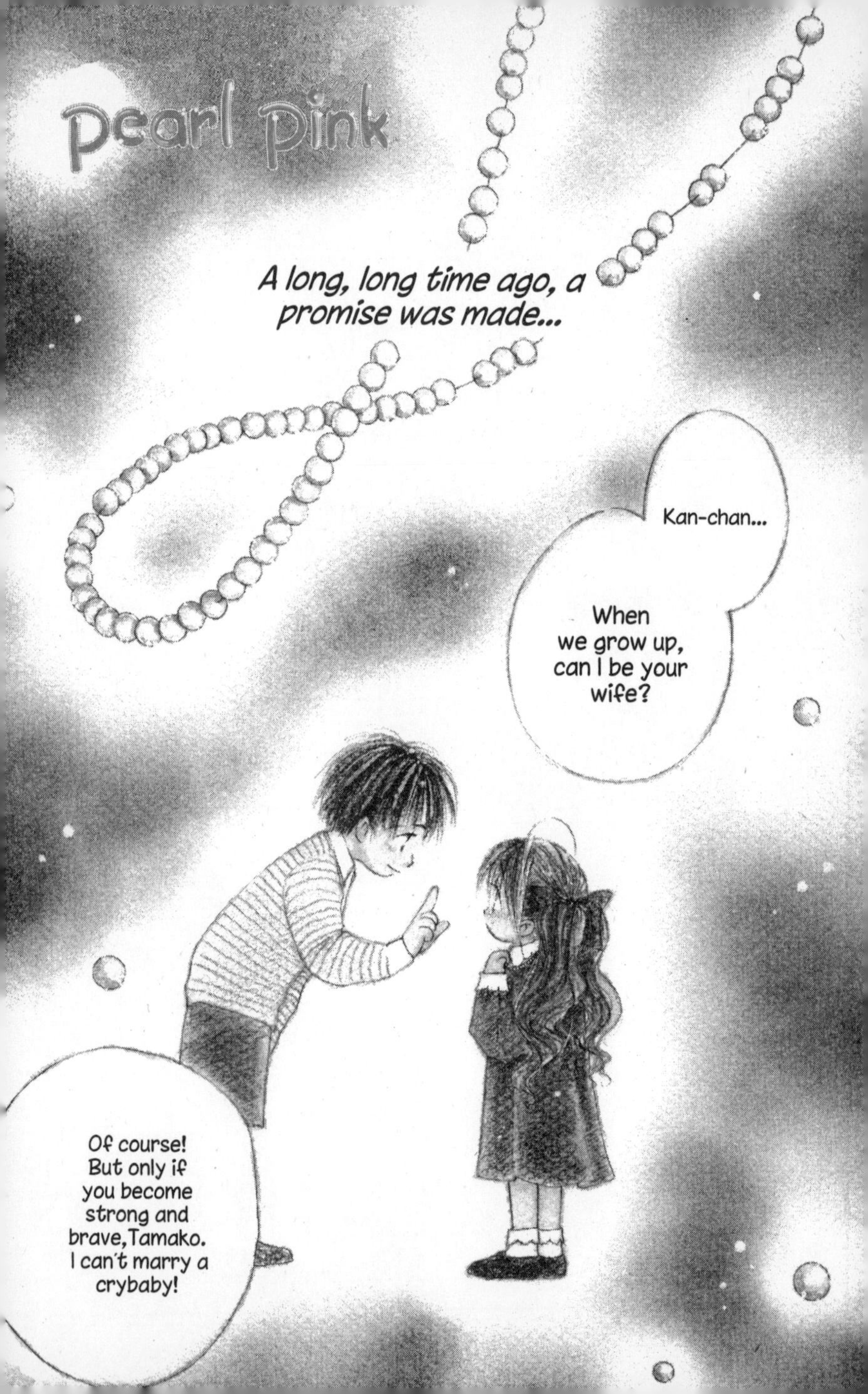
Pearl Pink
A long, long time ago, a promise was made...
Kan-chan...
When we grow up, can I be your wife?
Of course! But only if you become strong and brave, Tamako. I can't marry a crybaby!

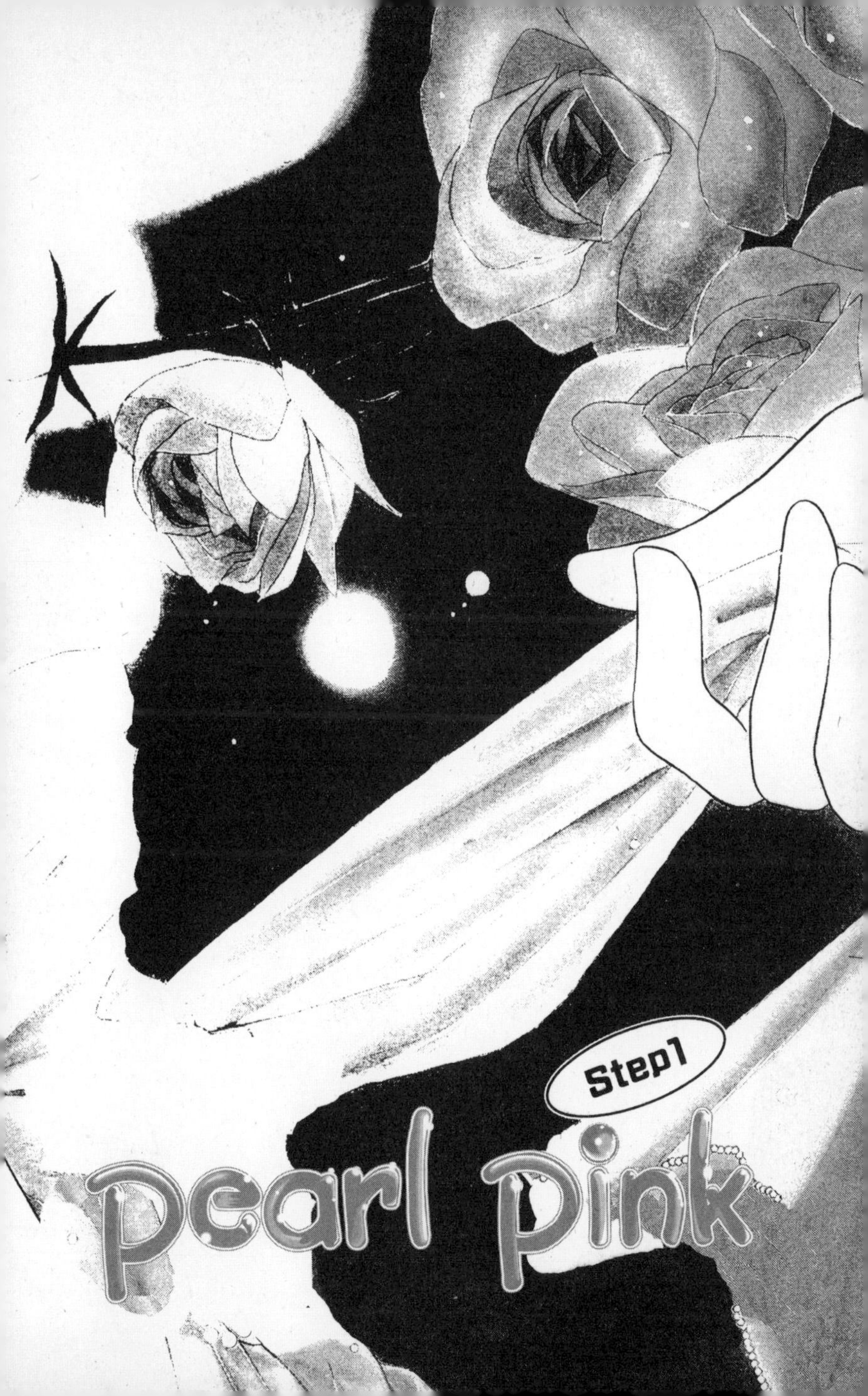
Step1
Pearl Pink

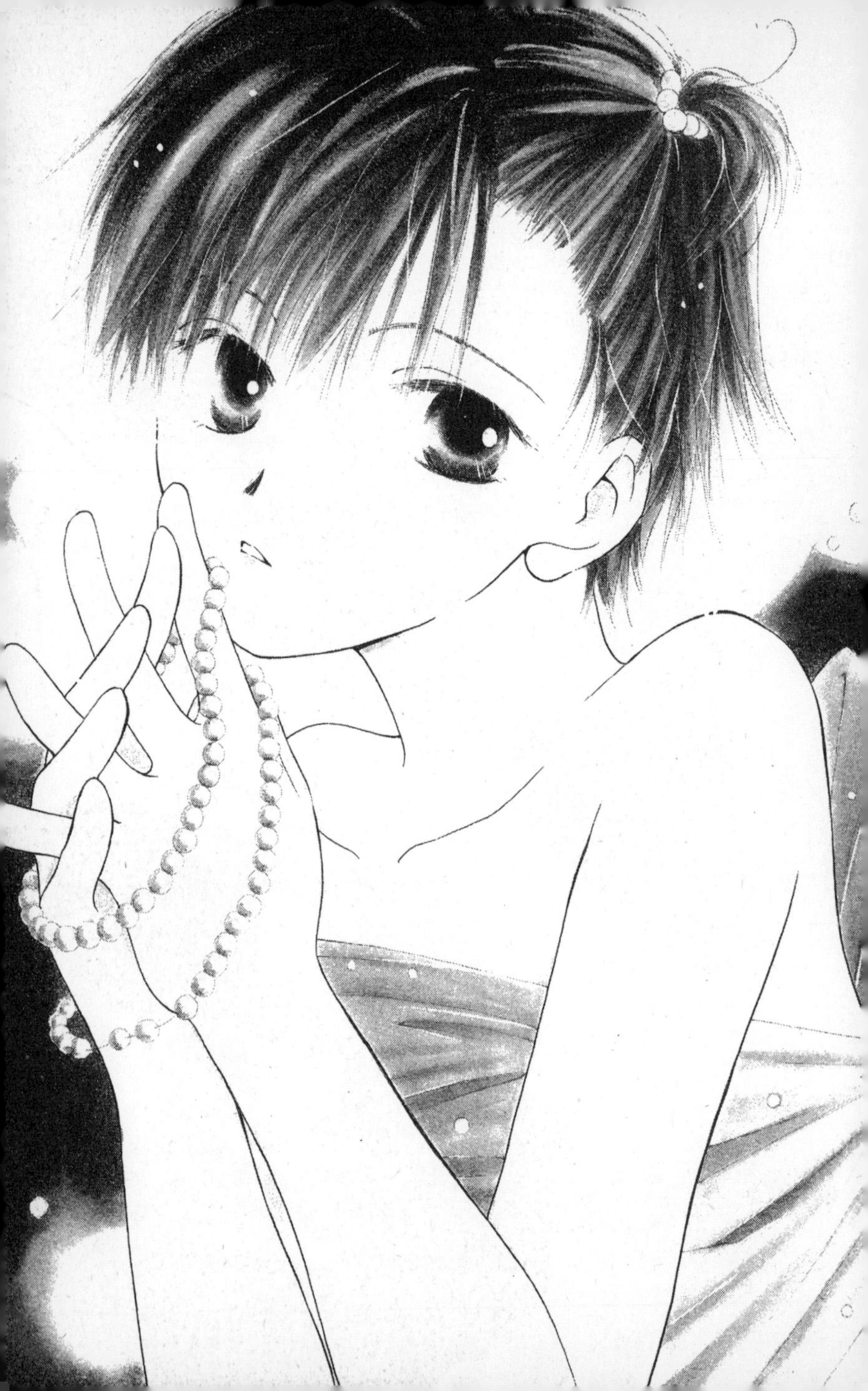

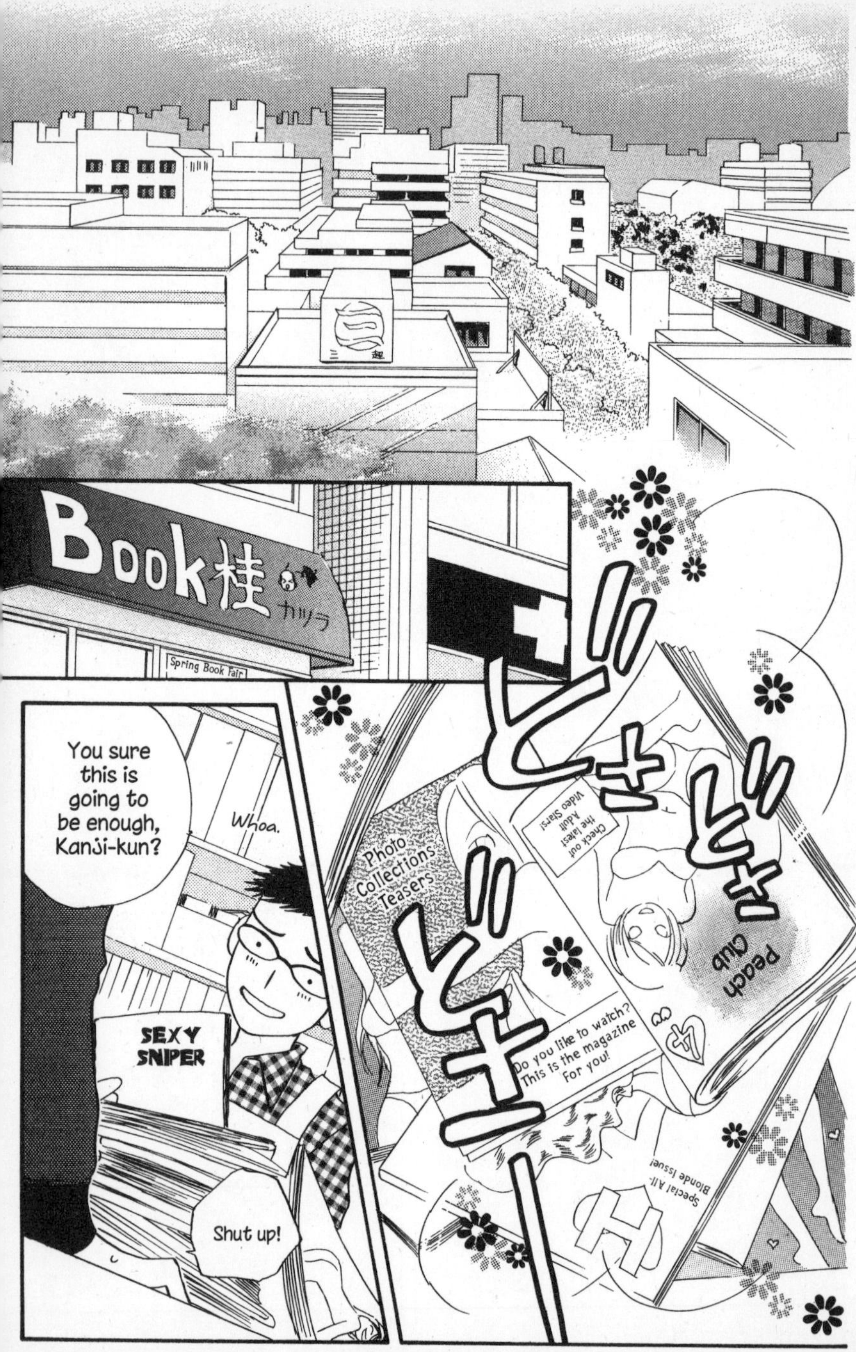

Book 桂
カツラ
Spring Book Fair
どき
どき
どきー
Check out the latest Adult Video Stars!
Peach Club
Photo Collections Teasers
Do you like to watch? This is the magazine For you!
Special All-Blonde Issue!
You sure this is going to be enough, Kanji-kun?
Whoa.
SEXY SNIPER
Shut up!

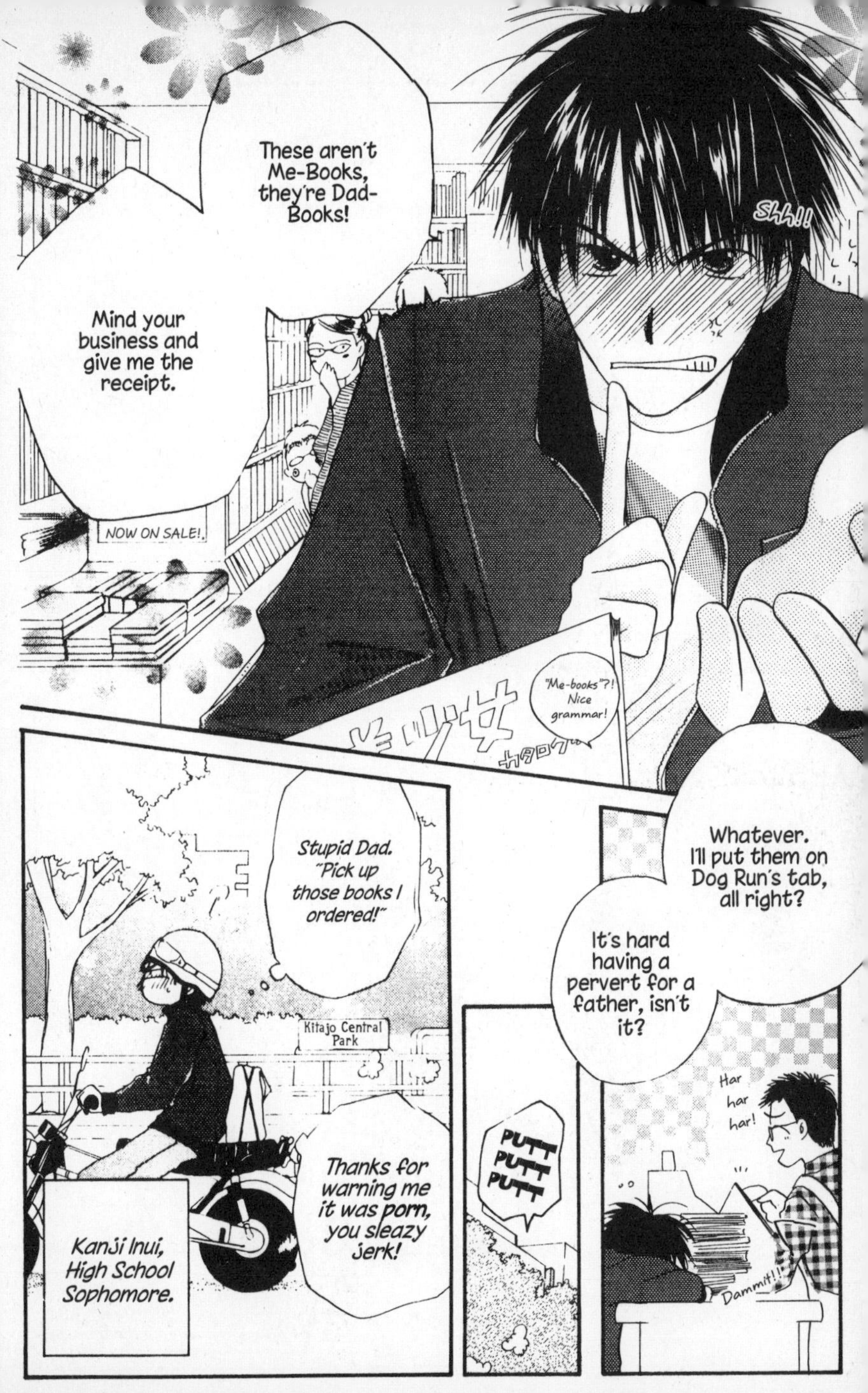

Shh!!
These aren't Me-Books, they're Dad-Books!
Mind your business and give me the receipt.
NOW ON SALE!
"Me-books"?! Nice grammar!
Whatever. I'll put them on Dog Run's tab, all right?
It's hard having a pervert for a father, isn't it?
Har har har!
Dammit!!
PUTT PUTT PUTT
Stupid Dad. "Pick up those books I ordered!"
Kitajo Central Park
Thanks for warning me it was porn, you sleazy jerk!
Kanji Inui, High School Sophomore.

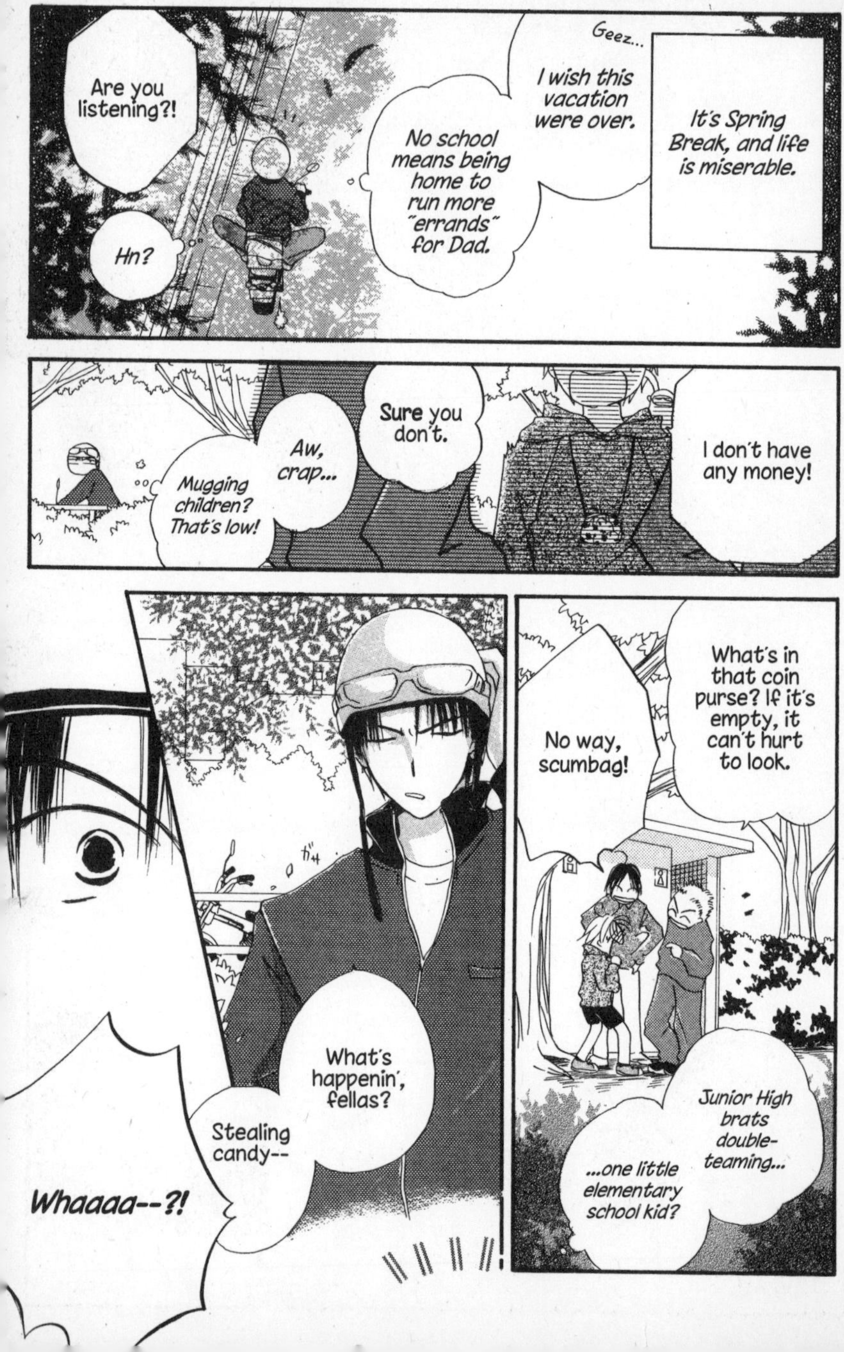

It's Spring Break, and life is miserable.
Geez...
I wish this vacation were over.
No school means being home to run more "errands" for Dad.
Are you listening?!
Hn?
I don't have any money!
Sure you don't.
Aw, crap...
Mugging children? That's low!
What's in that coin purse? If it's empty, it can't hurt to look.
No way, scumbag!
Junior High brats double-teaming...
...one little elementary school kid?
What's happenin', fellas?
Stealing candy--
Whaaaa--?!

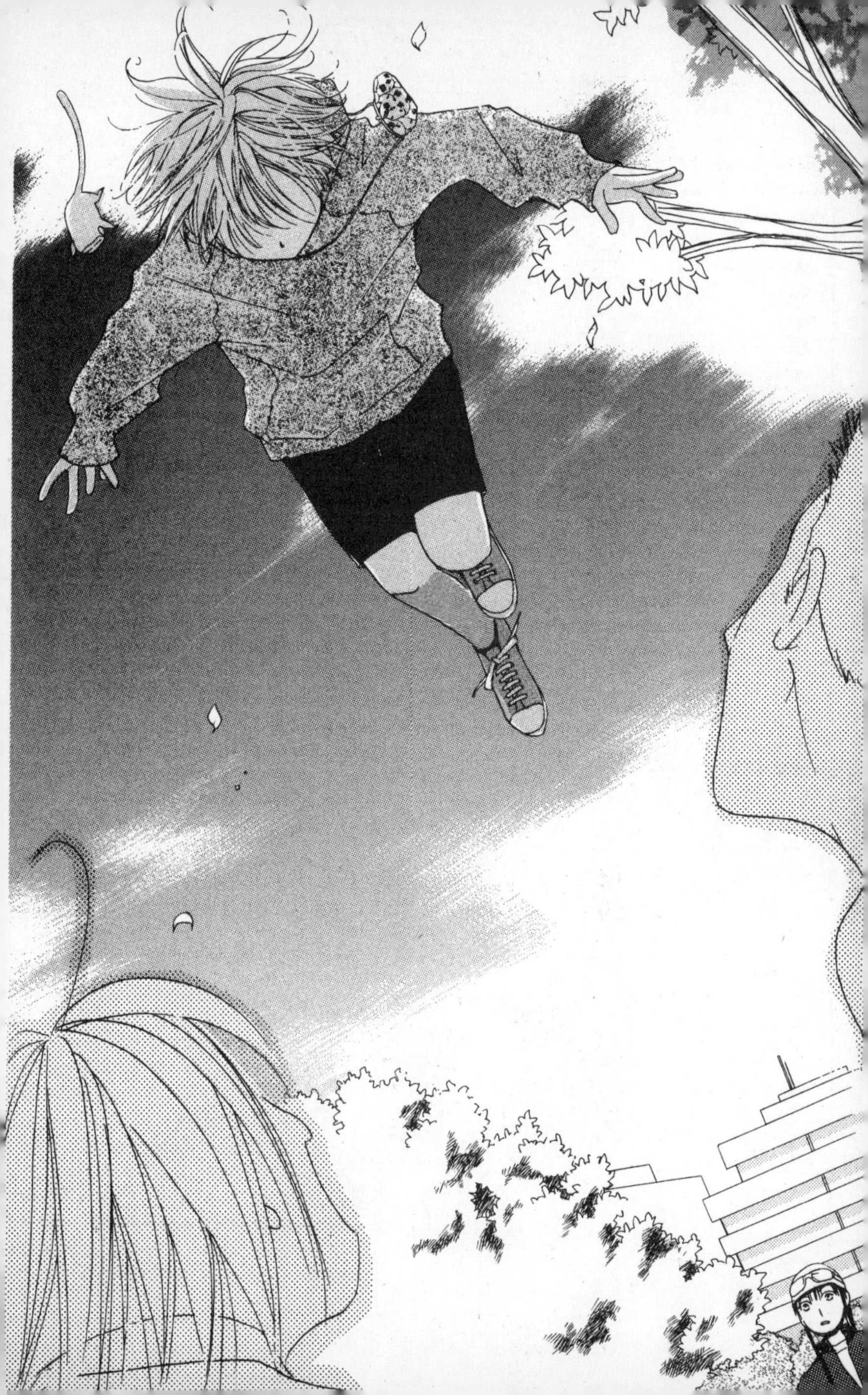

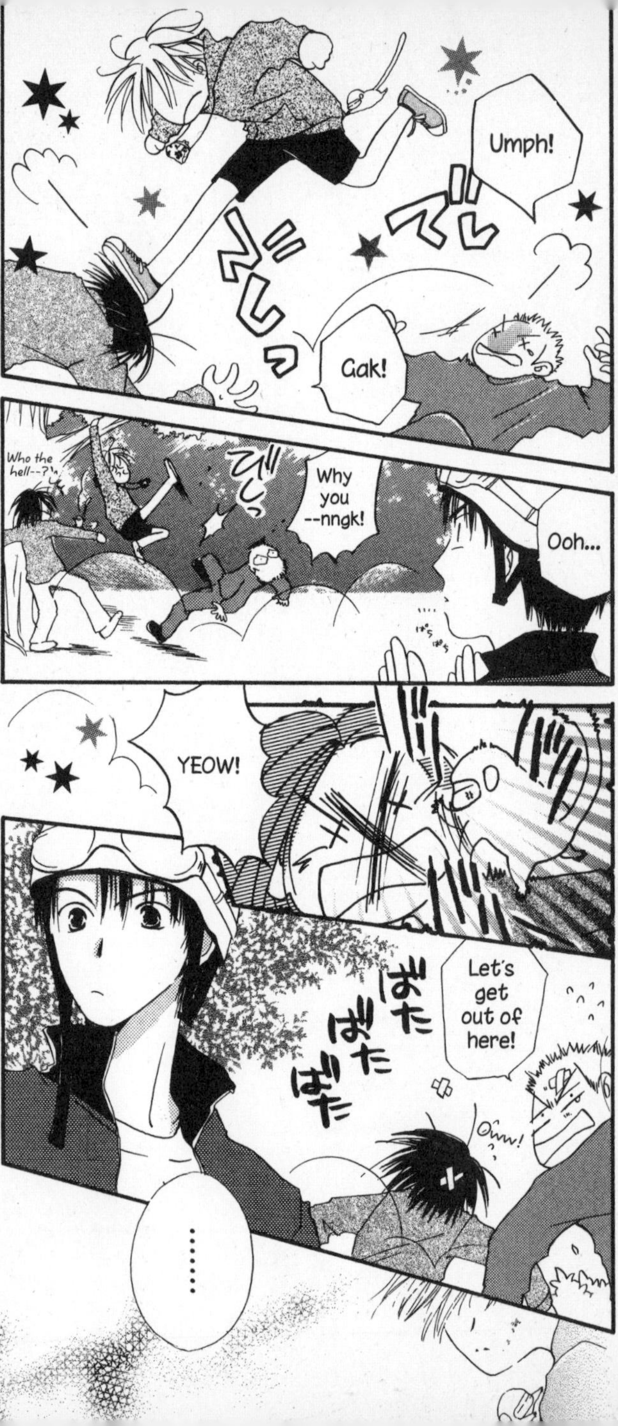
Umph!
Gak!
Ooh...
Why you --nngk!
Who the hell--?!
YEOW!
Let's get out of here!
ばた ばた ばた
Owww!
......

My 6th Manga. Woot!

Hello, everyone! How do you do? My name is Meca Tanaka, and this is the sixth collected volume of my comics. Yay! I'm so happy!

Pearl Pink is really different from my other stories, and so I imagine my old fans are kind of confused. My apologies, dear readers. I assure you that you're nowhere near as confused as I am.

Part of it is this is my very first "serial" manga. I've thrown myself so deep into this story, my assistants probably think I'm nuts. It will be worth it if you folks out there get into it, though.

All right, then! From here on out, I'll use this space for whatever strikes my fancy.

Woo hoo! Let's go!

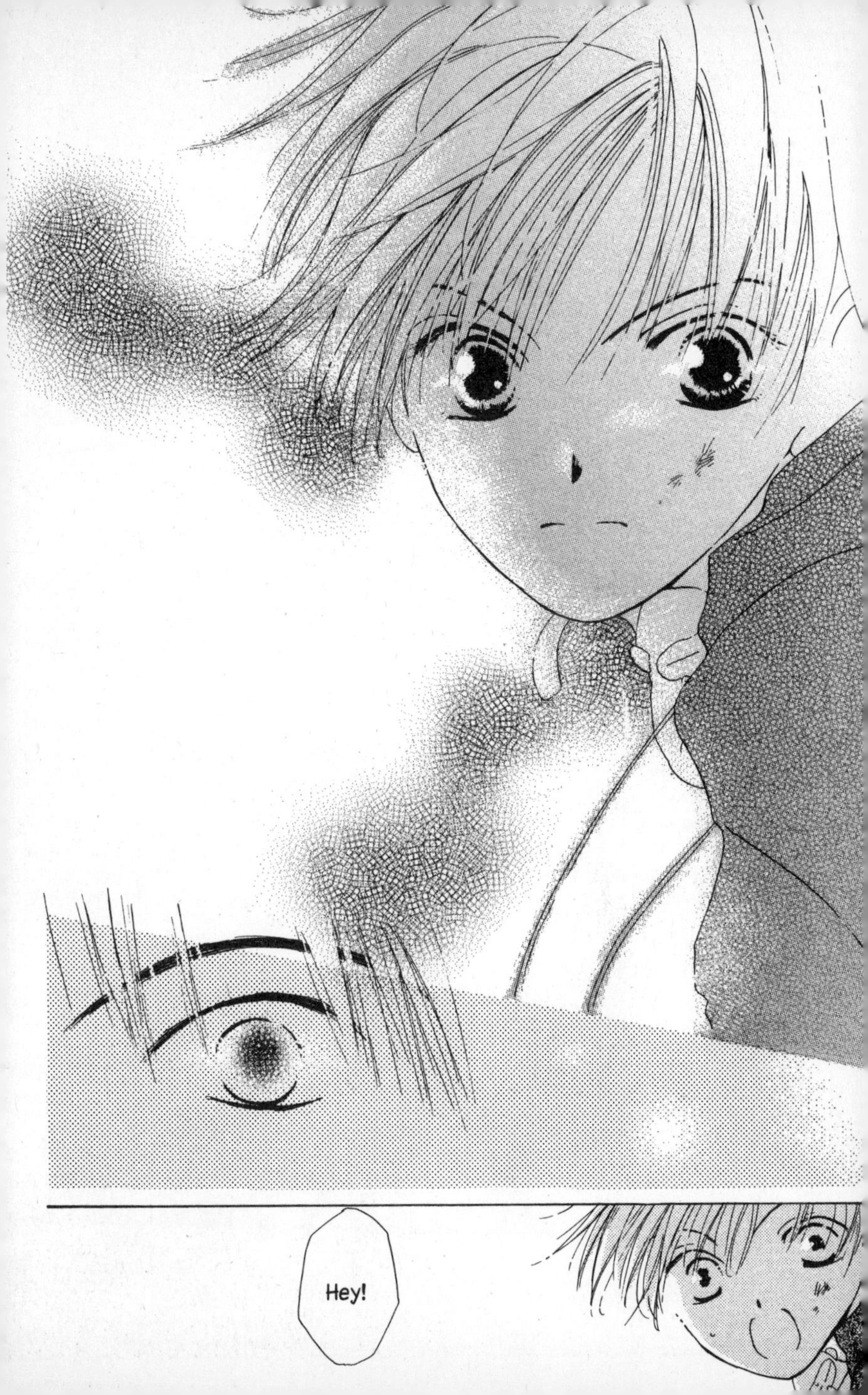
Hey!

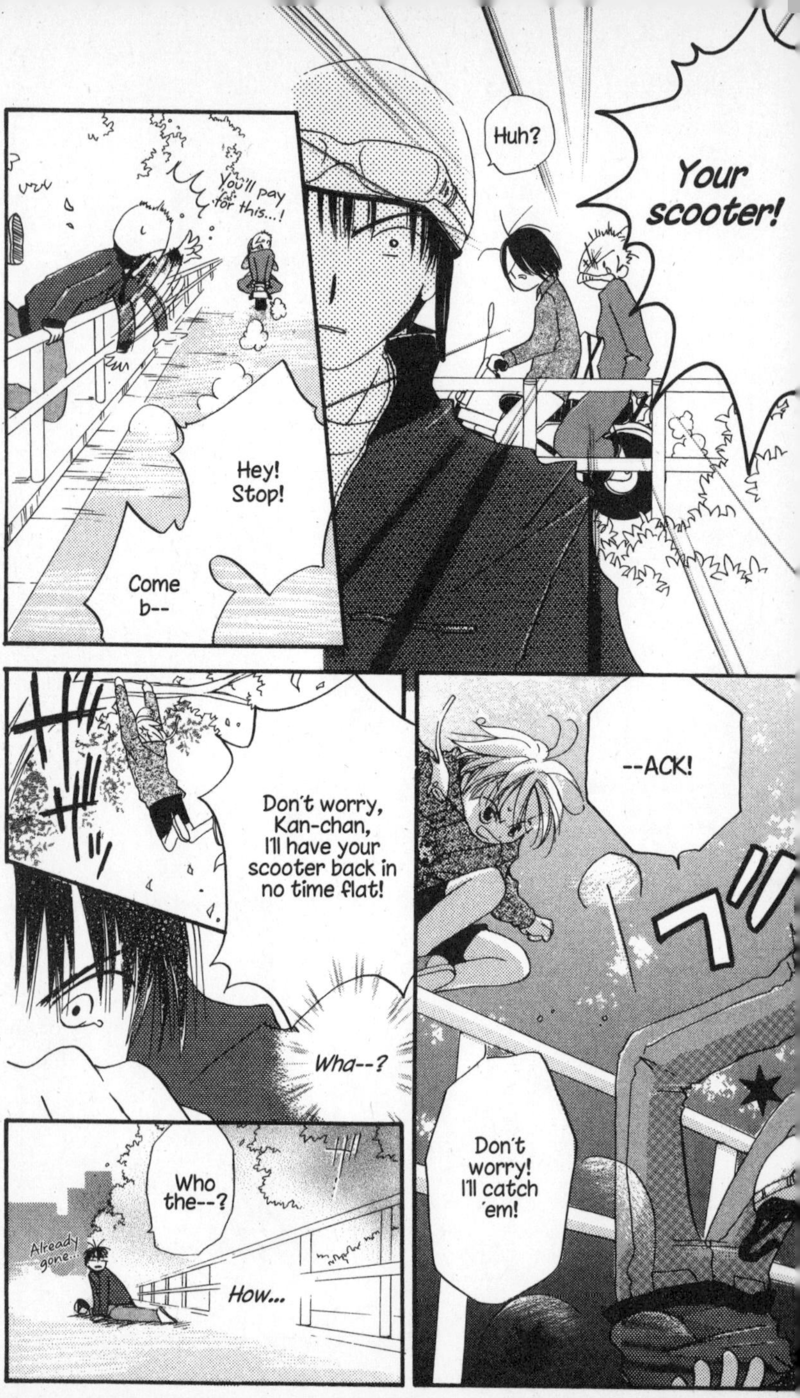
Your scooter!
Huh?
You'll pay for this...!
Hey! Stop!
Come b--
--ACK!
Don't worry! I'll catch 'em!
Don't worry, Kan-chan, I'll have your scooter back in no time flat!
Wha--?
Who the--?
Already gone...
How...

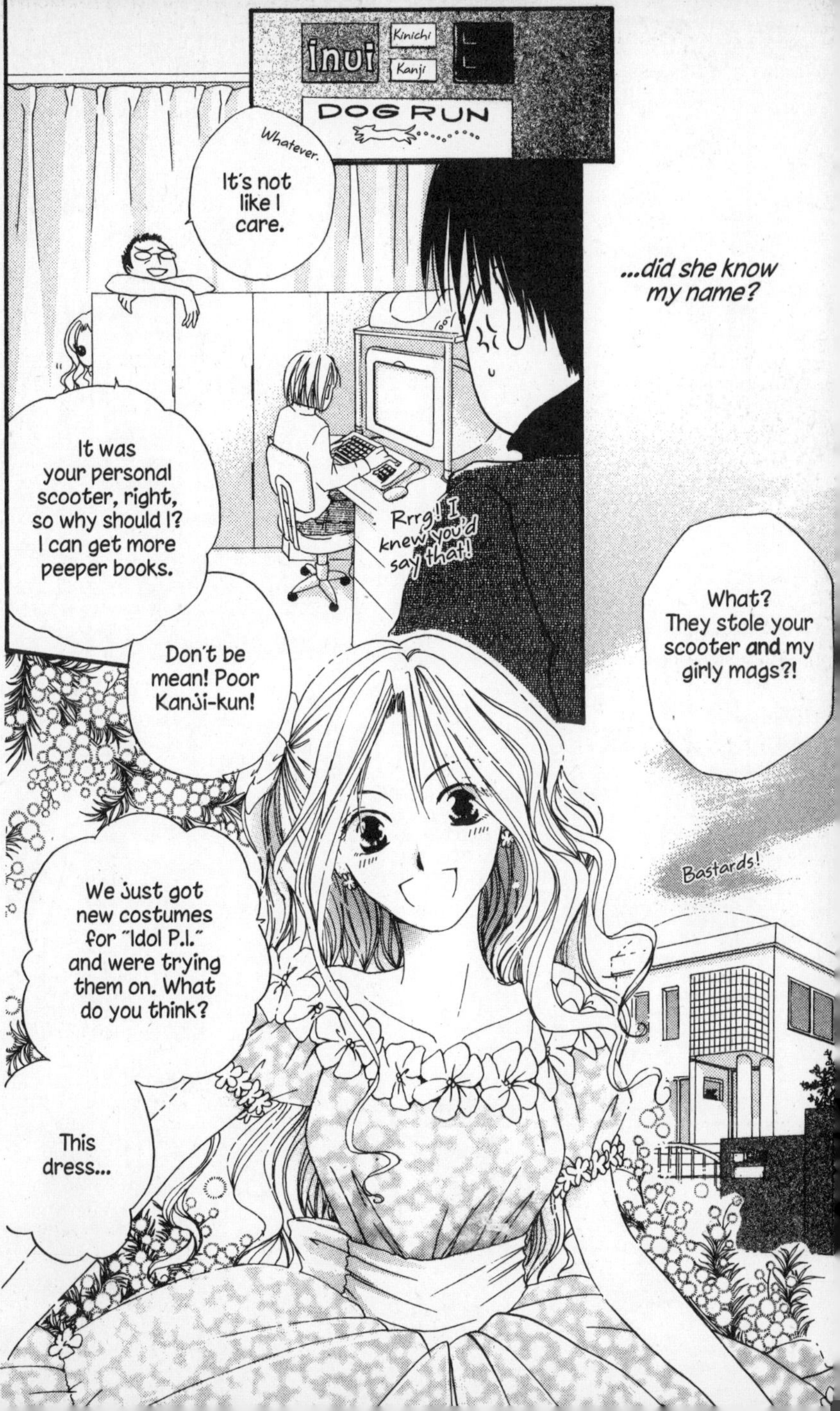
...did she know my name?
What? They stole your scooter and my girly mags?!
Bastards!
Inui
Kinichi
Kanji
DOG RUN
Whatever.
It's not like I care.
It was your personal scooter, right, so why should I? I can get more peeper books.
Rrrg! I knew you'd say that!
Don't be mean! Poor Kanji-kun!
We just got new costumes for "Idol P.I." and were trying them on. What do you think?
This dress...

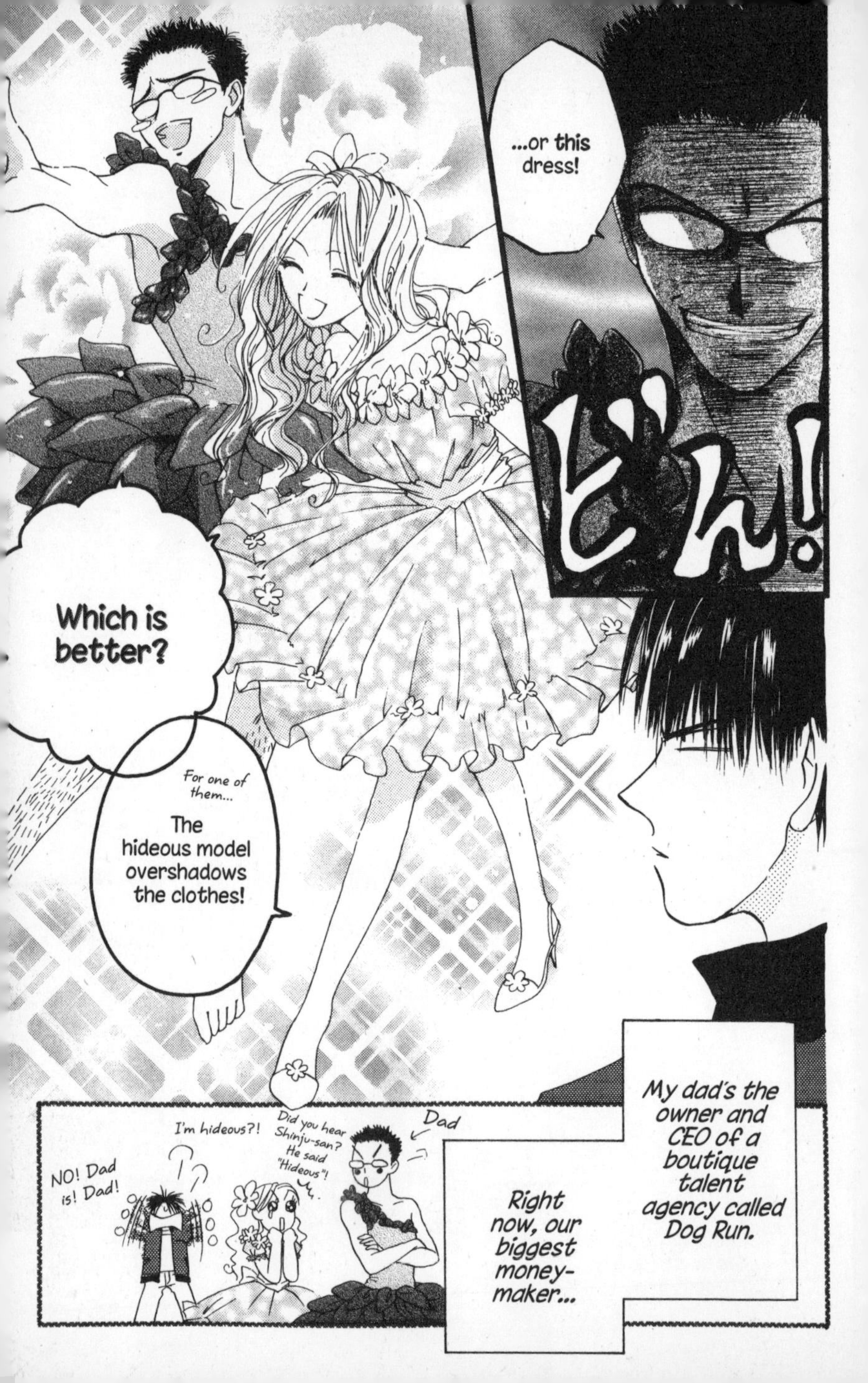
...or this dress!
どん!
Which is better?
For one of them...
The hideous model overshadows the clothes!
My dad's the owner and CEO of a boutique talent agency called Dog Run.
Right now, our biggest money-maker...
Dad
Did you hear Shinju-san? He said "Hideous"!
I'm hideous?!
NO! Dad is! Dad!

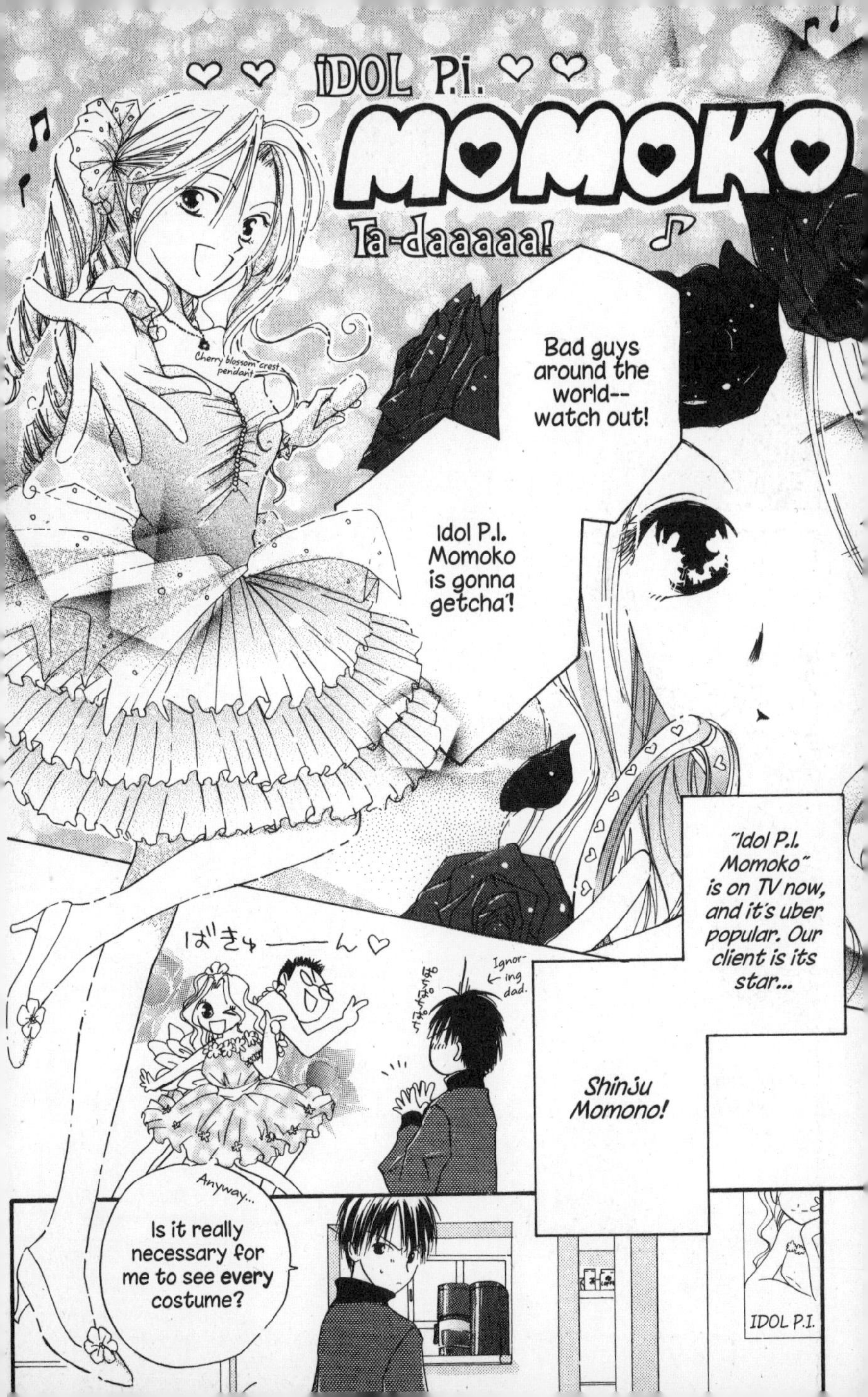
iDOL P.i.
MOMOKO
Ta-daaaaa!
Cherry blossom crest pendant
Bad guys around the world-- watch out!
Idol P.I. Momoko is gonna getcha'!
"Idol P.I. Momoko" is on TV now, and it's uber popular. Our client is its star...
Shinju Momono!
ばきゅーーん♡
Ignor-ing dad.
Anyway...
Is it really necessary for me to see every costume?
IDOL P.I.

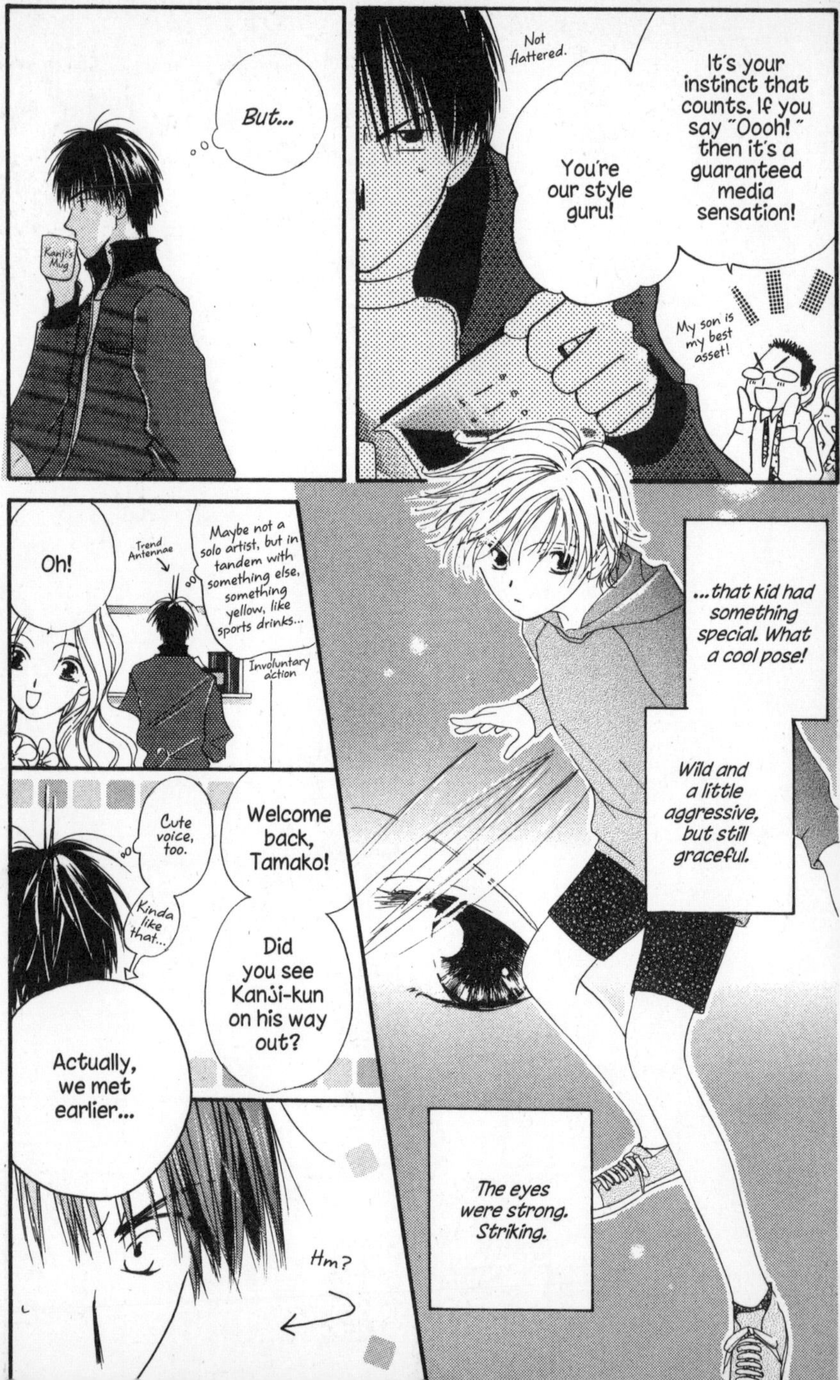
It's your instinct that counts. If you say "Oooh!" then it's a guaranteed media sensation!
You're our style guru!
Not flattered.
My son is my best asset!
But...
...that kid had something special. What a cool pose!
Wild and a little aggressive, but still graceful.
The eyes were strong. Striking.
Maybe not a solo artist, but in tandem with something else, something yellow, like sports drinks...
Trend Antennae
Oh!
Involuntary action
Kanji's Mug
Welcome back, Tamako!
Did you see Kanji-kun on his way out?
Cute voice, too.
Kinda like that...
Actually, we met earlier...
Hm?

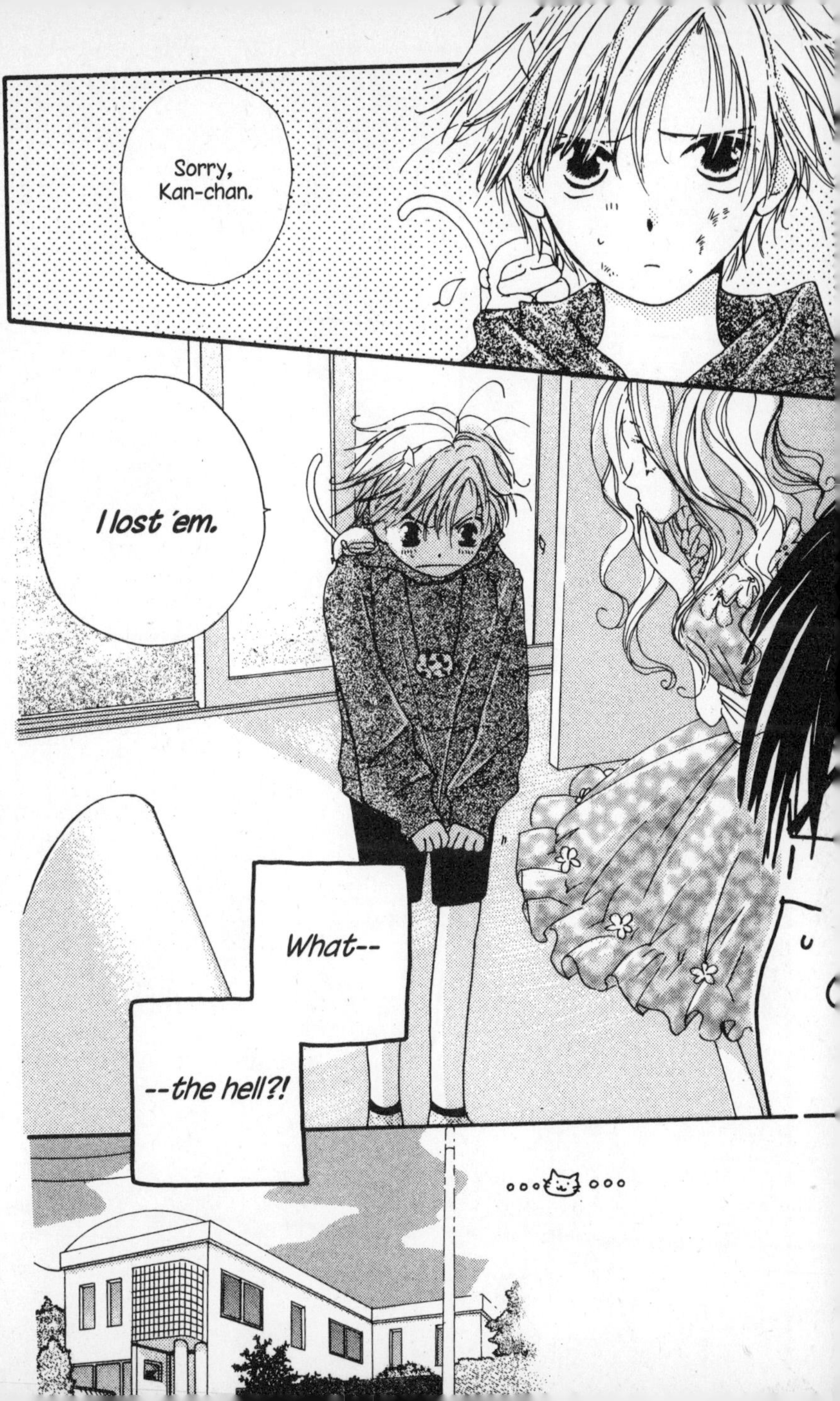
Sorry, Kan-chan.
I lost 'em.
What--
--the hell?!
ooo ooo

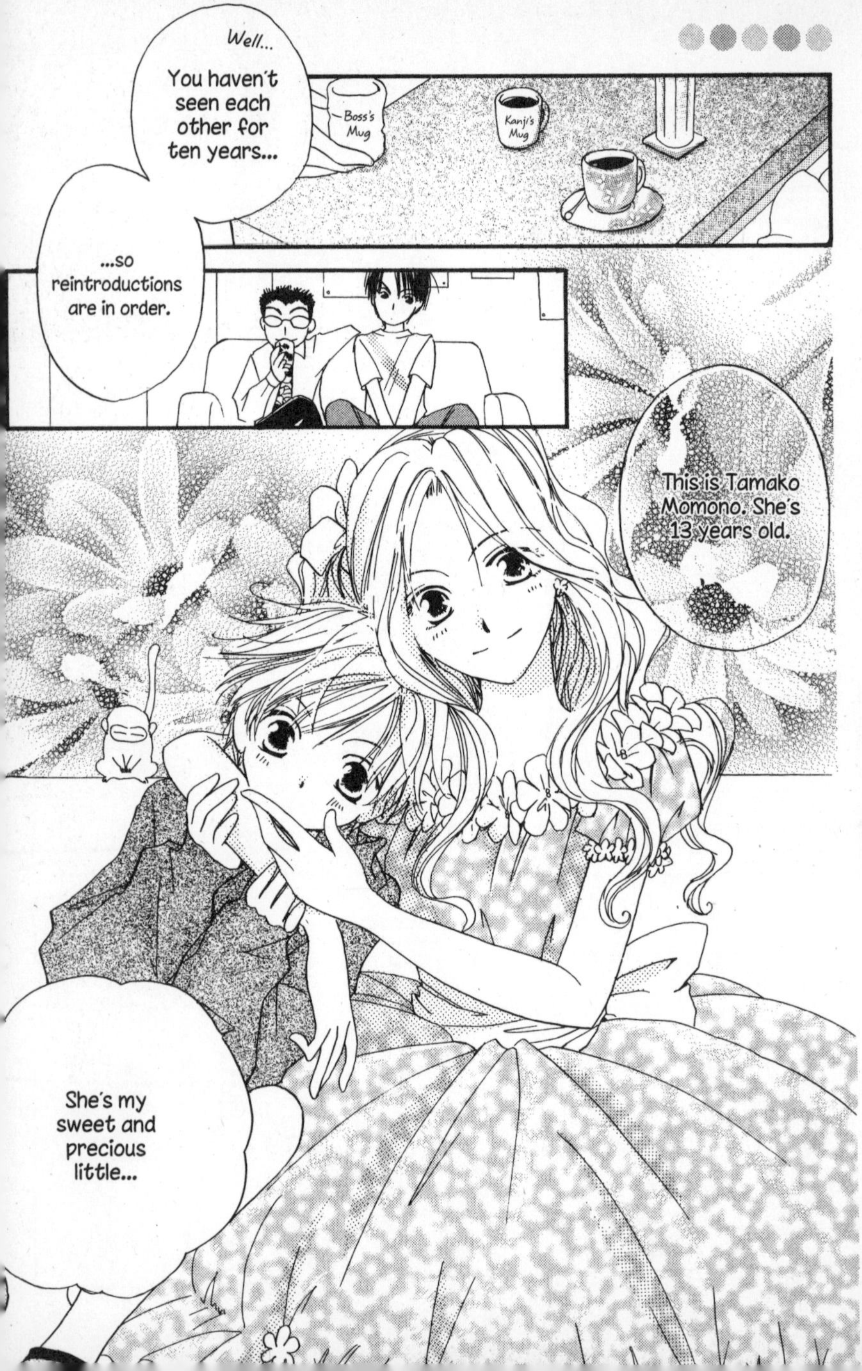
Kanji's Mug
Boss's Mug
Well...
You haven't seen each other for ten years...
...so reintroductions are in order.
This is Tamako Momono. She's 13 years old.
She's my sweet and precious little...

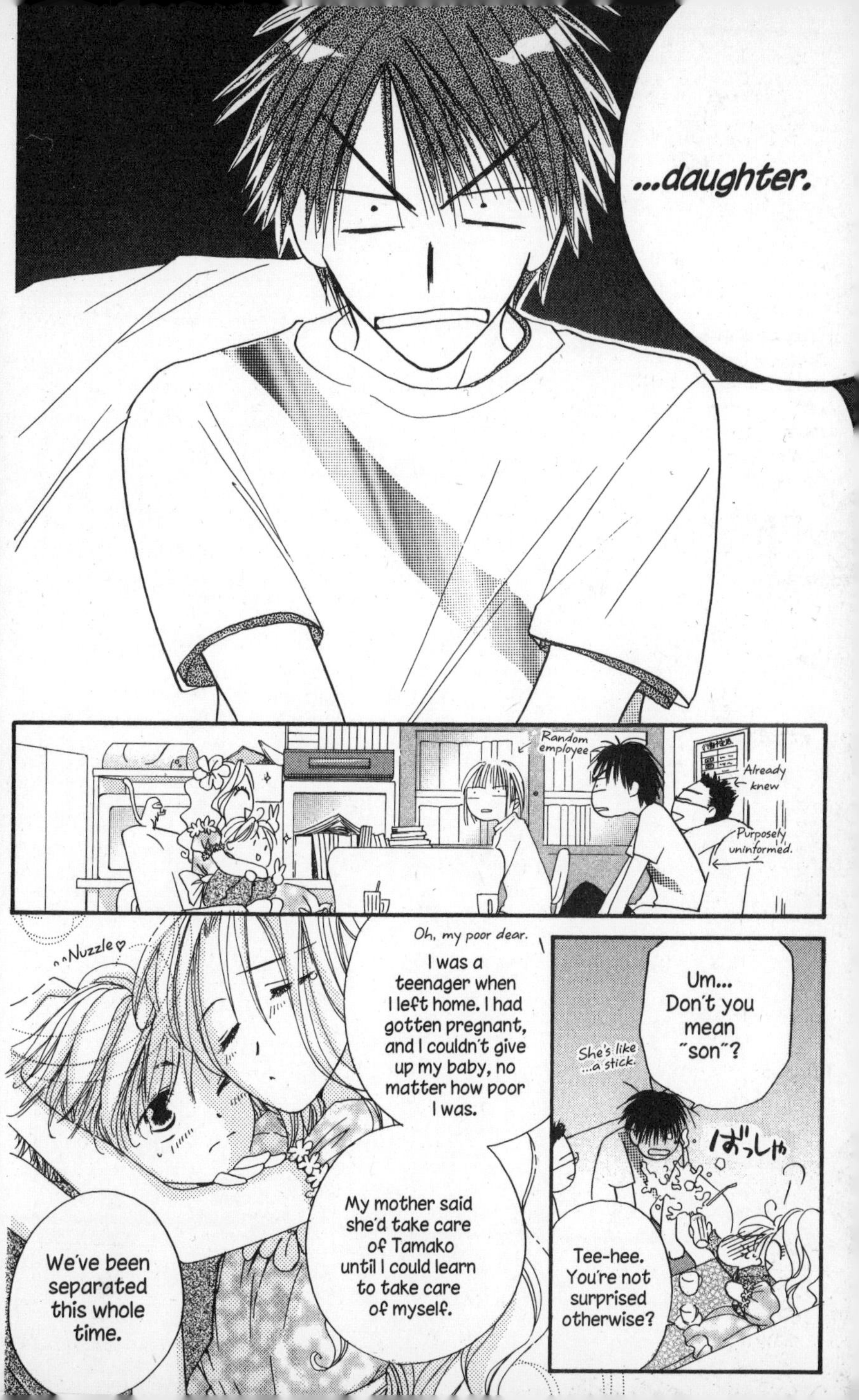
...daughter.
Already knew
Purposely uninformed.
Random employee
Um... Don't you mean "son"?
She's like ...a stick.
ぱっしゃ
Tee-hee. You're not surprised otherwise?
Oh, my poor dear.
I was a teenager when I left home. I had gotten pregnant, and I couldn't give up my baby, no matter how poor I was.
My mother said she'd take care of Tamako until I could learn to take care of myself.
We've been separated this whole time.
Nuzzle♡

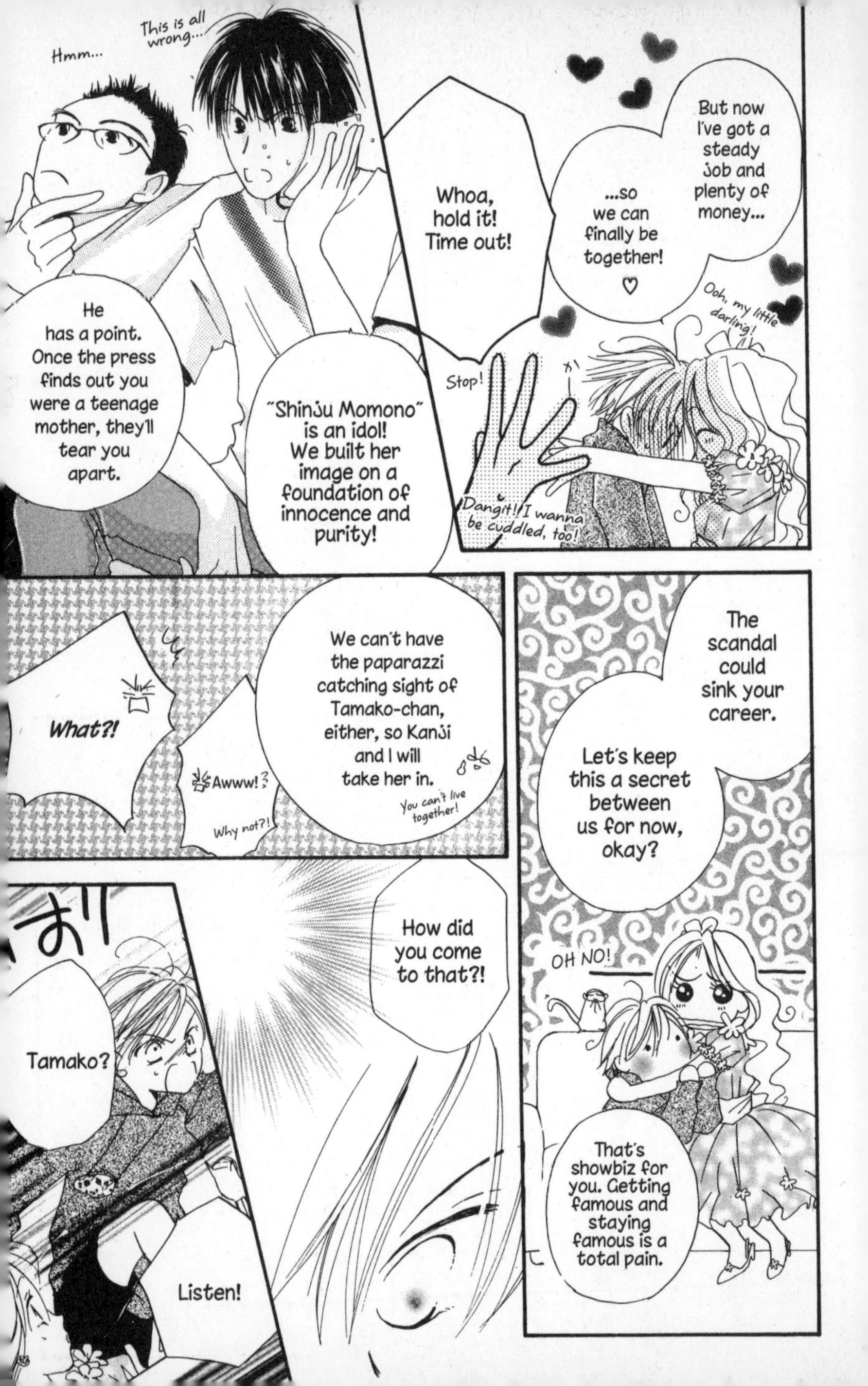
But now I've got a steady job and plenty of money...
...so we can finally be together! ♡
Ooh, my little darling!
Stop!
Dangit! I wanna be cuddled, too!
Whoa, hold it! Time out!
This is all wrong...
Hmm...
"Shinju Momono" is an idol! We built her image on a foundation of innocence and purity!
He has a point. Once the press finds out you were a teenage mother, they'll tear you apart.
The scandal could sink your career.
Let's keep this a secret between us for now, okay?
OH NO!
That's showbiz for you. Getting famous and staying famous is a total pain.
We can't have the paparazzi catching sight of Tamako-chan, either, so Kanji and I will take her in.
You can't live together!
Awww!
Why not?!
What?!
How did you come to that?!
Tamako?
Listen!

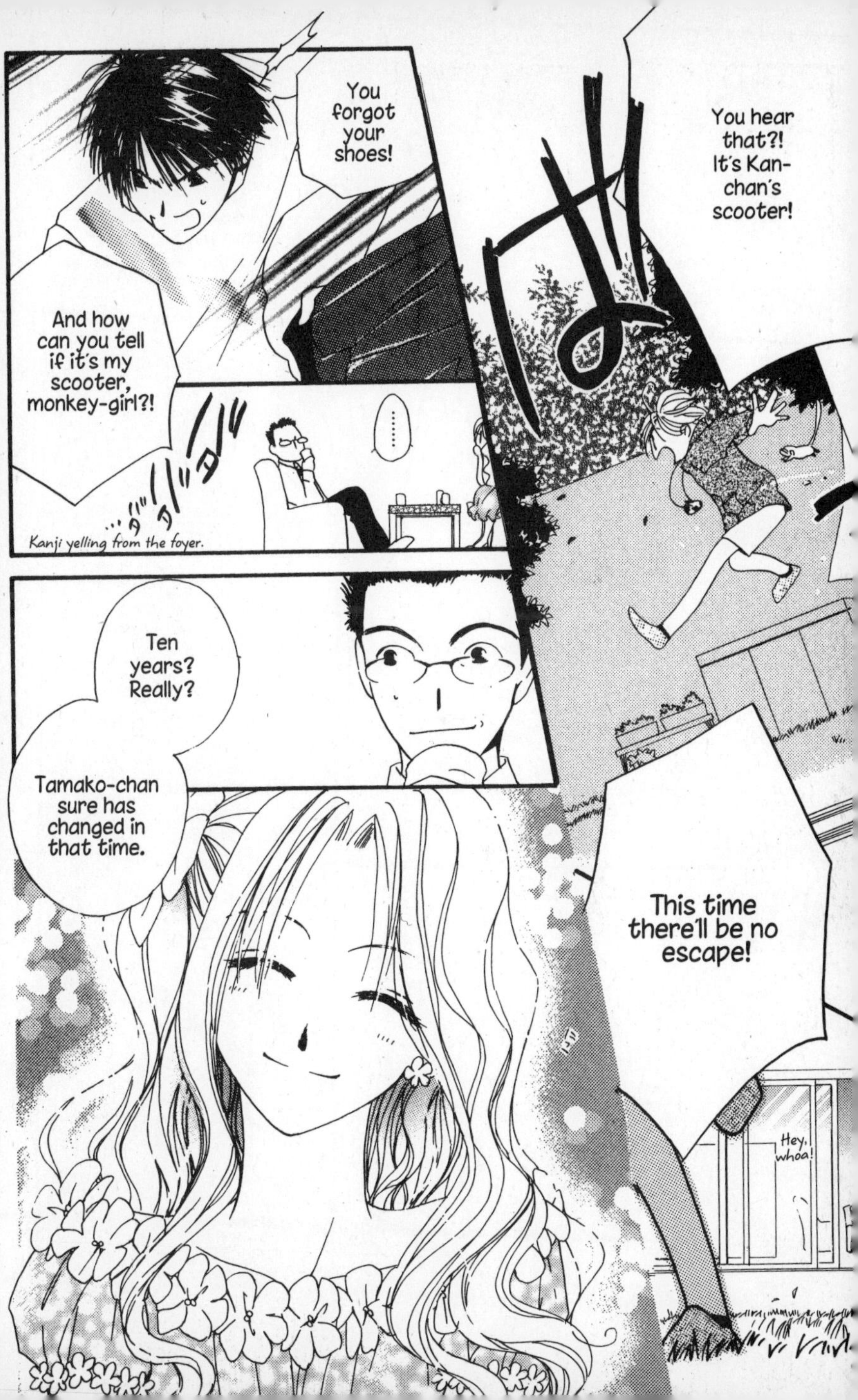
You hear that?! It's Kan-chan's scooter!
You forgot your shoes!
And how can you tell if it's my scooter, monkey-girl?!
......
Kanji yelling from the foyer.
Ten years? Really?
Tamako-chan sure has changed in that time.
This time there'll be no escape!
Hey, whoa!

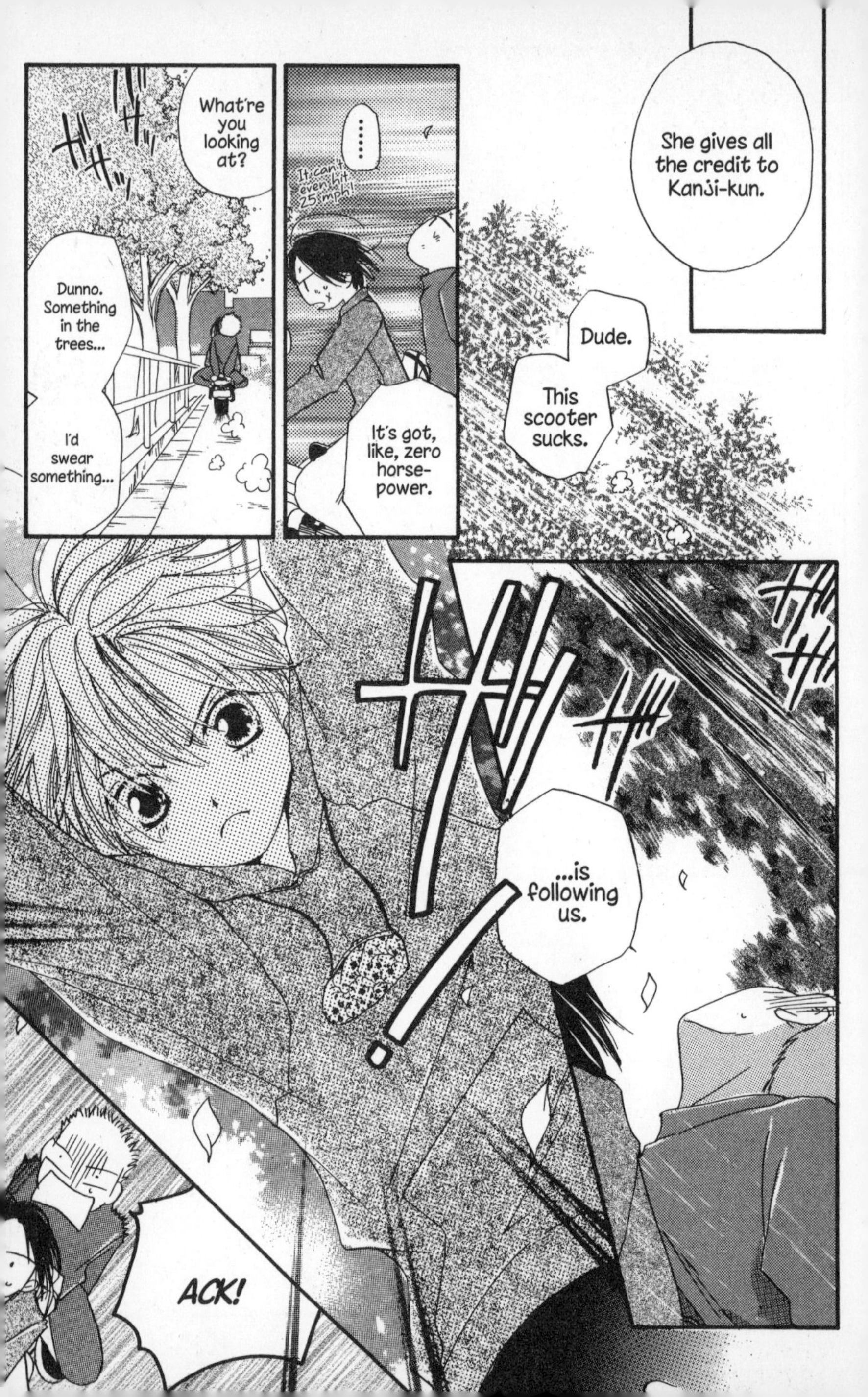
She gives all the credit to Kanji-kun.
Dude.
This scooter sucks.
......
It can't even hit 25 mph!
It's got, like, zero horsepower.
What're you looking at?
Dunno. Something in the trees...
I'd swear something...
...is following us.
ACK!

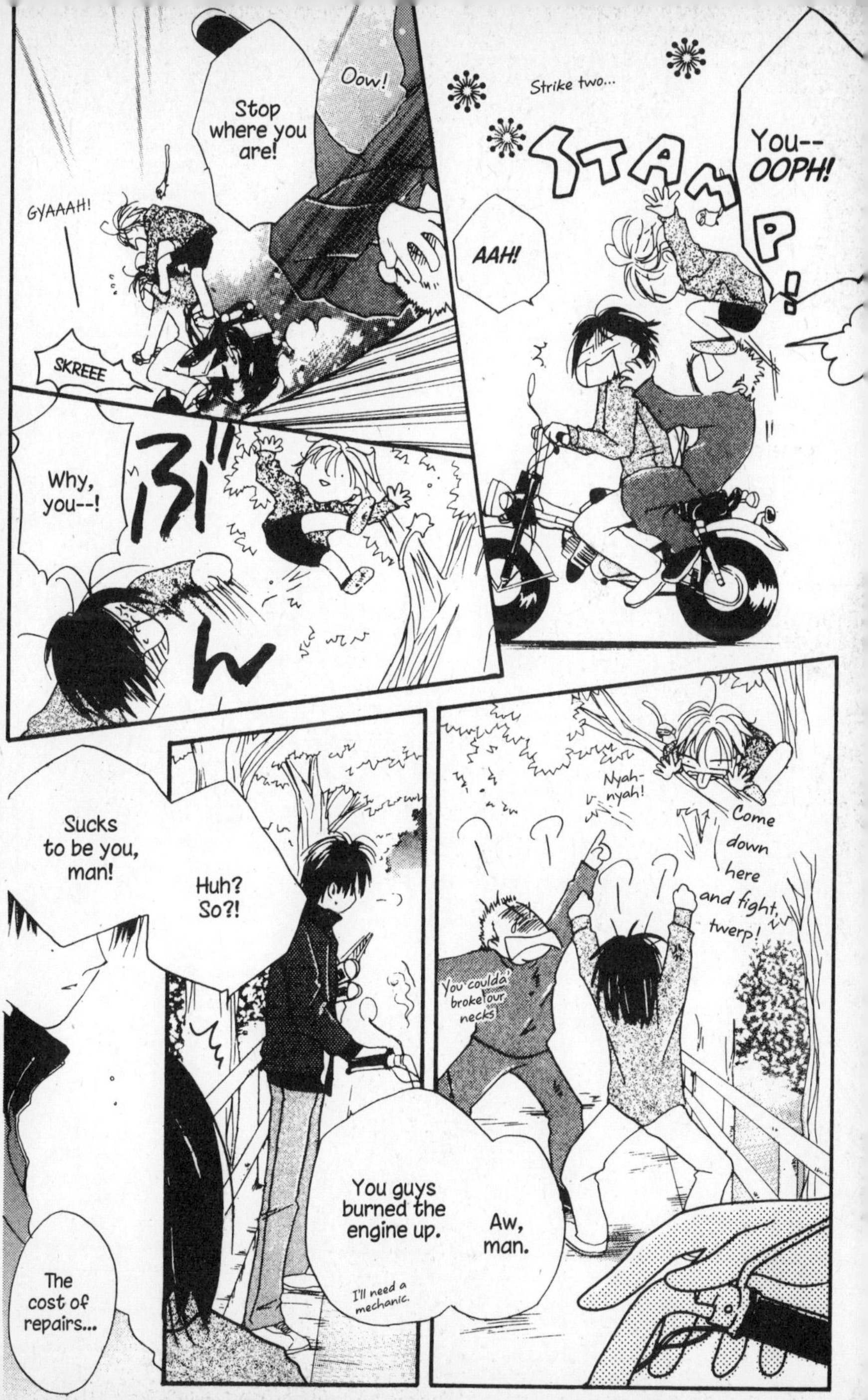
You--
OOPH!
Strike two...
STAMP!
AAH!
Oow!
Stop where you are!
GYAAAH!
SKREEE
Why, you--!
Nyah-nyah!
Come down here and fight, twerp!
You coulda' broke our necks
Huh? So?!
Aw, man.
You guys burned the engine up.
I'll need a mechanic.
Sucks to be you, man!
The cost of repairs...

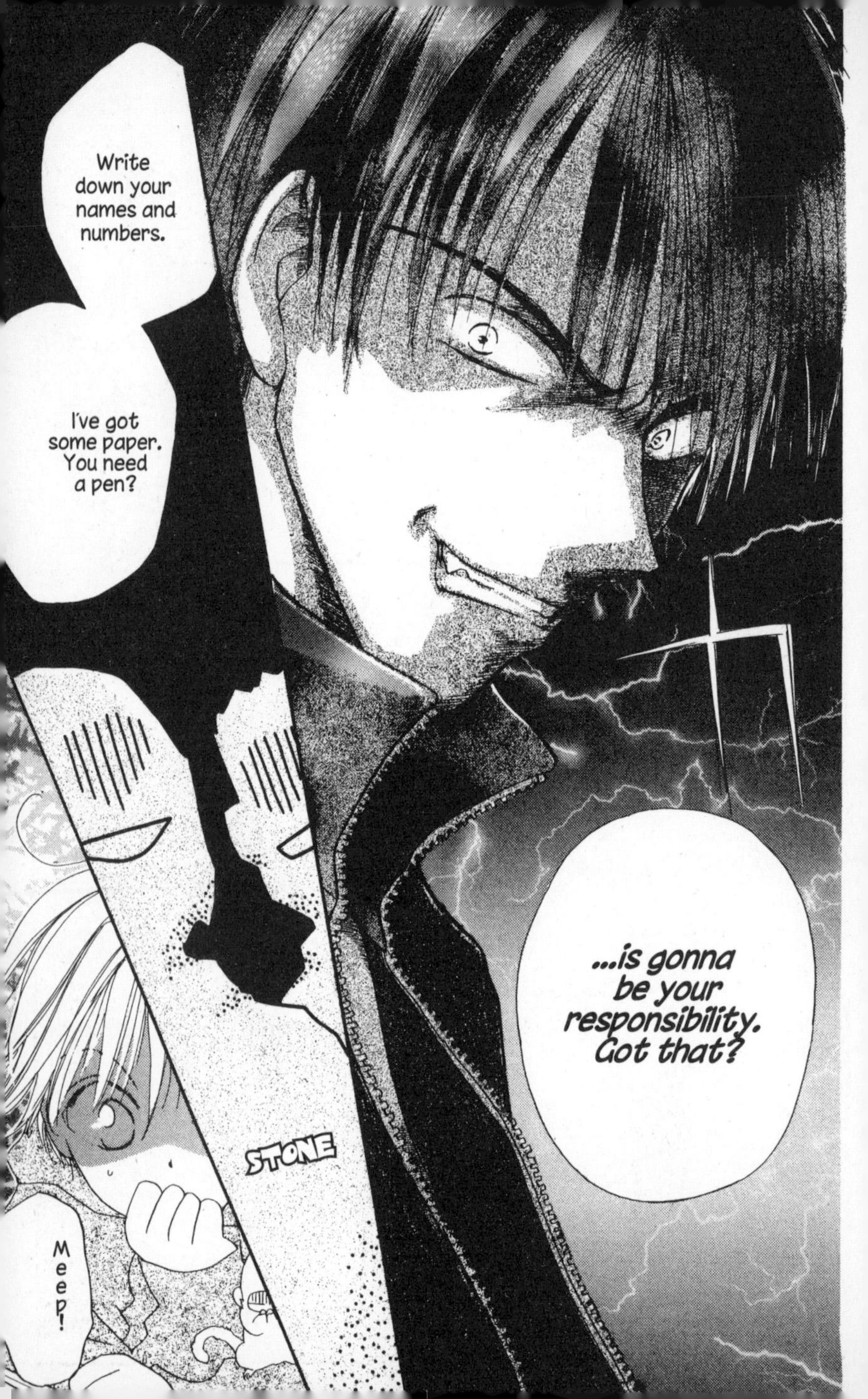
Write down your names and numbers.
I've got some paper. You need a pen?
...is gonna be your responsibility. Got that?
STONE
Meep!

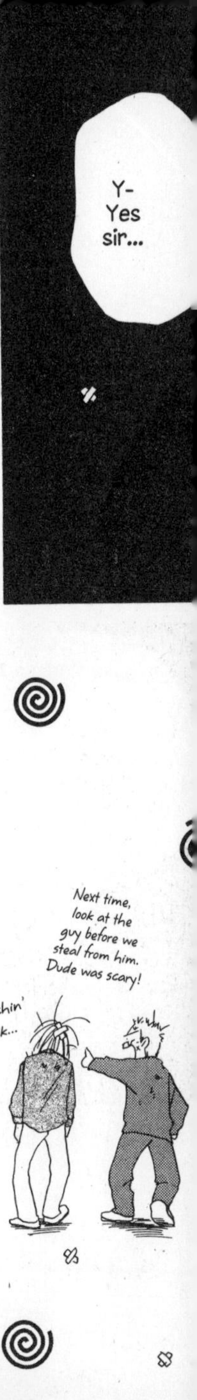

Y- Yes sir...
Next time, look at the guy before we steal from him. Dude was scary!
My achin' back...

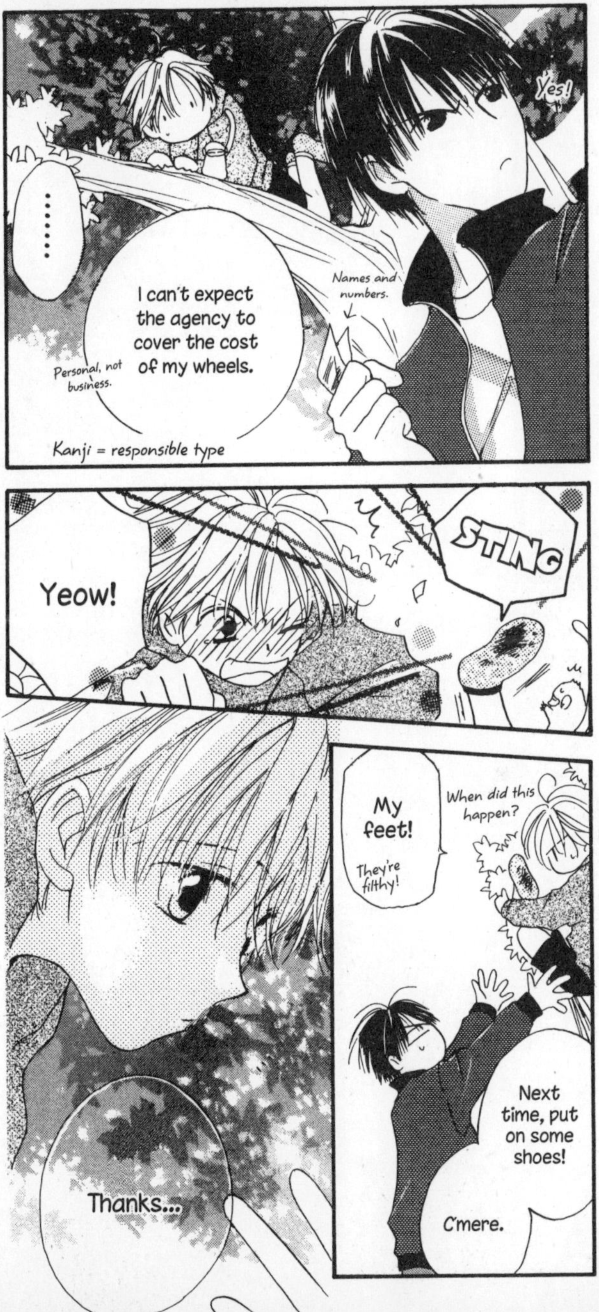

Yes!
Names and numbers.
I can't expect the agency to cover the cost of my wheels.
Personal, not business.
......
Kanji = responsible type
STING
Yeow!
When did this happen?
My feet!
They're filthy!
Next time, put on some shoes!
C'mere.
Thanks...

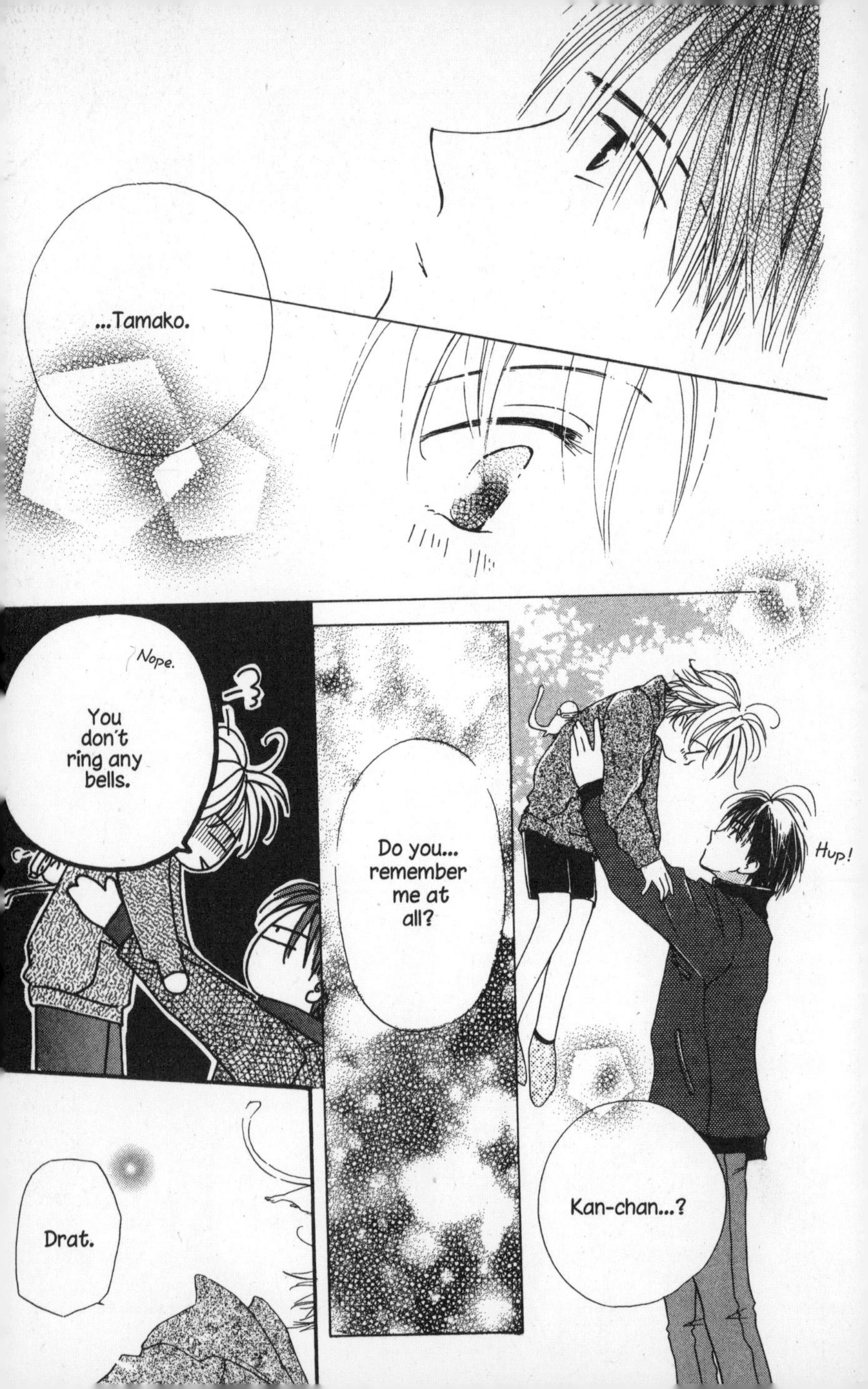
...Tamako.
Hup!
Kan-chan...?
Do you... remember me at all?
Nope.
You don't ring any bells.
Drat.

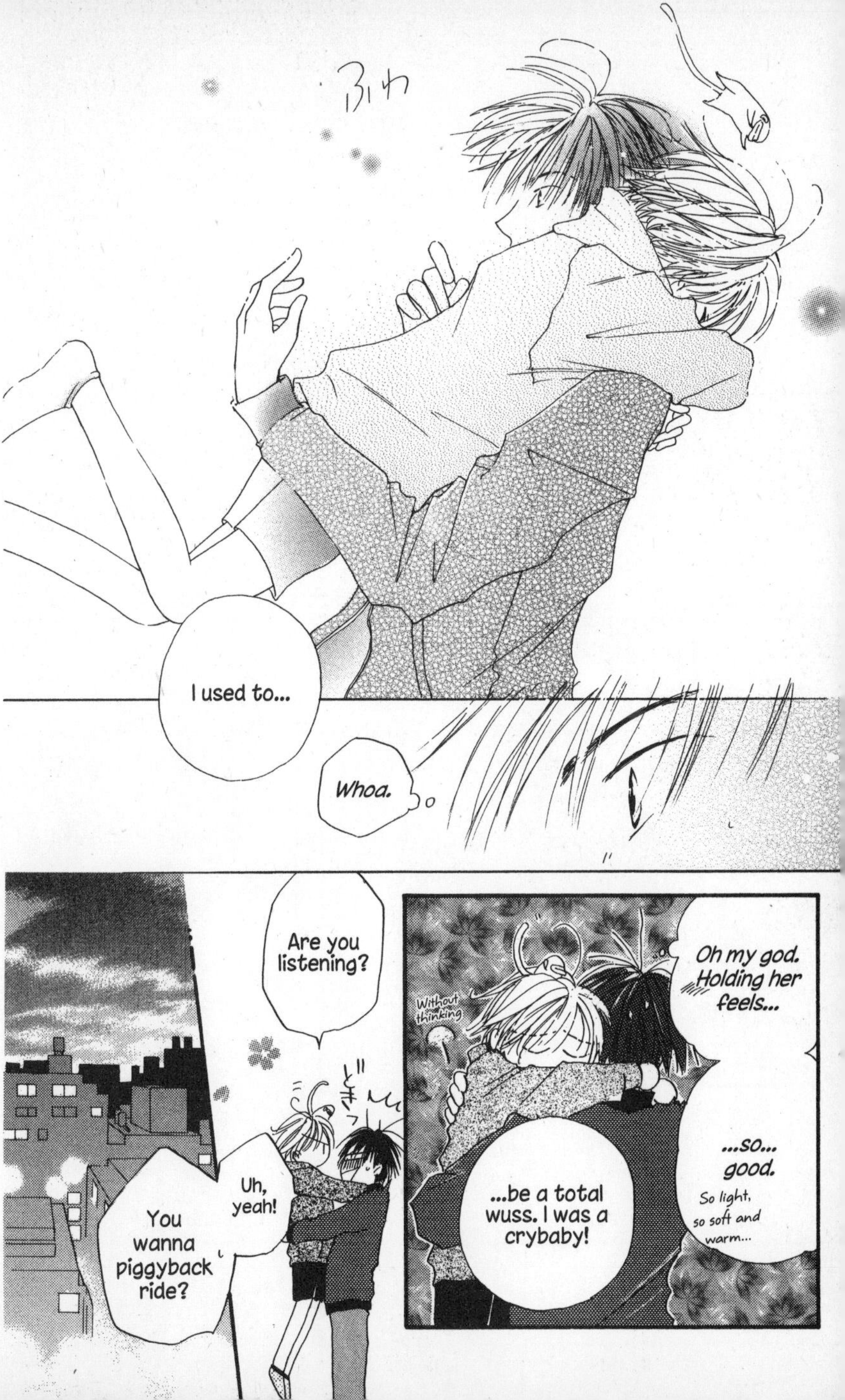
ふわ
I used to...
Whoa.
Oh my god. Holding her feels...
...so... good.
So light, so soft and warm...
Without thinking
...be a total wuss. I was a crybaby!
Are you listening?
Uh, yeah!
You wanna piggyback ride?

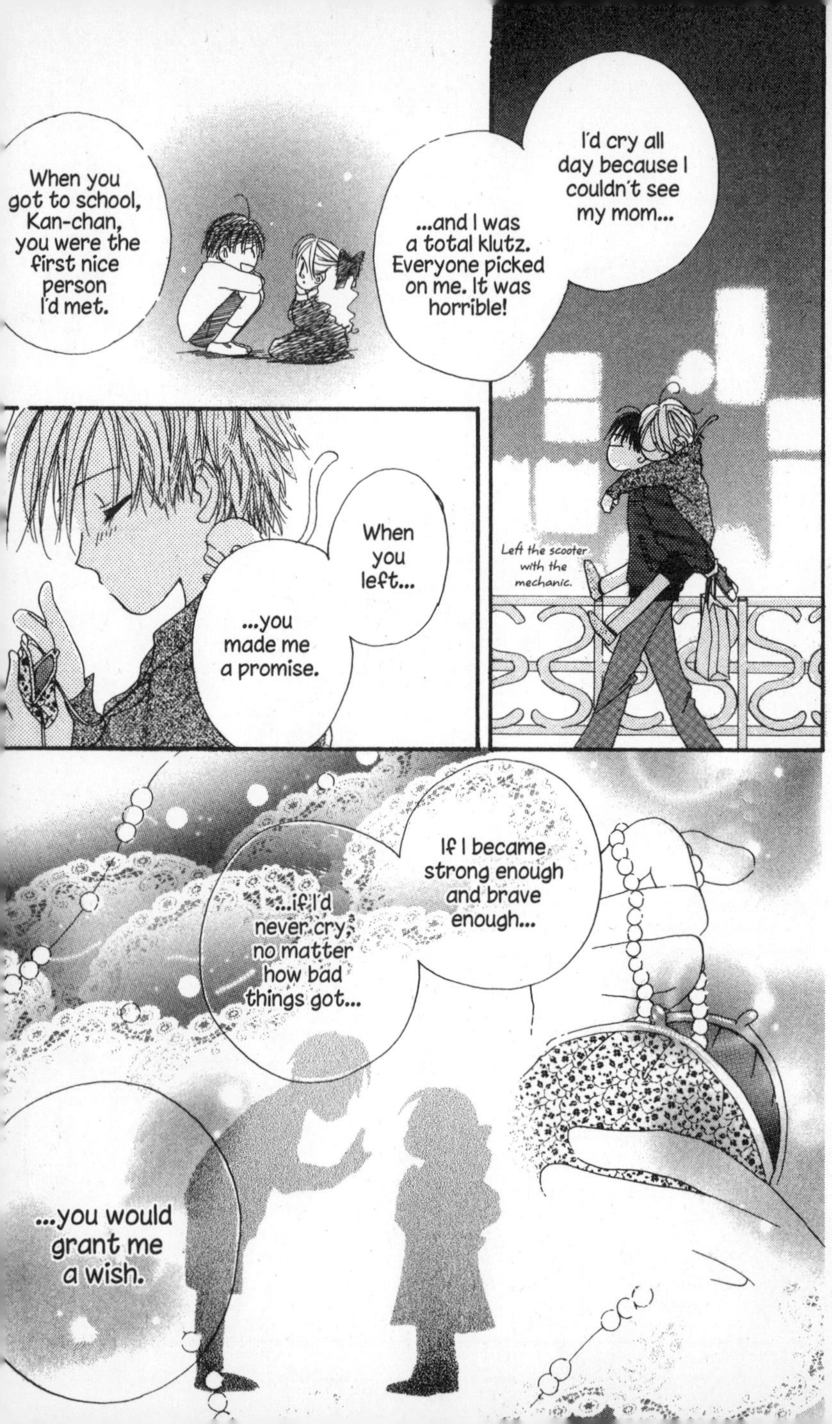
I'd cry all day because I couldn't see my mom...
...and I was a total klutz. Everyone picked on me. It was horrible!
Left the scooter with the mechanic.
When you got to school, Kan-chan, you were the first nice person I'd met.
When you left...
...you made me a promise.
If I became strong enough and brave enough...
...if I'd never cry, no matter how bad things got...
...you would grant me a wish.

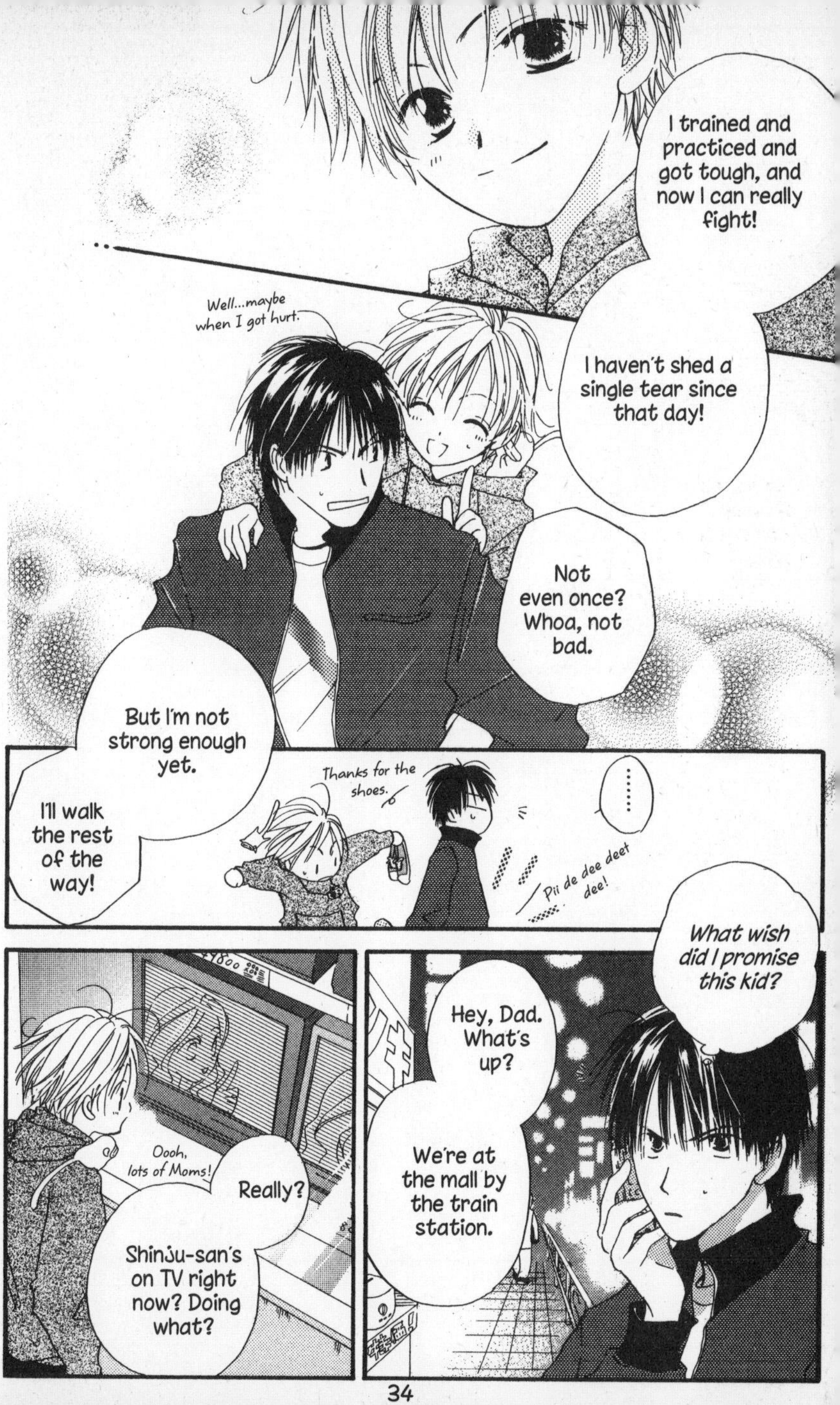
I trained and practiced and got tough, and now I can really fight!
I haven't shed a single tear since that day!
Well...maybe when I got hurt.
Not even once? Whoa, not bad.
But I'm not strong enough yet.
......
Pii de dee deet dee!
Thanks for the shoes.
I'll walk the rest of the way!
What wish did I promise this kid?
Hey, Dad. What's up?
We're at the mall by the train station.
Really?
Oooh, lots of Moms!
Shinju-san's on TV right now? Doing what?

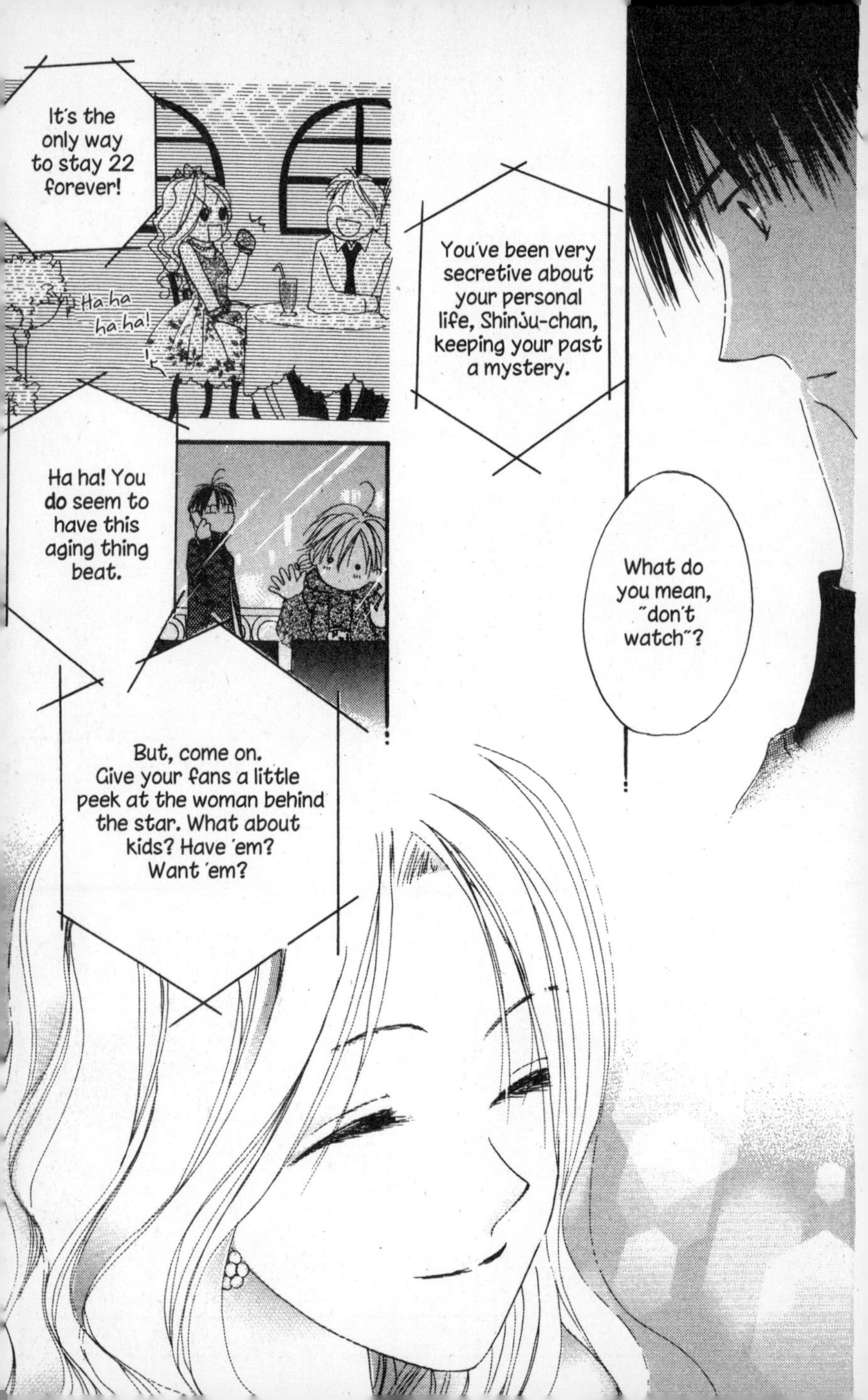
What do you mean, "don't watch"?
It's the only way to stay 22 forever!
Ha ha ha ha!
Ha ha! You do seem to have this aging thing beat.
You've been very secretive about your personal life, Shinju-chan, keeping your past a mystery.
But, come on. Give your fans a little peek at the woman behind the star. What about kids? Have 'em? Want 'em?

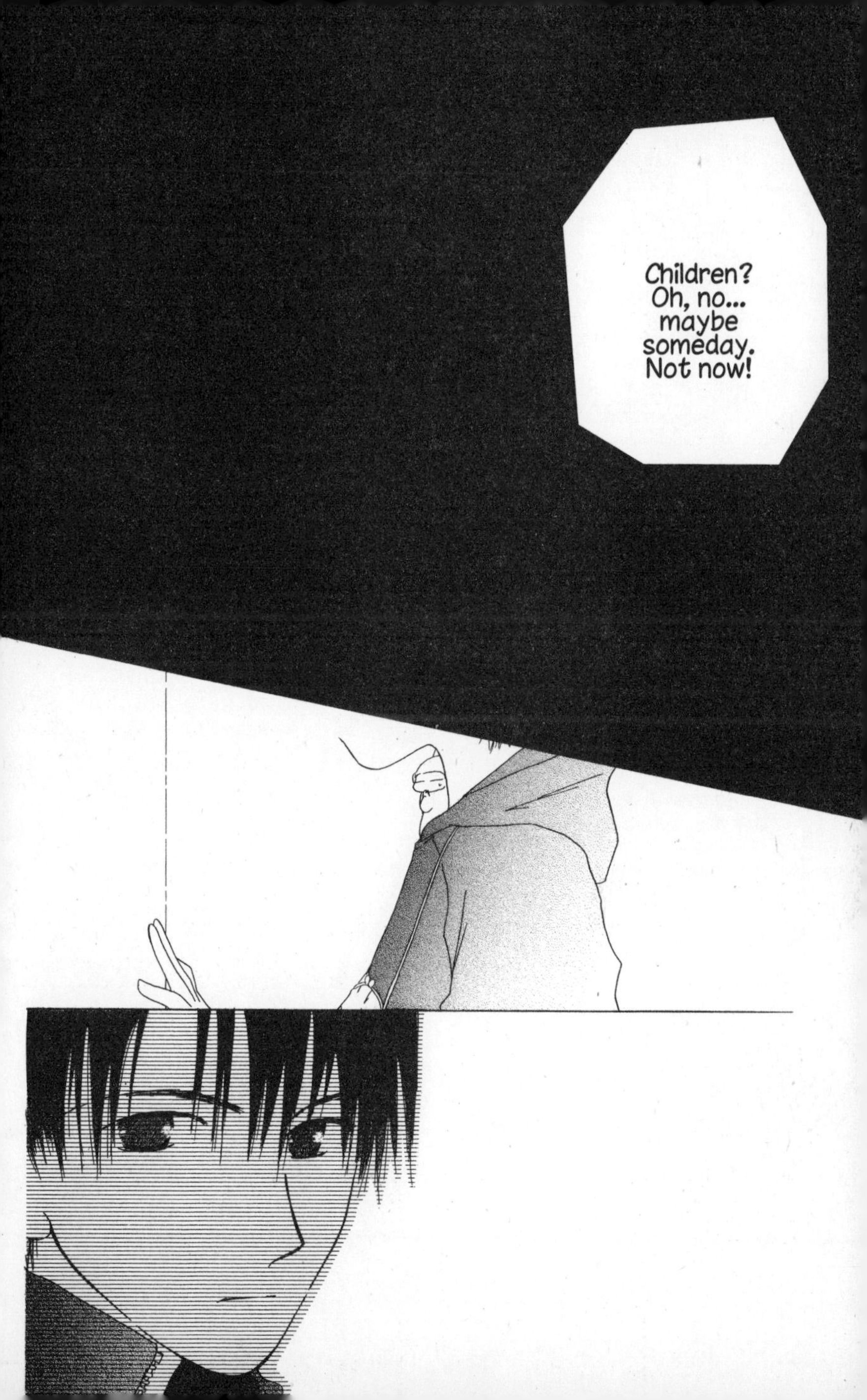
Children? Oh, no... maybe someday. Not now!

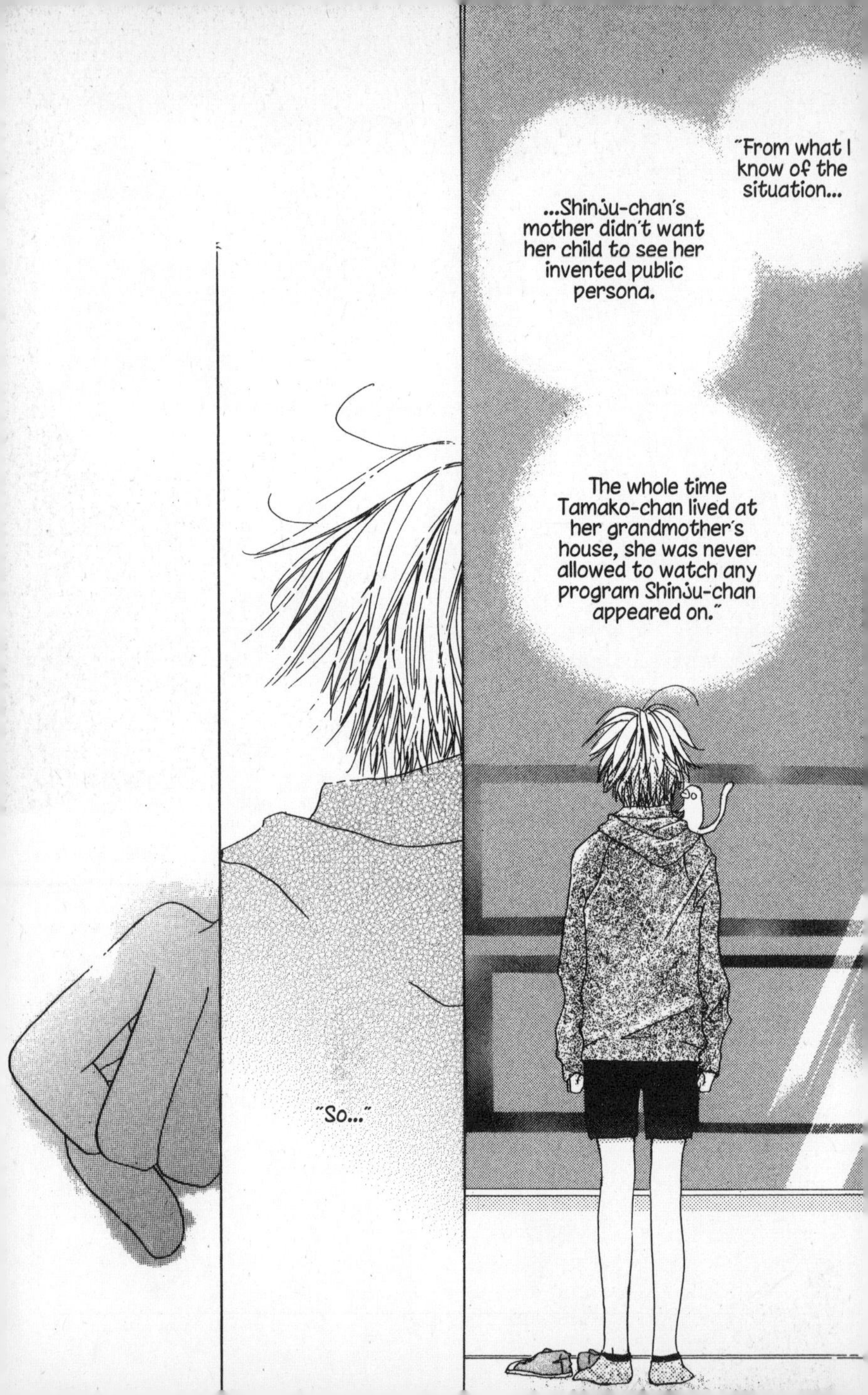
"From what I know of the situation...
...Shinju-chan's mother didn't want her child to see her invented public persona.
The whole time Tamako-chan lived at her grandmother's house, she was never allowed to watch any program Shinju-chan appeared on."
"So..."

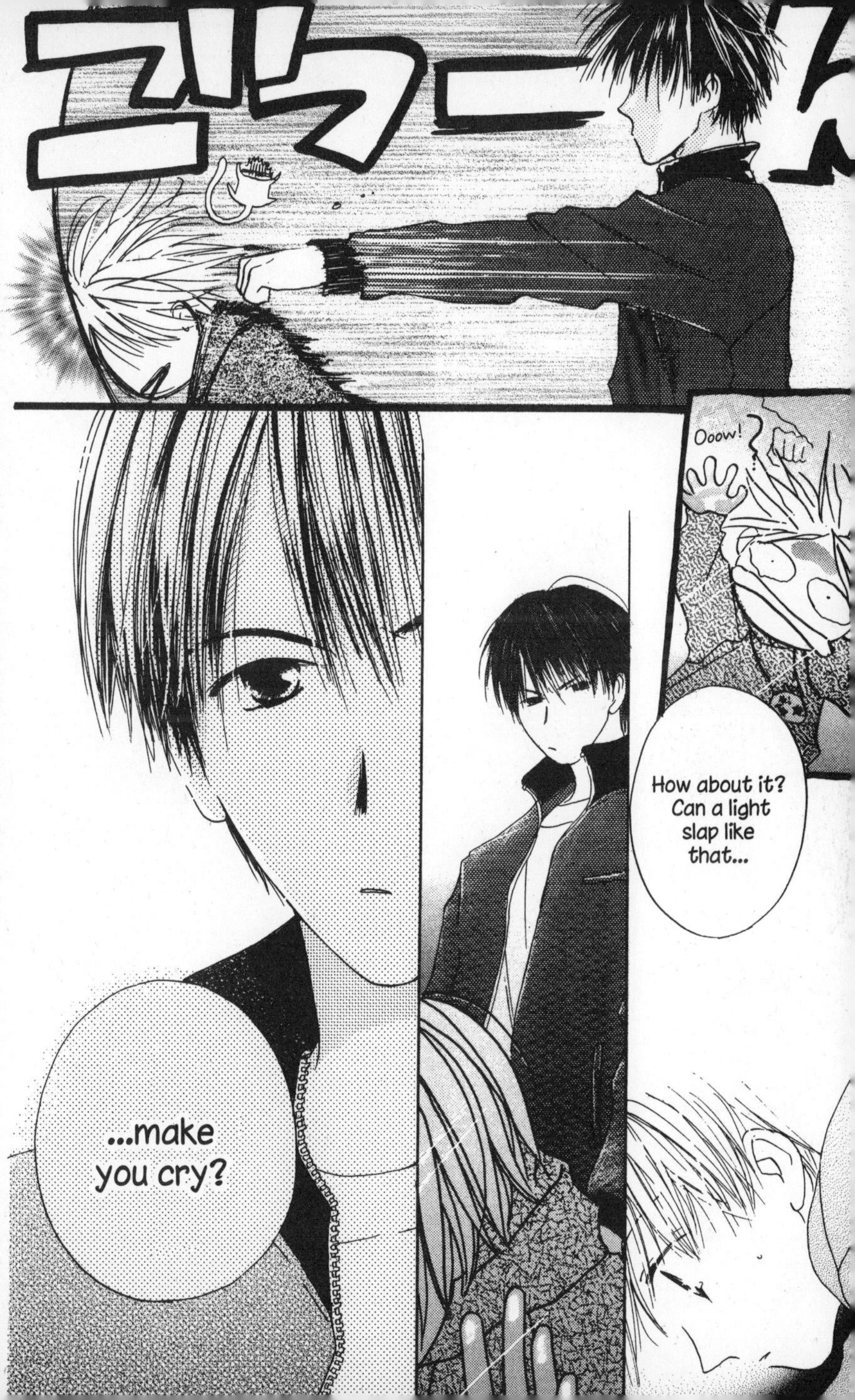
Ooow!
How about it? Can a light slap like that...
...make you cry?

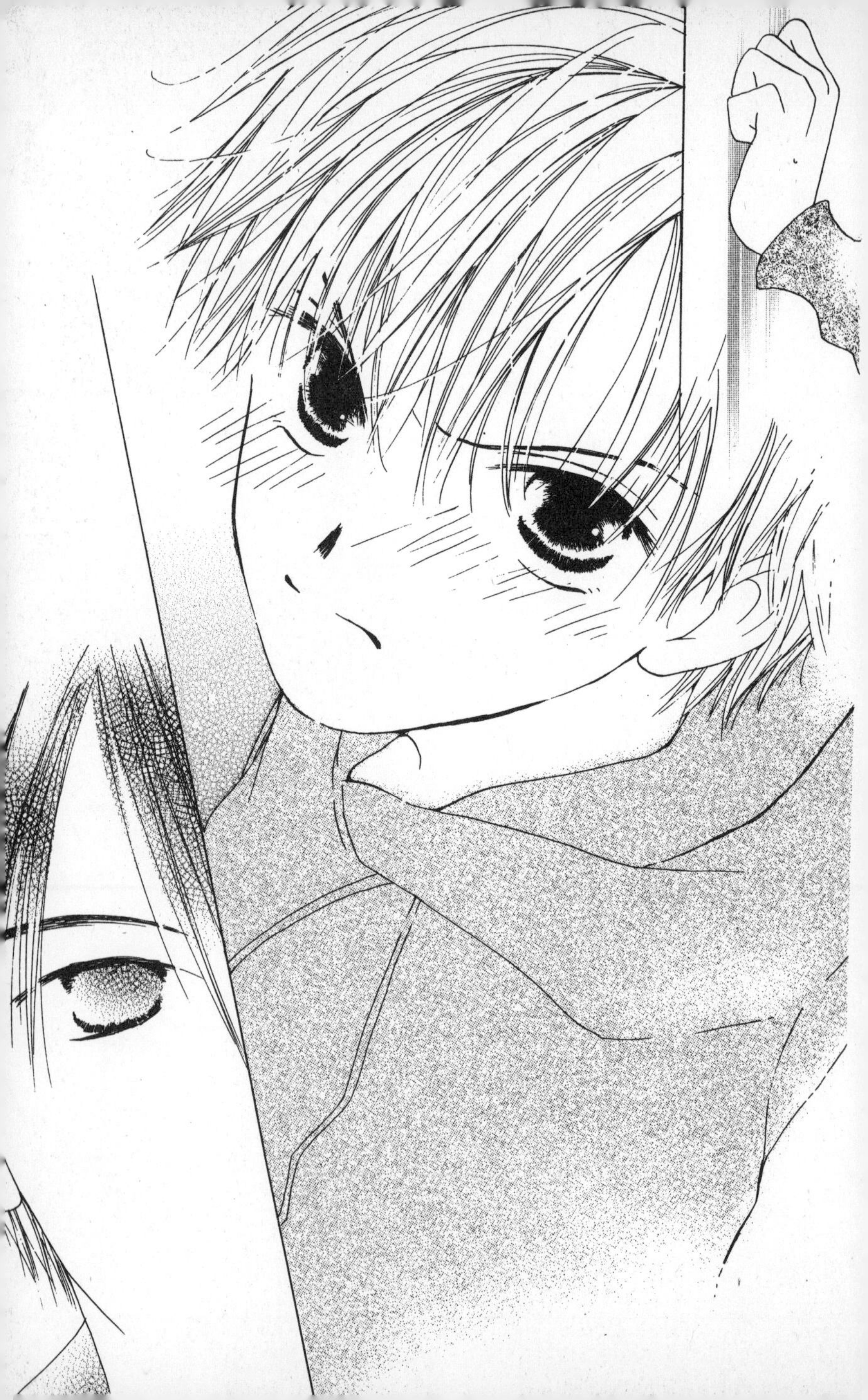

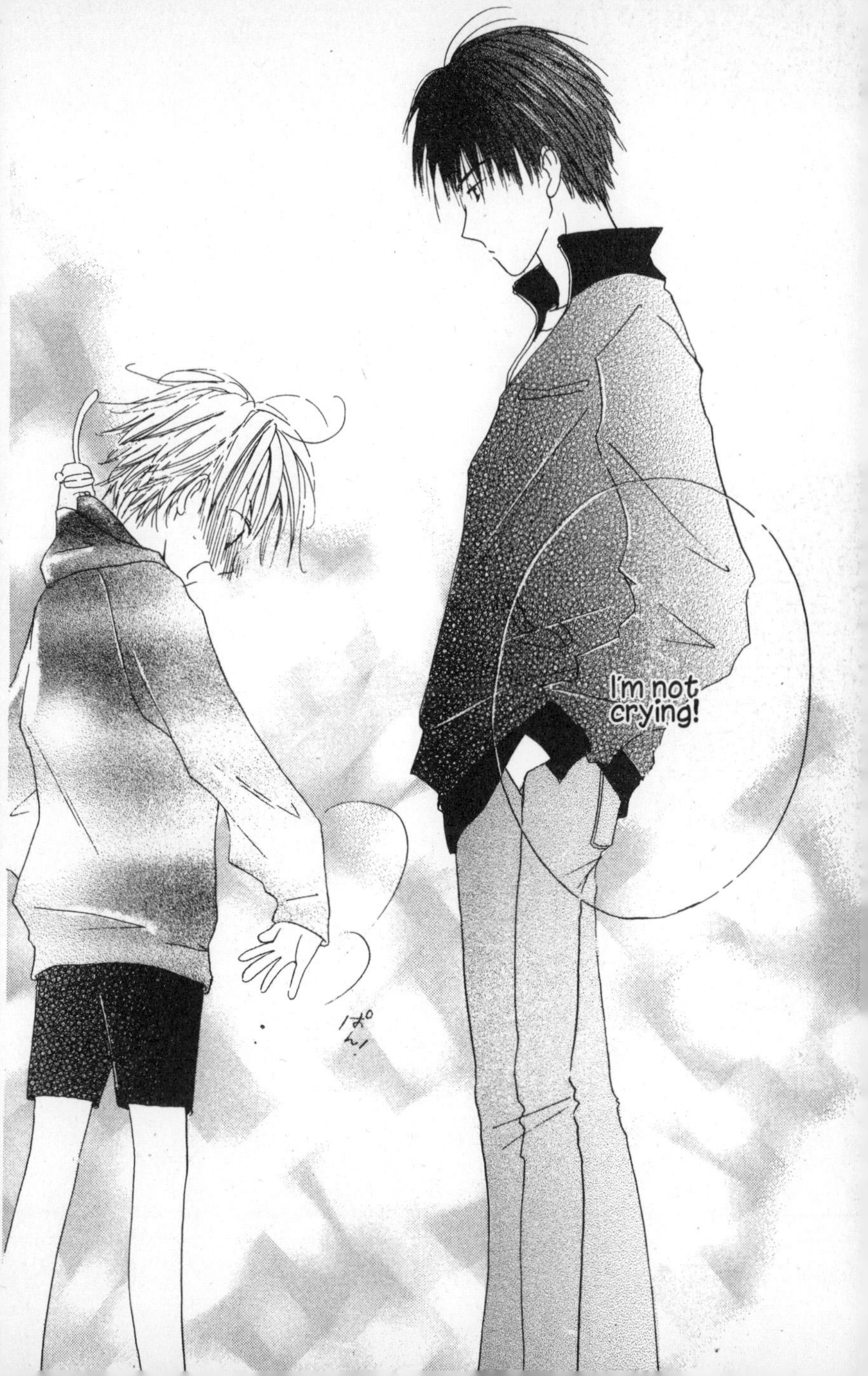
I'm not crying!
ぱん!

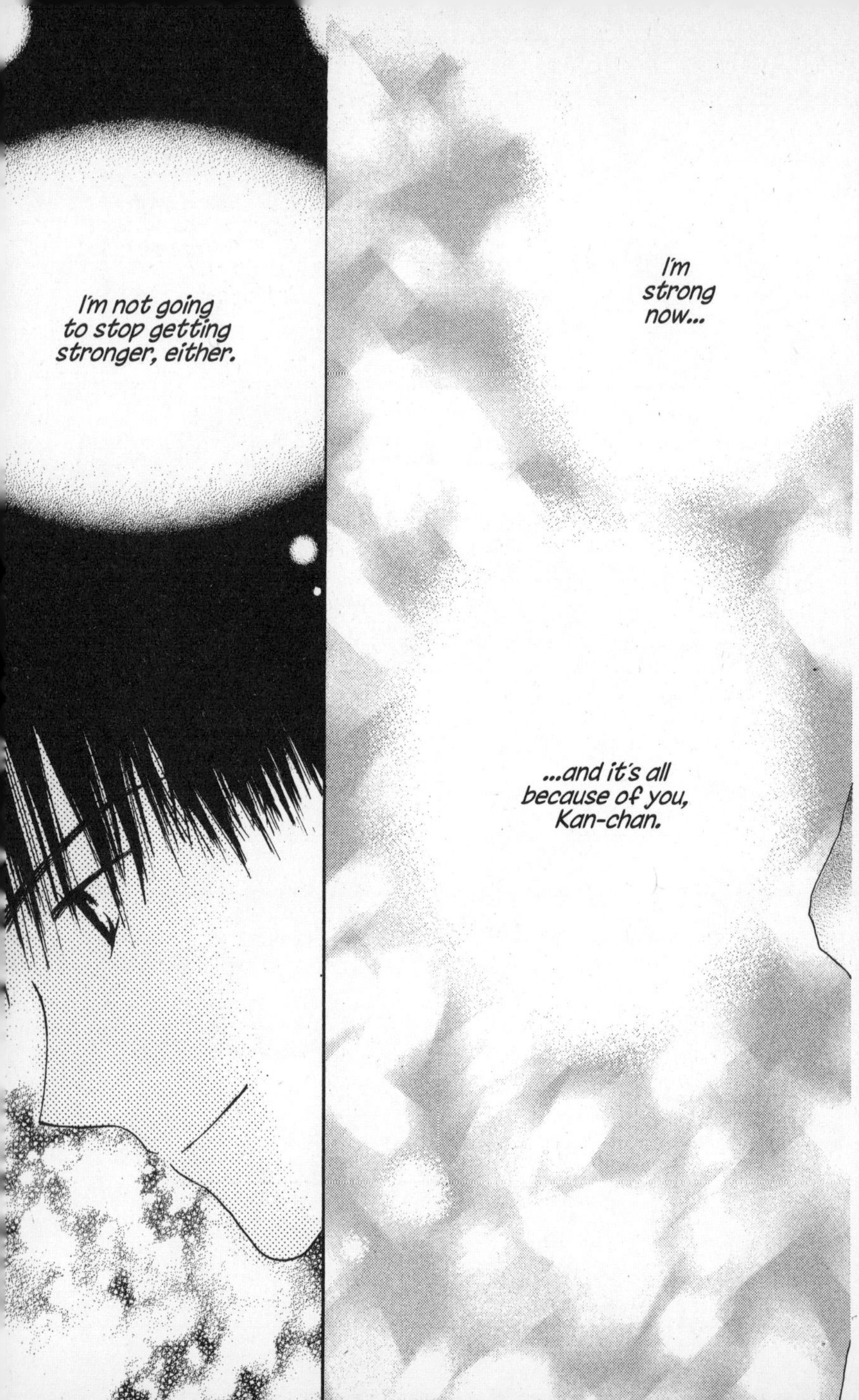
I'm strong now...
...and it's all because of you, Kan-chan.
I'm not going to stop getting stronger, either.

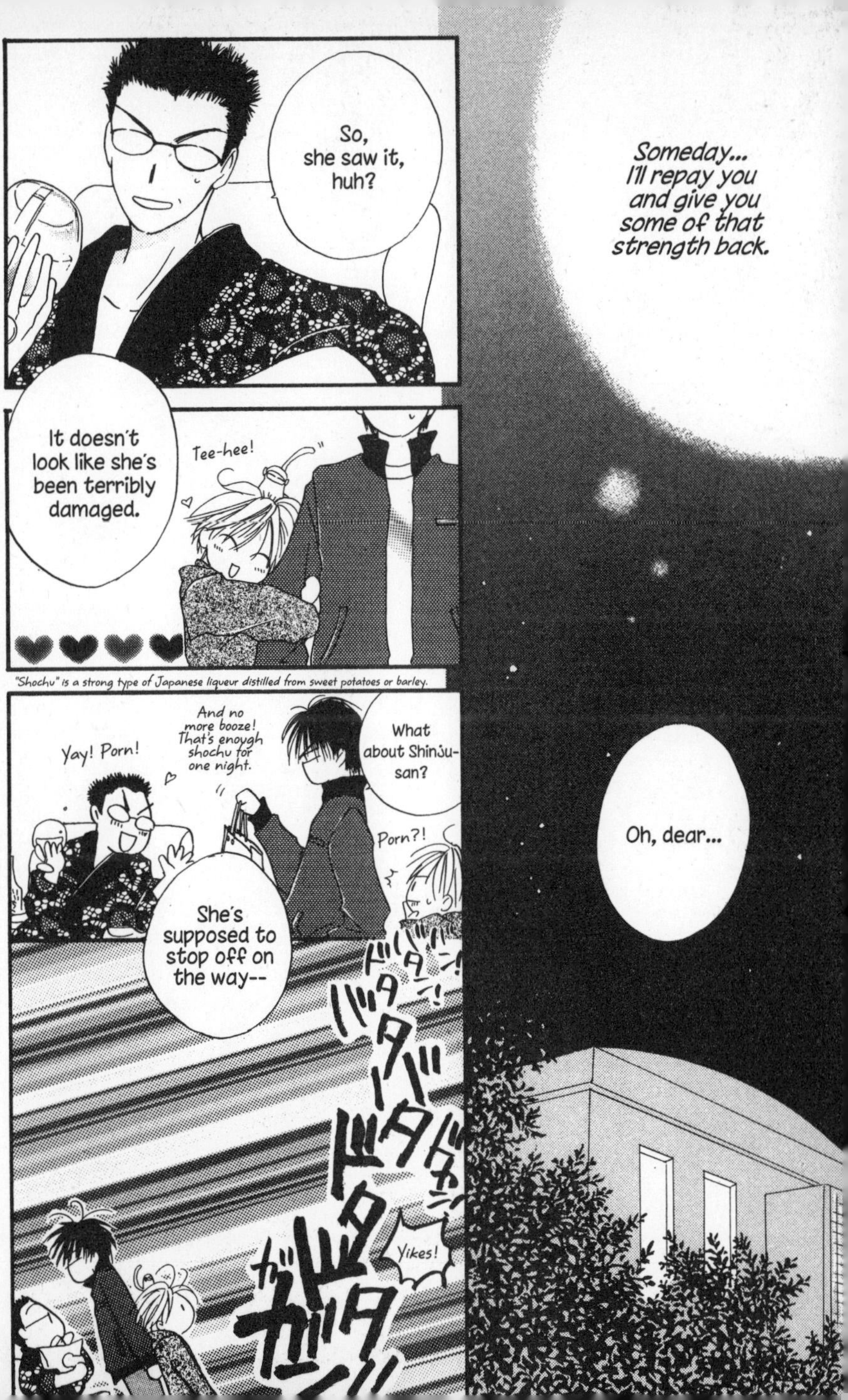
Someday... I'll repay you and give you some of that strength back.
Oh, dear...
So, she saw it, huh?
Tee-hee!
It doesn't look like she's been terribly damaged.
What about Shinju-san?
And no more booze! That's enough shochu for one night.
Yay! Porn!
Porn?!
She's supposed to stop off on the way--
Yikes!

"Shochu" is a strong type of Japanese liqueur distilled from sweet potatoes or barley.

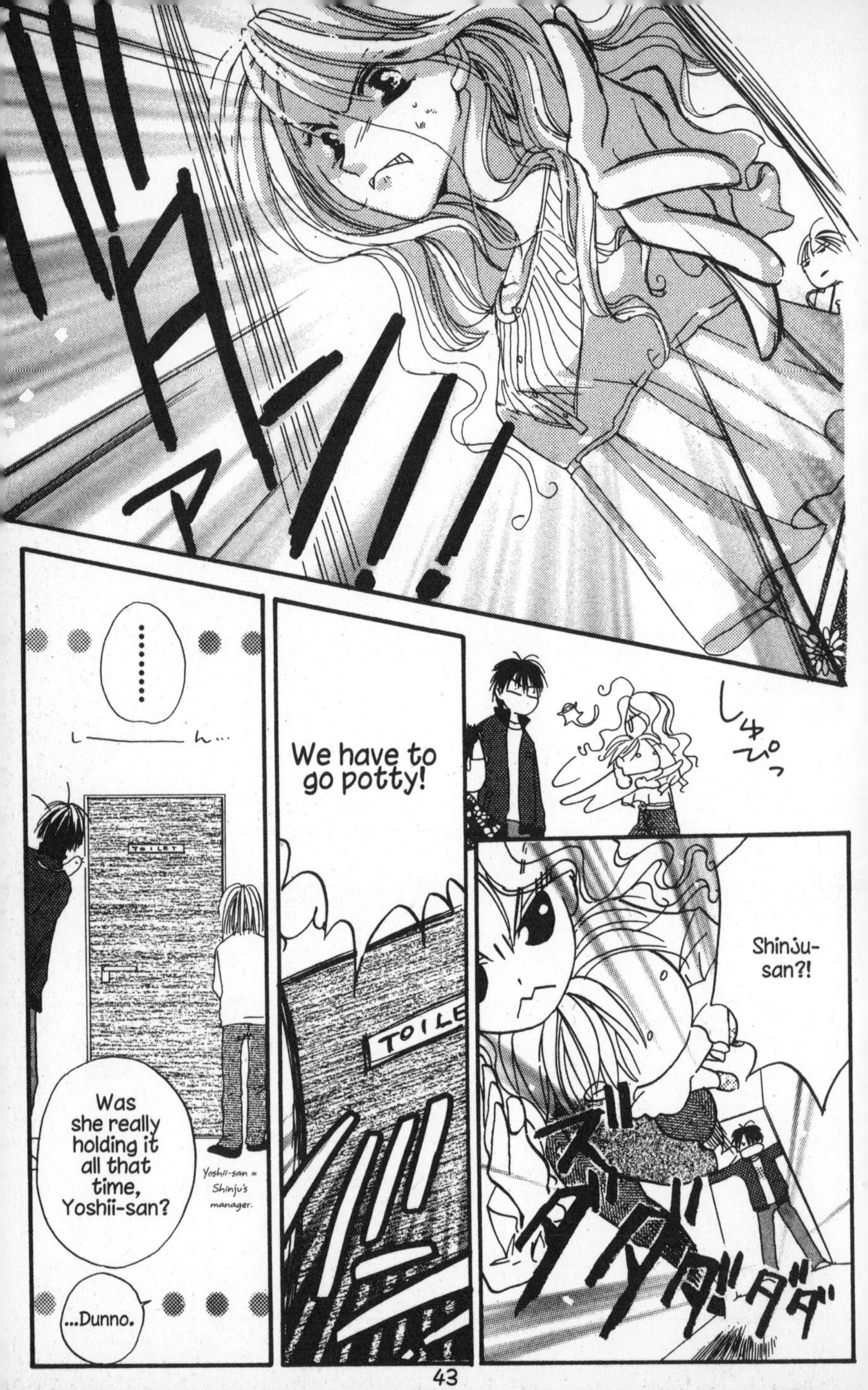
しゅぴっ
Shinju-san?!
We have to go potty!
TOILE
......
し————ん…
TOILET
Was she really holding it all that time, Yoshii-san?
Yoshii-san = Shinju's manager.
...Dunno.

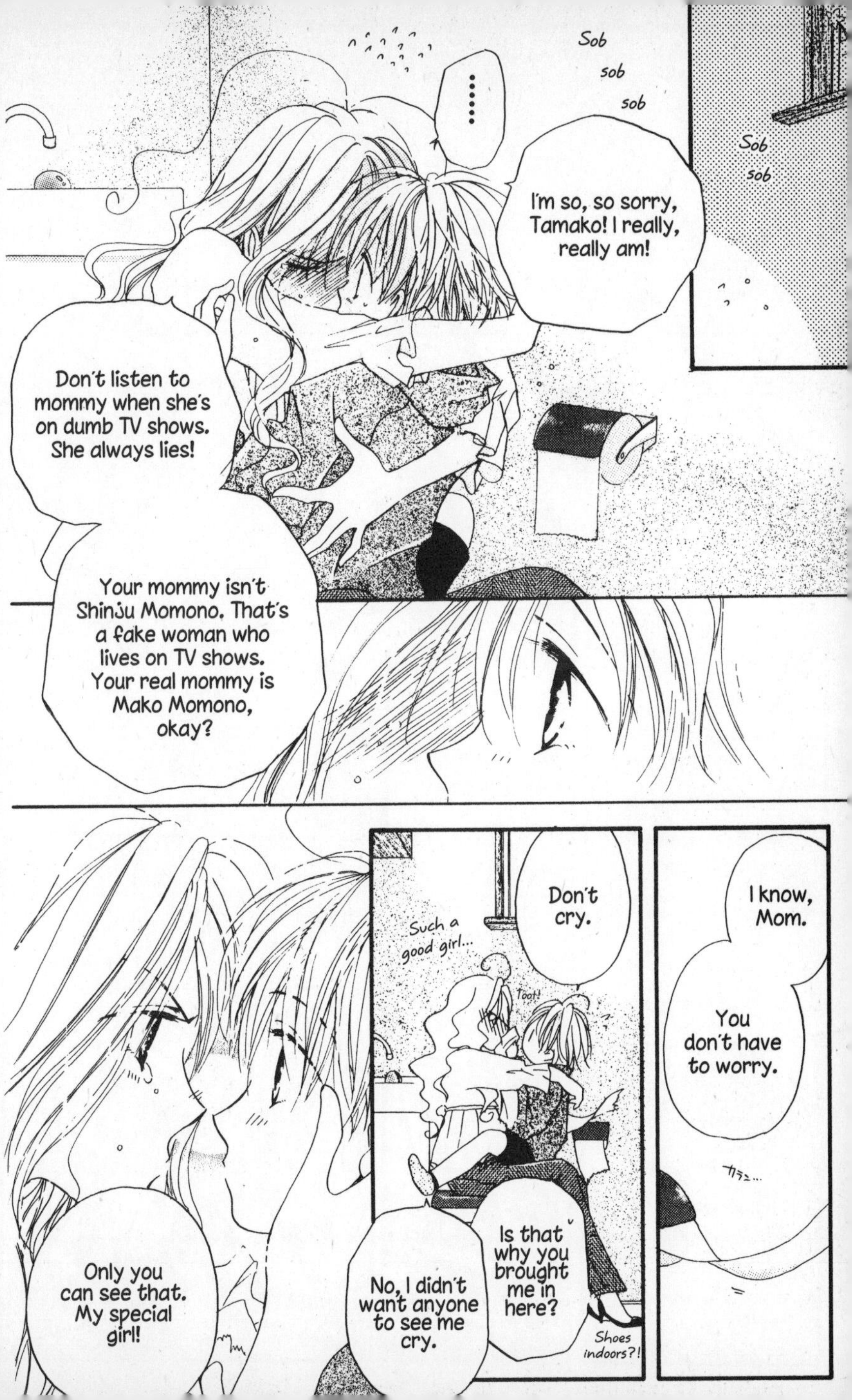
Sob
sob
sob
Sob
sob
......
I'm so, so sorry, Tamako! I really, really am!
Don't listen to mommy when she's on dumb TV shows. She always lies!
Your mommy isn't Shinju Momono. That's a fake woman who lives on TV shows. Your real mommy is Mako Momono, okay?
I know, Mom.
You don't have to worry.
カラン...
Don't cry.
Such a good girl...
Toot!
Is that why you brought me in here?
Shoes indoors?!
No, I didn't want anyone to see me cry.
Only you can see that. My special girl!

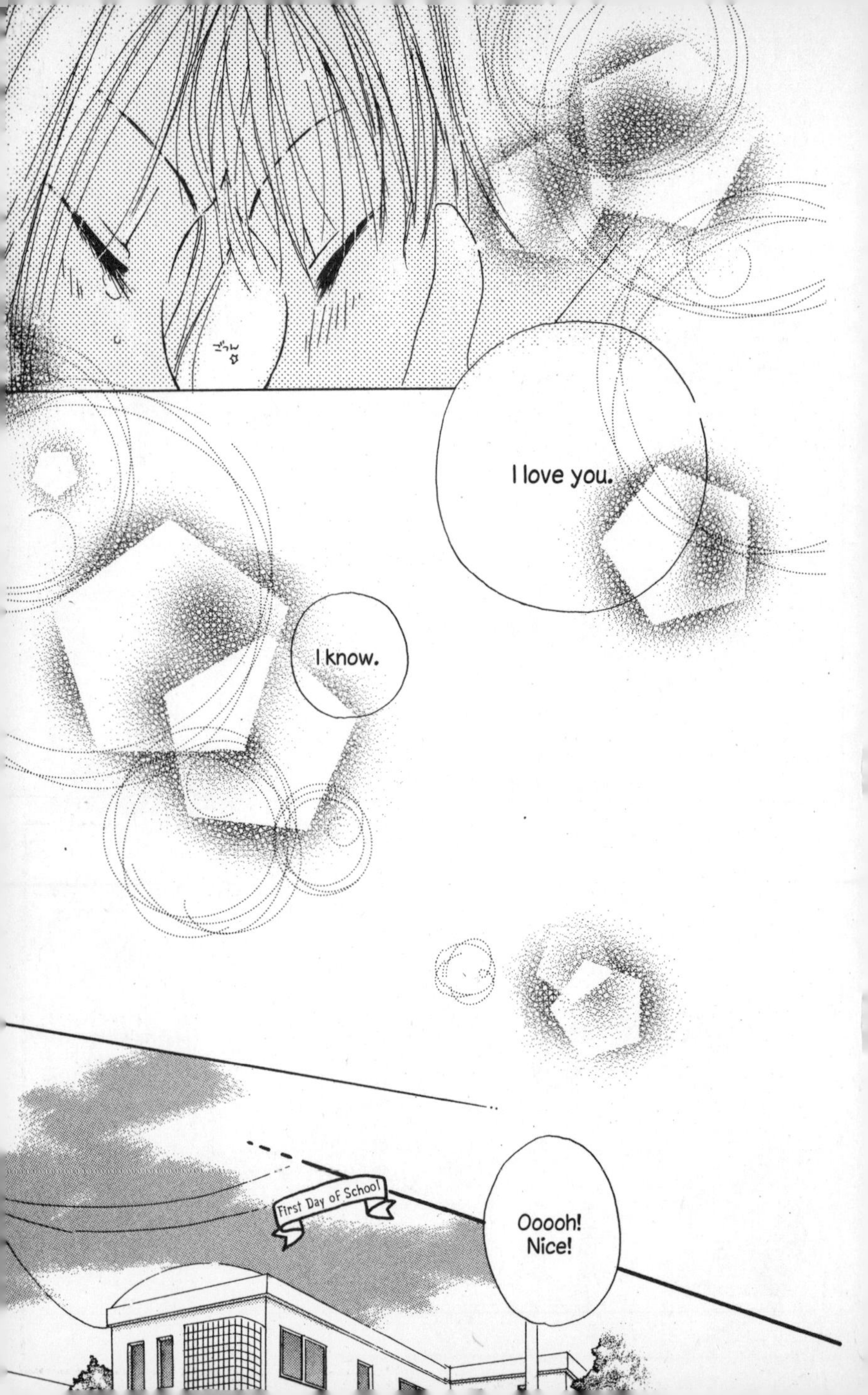
ごつん☆
I love you.
I know.
First Day of School
Ooooh!
Nice!

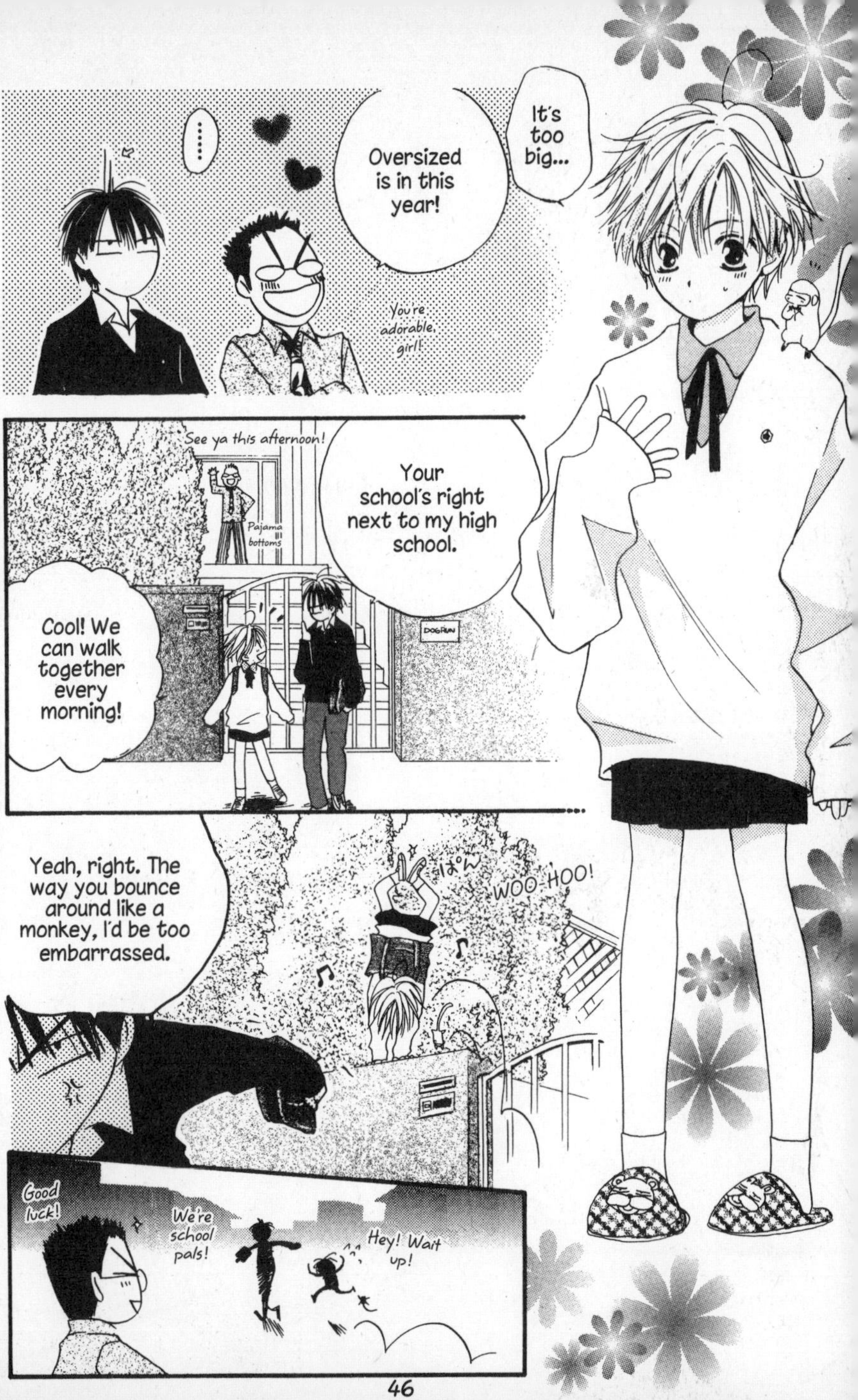
It's too big...
Oversized is in this year!
......
You're adorable, girl!
Your school's right next to my high school.
Cool! We can walk together every morning!
See ya this afternoon!
Pajama bottoms
WOO-HOO!
ぱん
Yeah, right. The way you bounce around like a monkey, I'd be too embarrassed.
Hey! Wait up!
We're school pals!
Good luck!

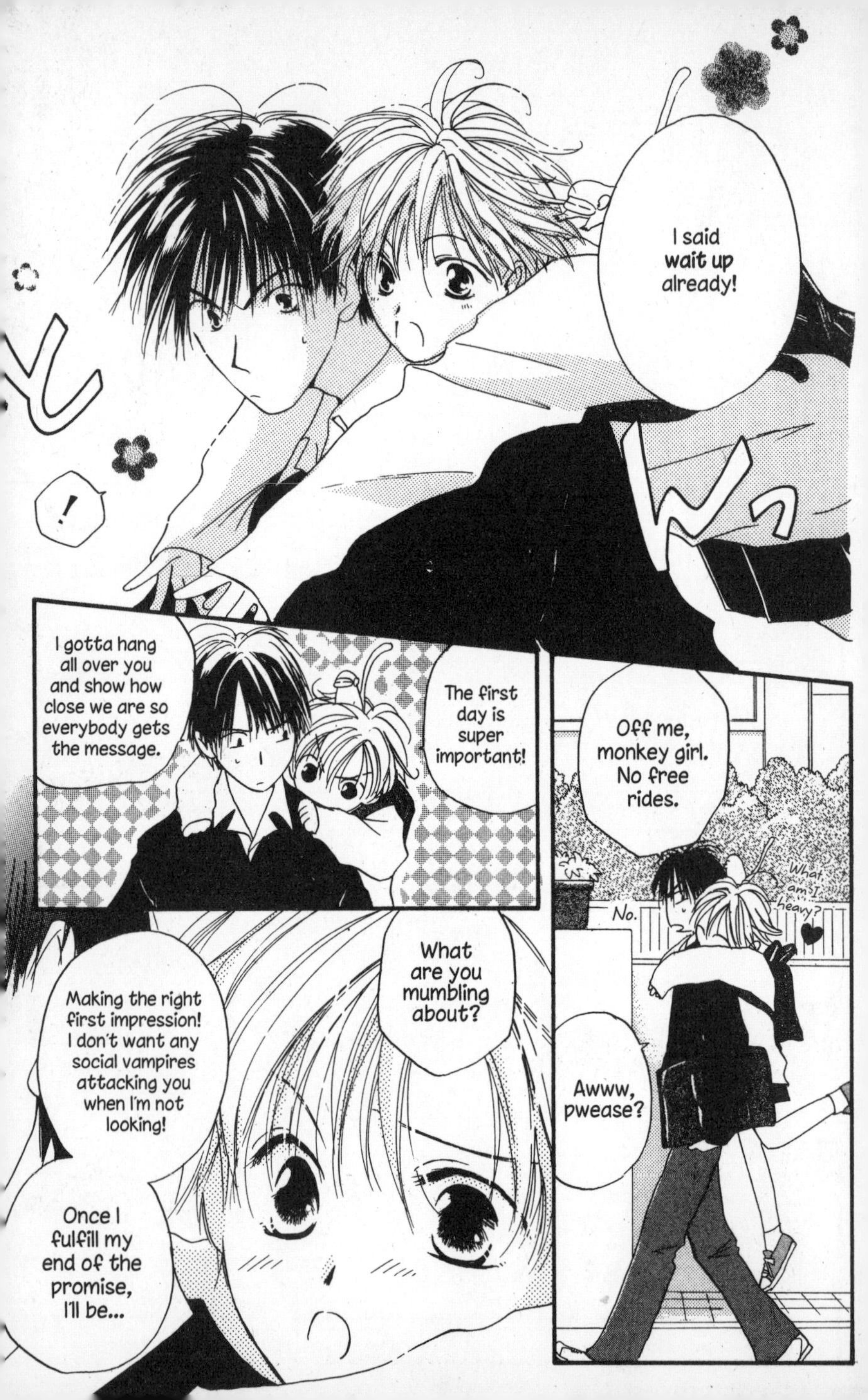
I said wait up already!
!
Off me, monkey girl. No free rides.
What, am I heavy?
No.
Awww, pwease?
The first day is super important!
I gotta hang all over you and show how close we are so everybody gets the message.
What are you mumbling about?
Making the right first impression! I don't want any social vampires attacking you when I'm not looking!
Once I fulfill my end of the promise, I'll be...

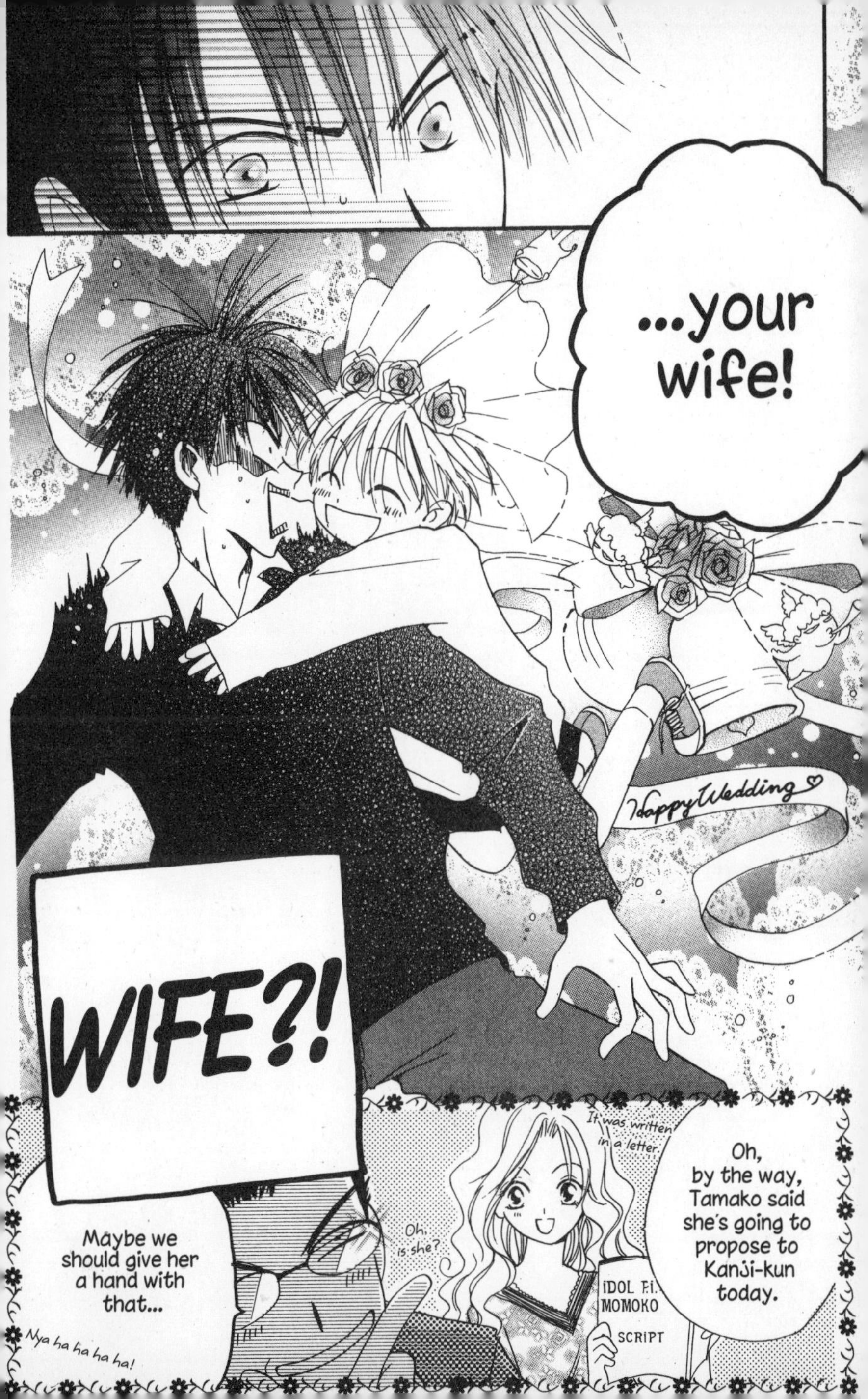
...your wife!
Happy Wedding
WIFE?!
Oh, by the way, Tamako said she's going to propose to Kanji-kun today.
It was written in a letter.
IDOL F.I. MOMOKO SCRIPT
Oh, is she?
Maybe we should give her a hand with that...
Nya ha ha ha ha!

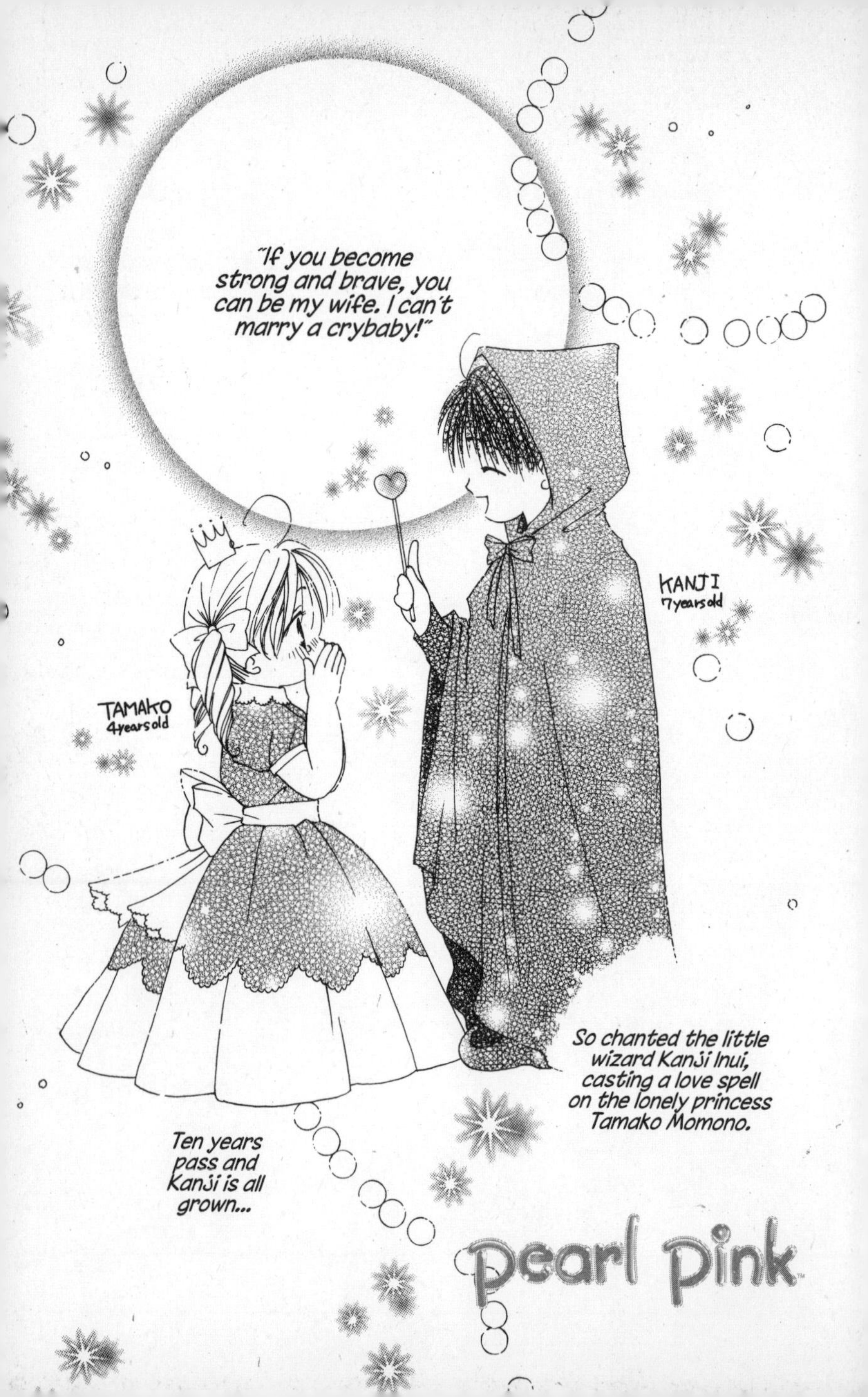
"If you become strong and brave, you can be my wife. I can't marry a crybaby!"
KANJI 7 years old
TAMAKO 4 years old
So chanted the little wizard Kanji Inui, casting a love spell on the lonely princess Tamako Momono.
Ten years pass and Kanji is all grown...
pearl pink™

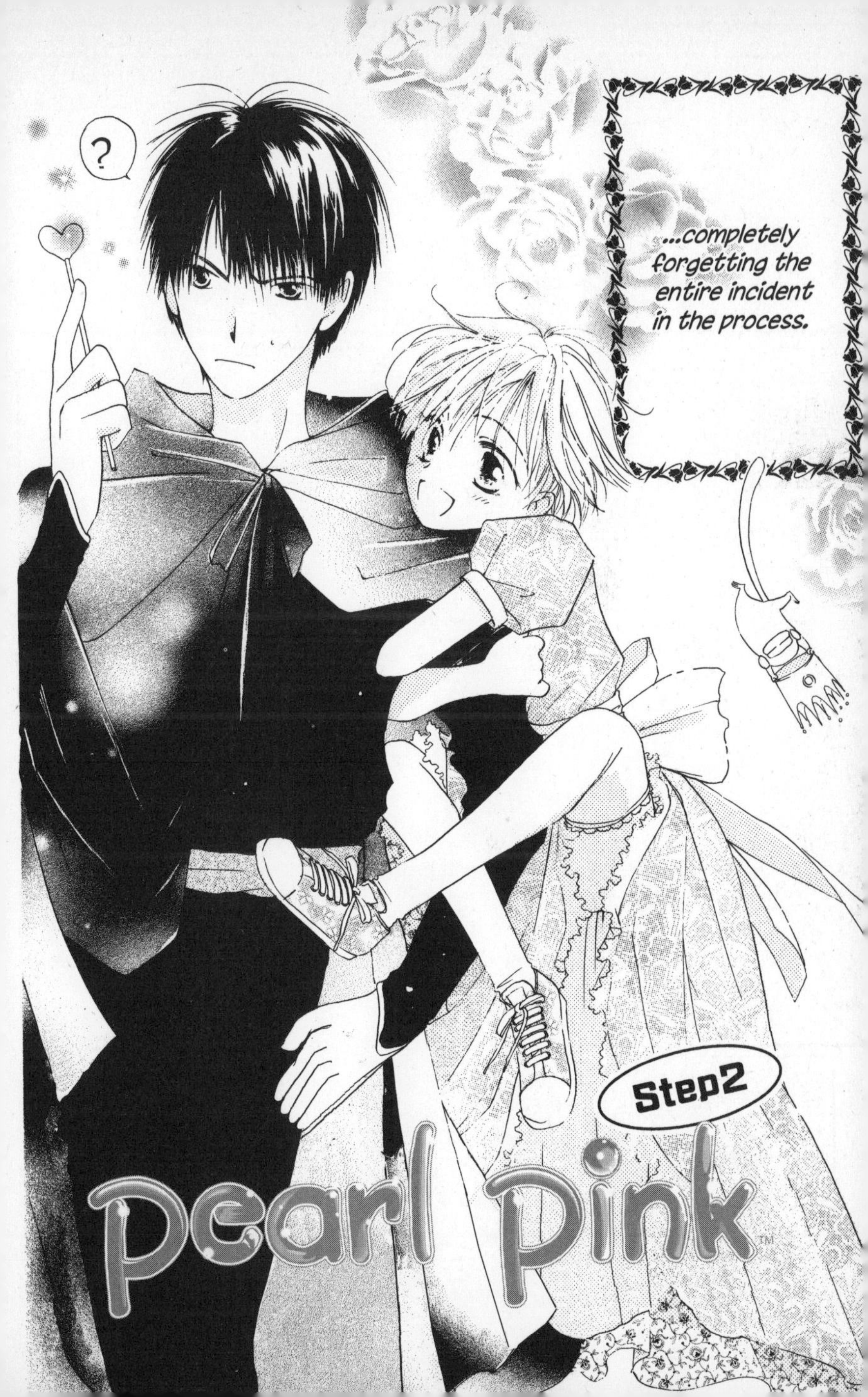
...completely forgetting the entire incident in the process.
?
Step2
pearl pink™

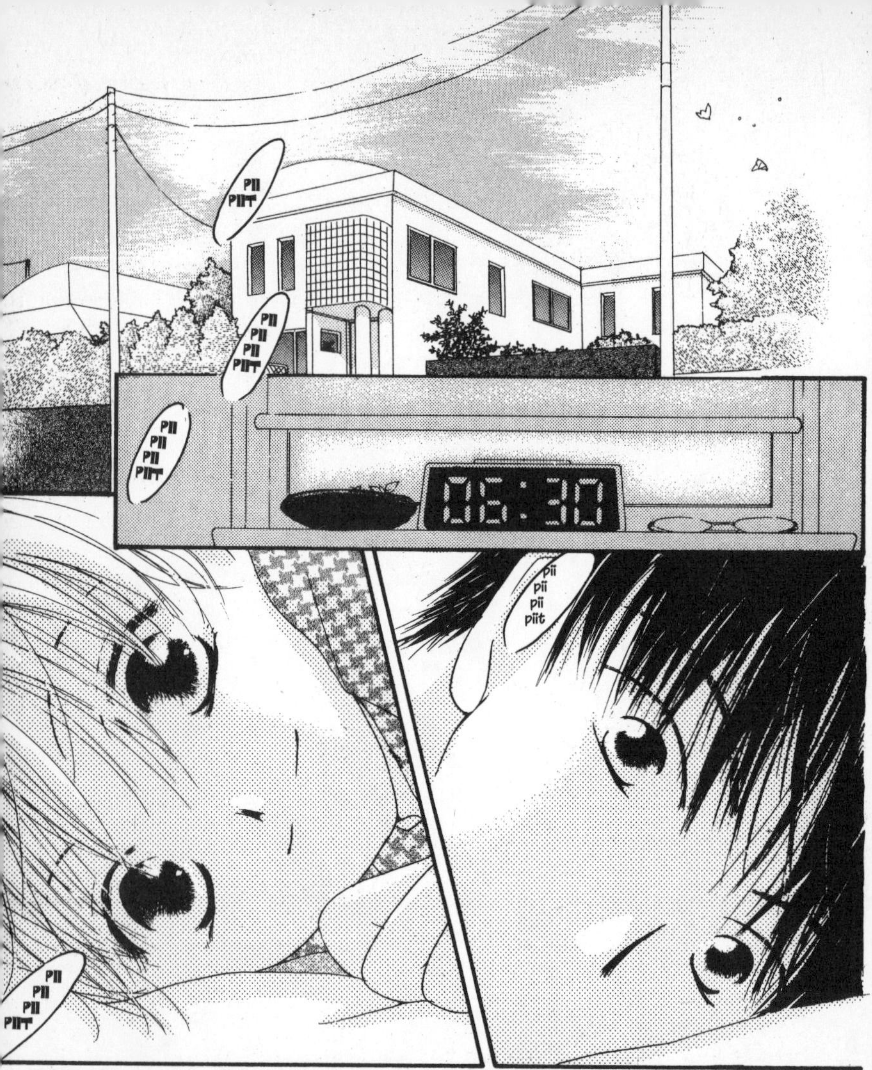
PII PIIT
PII PII PII PIIT
PII PII PII PIIT
06:30
pii pii pii piit
PII PII PII PIIT

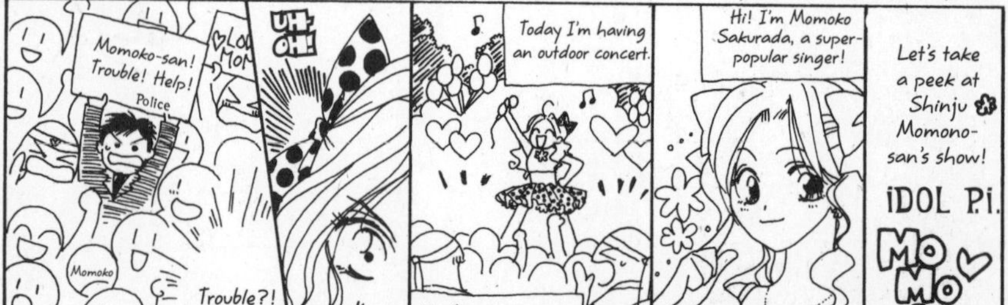
Let's take a peek at Shinju Momono-san's show!
iDOL P.i.
MOMOKO
1.
Hi! I'm Momoko Sakurada, a super-popular singer!
Today I'm having an outdoor concert.
My fans scream and dance and have a great time!
UH-OH!
Momoko-san! Trouble! Help!
Police
Momoko
Trouble?!
TBC...

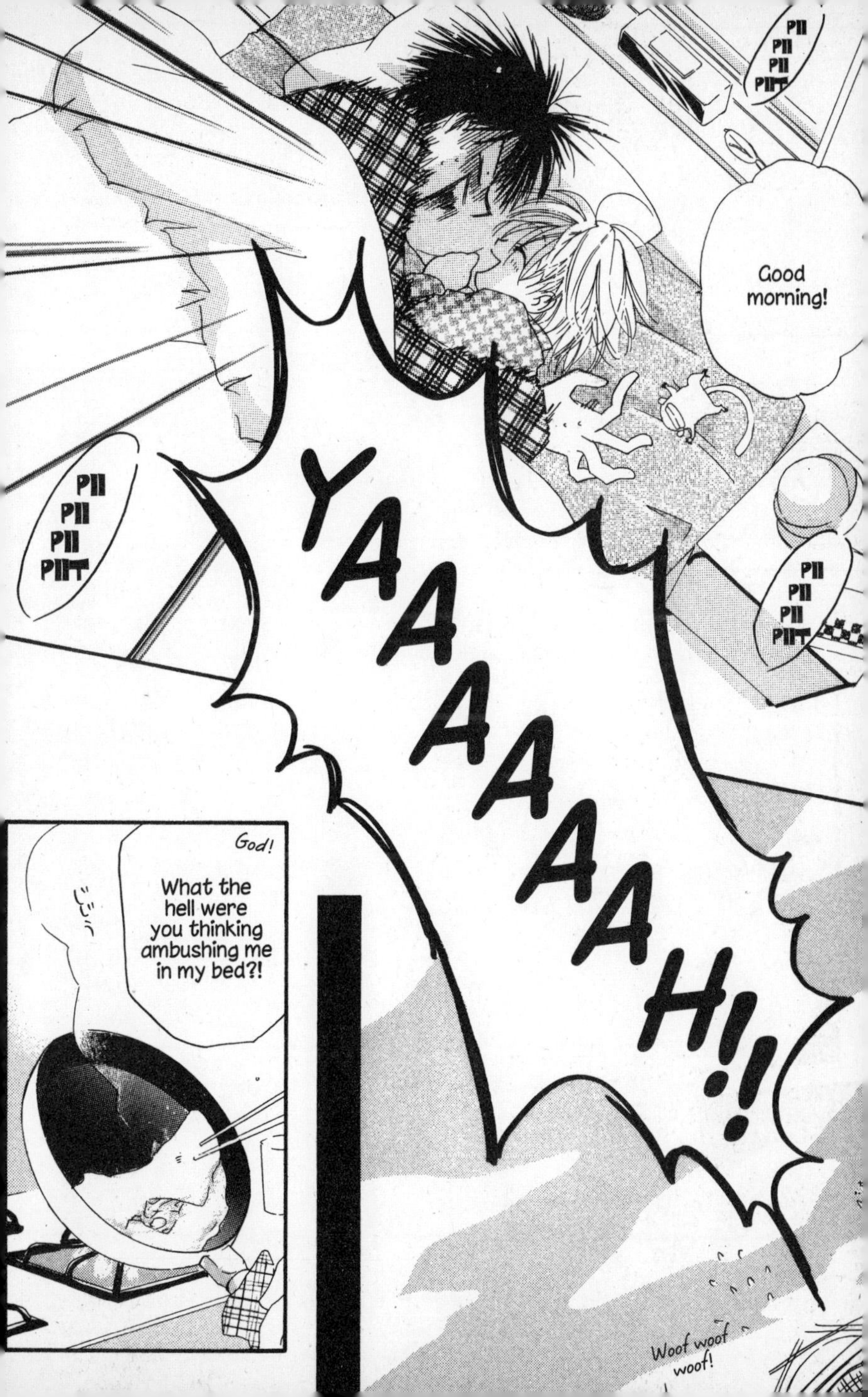
PII PII PII PIIT
Good morning!
PII PII PII PIIT
YAAAAAAH!!
PII PII PII PIIT
Woof woof woof!
God!
What the hell were you thinking ambushing me in my bed?!

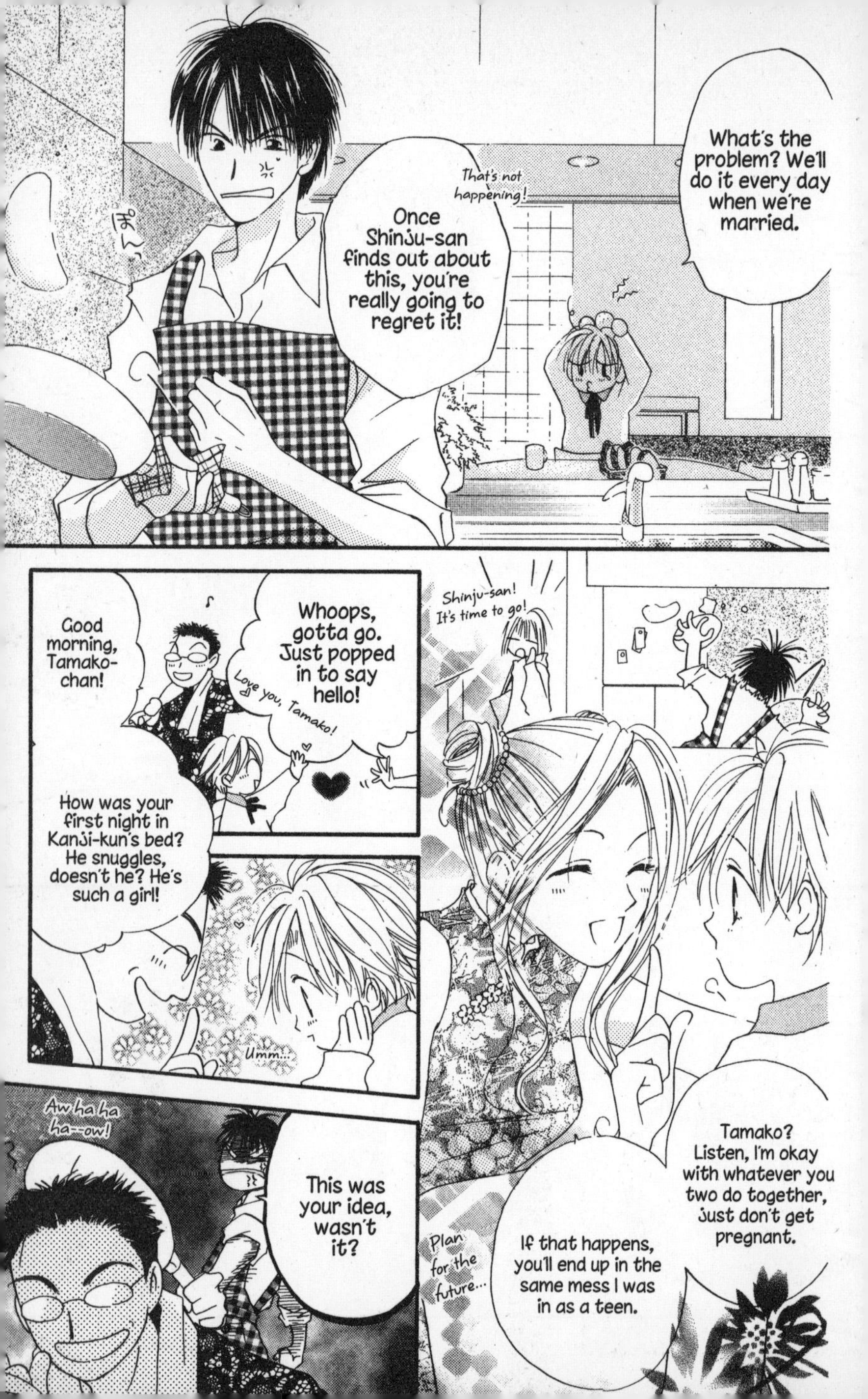
What's the problem? We'll do it every day when we're married.
That's not happening!
Once Shinju-san finds out about this, you're really going to regret it!
ぽん、
Shinju-san! It's time to go!
Tamako? Listen, I'm okay with whatever you two do together, just don't get pregnant.
If that happens, you'll end up in the same mess I was in as a teen.
Plan for the future...
Whoops, gotta go. Just popped in to say hello!
Love you, Tamako!
Good morning, Tamako-chan!
How was your first night in Kanji-kun's bed? He snuggles, doesn't he? He's such a girl!
Umm...
This was your idea, wasn't it?
Aw ha ha ha--ow!

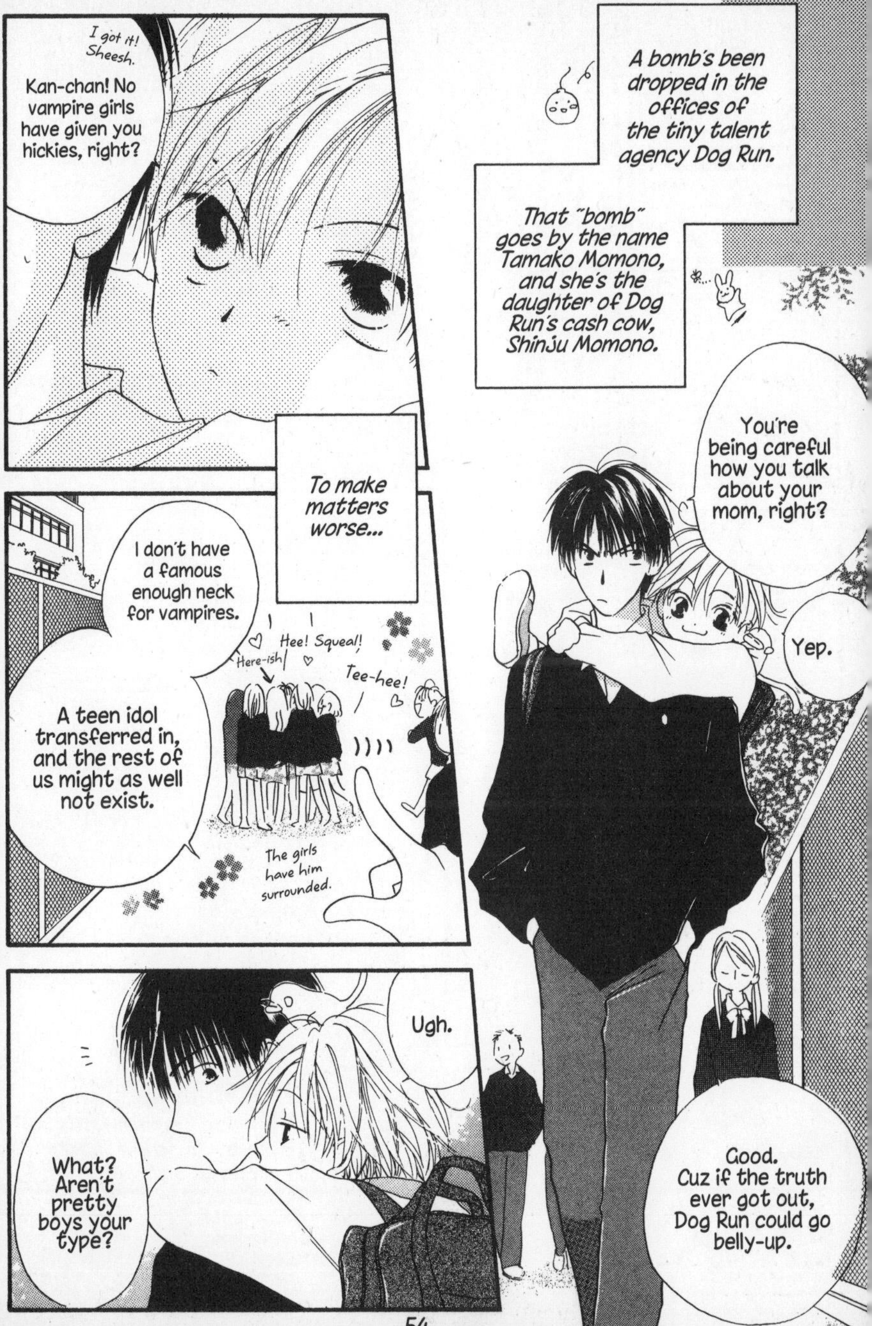
A bomb's been dropped in the offices of the tiny talent agency Dog Run.
That "bomb" goes by the name Tamako Momono, and she's the daughter of Dog Run's cash cow, Shinju Momono.
You're being careful how you talk about your mom, right?
Yep.
Good. Cuz if the truth ever got out, Dog Run could go belly-up.
Kan-chan! No vampire girls have given you hickies, right?
I got it! Sheesh.
To make matters worse...
I don't have a famous enough neck for vampires.
Hee! Squeal!
Here-ish
Tee-hee!
A teen idol transferred in, and the rest of us might as well not exist.
The girls have him surrounded.
Ugh.
What? Aren't pretty boys your type?

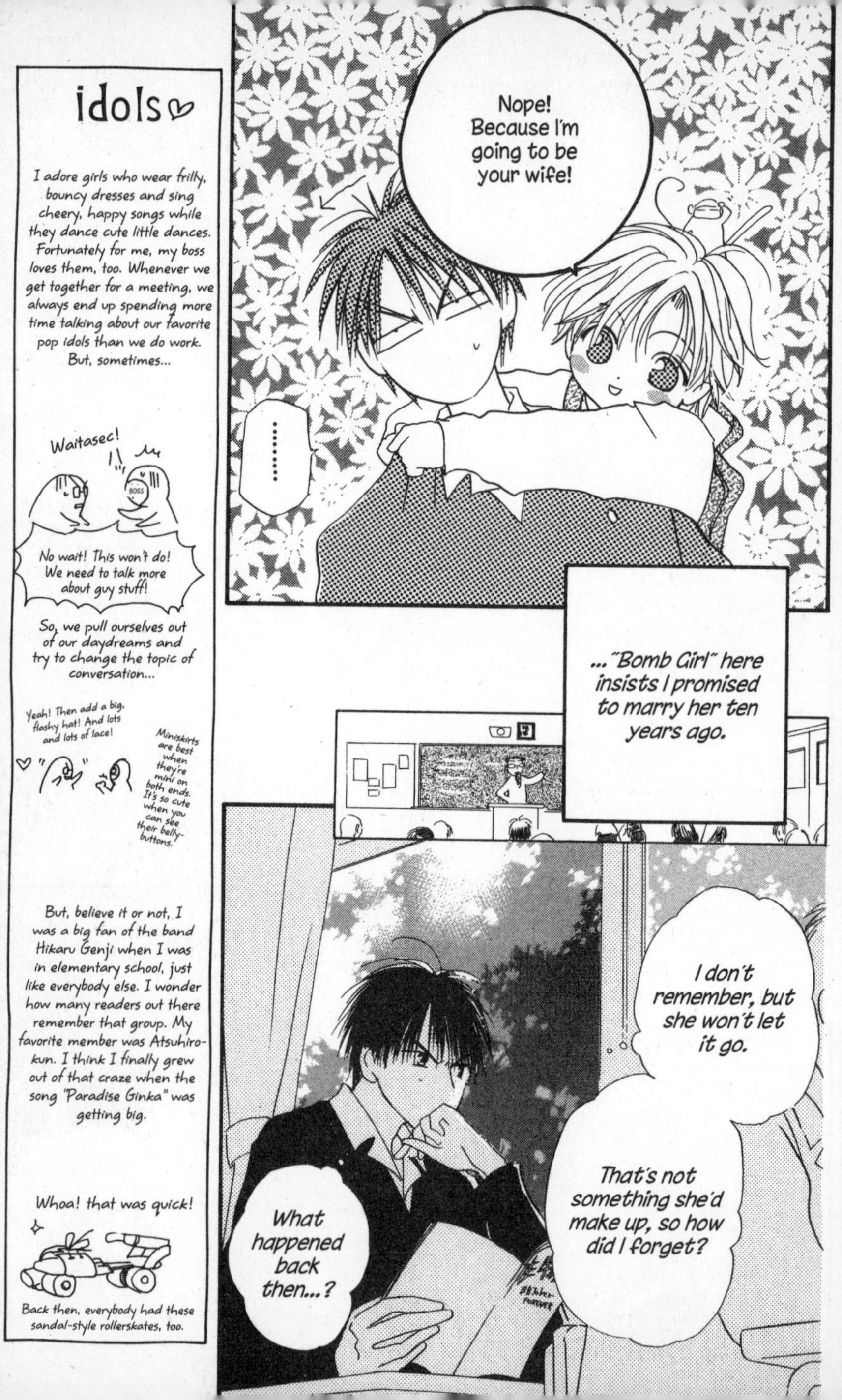
Nope! Because I'm going to be your wife!
....
..."Bomb Girl" here insists I promised to marry her ten years ago.
I don't remember, but she won't let it go.
That's not something she'd make up, so how did I forget?
What happened back then...?

idols♡

I adore girls who wear frilly, bouncy dresses and sing cheery, happy songs while they dance cute little dances. Fortunately for me, my boss loves them, too. Whenever we get together for a meeting, we always end up spending more time talking about our favorite pop idols than we do work. But, sometimes...

Waitasec!

BOSS

No wait! This won't do! We need to talk more about guy stuff!

So, we pull ourselves out of our daydreams and try to change the topic of conversation...

Yeah! Then add a big, flashy hat! And lots and lots of lace!

Miniskirts are best when they're mini on both ends. It's so cute when you can see their belly-buttons.

But, believe it or not, I was a big fan of the band Hikaru Genji when I was in elementary school, just like everybody else. I wonder how many readers out there remember that group. My favorite member was Atsuhiro-kun. I think I finally grew out of that craze when the song "Paradise Ginka" was getting big.

Whoa! that was quick!

Back then, everybody had these sandal-style rollerskates, too.

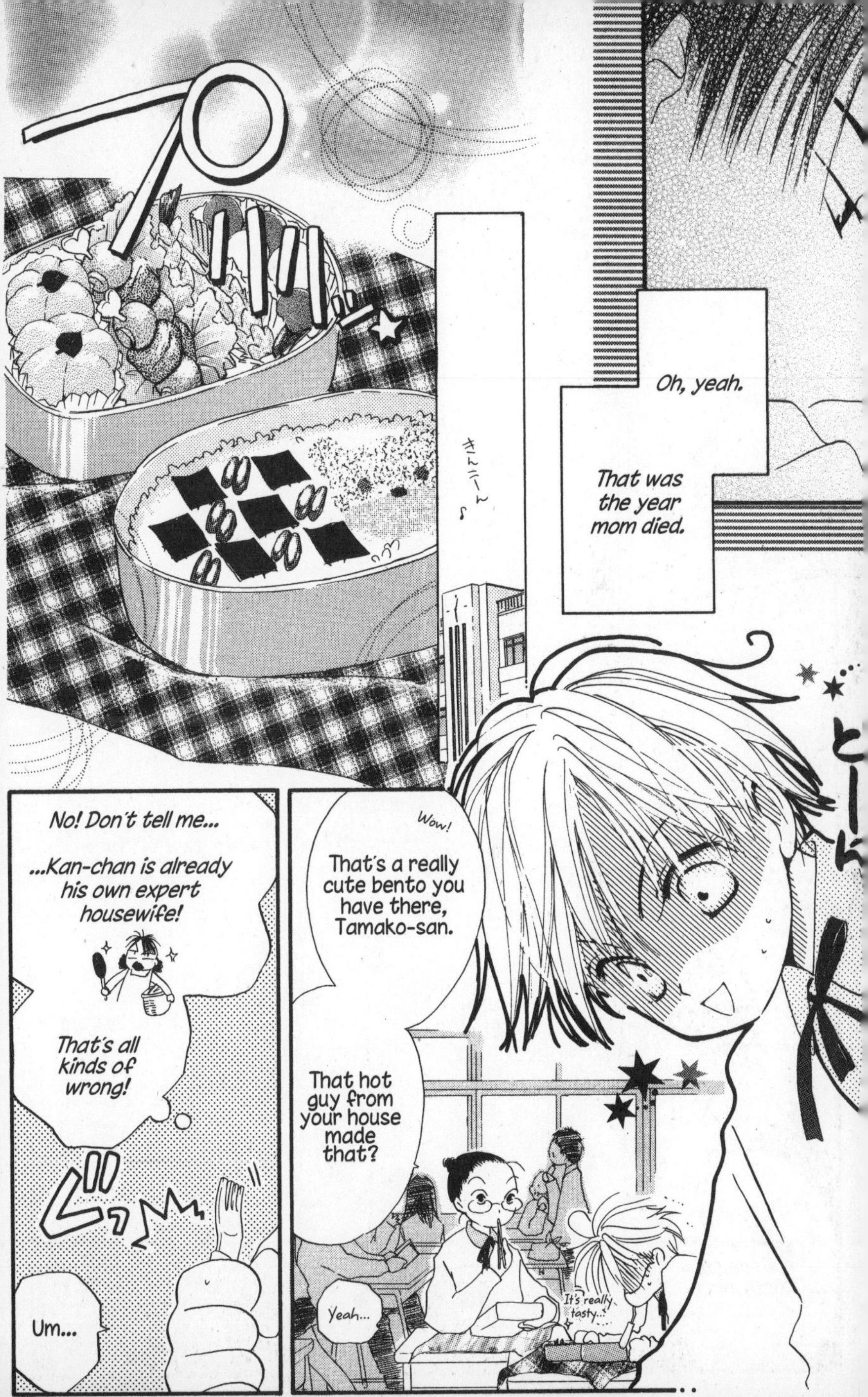
Oh, yeah.
That was the year mom died.
きんこーん♪
どーん
Wow!
That's a really cute bento you have there, Tamako-san.
That hot guy from your house made that?
Yeah...
It's really tasty...
No! Don't tell me...
...Kan-chan is already his own expert housewife!
That's all kinds of wrong!
Um...

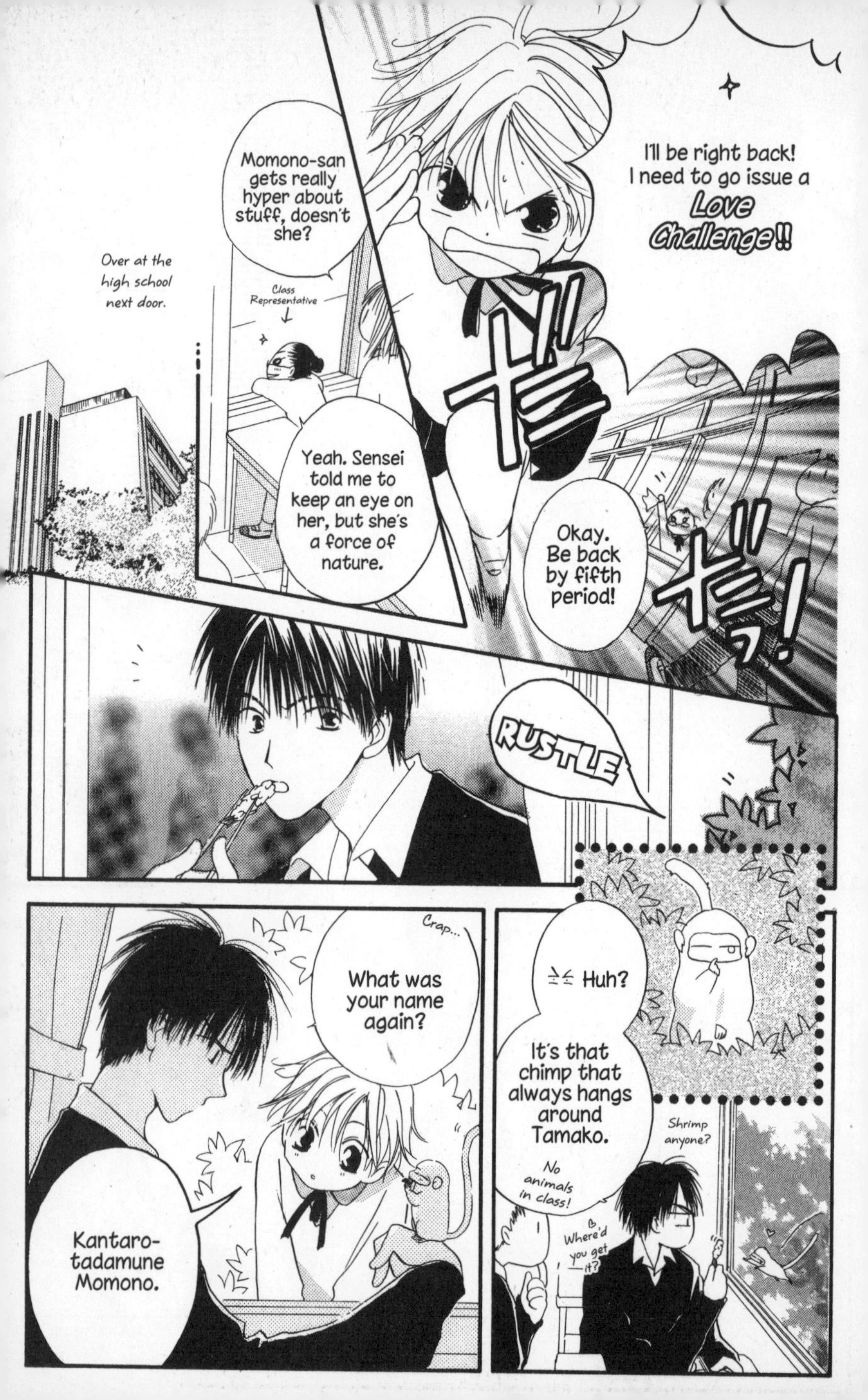
I'll be right back! I need to go issue a Love Challenge!!
Okay. Be back by fifth period!
Over at the high school next door.
Momono-san gets really hyper about stuff, doesn't she?
Class Representative
Yeah. Sensei told me to keep an eye on her, but she's a force of nature.
RUSTLE
Huh?
It's that chimp that always hangs around Tamako.
Shrimp anyone?
No animals in class!
Where'd you get it?
Crap...
What was your name again?
Kantaro-tadamune Momono.

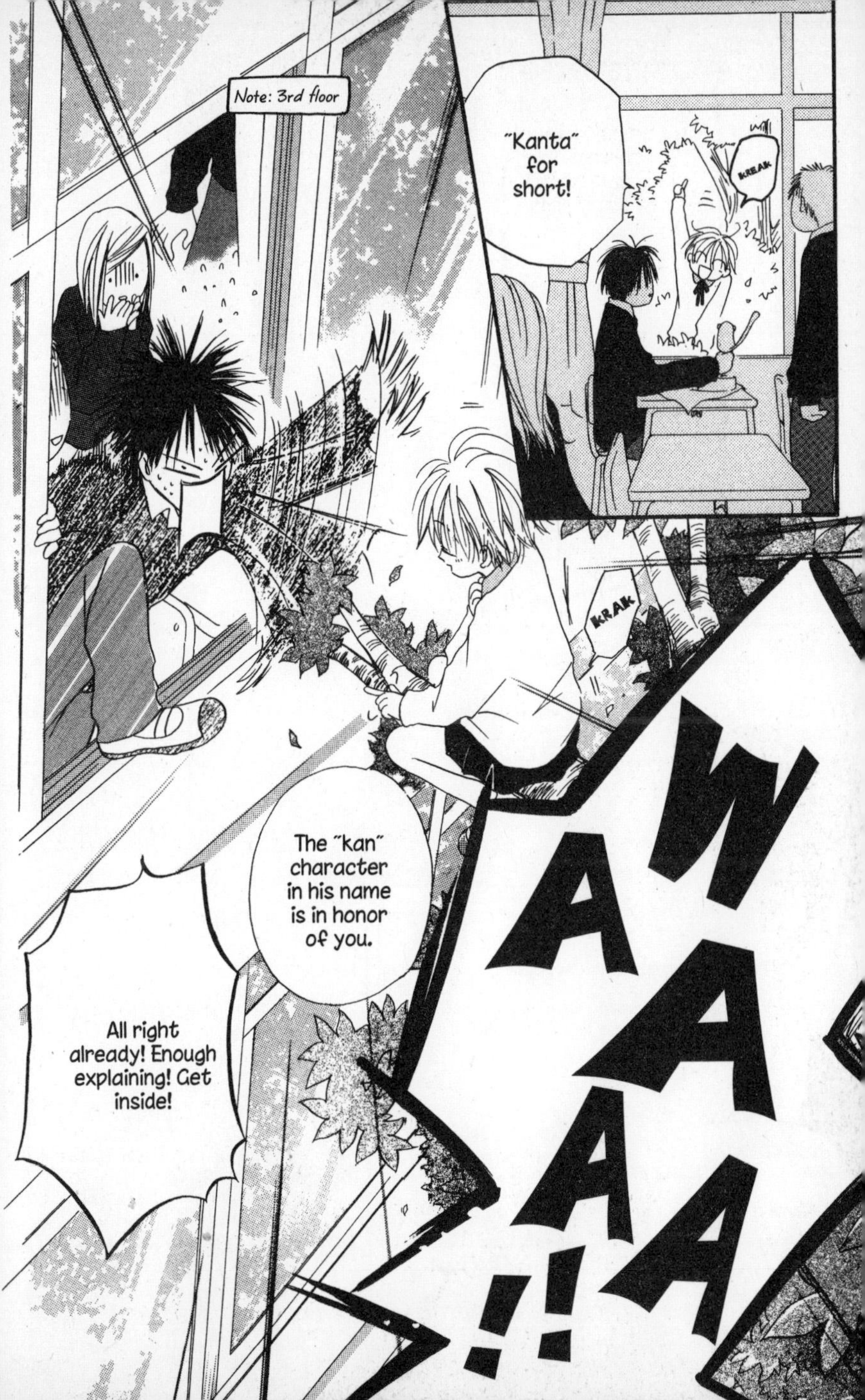
"Kanta" for short!
KREAK
Note: 3rd floor
KRAK
WAAAA!!
The "kan" character in his name is in honor of you.
All right already! Enough explaining! Get inside!

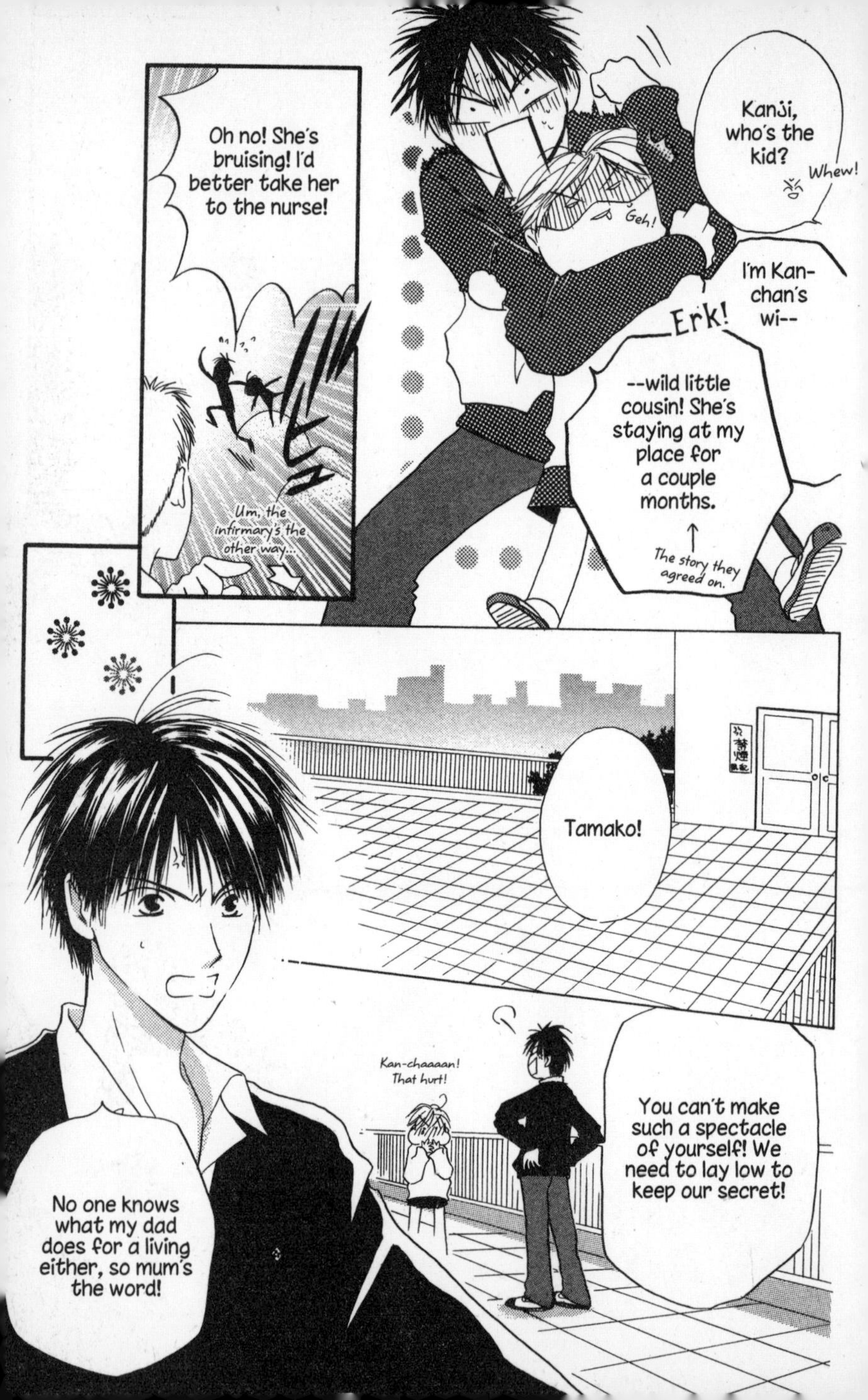
Kanji, who's the kid?
Whew!
Geh!
I'm Kan-chan's wi--
Erk!
--wild little cousin! She's staying at my place for a couple months.
The story they agreed on.
Oh no! She's bruising! I'd better take her to the nurse!
Um, the infirmary's the other way...
Tamako!
You can't make such a spectacle of yourself! We need to lay low to keep our secret!
Kan-chaaaan! That hurt!
No one knows what my dad does for a living either, so mum's the word!

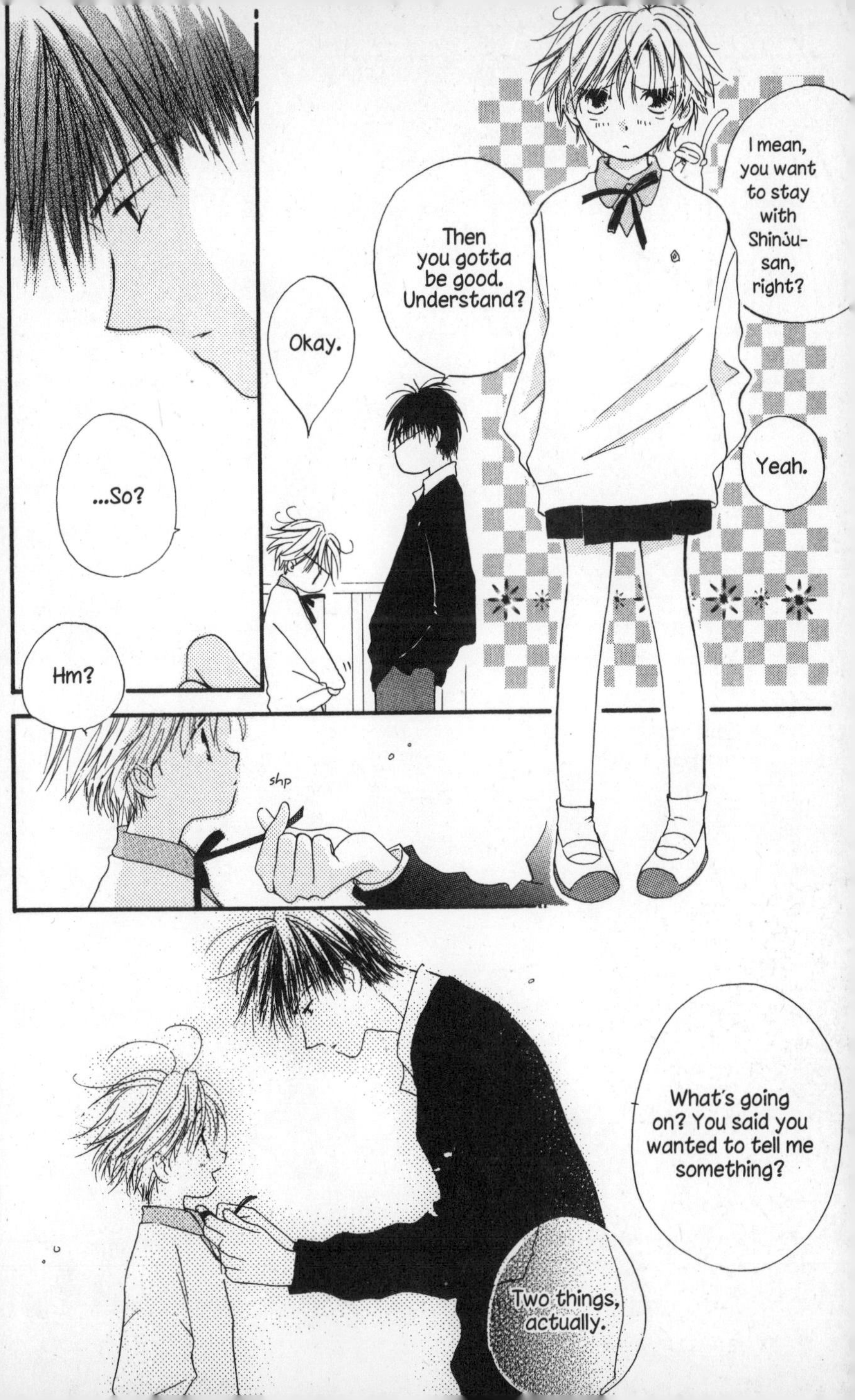
I mean, you want to stay with Shinju-san, right?
Yeah.
Then you gotta be good. Understand?
Okay.
...So?
Hm?
shp
What's going on? You said you wanted to tell me something?
Two things, actually.

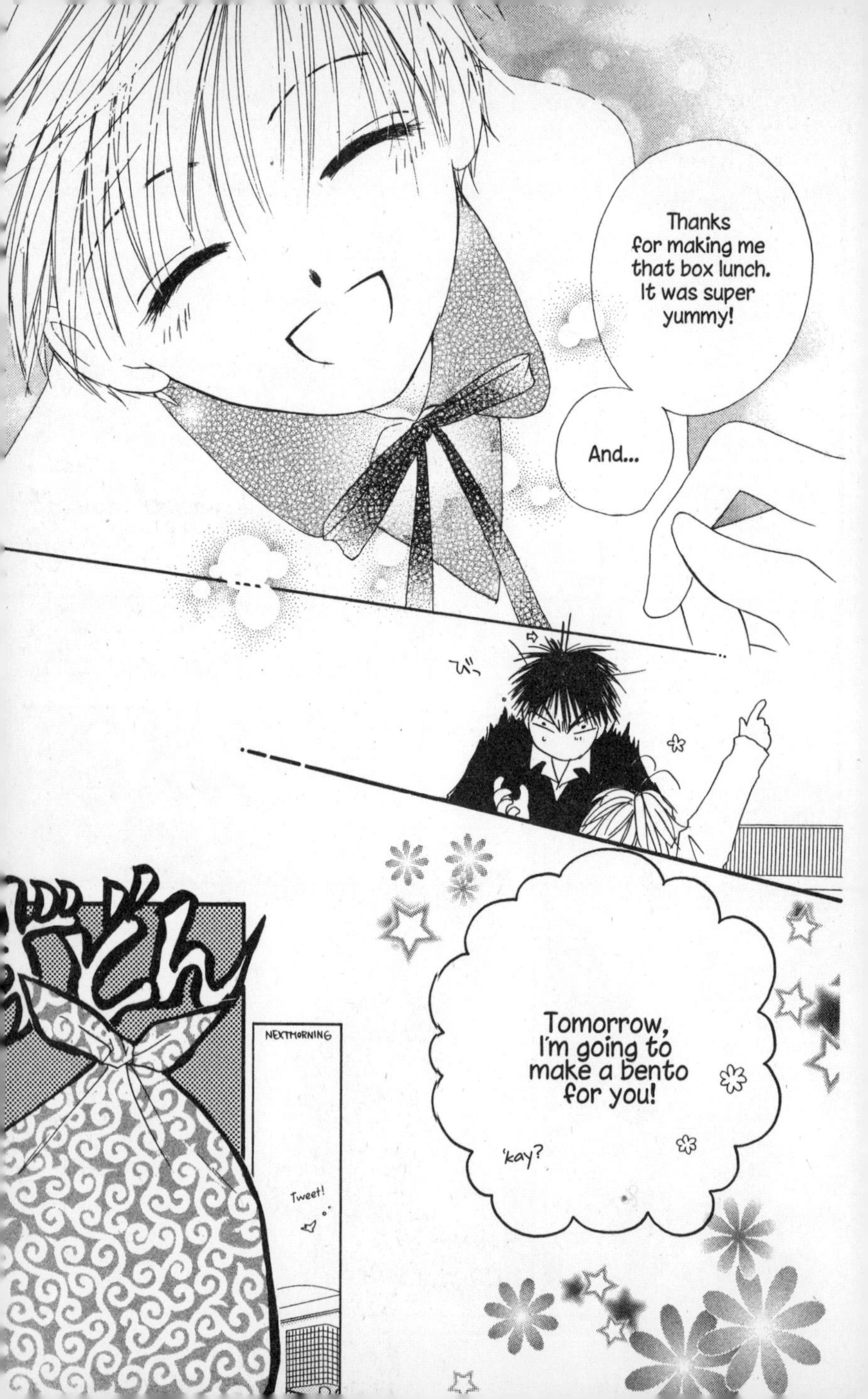
Thanks for making me that box lunch. It was super yummy!
And...
びっ
Tomorrow, I'm going to make a bento for you!
'kay?
NEXTMORNING
Tweet!

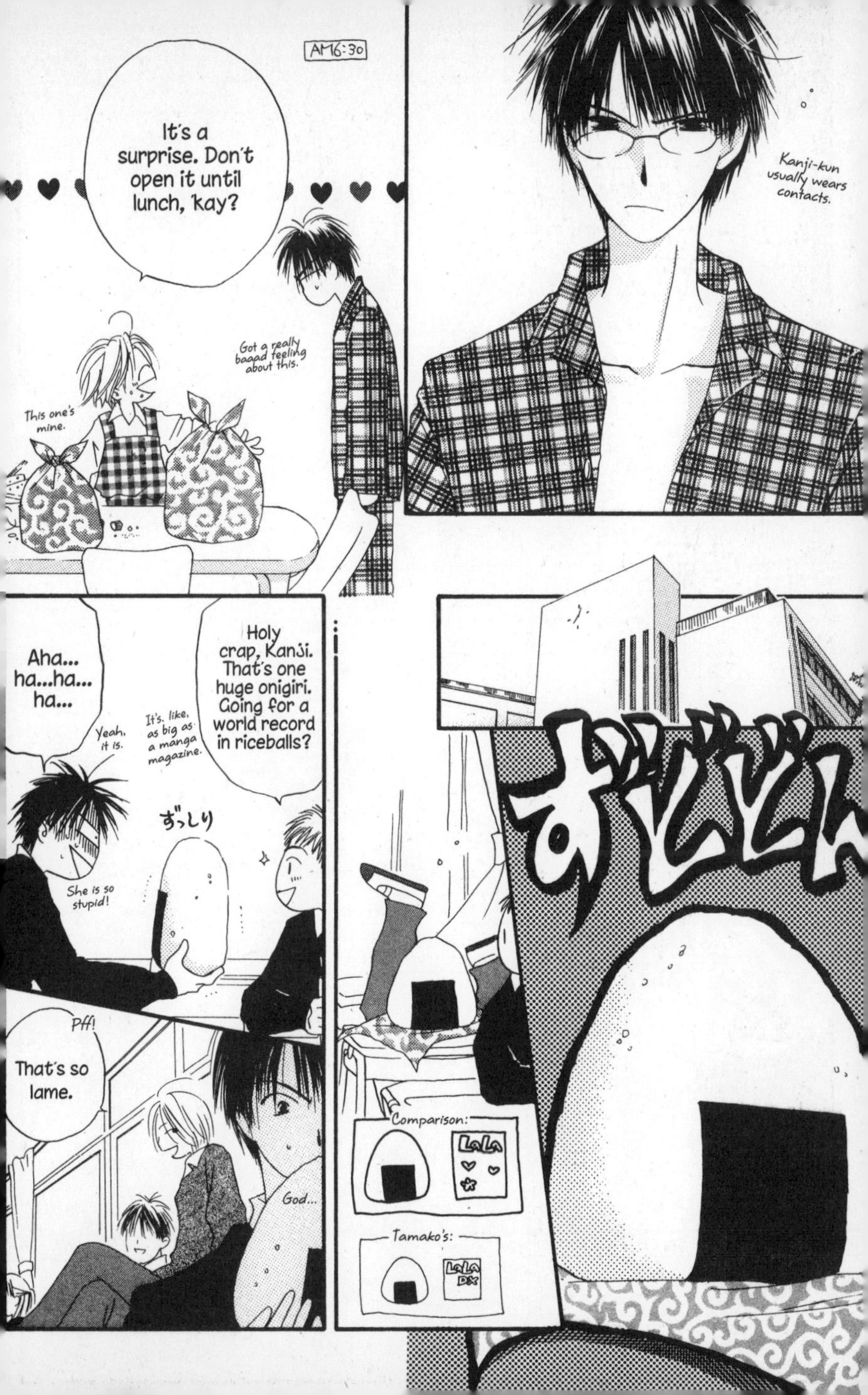
Kanji-kun usually wears contacts.
AM6:30
It's a surprise. Don't open it until lunch, 'kay?
Got a really baaad feeling about this.
This one's mine.
Comparison:
LaLa
Tamako's:
LaLa DX
Holy crap, Kanji. That's one huge onigiri. Going for a world record in riceballs?
It's, like, as big as a manga magazine.
Yeah, it is.
Aha... ha...ha... ha...
ずっしり
She is so stupid!
God...
Pff!
That's so lame.

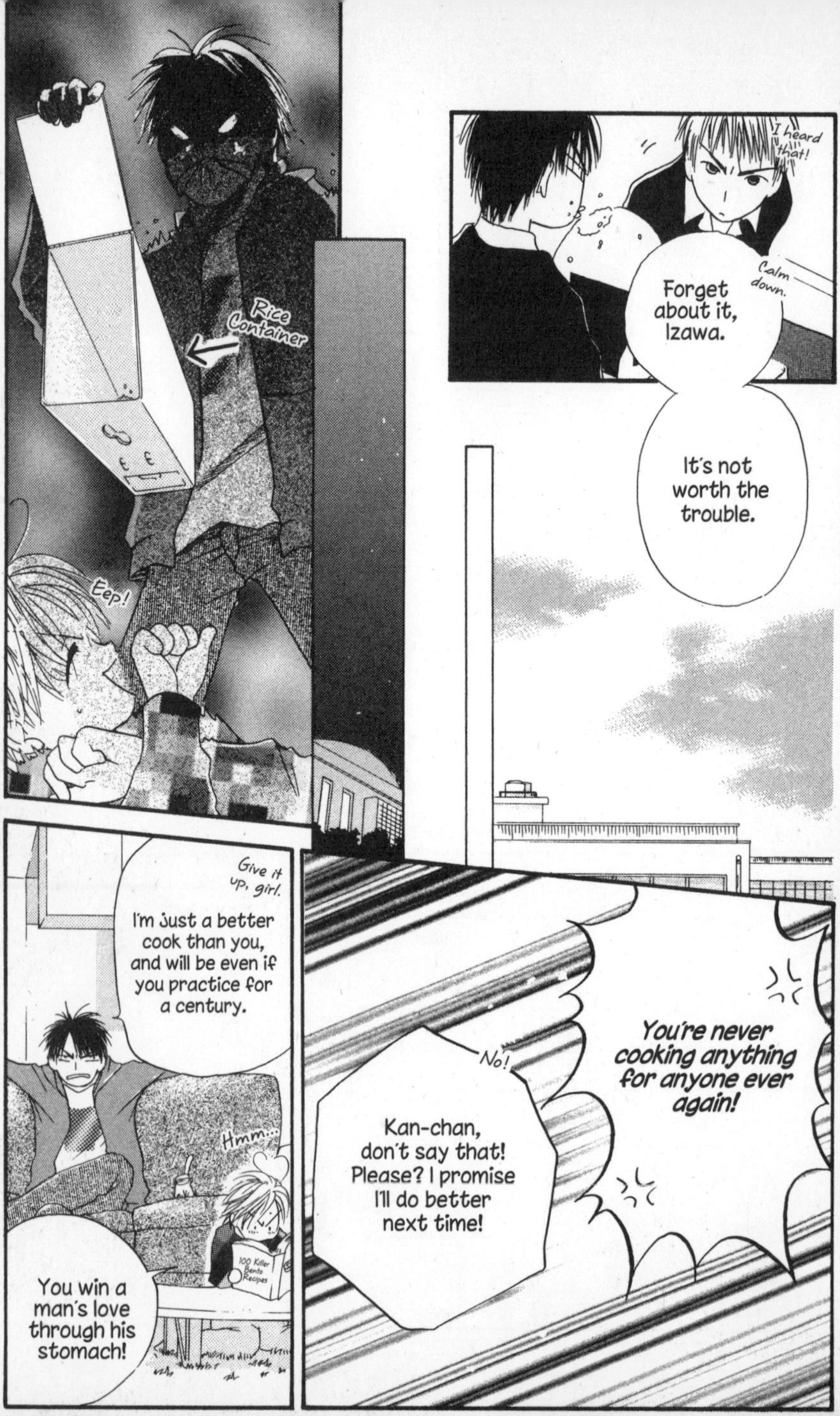
I heard that!
Calm down.
Forget about it, Izawa.
It's not worth the trouble.
Rice Container
Eep!
You're never cooking anything for anyone ever again!
No!
Kan-chan, don't say that! Please? I promise I'll do better next time!
Give it up, girl.
I'm just a better cook than you, and will be even if you practice for a century.
Hmm...
100 Killer Bento Recipes
You win a man's love through his stomach!

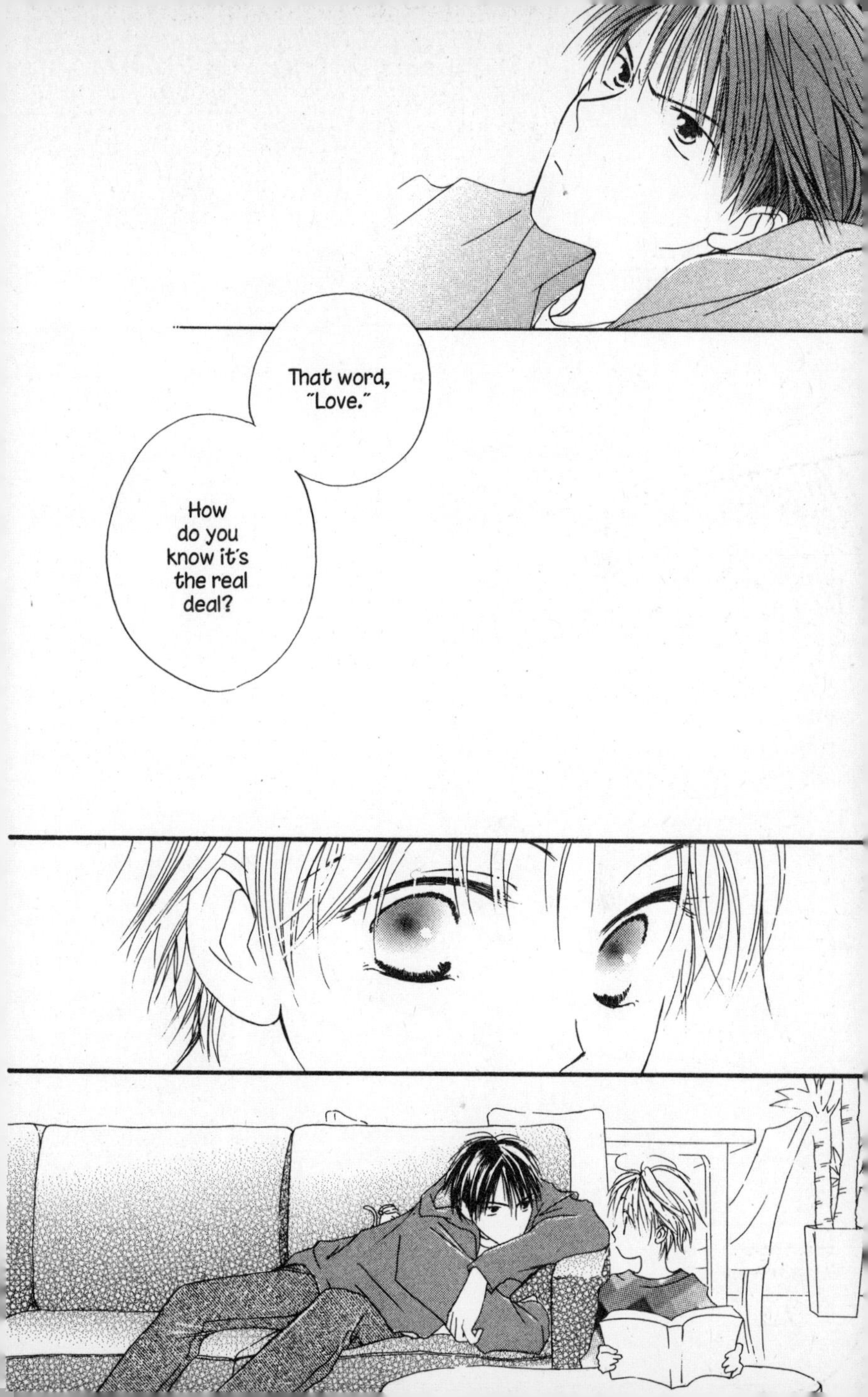
That word, "Love."
How do you know it's the real deal?

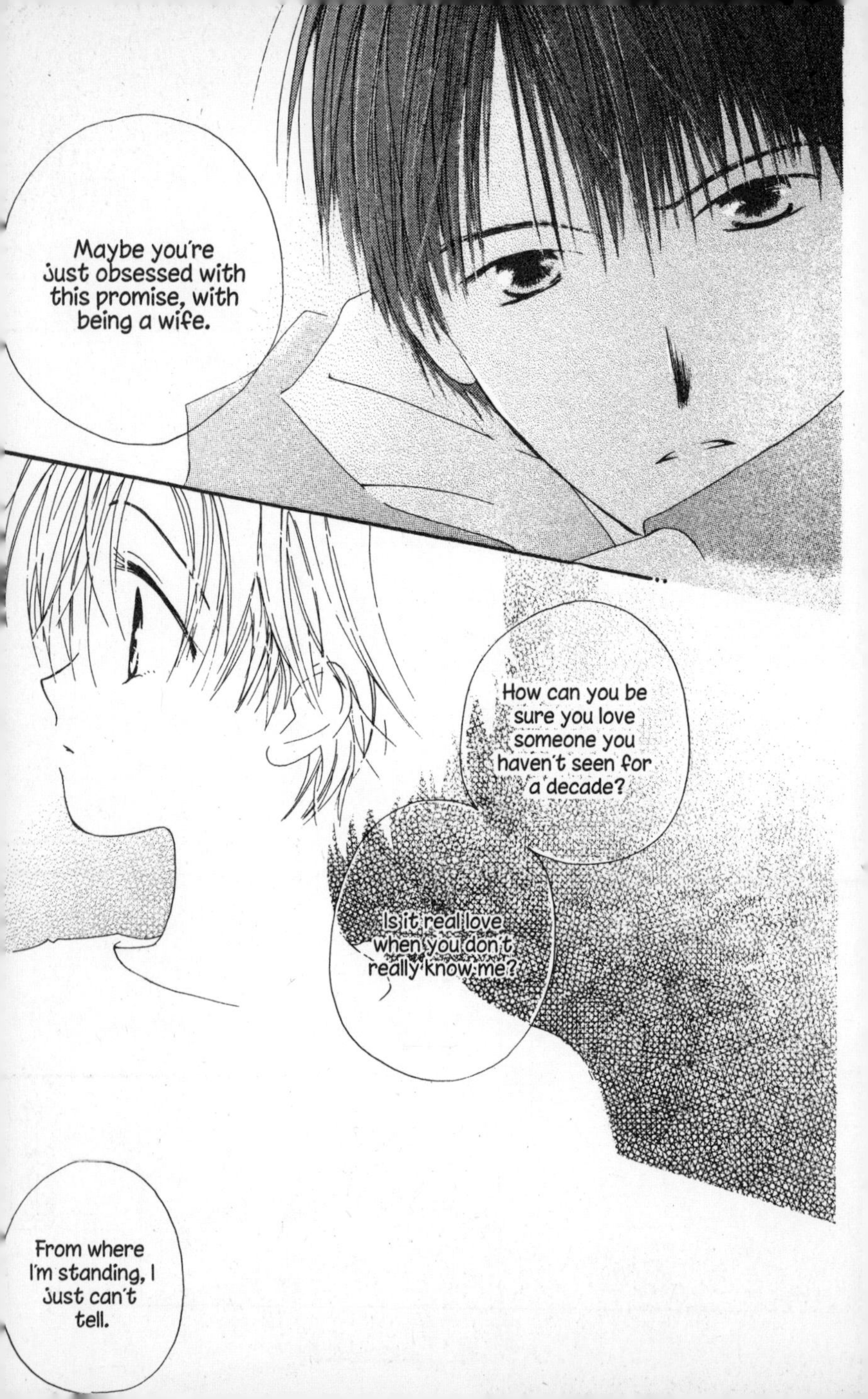

Maybe you're just obsessed with this promise, with being a wife.
How can you be sure you love someone you haven't seen for a decade?
Is it real love when you don't really know me?
From where I'm standing, I just can't tell.

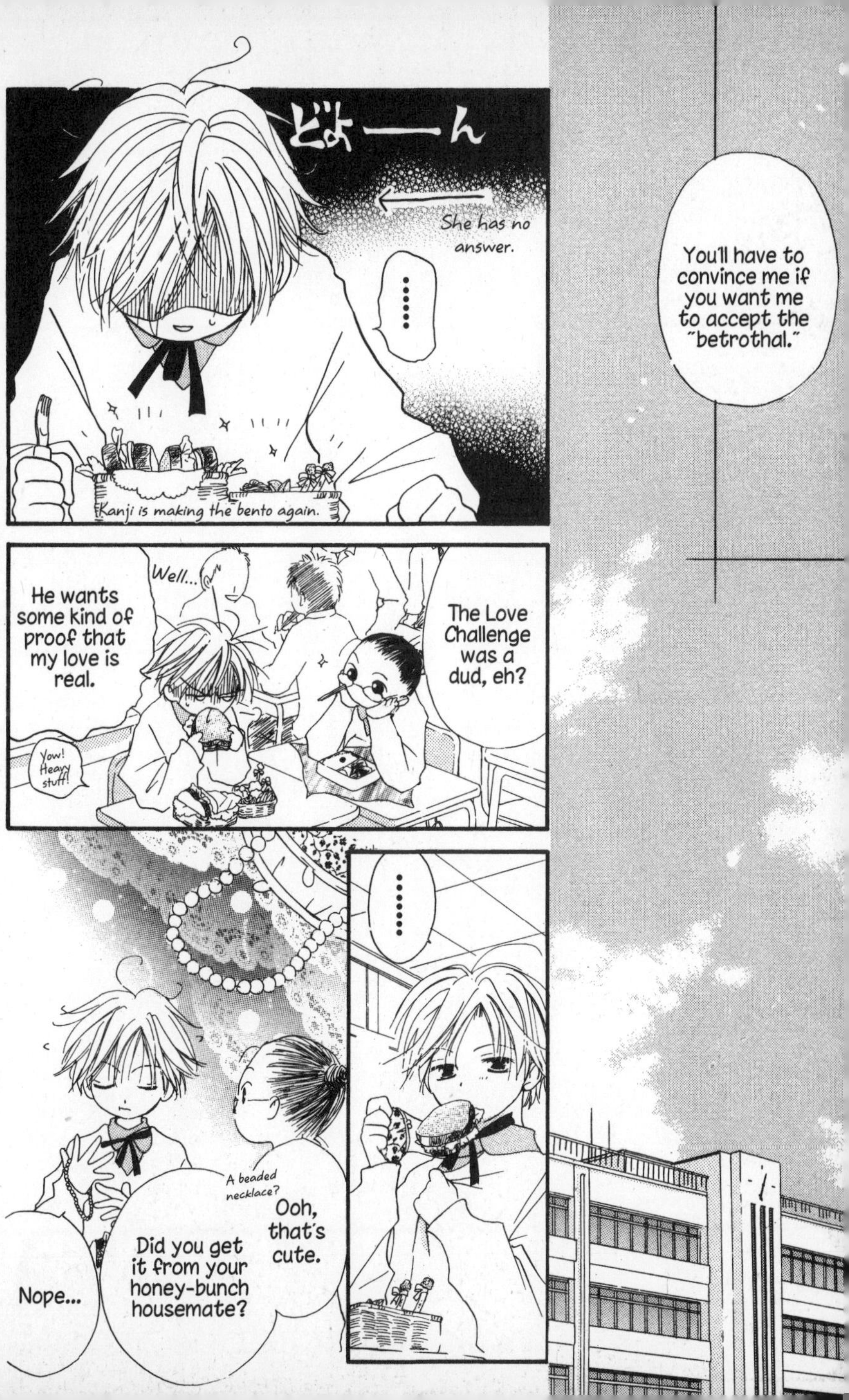
You'll have to convince me if you want me to accept the "betrothal."
どよーん
......
She has no answer.
Kanji is making the bento again.
The Love Challenge was a dud, eh?
Well...
He wants some kind of proof that my love is real.
Yow! Heavy stuff!
......
Ooh, that's cute.
A beaded necklace?
Did you get it from your honey-bunch housemate?
Nope...

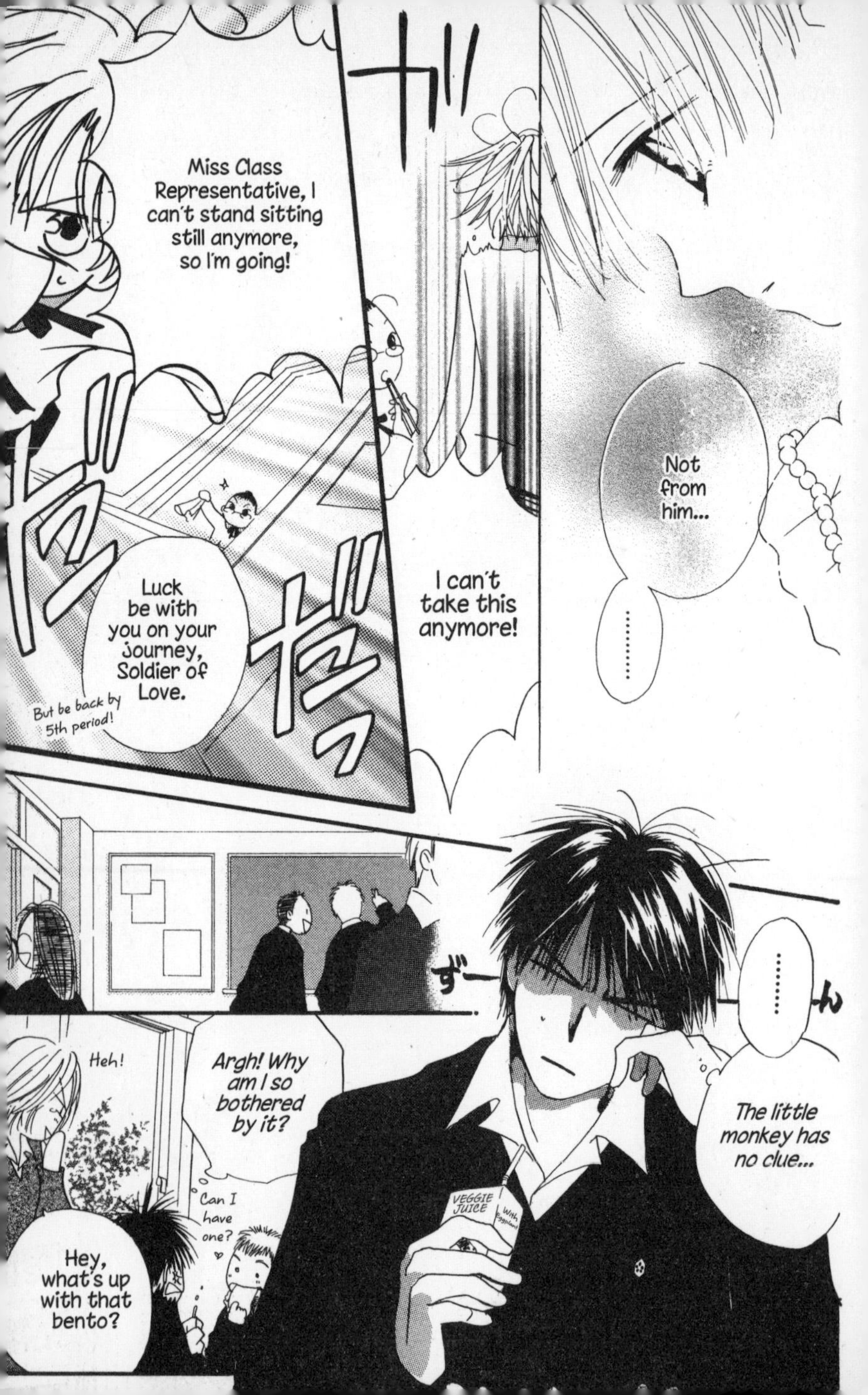
Not from him...
......
I can't take this anymore!
Miss Class Representative, I can't stand sitting still anymore, so I'm going!
Luck be with you on your journey, Soldier of Love.
But be back by 5th period!
......
The little monkey has no clue...
Argh! Why am I so bothered by it?
Heh!
VEGGIE JUICE
With Eggplant
Can I have one?
Hey, what's up with that bento?

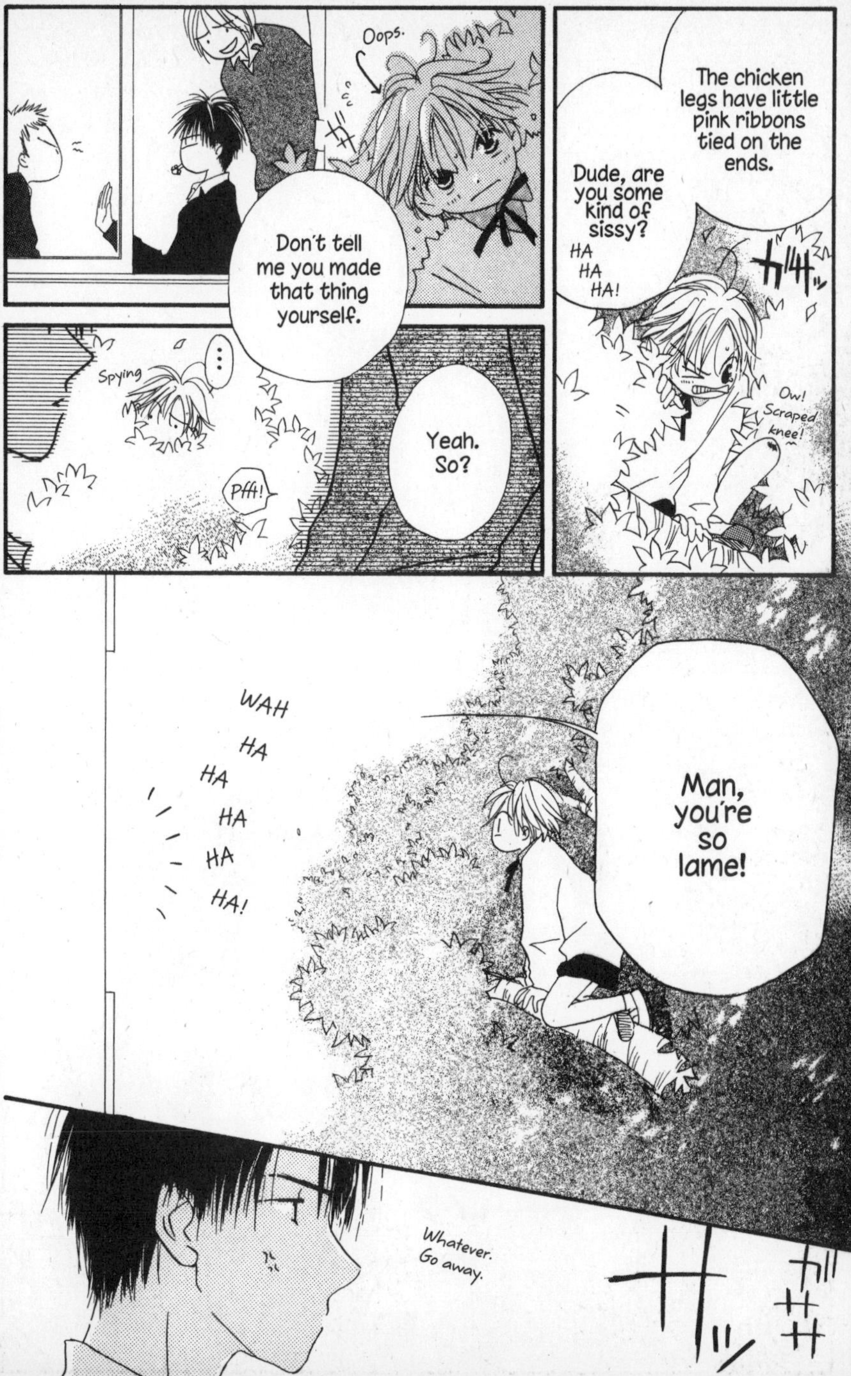
The chicken legs have little pink ribbons tied on the ends.
Dude, are you some kind of sissy?
HA HA HA!
Ow! Scraped knee!
Oops.
Don't tell me you made that thing yourself.
Spying
...
Pff!
Yeah. So?
Man, you're so lame!
WAH HA HA HA HA HA!
Whatever. Go away.

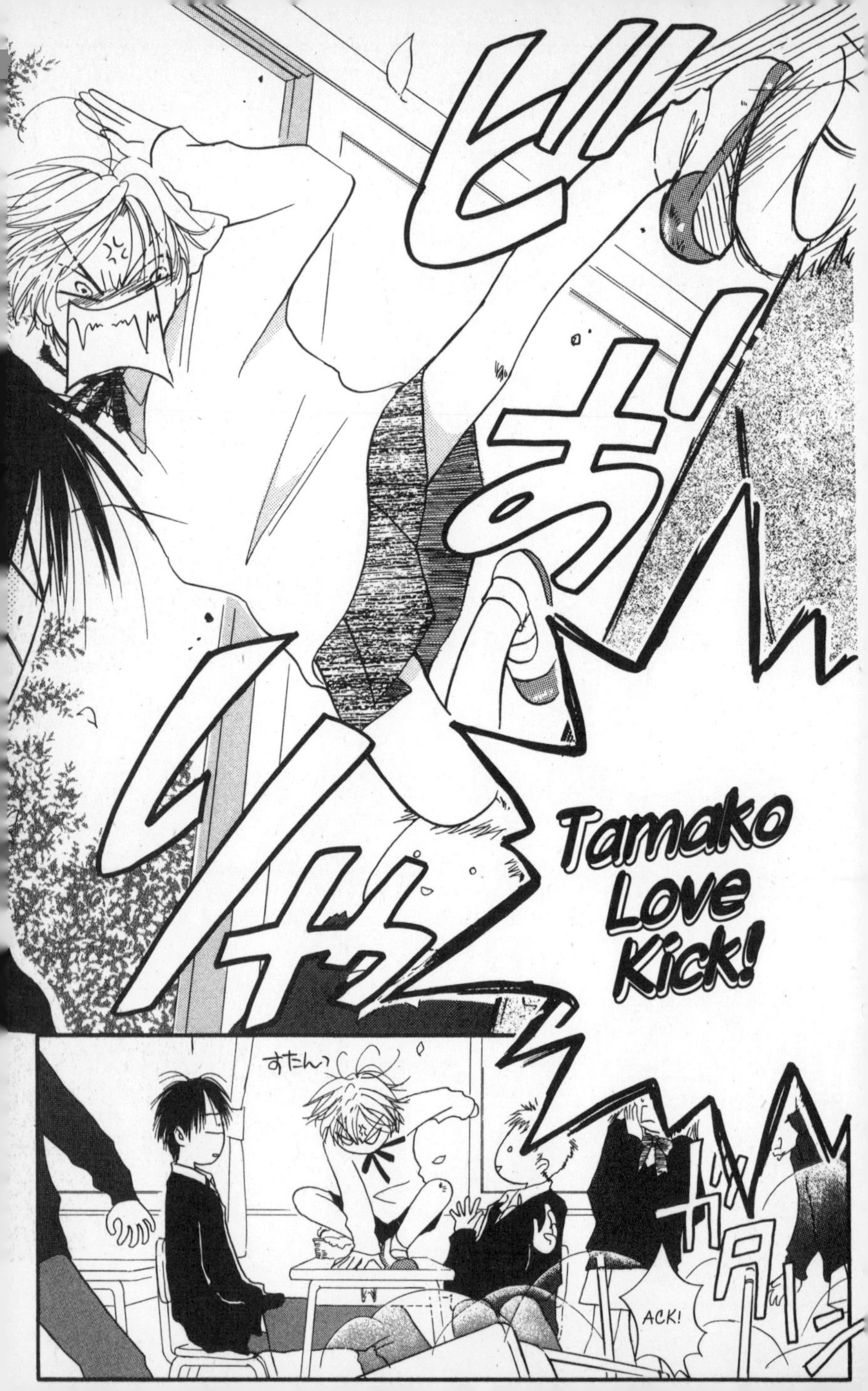
Tamako Love Kick!
ガタ
ACK!
すたんっ

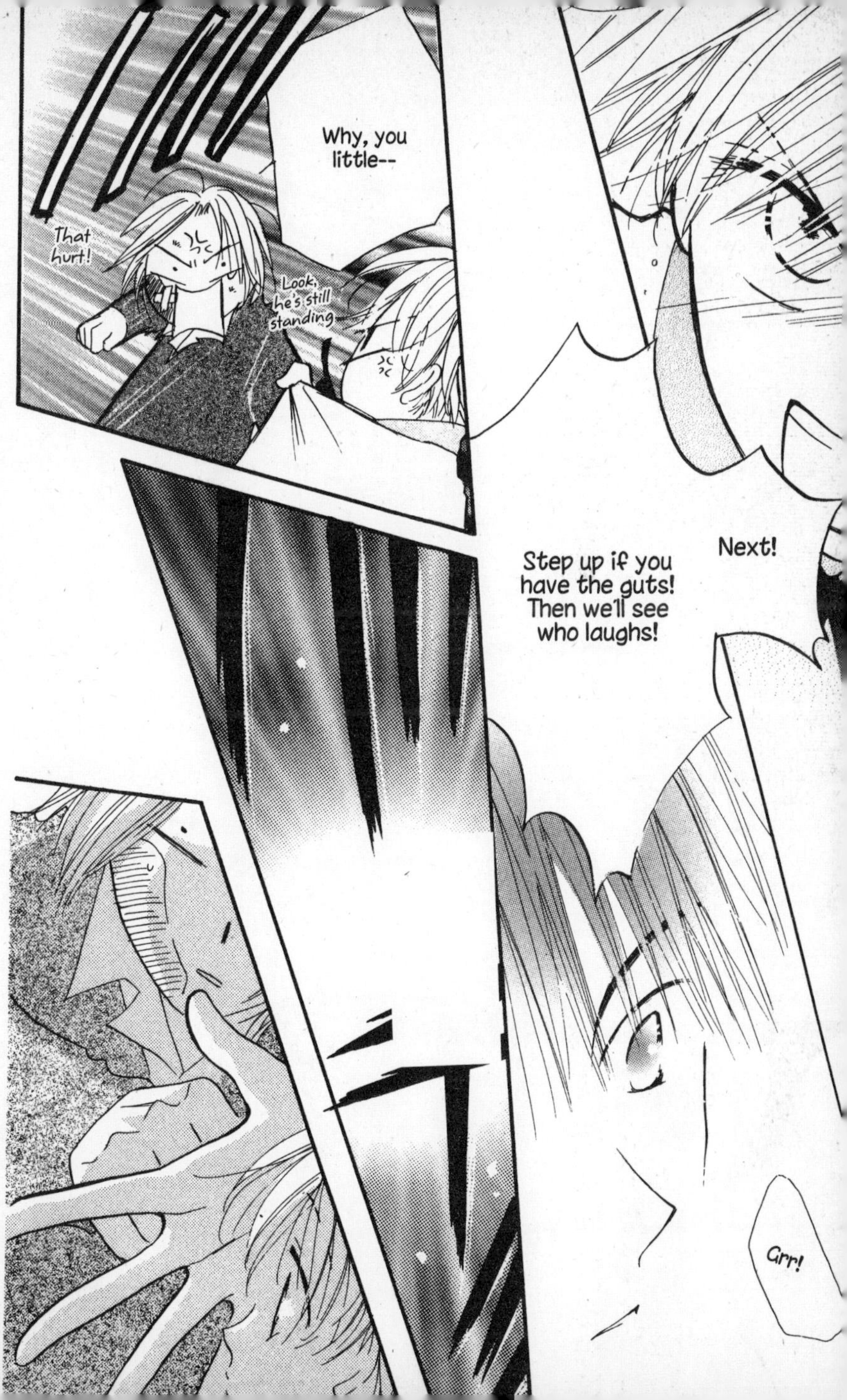
Next!
Step up if you have the guts! Then we'll see who laughs!
Why, you little--
That hurt!
Look, he's still standing
Grr!

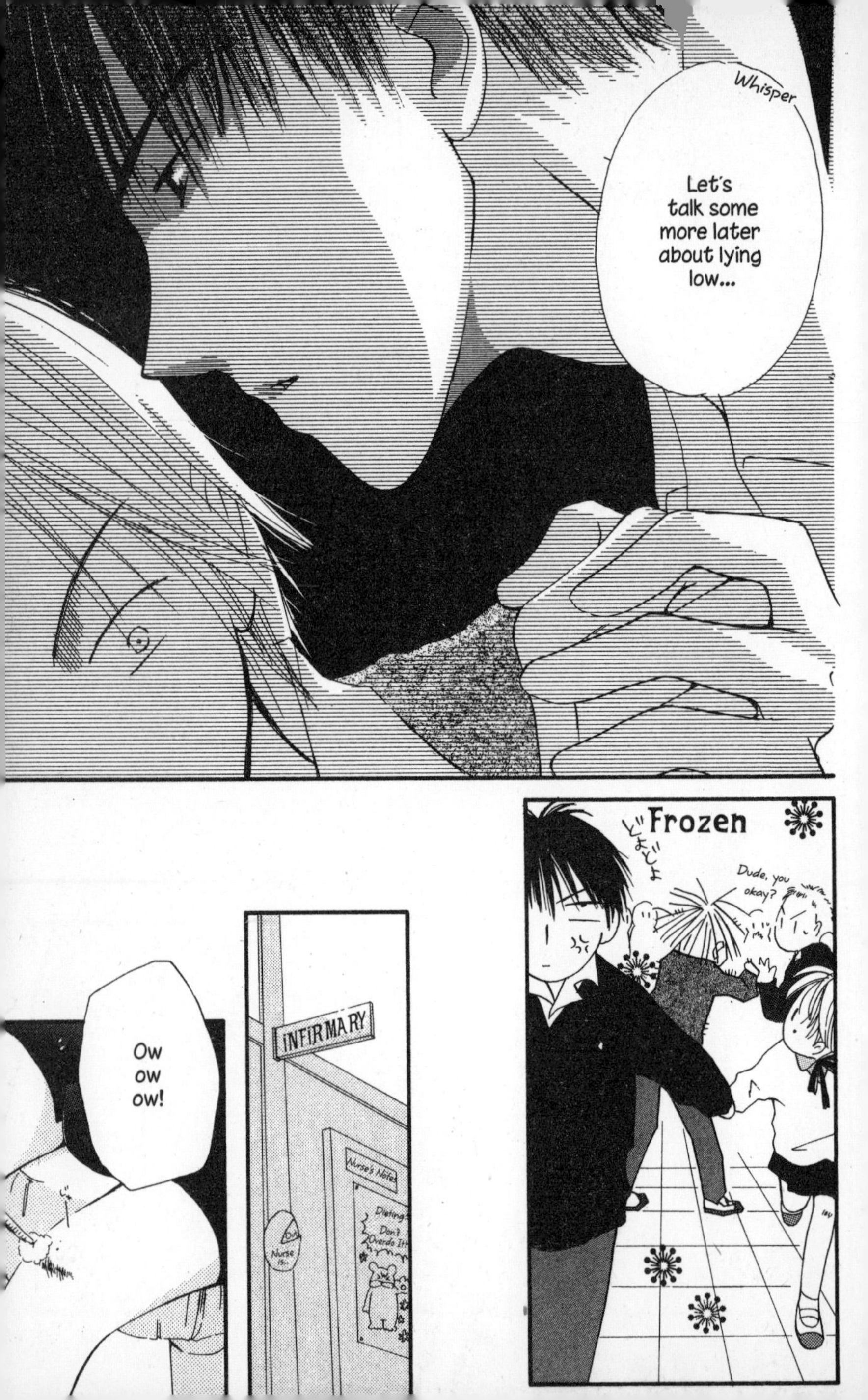
Whisper
Let's talk some more later about lying low...
Frozen
どよどよ
Dude, you okay?
INFIRMARY
Ow ow ow!

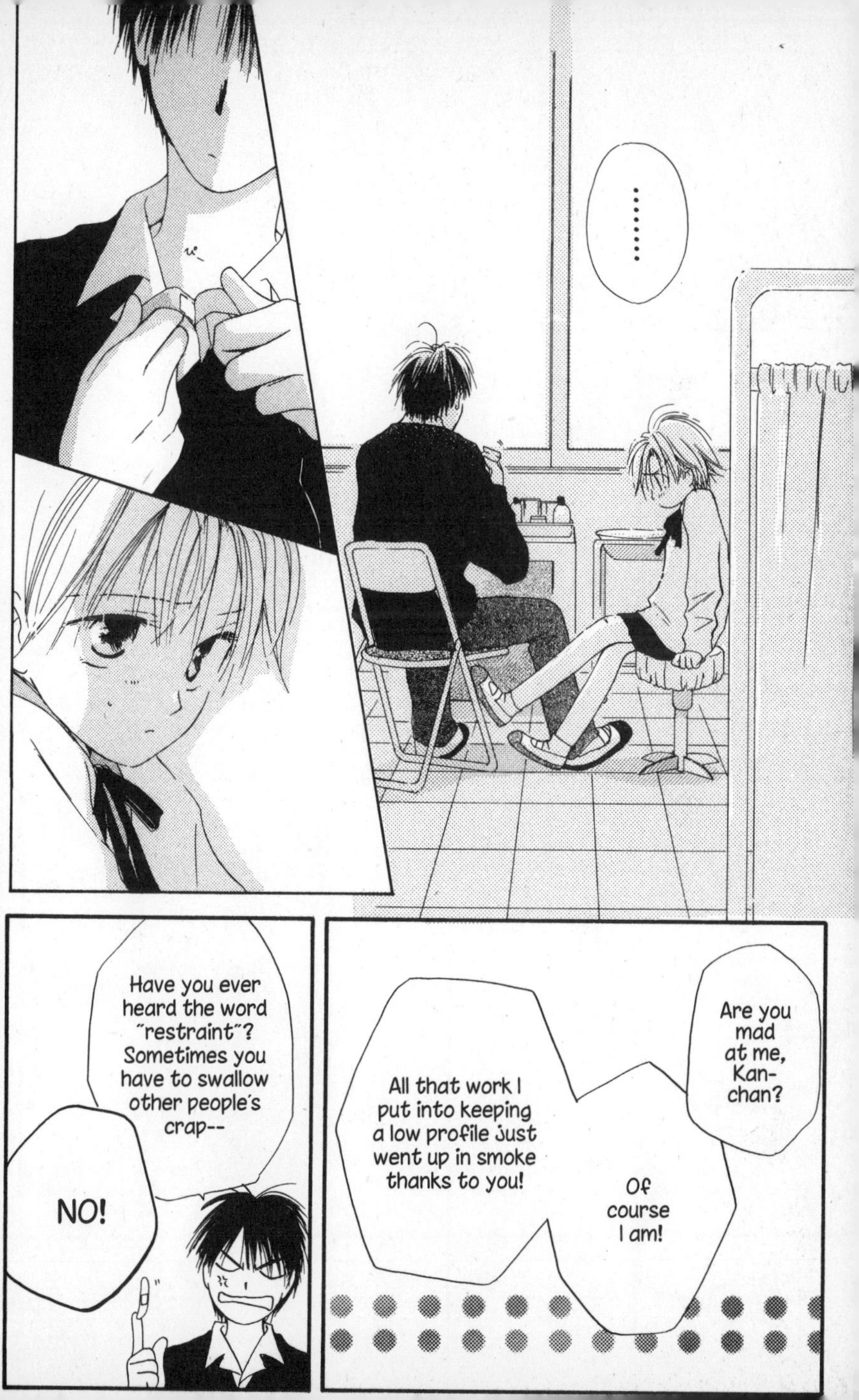
....
Are you mad at me, Kan-chan?
Of course I am!
All that work I put into keeping a low profile just went up in smoke thanks to you!
Have you ever heard the word "restraint"? Sometimes you have to swallow other people's crap--
NO!

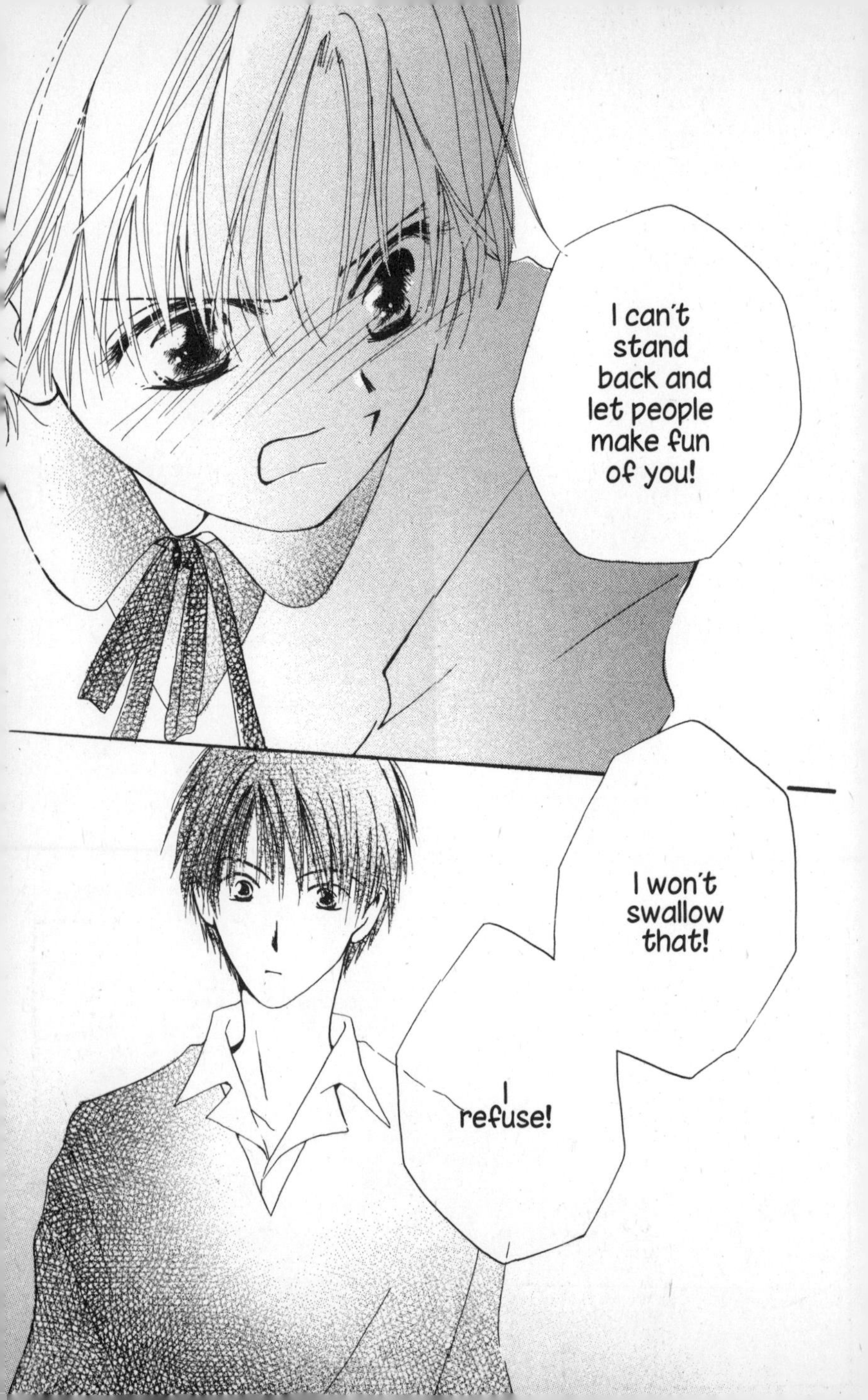
I can't stand back and let people make fun of you!
I won't swallow that!
I refuse!

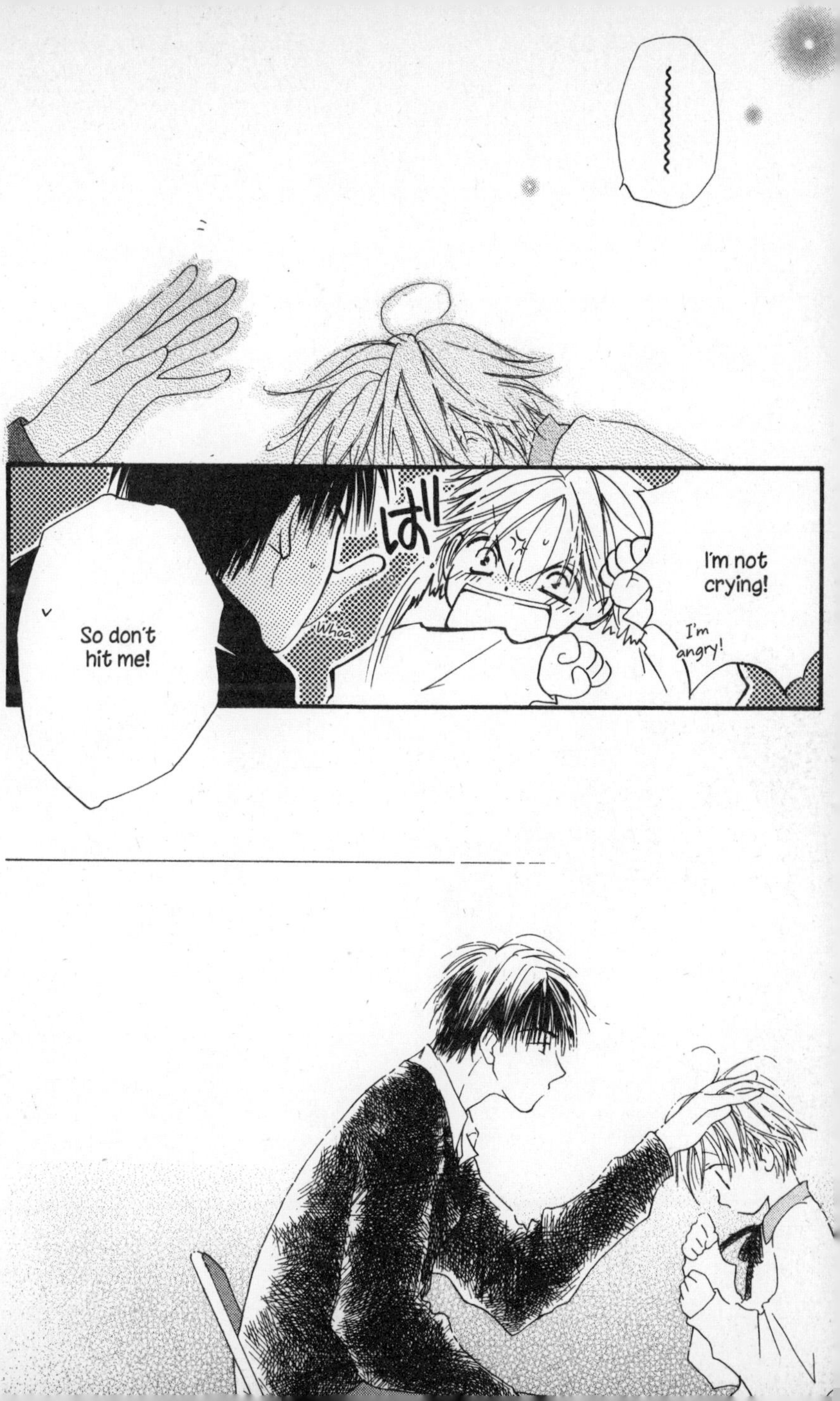
I'm not crying!
I'm angry!
Whoa
So don't hit me!

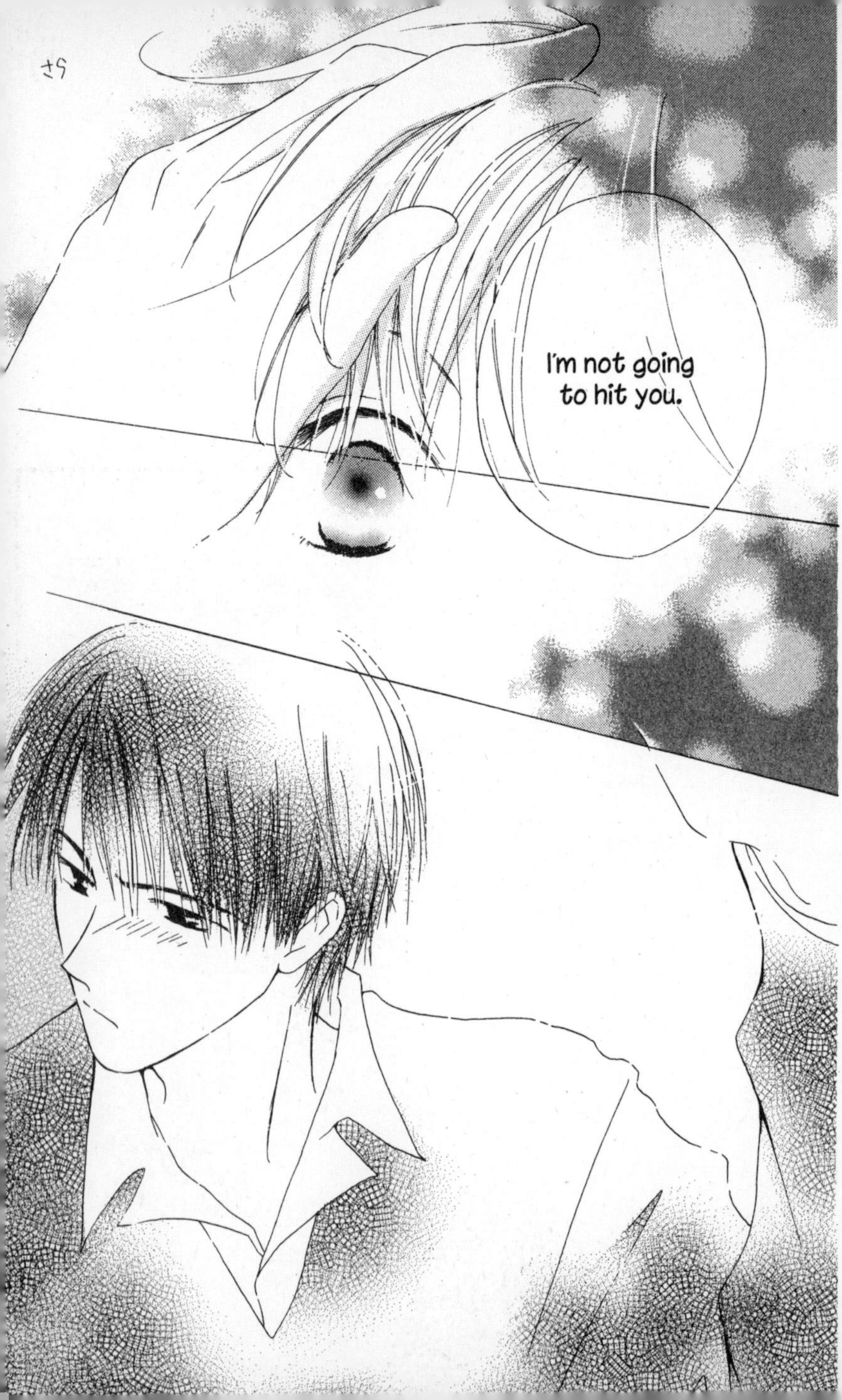
I'm not going to hit you.

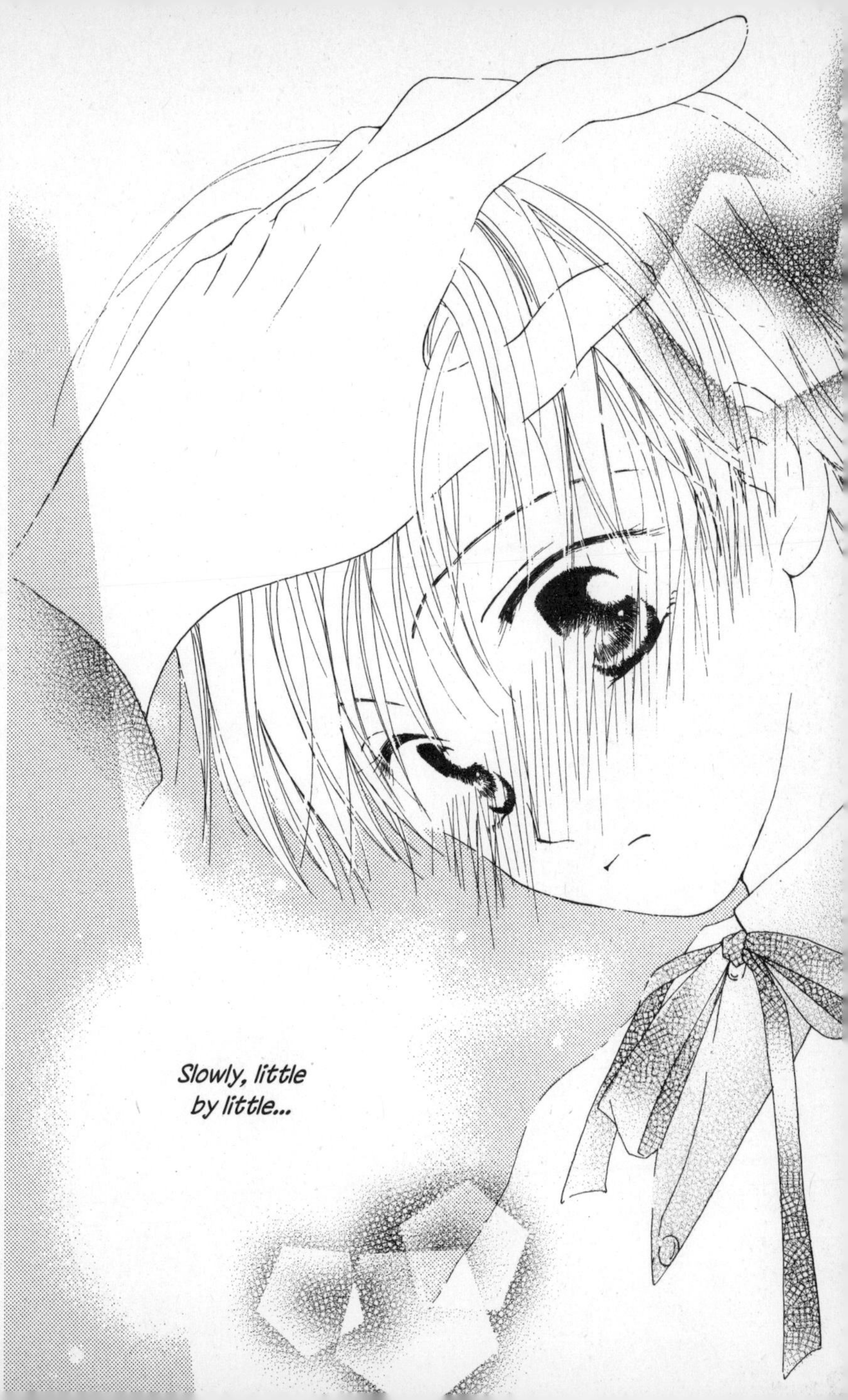
Slowly, little by little...

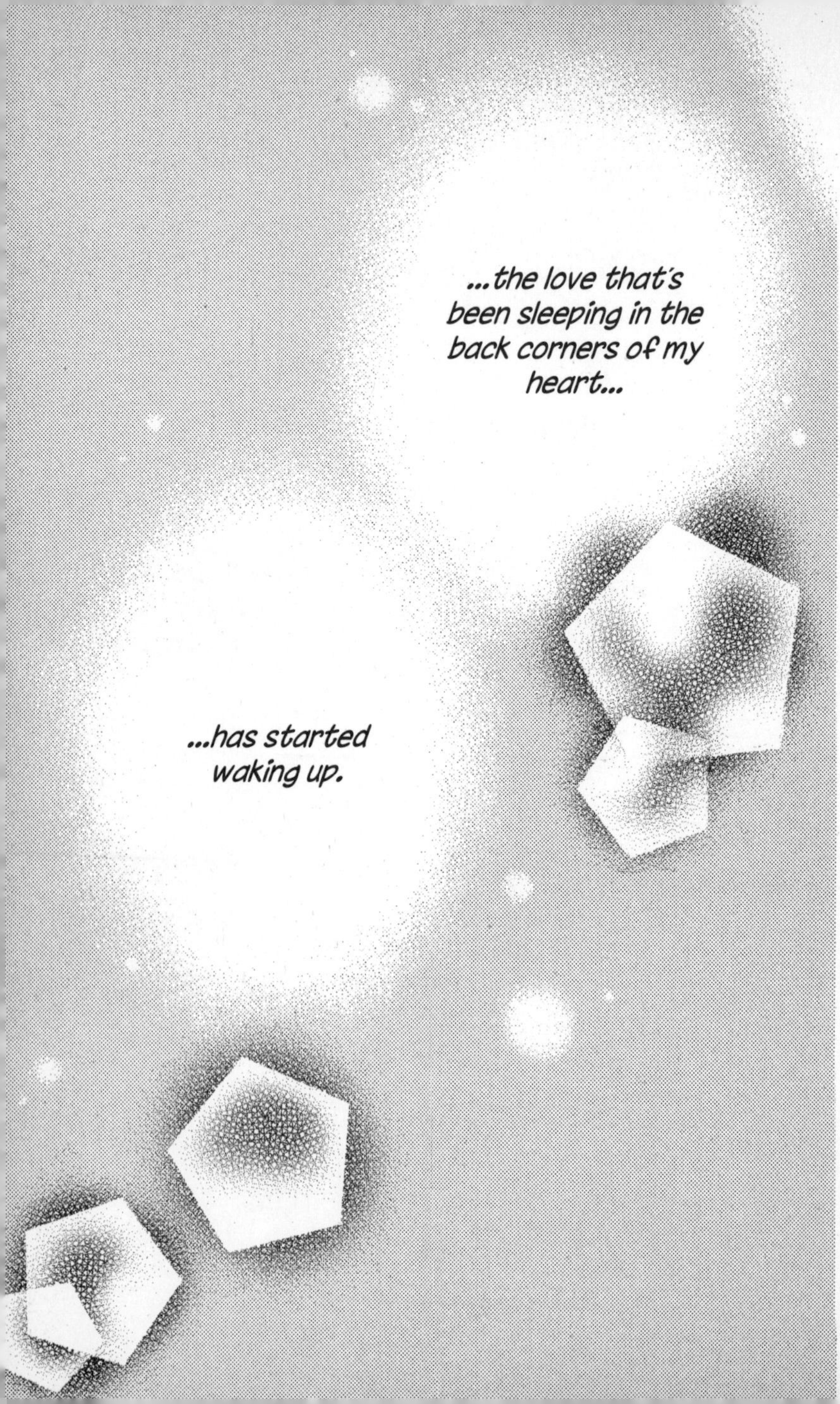
...the love that's been sleeping in the back corners of my heart...
...has started waking up.

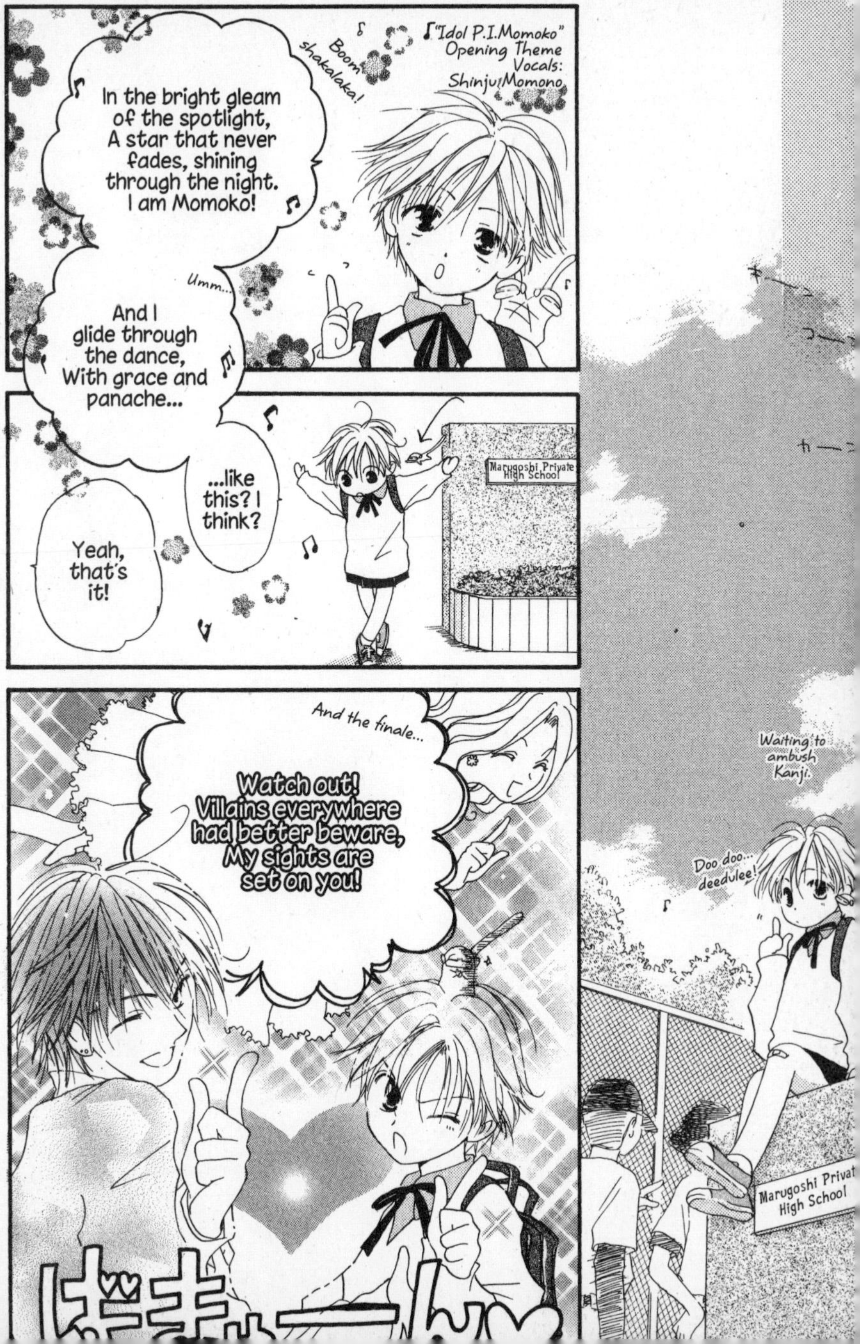
Waiting to ambush Kanji.
Doo doo... deedulee!
Marugoshi Private High School
"Idol P.I. Momoko" Opening Theme Vocals: Shinju Momono
Boom shakalaka!
In the bright gleam of the spotlight, A star that never fades, shining through the night. I am Momoko!
Umm...
And I glide through the dance, With grace and panache...
Marugoshi Private High School
...like this? I think?
Yeah, that's it!
And the finale...
Watch out! Villains everywhere had better beware, My sights are set on you!

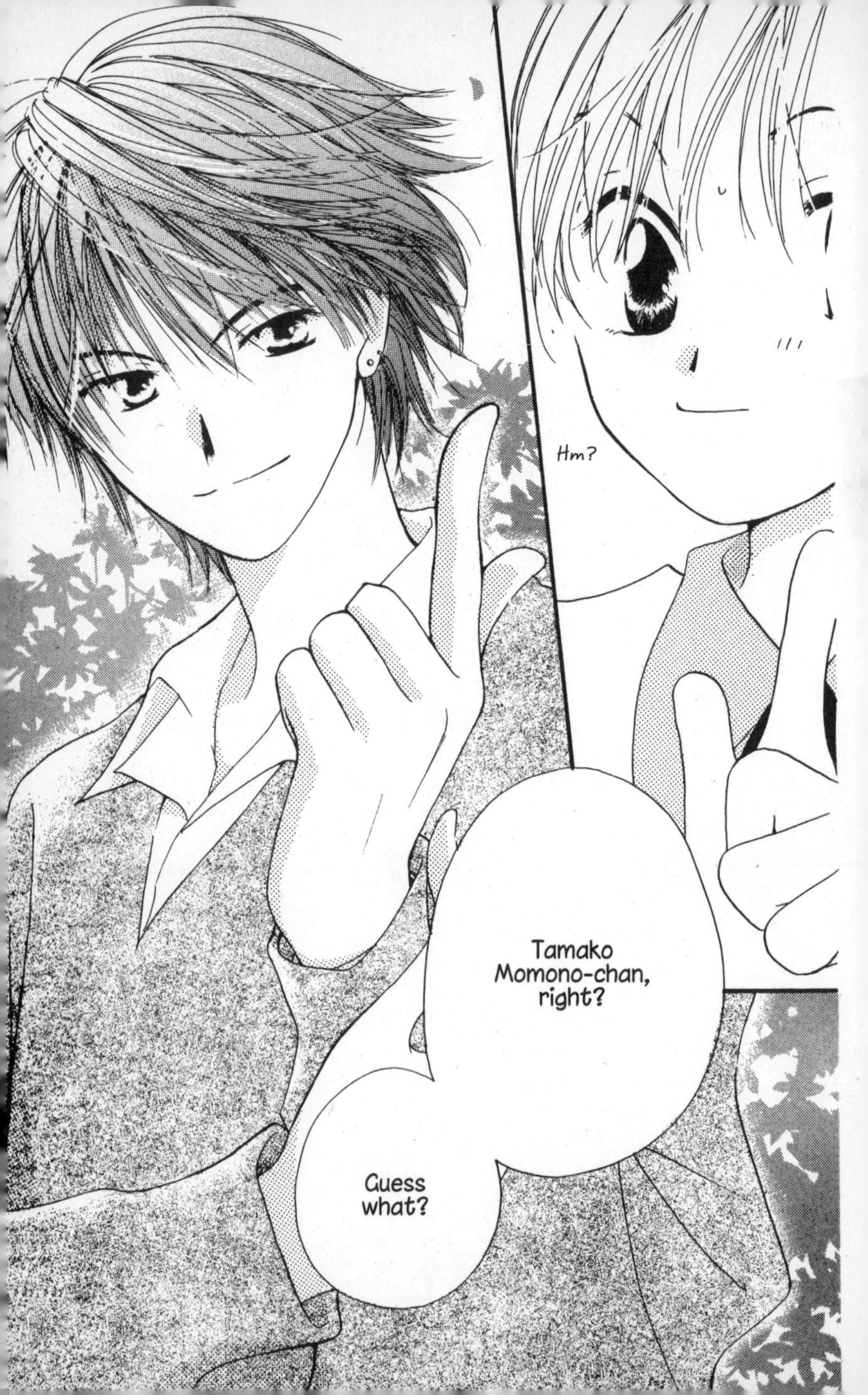
Hm?
Tamako Momono-chan, right?
Guess what?

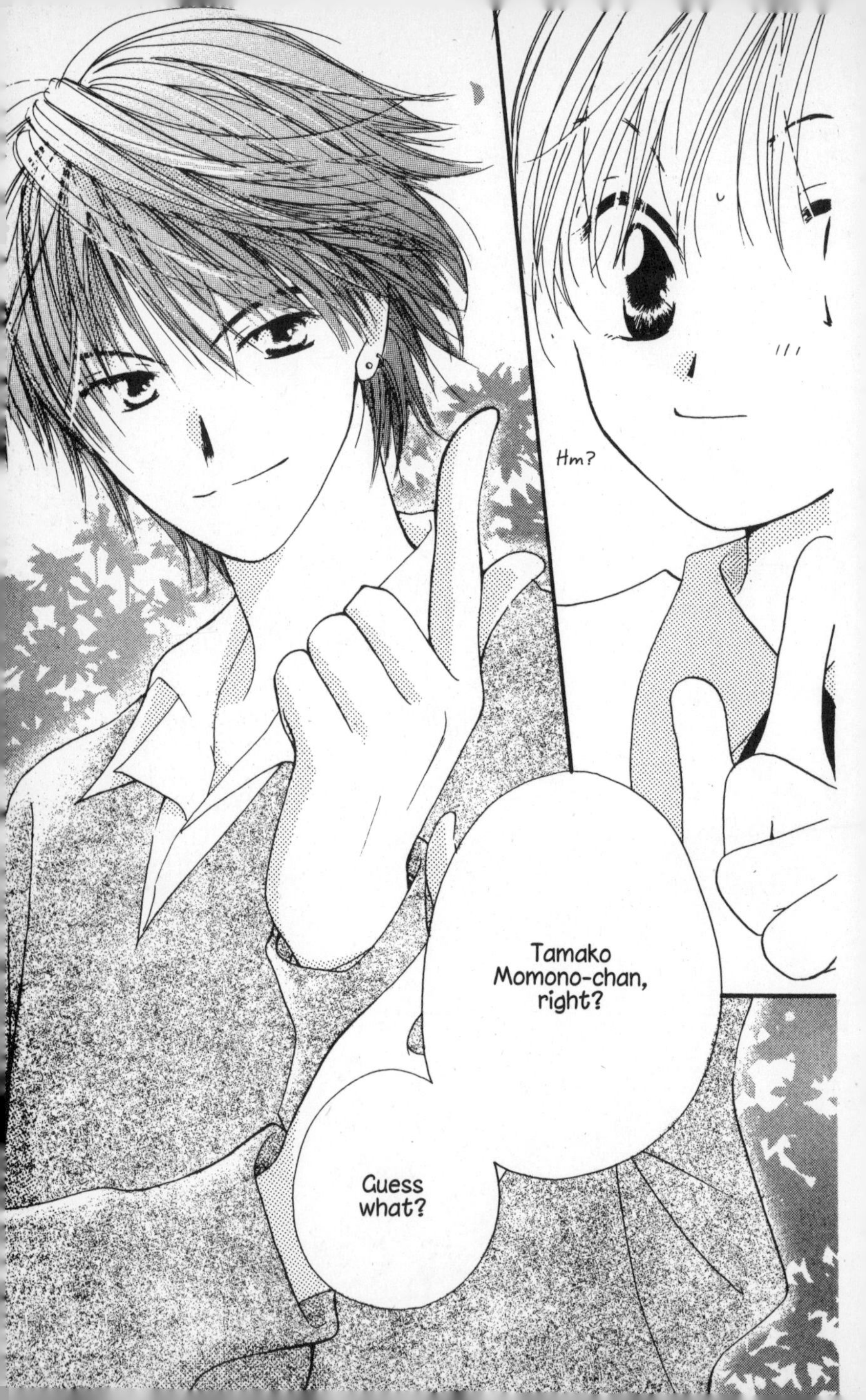
Hm?
Tamako Momono-chan, right?
Guess what?

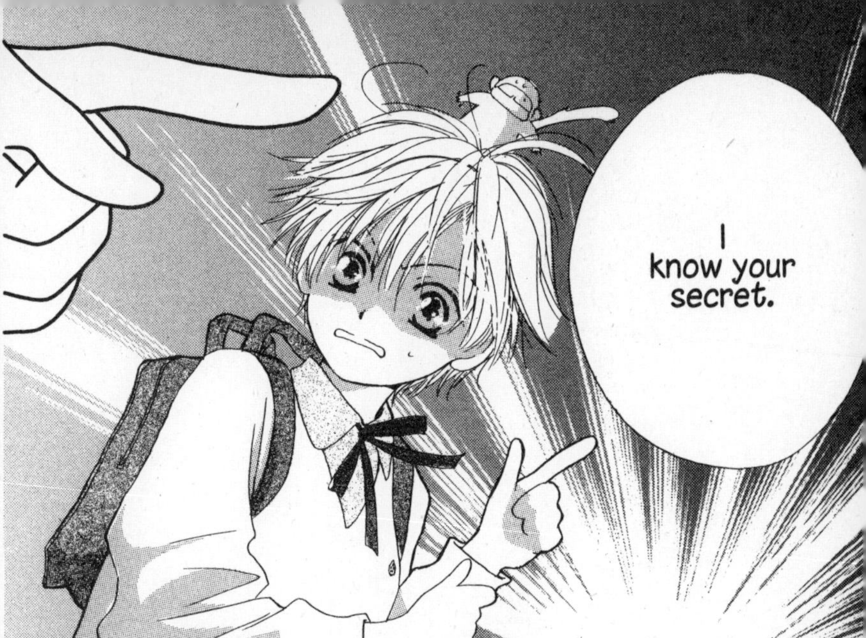
I know your secret.
WHAT?!

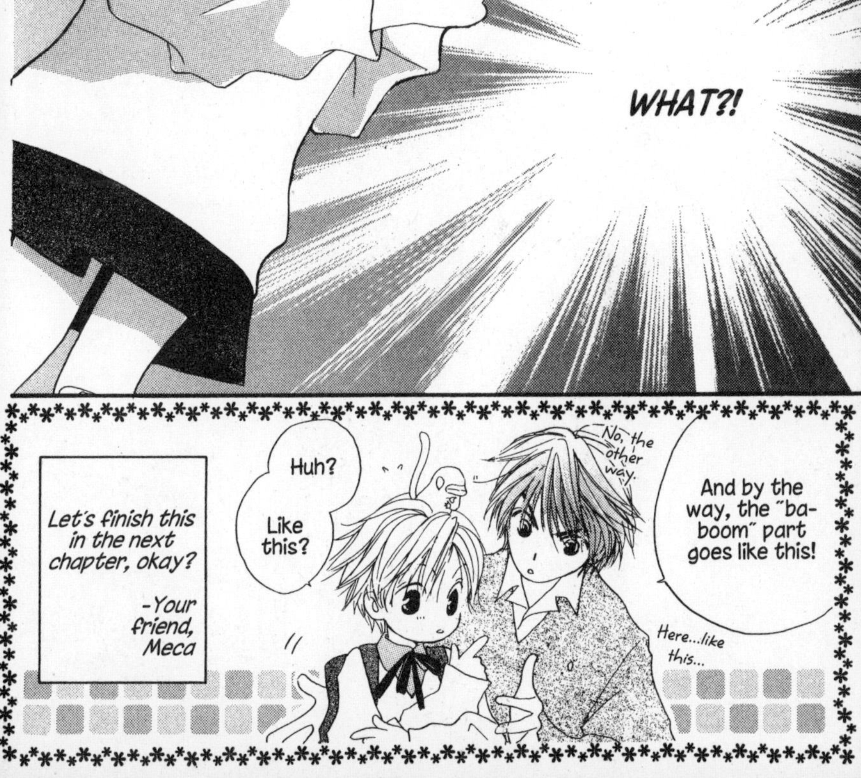
And by the way, the "ba-boom" part goes like this!
Here...like this...
Huh?
Like this?
No, the other way.
Let's finish this in the next chapter, okay?
-Your friend, Meca

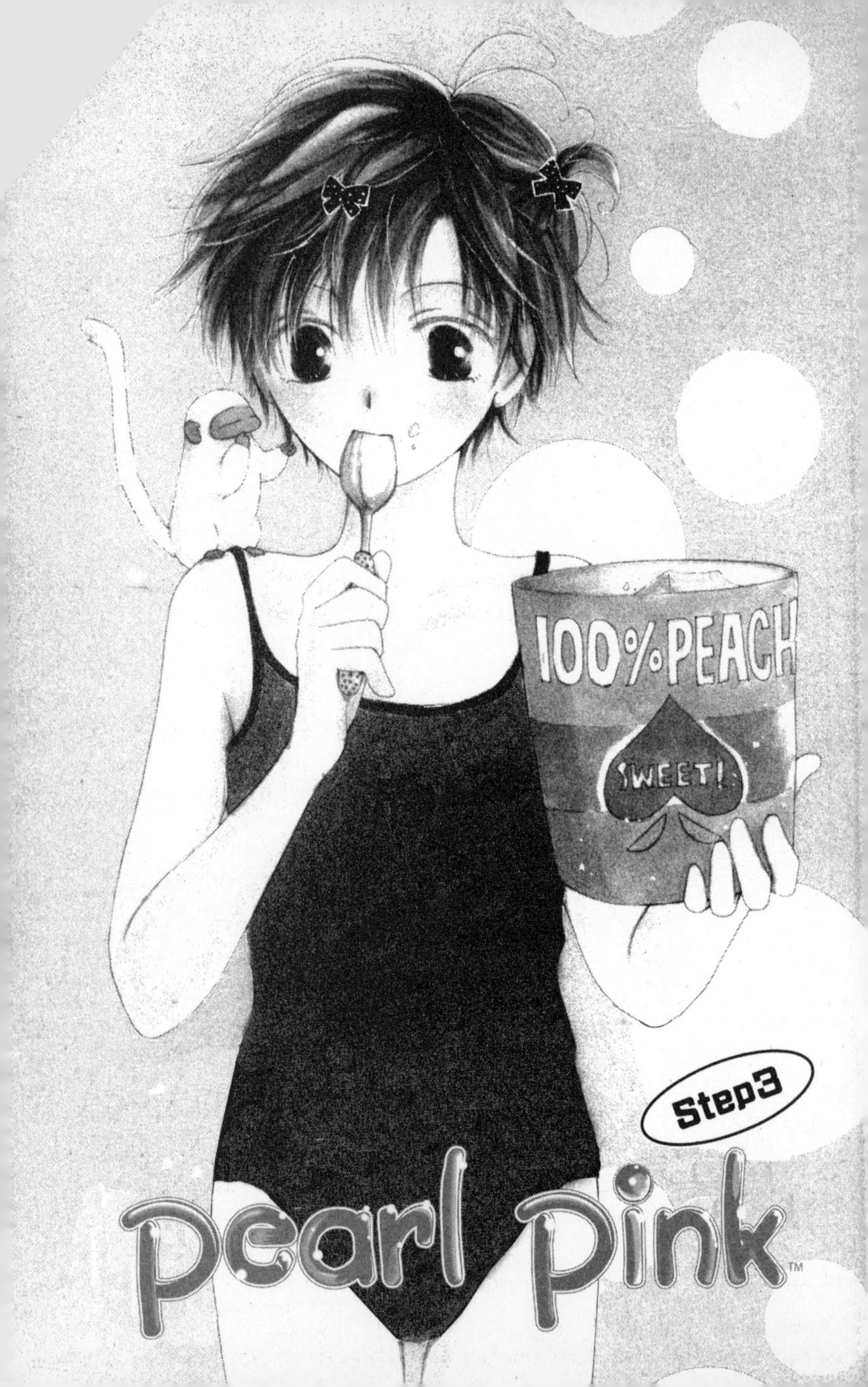
100% PEACH
SWEET!
Step3
Pearl Pink™

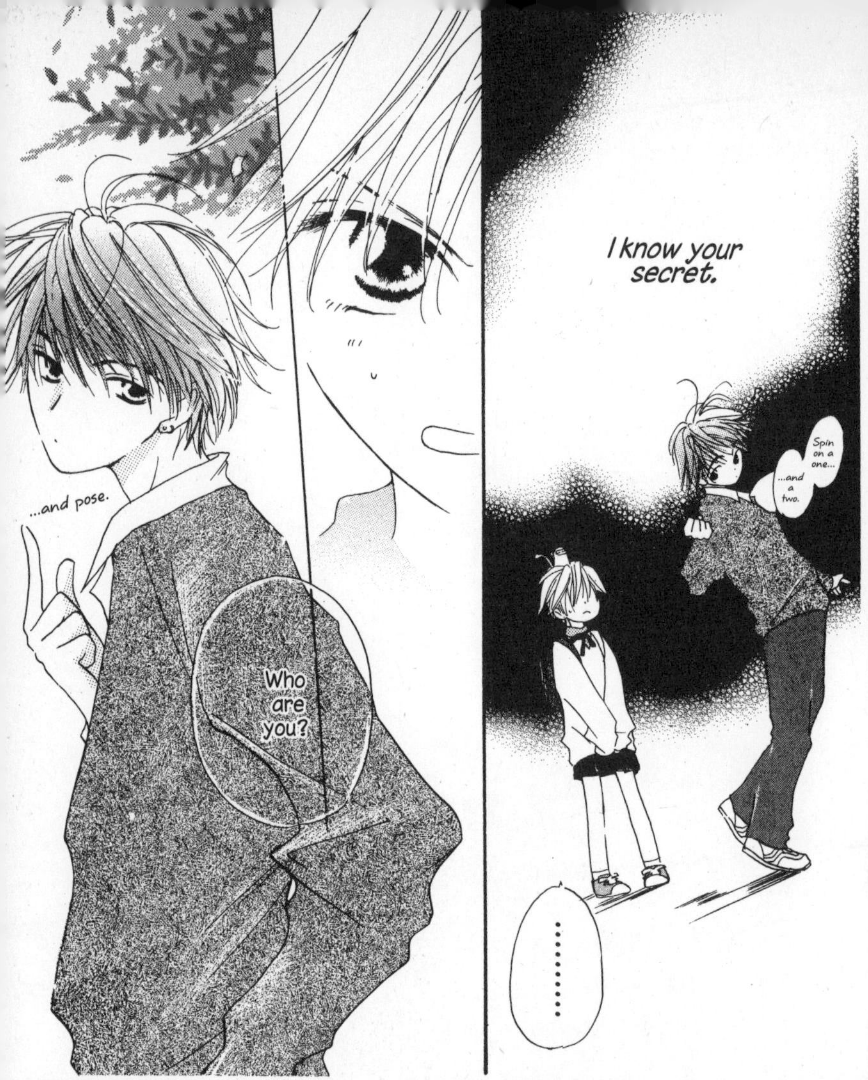
I know your secret.
Spin on a one...
...and a two.
......
...and pose.
Who are you?

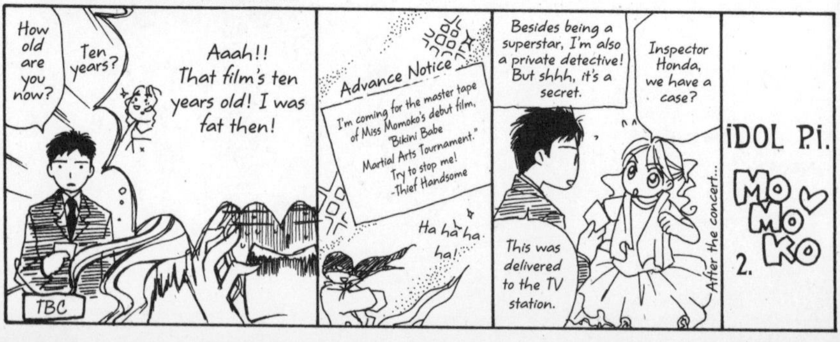
iDOL P.i. MOMOKO 2.
Inspector Honda, we have a case?
Besides being a superstar, I'm also a private detective! But shhh, it's a secret.
After the concert...
This was delivered to the TV station.
Advance Notice
I'm coming for the master tape of Miss Momoko's debut film, "Bikini Babe Martial Arts Tournament." Try to stop me! -Thief Handsome
Ha ha ha ha!
Aaah!! That film's ten years old! I was fat then!
Ten years?
How old are you now?
TBC

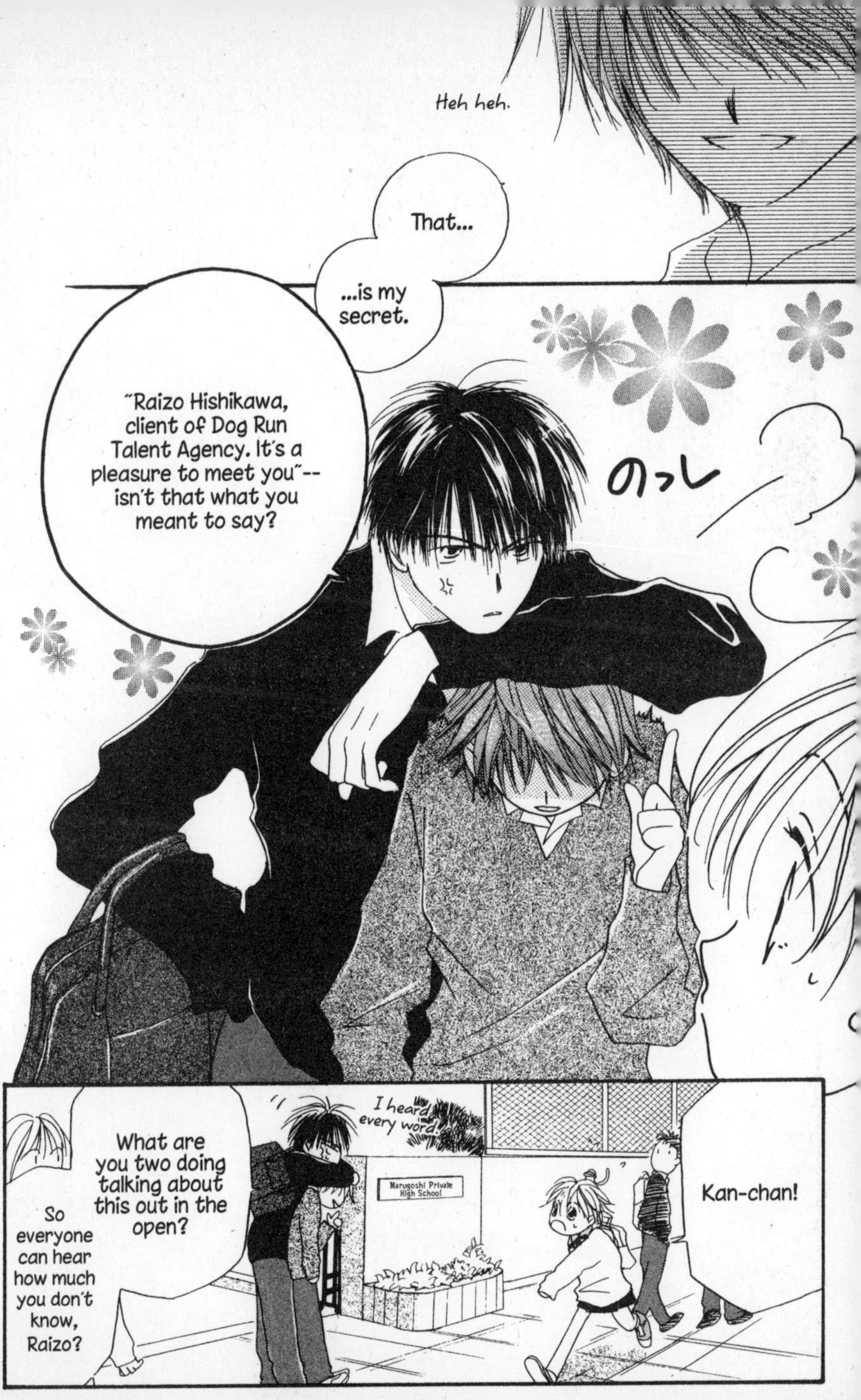
Heh heh.
That...
...is my secret.
のっし
"Raizo Hishikawa, client of Dog Run Talent Agency. It's a pleasure to meet you"--isn't that what you meant to say?
Kan-chan!
Marugoshi Private High School
I heard every word.
What are you two doing talking about this out in the open?
So everyone can hear how much you don't know, Raizo?

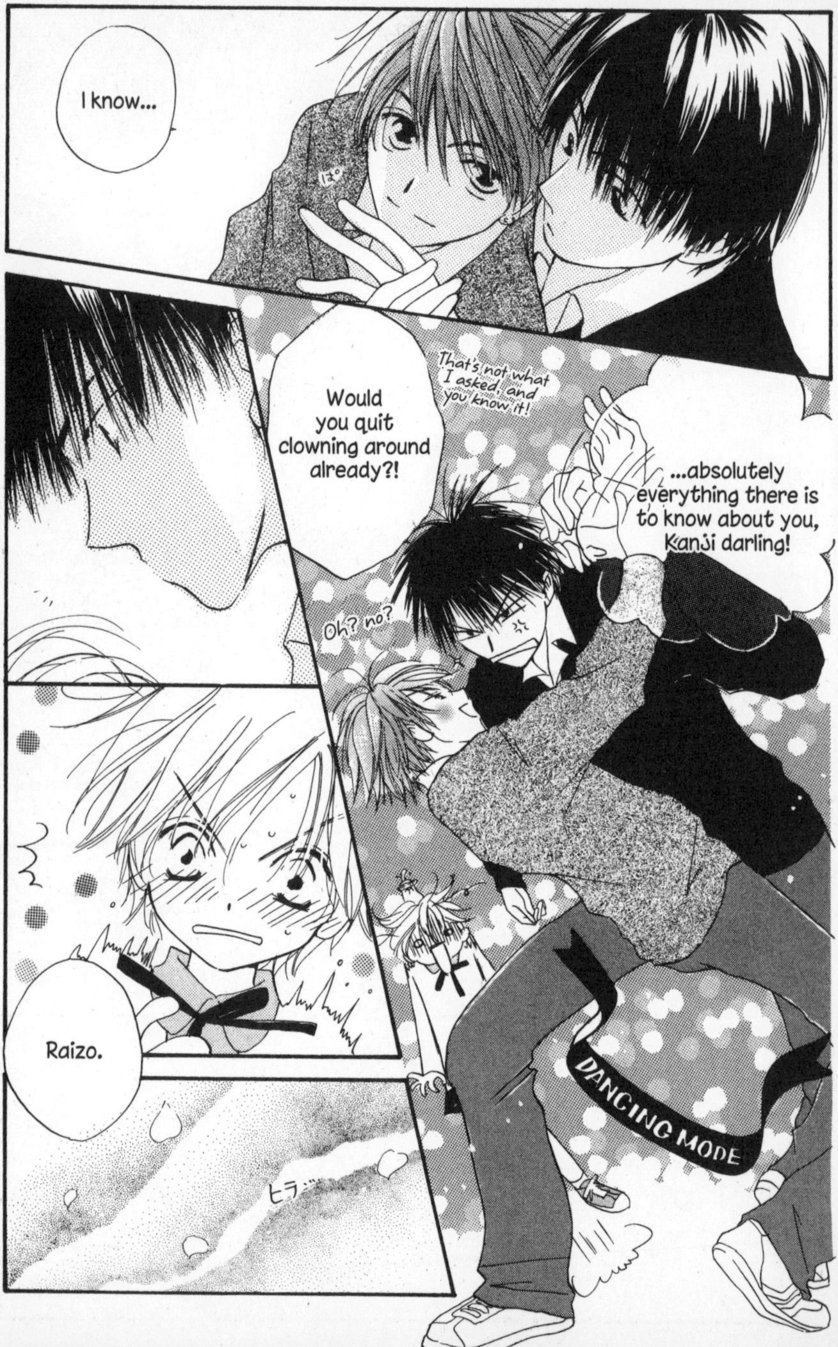
I know...
ぱ
...absolutely everything there is to know about you, Kanji darling!
That's not what I asked, and you know it!
Oh? no?
DANCING MODE
Would you quit clowning around already?!
Raizo.
ヒラ…

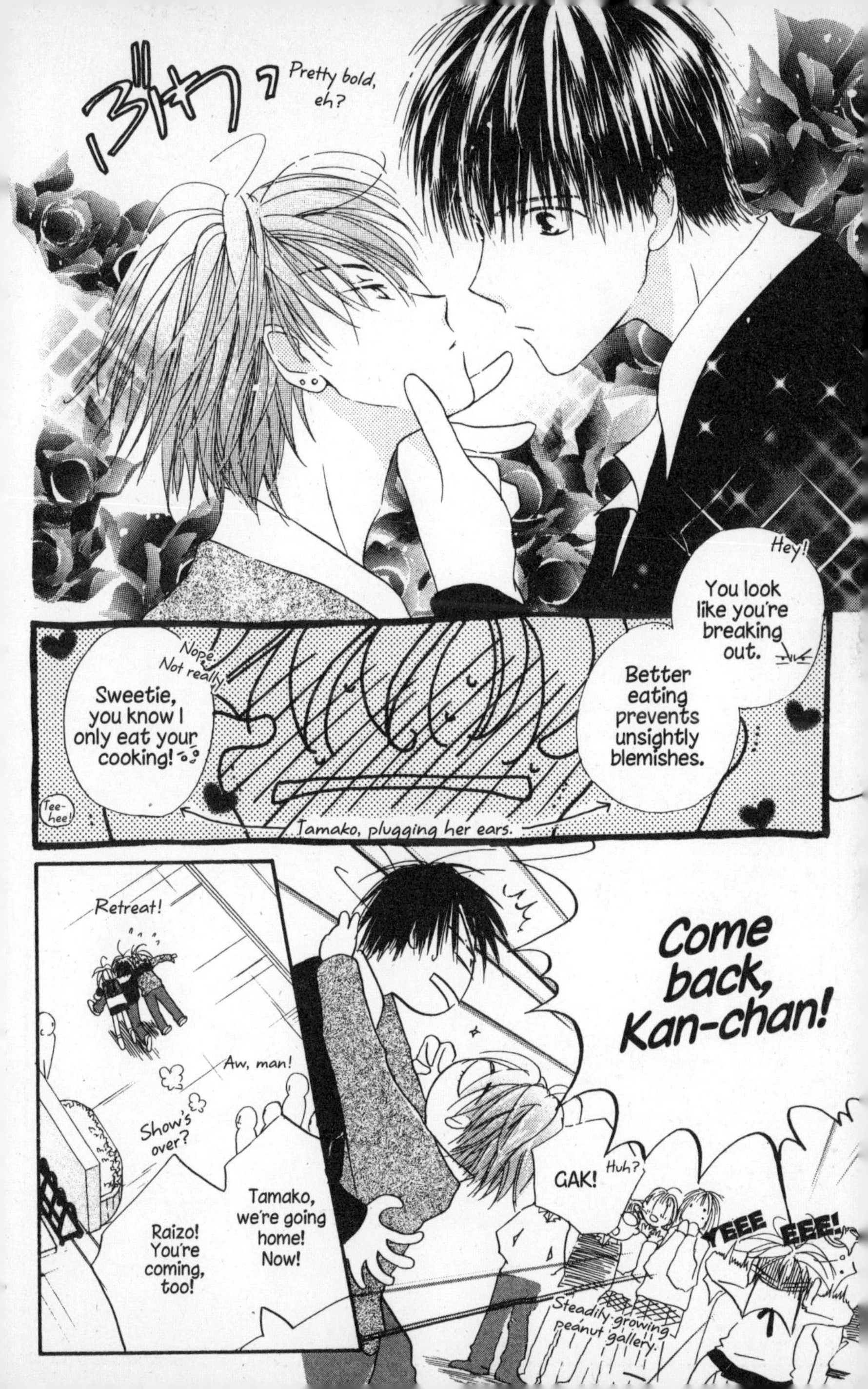
Pretty bold, eh?
Hey! You look like you're breaking out.
Better eating prevents unsightly blemishes.
Nope. Not really.
Sweetie, you know I only eat your cooking!
Tee-hee!
Tamako, plugging her ears.
Come back, Kan-chan!
Huh?
GAK!
YEEE EEE!
Steadily growing peanut gallery.
Tamako, we're going home! Now!
Raizo! You're coming, too!
Retreat!
Aw, man!
Show's over?

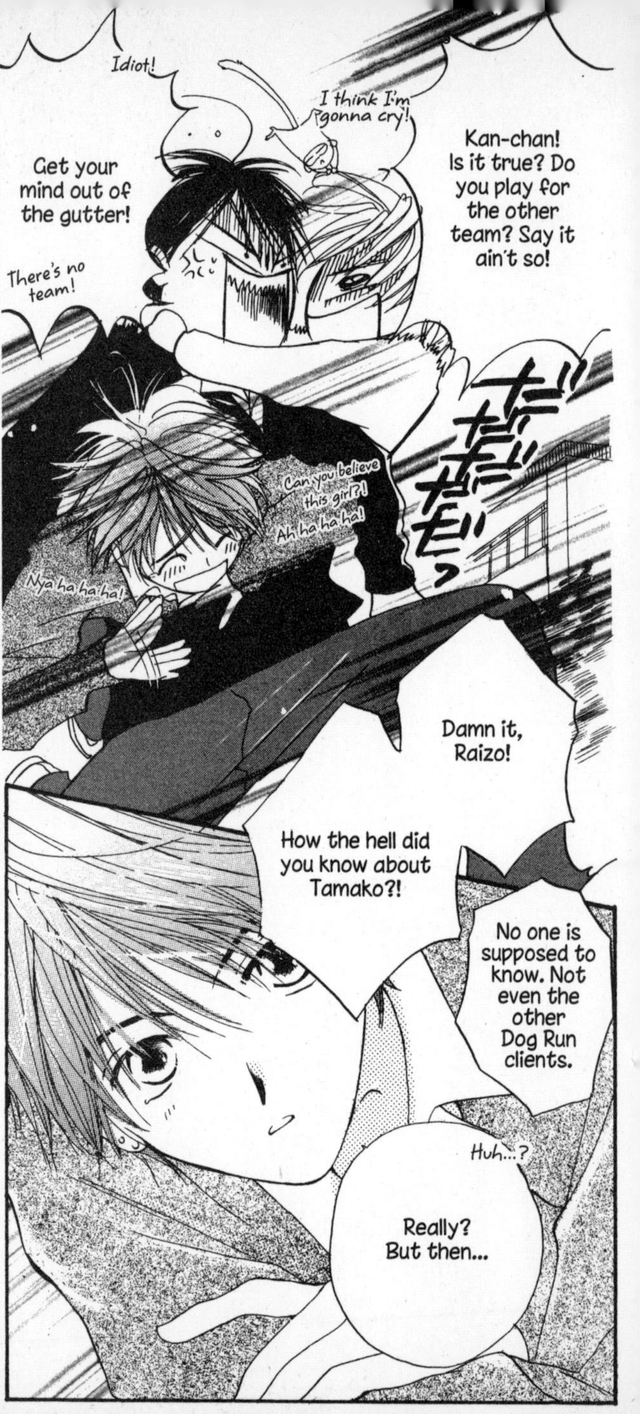
Kan-chan! Is it true? Do you play for the other team? Say it ain't so!
I think I'm gonna cry!
Idiot!
Get your mind out of the gutter!
There's no team!
Can you believe this girl?! Ah ha ha ha!
Nya ha ha ha!
Damn it, Raizo!
How the hell did you know about Tamako?!
No one is supposed to know. Not even the other Dog Run clients.
Huh...?
Really? But then...

idols, part 2

Where'd I get the idea for "Rain"? Hmm... Well, all sorts of different places, really. At the time, I noticed that a lot of the mega-popular idols on TV had names that had to do with the weather, so I figured, "Hey, if it works for them, it'll work for me." I hope I'll get the chance to give a proper amount of space to the other two members of Rain at some point. Raizo's not the only one, you know.

When I first created Raizo, I envisioned him as the sort of character who could nail every routine perfectly in rehearsals, but would get so nervous right before the real deal that he'd always get a bad case of diarrhea. Poor guy, huh? From there, I thought: rumbling guts -> rumbling sky -> thunder -> Raizo.

The "rai" part of his name uses the character meaning "thunder." The other two members of Rain got names that had something to do with... well, rain.
Ah! Waitaminute! You don't find out about any of this until the page after this one!

First-time readers, skip this part!

...After we've already read most of it?

By the way, the second half of Tamako's monkey's name is Tadamune. Kantaro-Tadamune. I got it from the traitor who killed the historical figure Yoshitomo Minamoto. I was at the local shrine watching a play about the Minamoto legend, and that name just sounded so cool. Kind of a morbid source for a name for a cute critter, though.

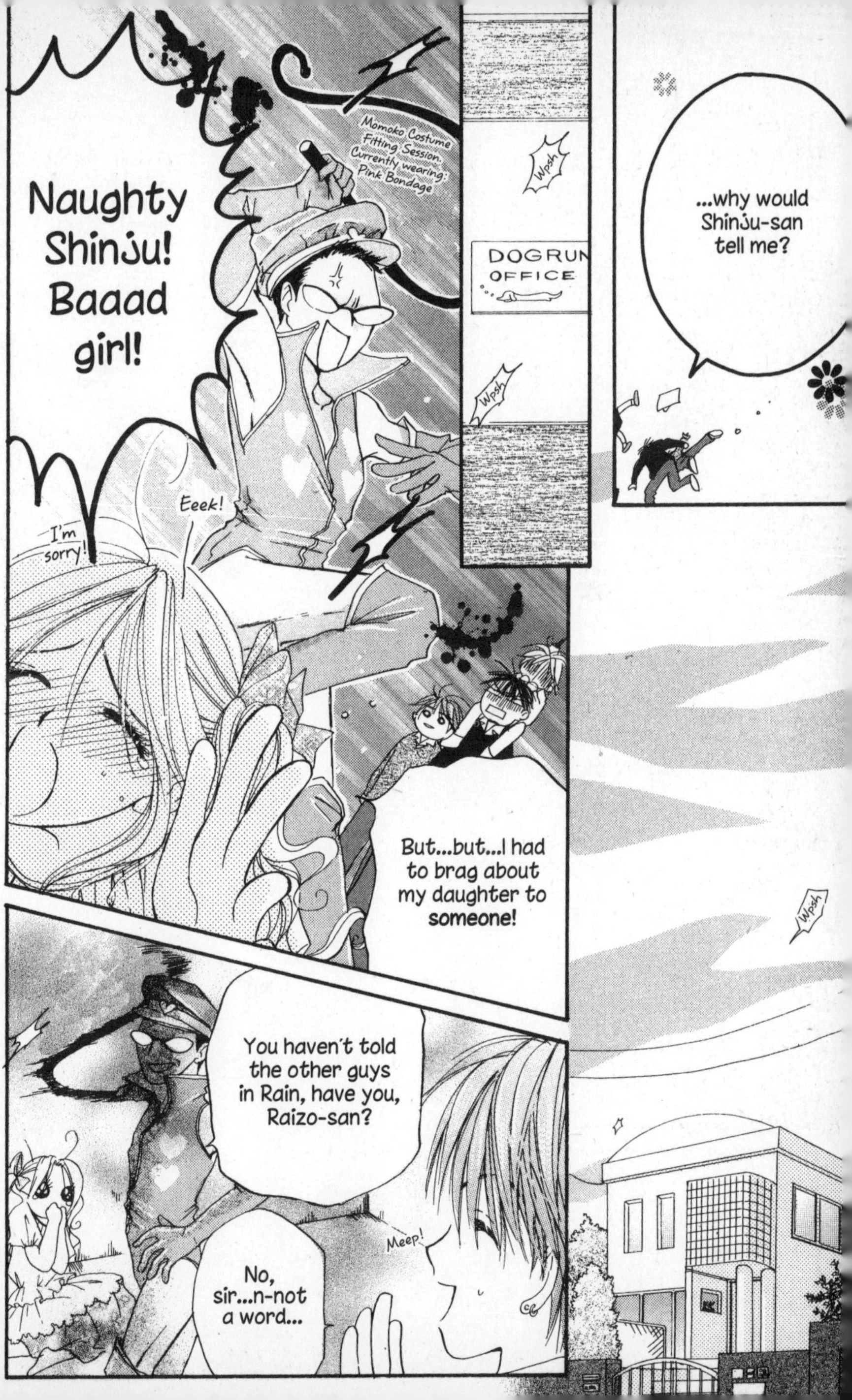
...why would Shinju-san tell me?
Wpsh
Wpsh
DOGRUN OFFICE
Wpsh
Momoko Costume Fitting Session. Currently wearing: Pink Bondage
Naughty Shinju! Baaad girl!
Eeek!
I'm sorry!
But...but...I had to brag about my daughter to someone!
You haven't told the other guys in Rain, have you, Raizo-san?
Meep!
No, sir...n-not a word...

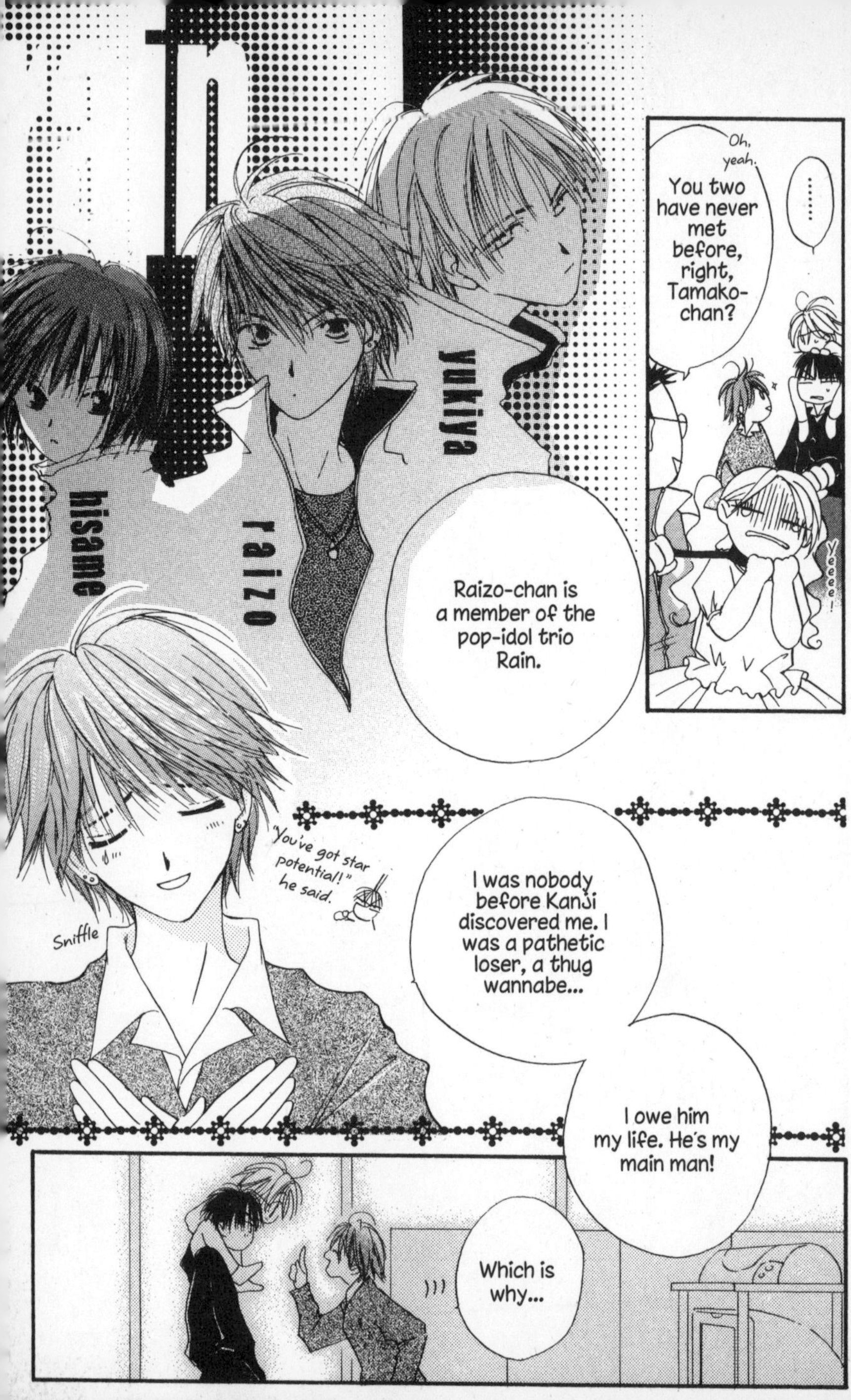
Oh, yeah.
You two have never met before, right, Tamako-chan?
......
Yeeee!
yukiya
raizo
hisame
Raizo-chan is a member of the pop-idol trio Rain.
I was nobody before Kanji discovered me. I was a pathetic loser, a thug wannabe...
"You've got star potential!" he said.
Sniffle
I owe him my life. He's my main man!
Which is why...

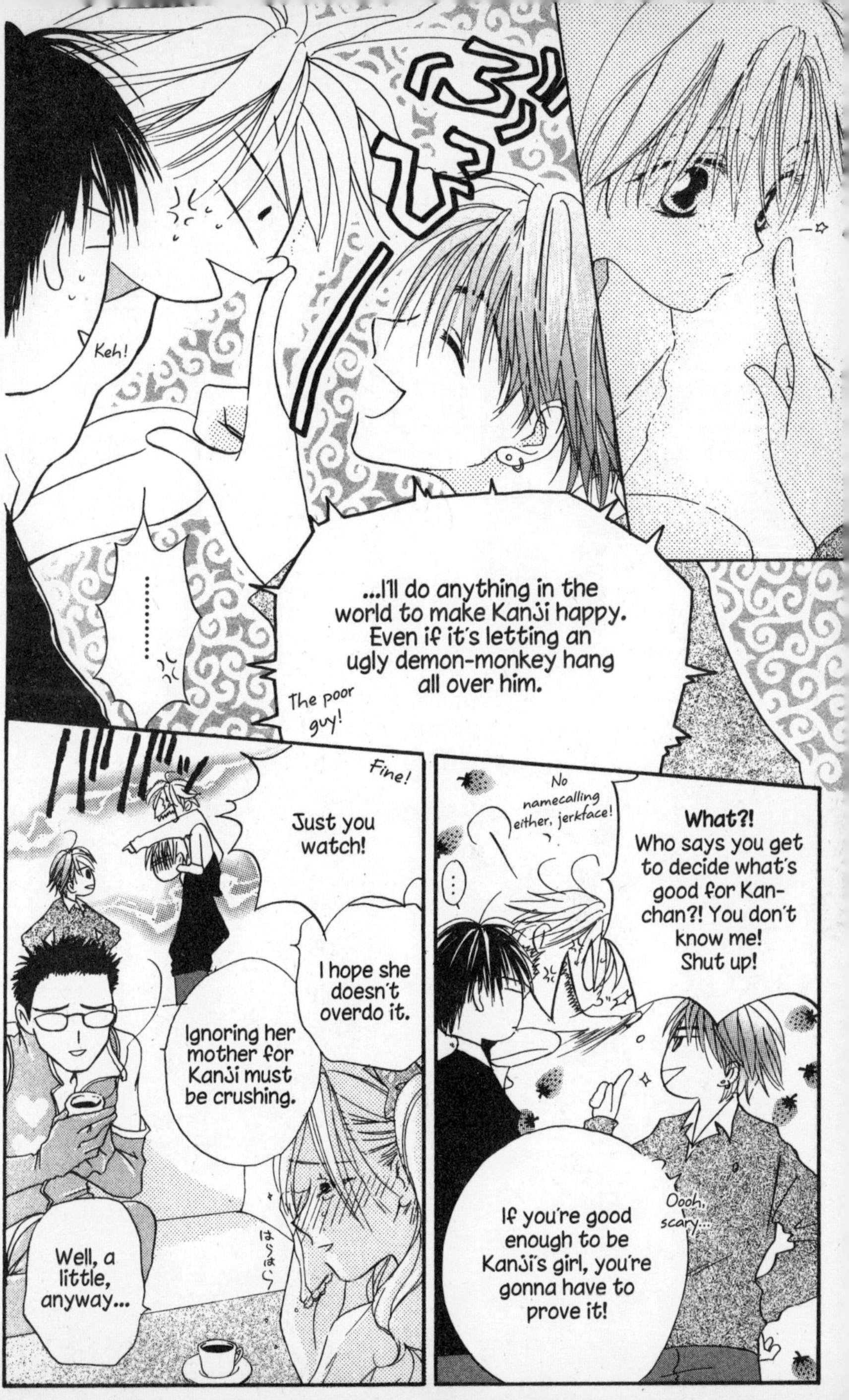
Keh!
...I'll do anything in the world to make Kanji happy. Even if it's letting an ugly demon-monkey hang all over him.
......
The poor guy!
What?! Who says you get to decide what's good for Kan-chan?! You don't know me! Shut up!
No namecalling either, jerkface!
...
Oooh, scary...
If you're good enough to be Kanji's girl, you're gonna have to prove it!
Fine!
Just you watch!
I hope she doesn't overdo it.
Ignoring her mother for Kanji must be crushing.
はらはら
Well, a little, anyway...

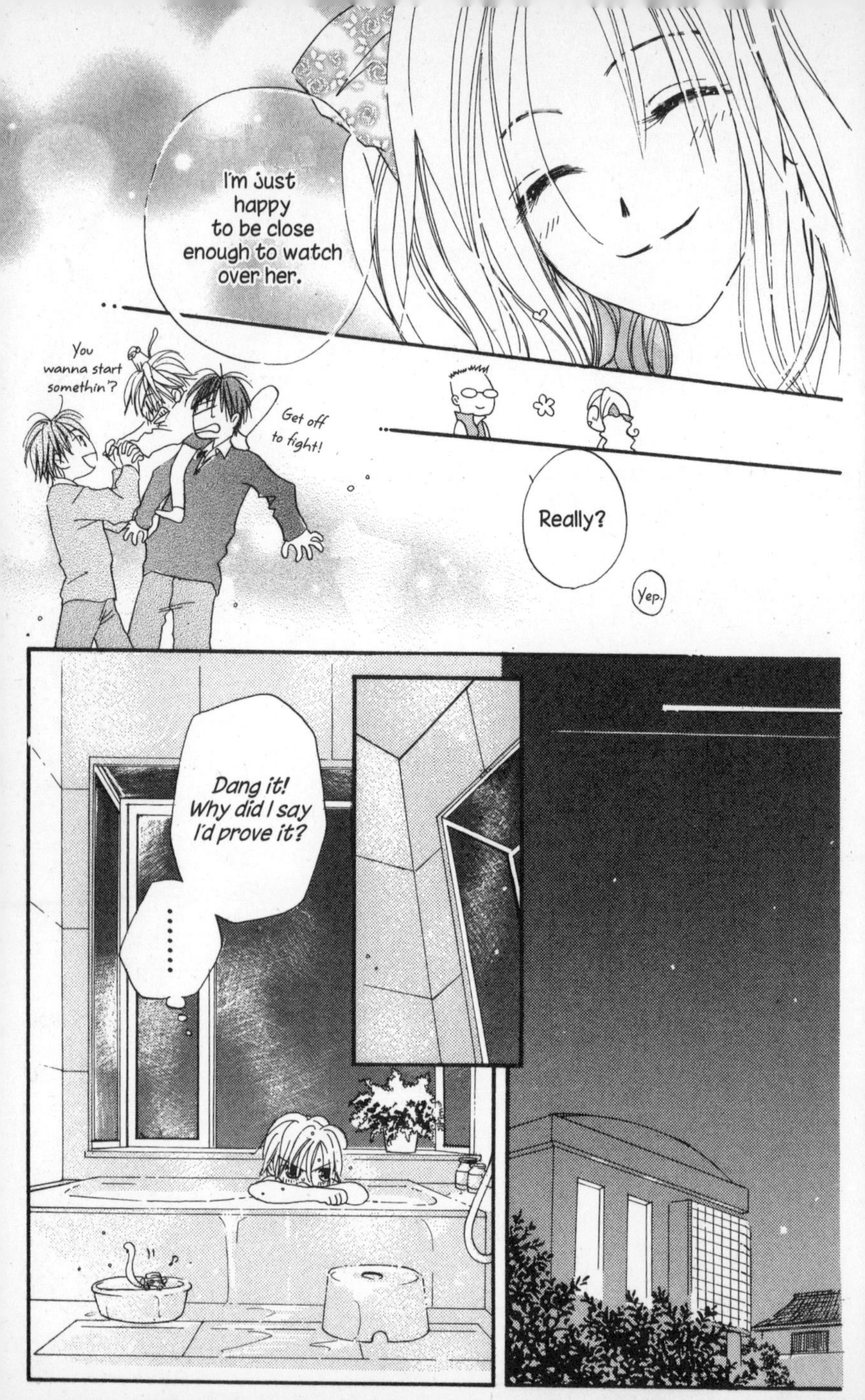
I'm just happy to be close enough to watch over her.
You wanna start somethin'?
Get off to fight!
Really?
Yep.
Dang it! Why did I say I'd prove it?
......

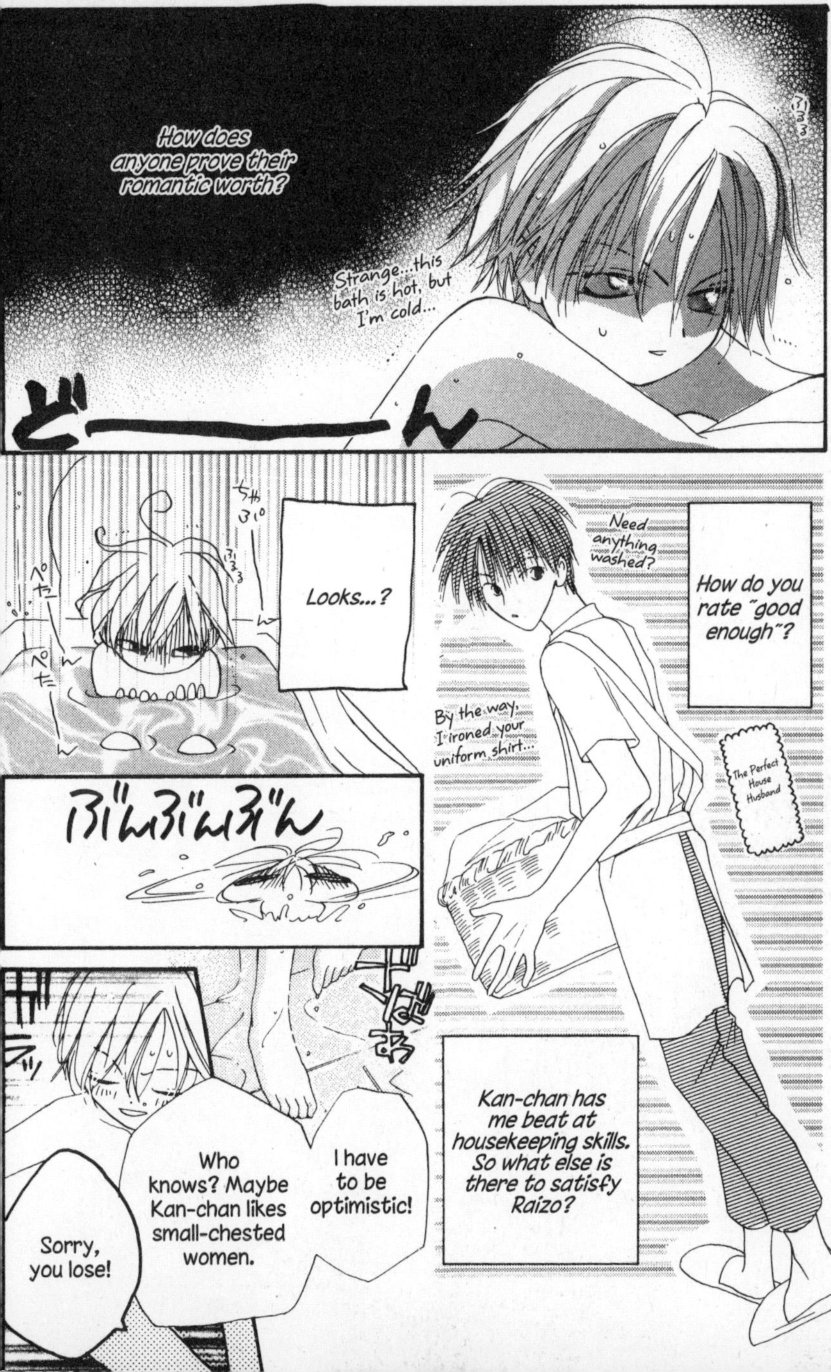
How does anyone prove their romantic worth?
Strange...this bath is hot, but I'm cold...
どーーーん
How do you rate "good enough"?
Need anything washed?
By the way, I ironed your uniform shirt...
The Perfect House Husband
Looks...?
Kan-chan has me beat at housekeeping skills. So what else is there to satisfy Raizo?
I have to be optimistic!
Who knows? Maybe Kan-chan likes small-chested women.
Sorry, you lose!

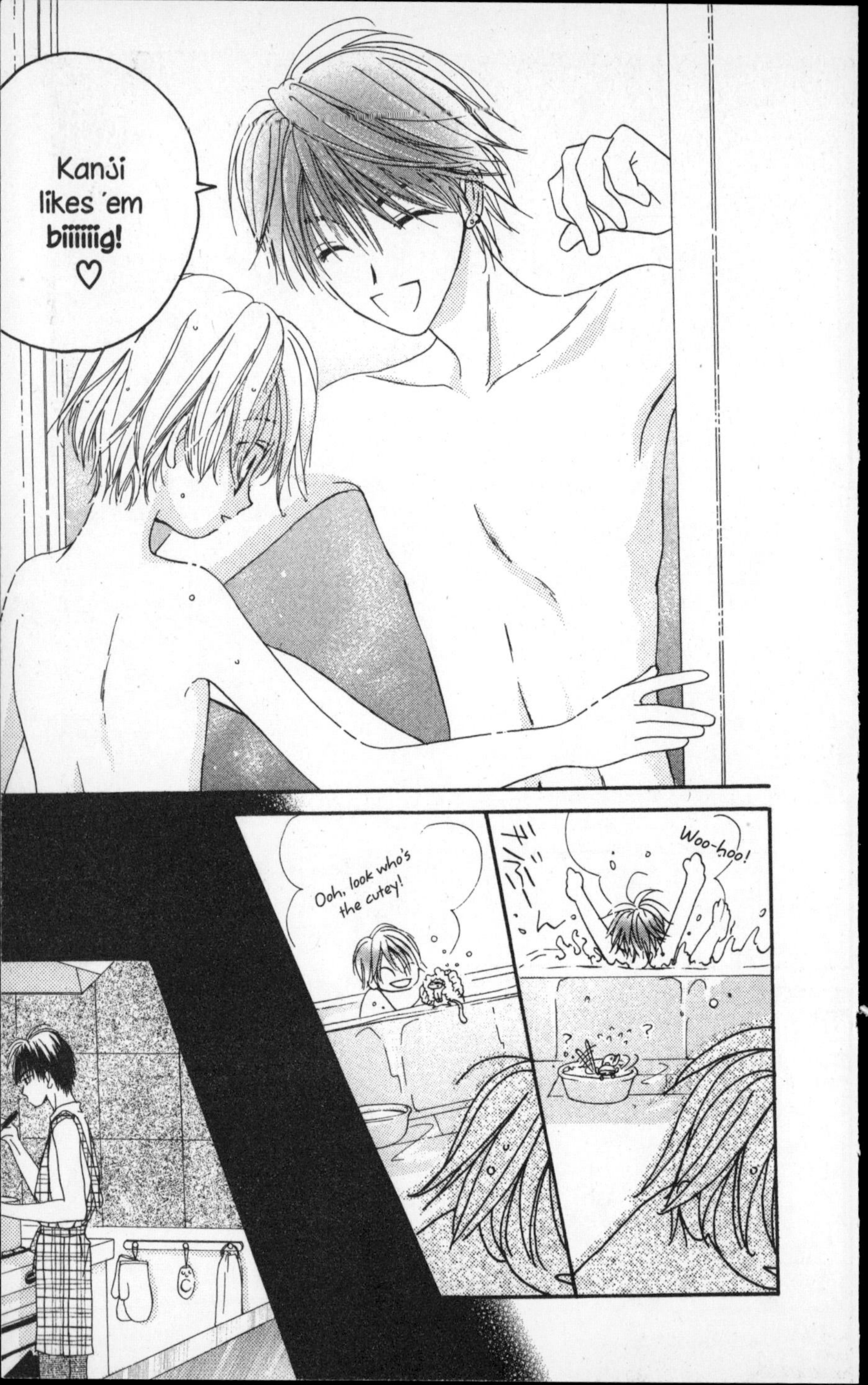
Kanji likes 'em biiiiiig! ♡
Woo-hoo!
Ooh, look who's the cutey!

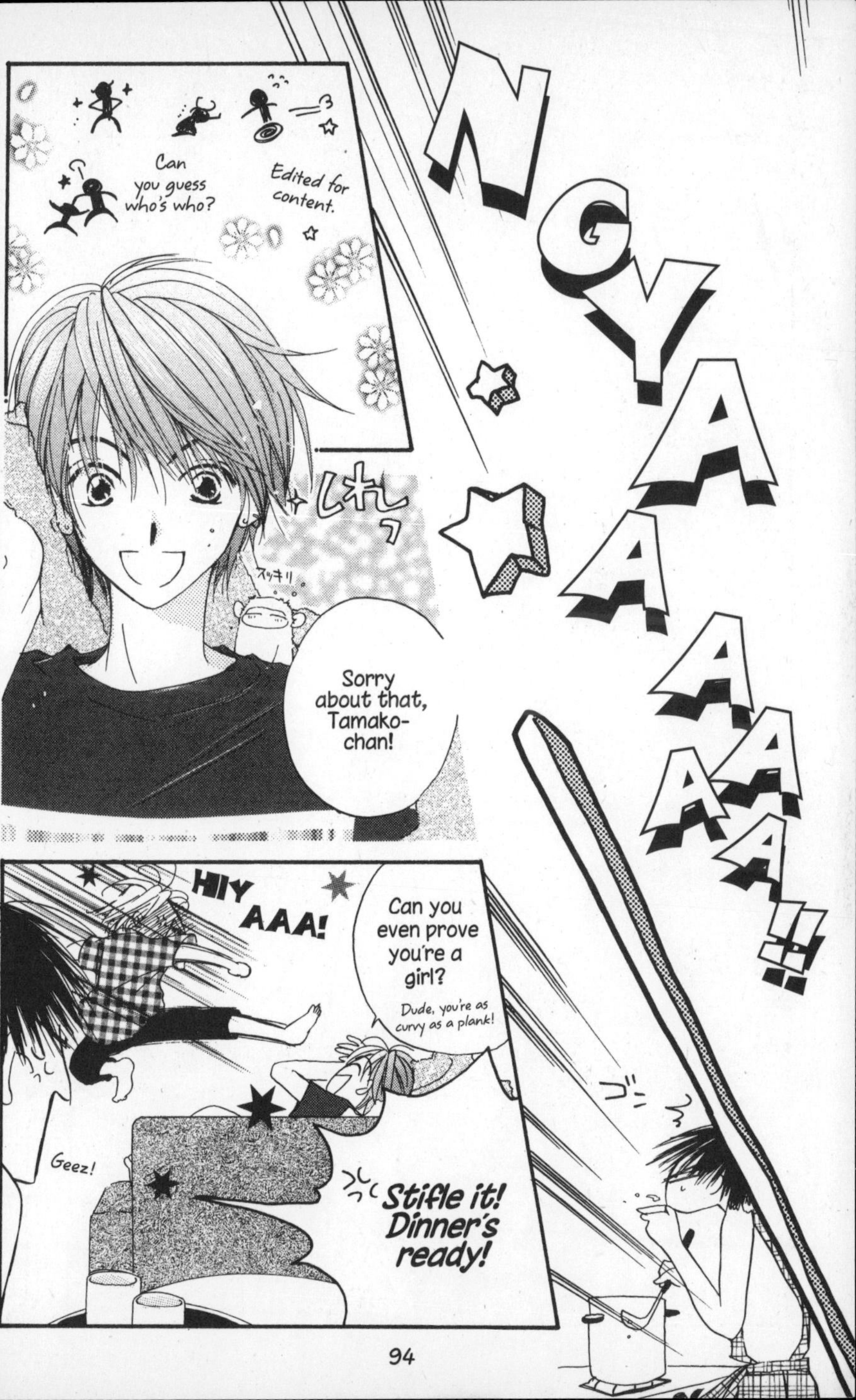

NGYAAAAAAA!!
Can you guess who's who?
Edited for content.
しれっ
スッキリ
Sorry about that, Tamako-chan!
Can you even prove you're a girl?
Dude, you're as curvy as a plank!
HIYAAA!
Stifle it! Dinner's ready!
Geez!

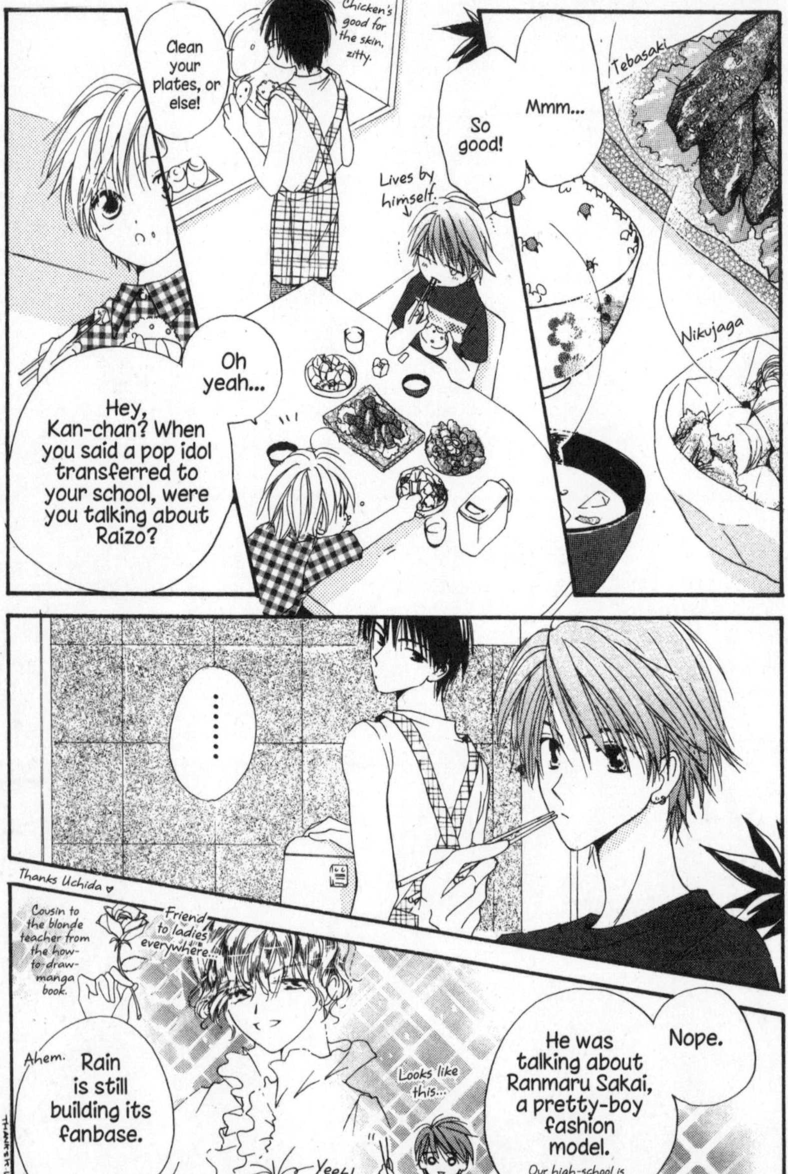

Mmm...
So good!
Tebasaki
Nikujaga
Chicken's good for the skin, zitty.
Clean your plates, or else!
Lives by himself.
Oh yeah...
Hey, Kan-chan? When you said a pop idol transferred to your school, were you talking about Raizo?
......
Nope.
He was talking about Ranmaru Sakai, a pretty-boy fashion model.
Our high-school is crawling with stars and idols...
Looks like this...
Yeek!
Rain is still building its fanbase.
Ahem.
Friend to ladies everywhere...
Cousin to the blonde teacher from the how-to-draw-manga book.
Thanks Uchida ♥

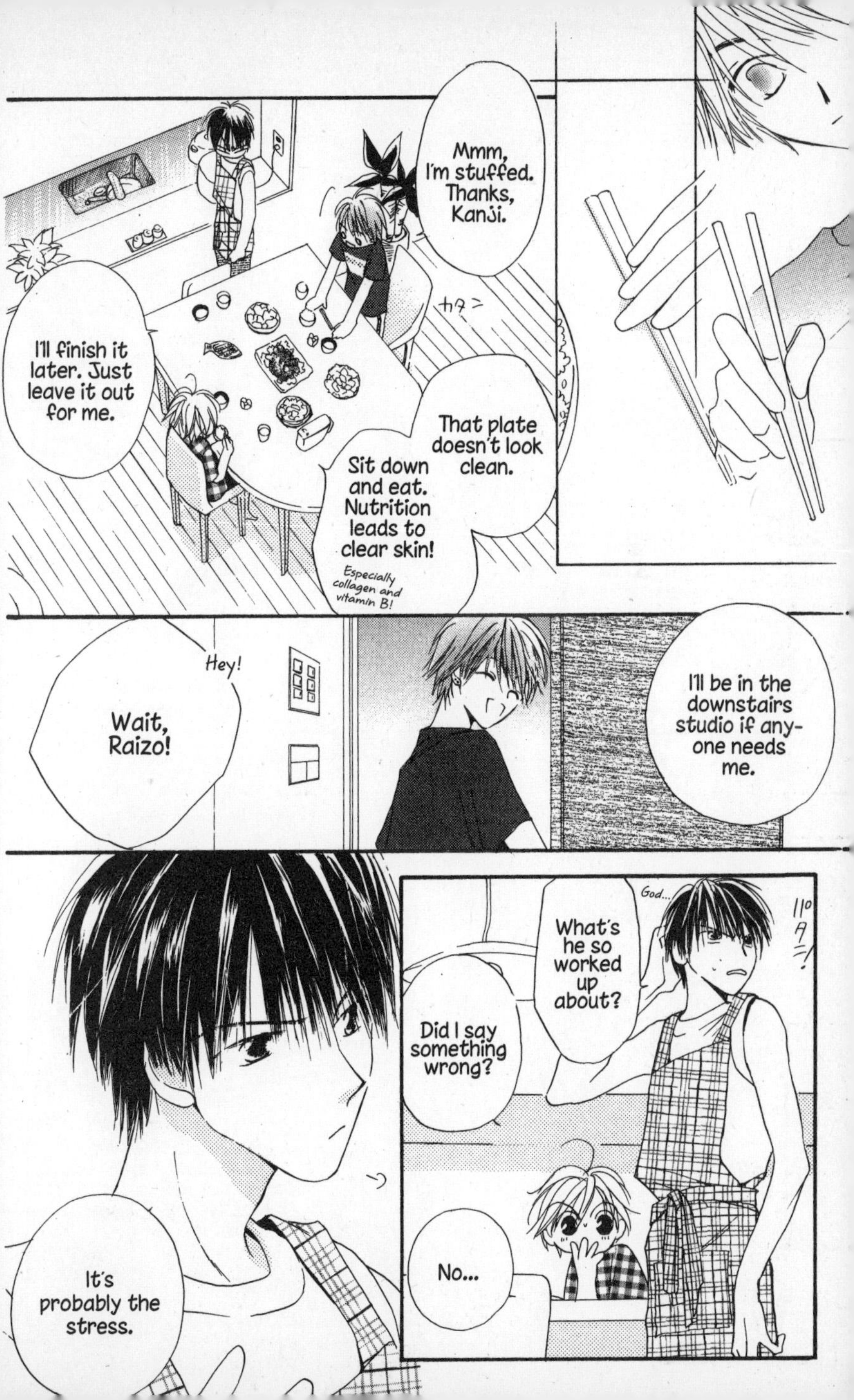
Mmm, I'm stuffed. Thanks, Kanji.
That plate doesn't look clean.
Sit down and eat. Nutrition leads to clear skin!
Especially collagen and vitamin B!
I'll finish it later. Just leave it out for me.
I'll be in the downstairs studio if any-one needs me.
Hey!
Wait, Raizo!
God...
What's he so worked up about?
Did I say something wrong?
No...
It's probably the stress.

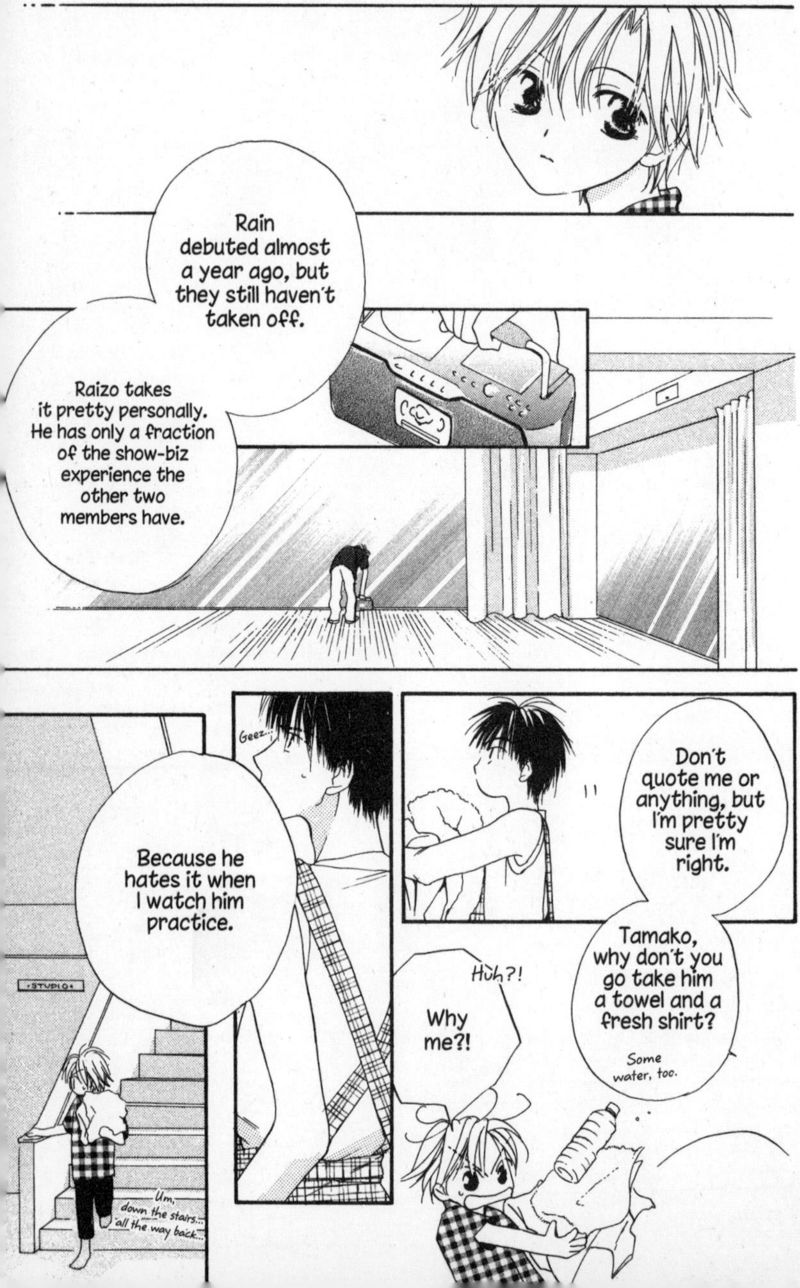
Rain debuted almost a year ago, but they still haven't taken off.
Raizo takes it pretty personally. He has only a fraction of the show-biz experience the other two members have.
Don't quote me or anything, but I'm pretty sure I'm right.
Geez...
Because he hates it when I watch him practice.
Tamako, why don't you go take him a towel and a fresh shirt?
Some water, too.
Huh?!
Why me?!
Um, down the stairs... all the way back...
STUDIO

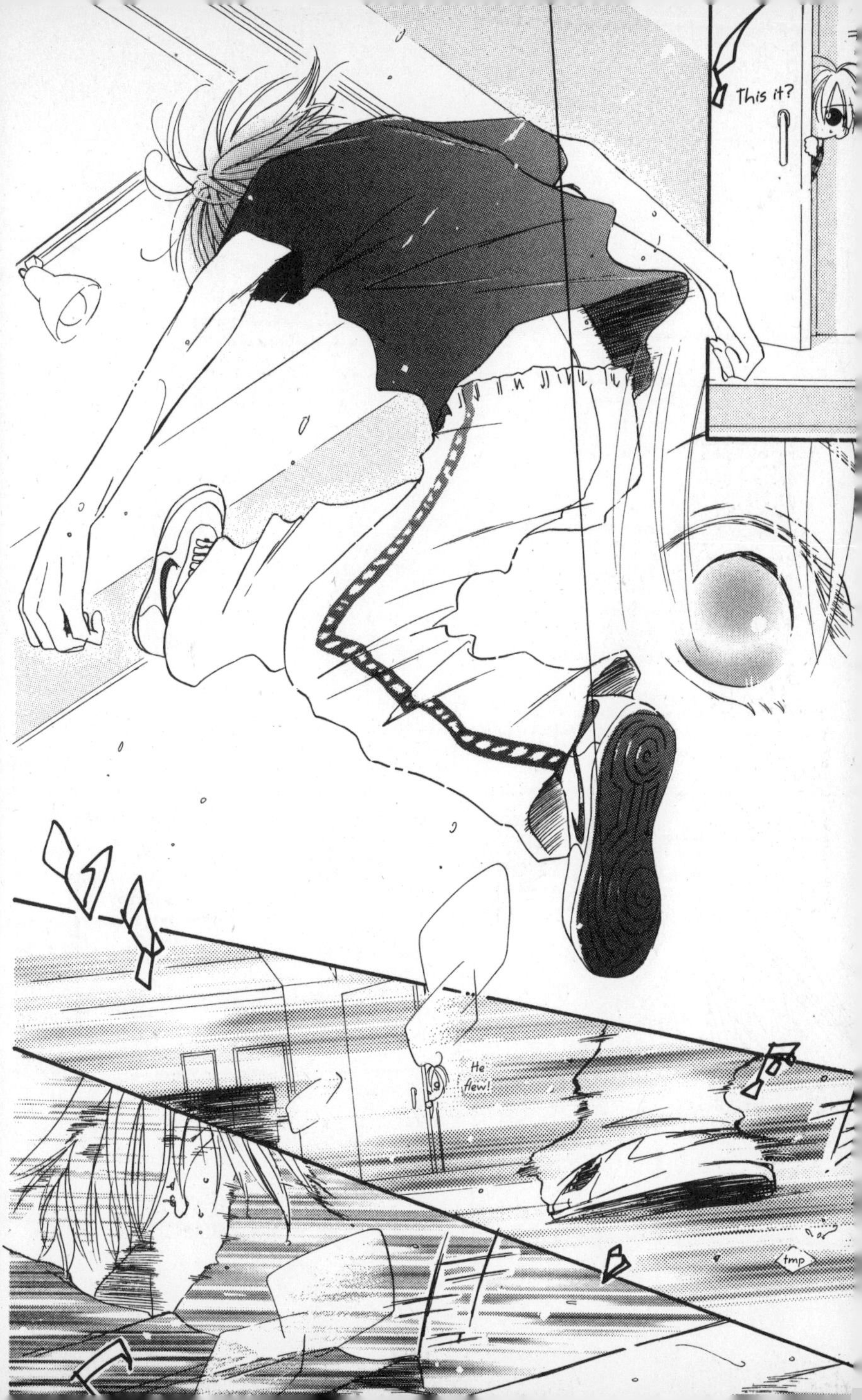
This it?
He flew!
tmp

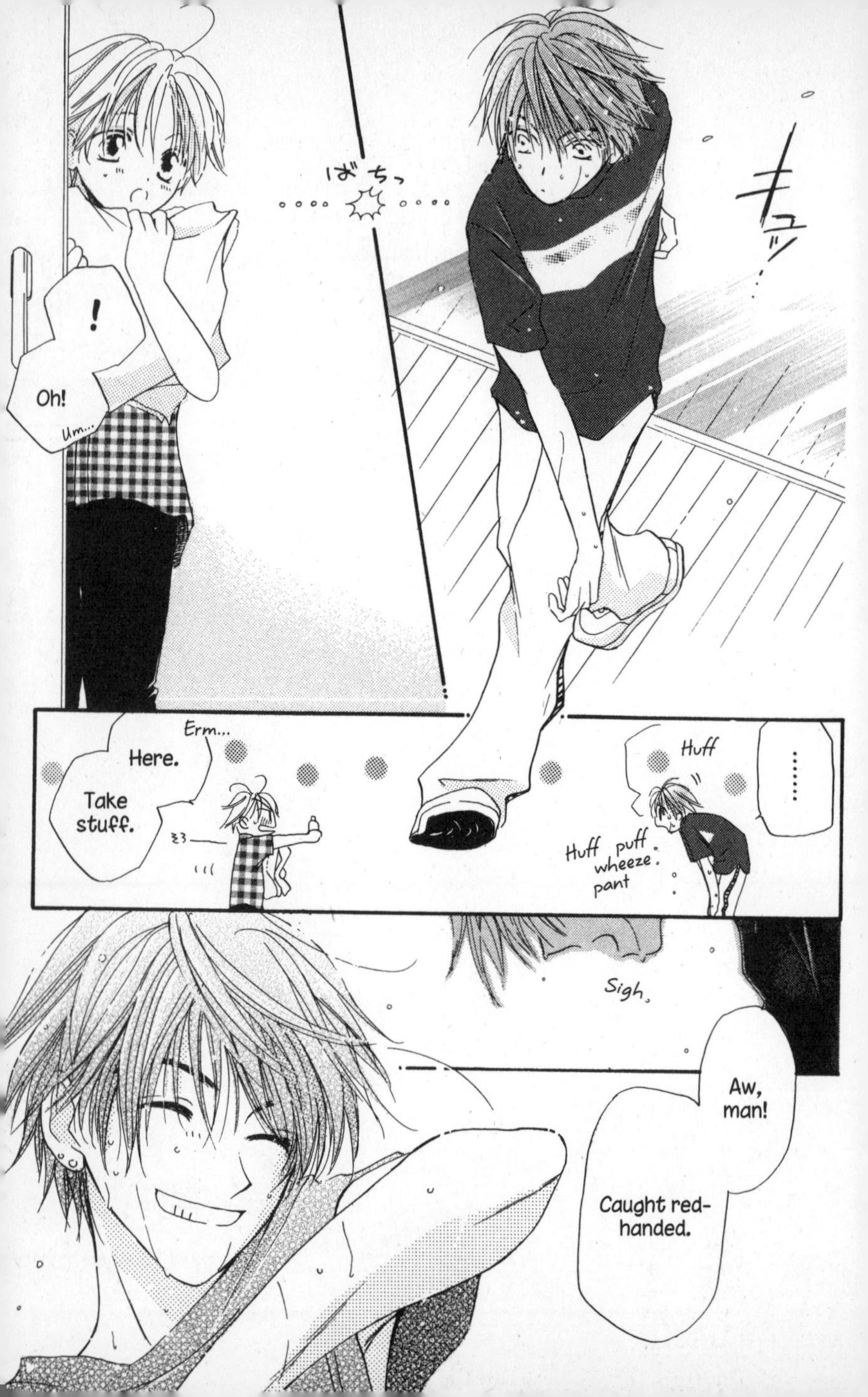
キュッ
ばちっ
!
Oh!
Um...
......
Huff
Huff puff wheeze pant
Erm...
Here.
Take stuff.
Sigh.
Aw, man!
Caught red-handed.

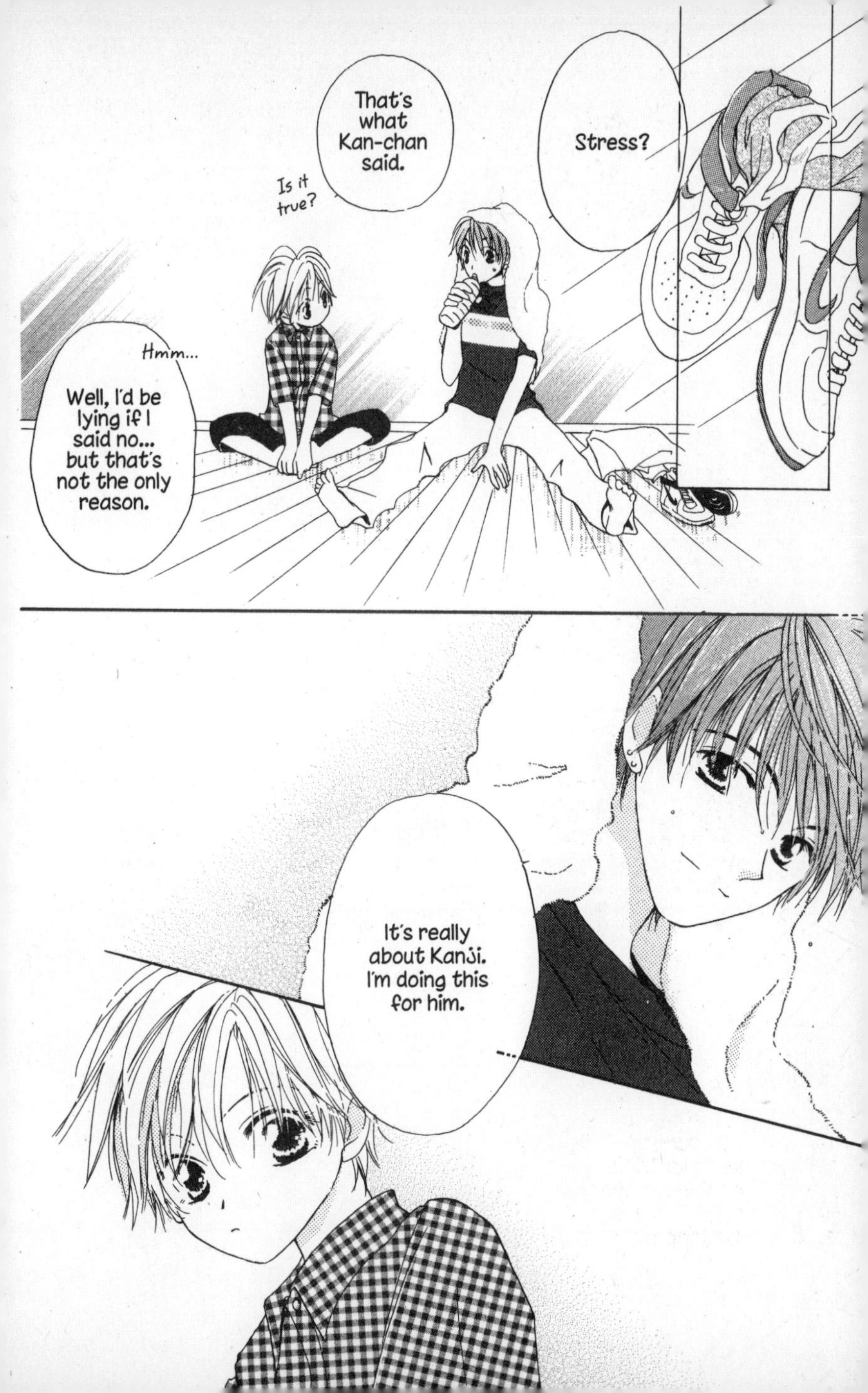
Stress?
That's what Kan-chan said.
Is it true?
Hmm...
Well, I'd be lying if I said no... but that's not the only reason.
It's really about Kanji. I'm doing this for him.

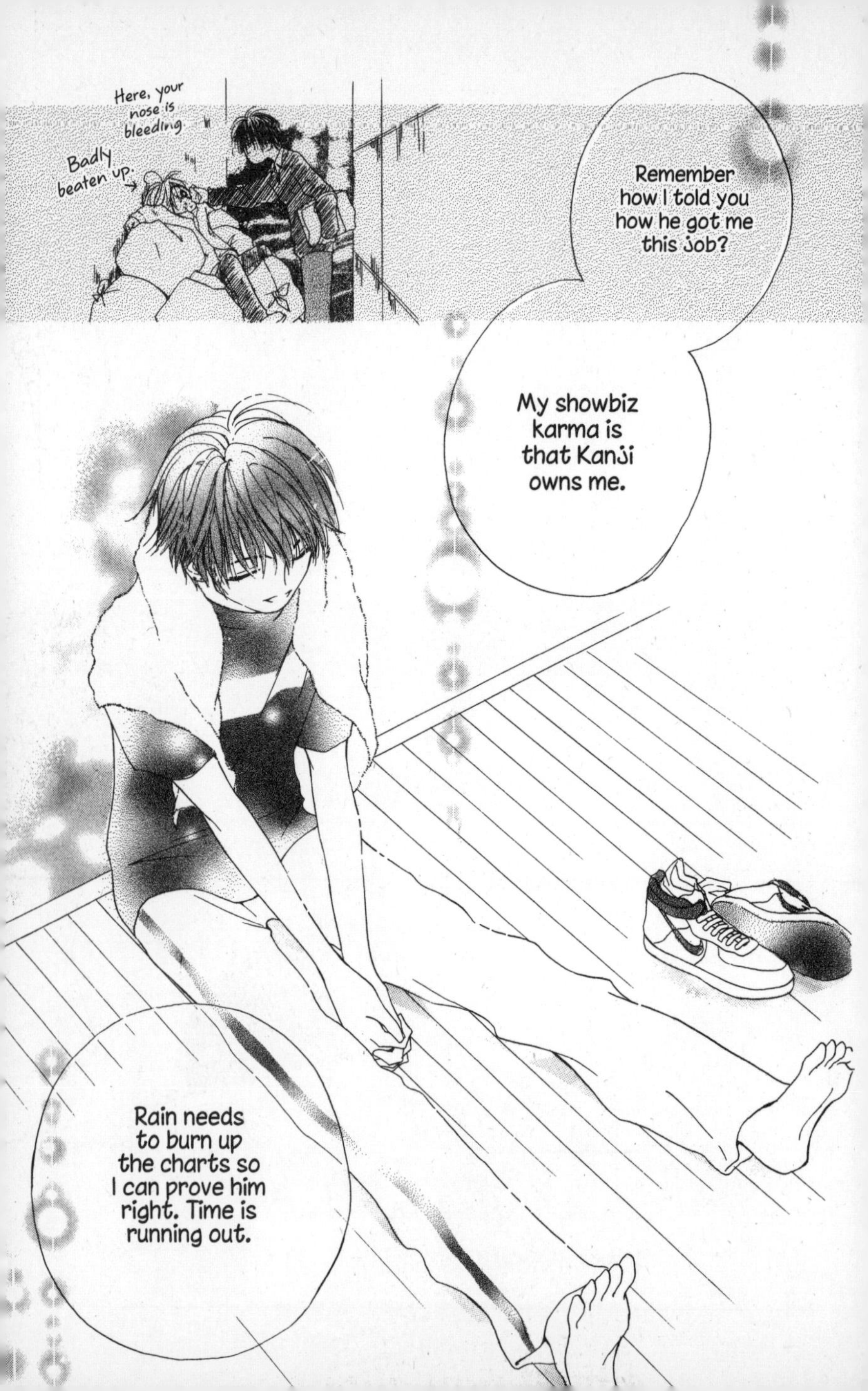
Remember how I told you how he got me this job?
Here, your nose is bleeding.
Badly beaten up.
My showbiz karma is that Kanji owns me.
Rain needs to burn up the charts so I can prove him right. Time is running out.

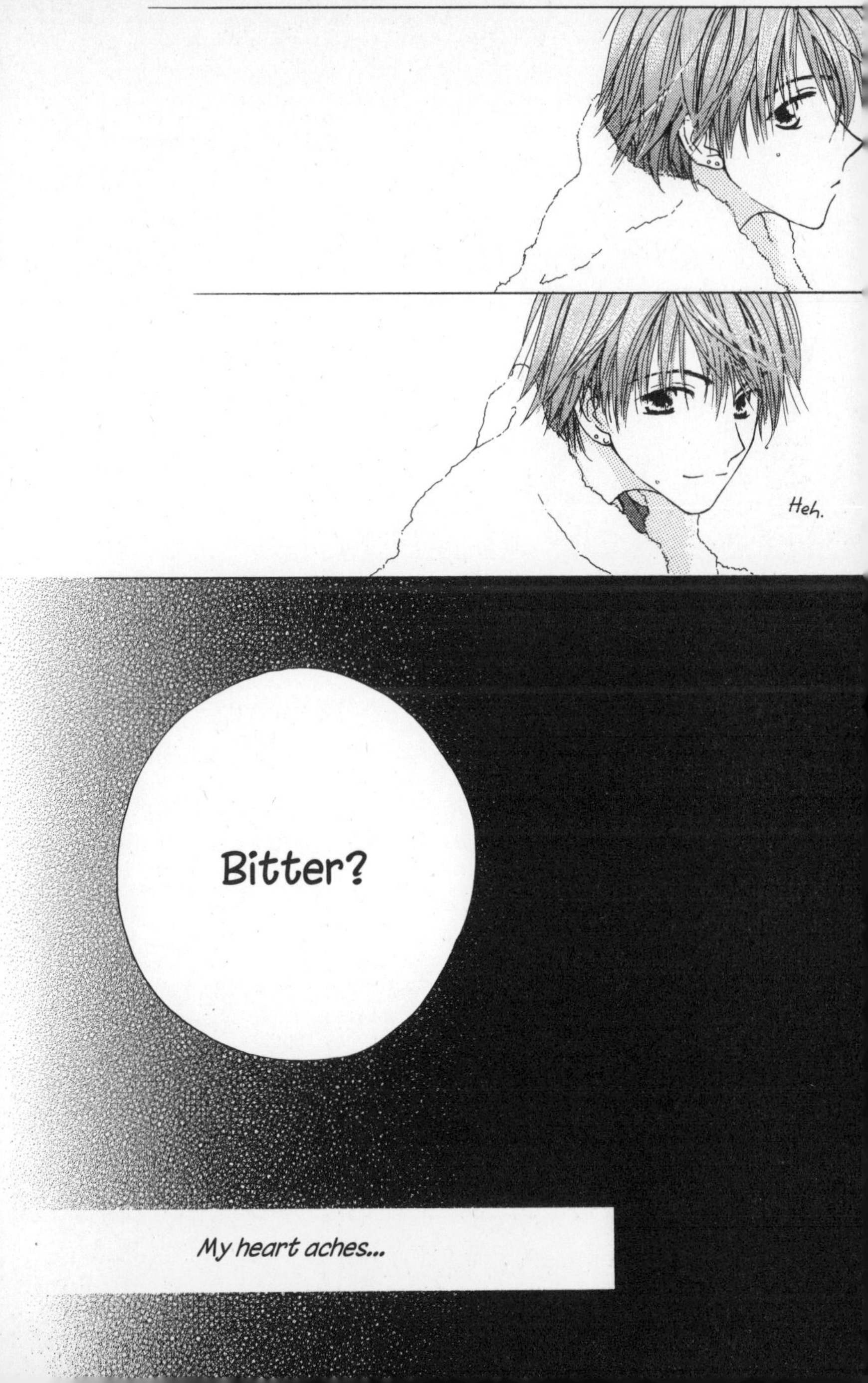
Heh.
Bitter?
My heart aches...

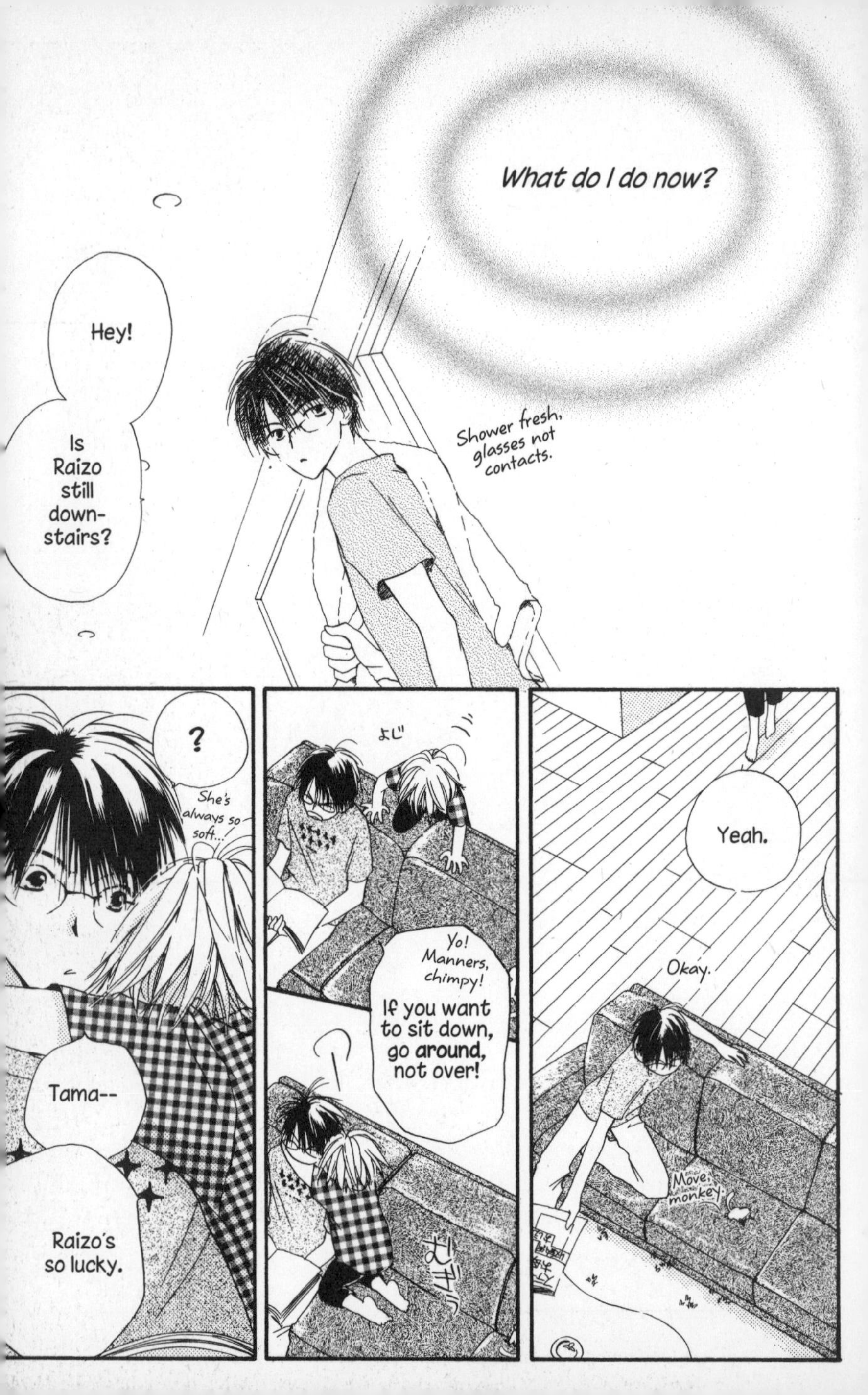
What do I do now?
Shower fresh, glasses not contacts.
Hey!
Is Raizo still downstairs?
Yeah.
Okay.
Move, monkey.
よじ
Yo! Manners, chimpy!
If you want to sit down, go around, not over!
?
She's always so soft...!
Tama--
Raizo's so lucky.

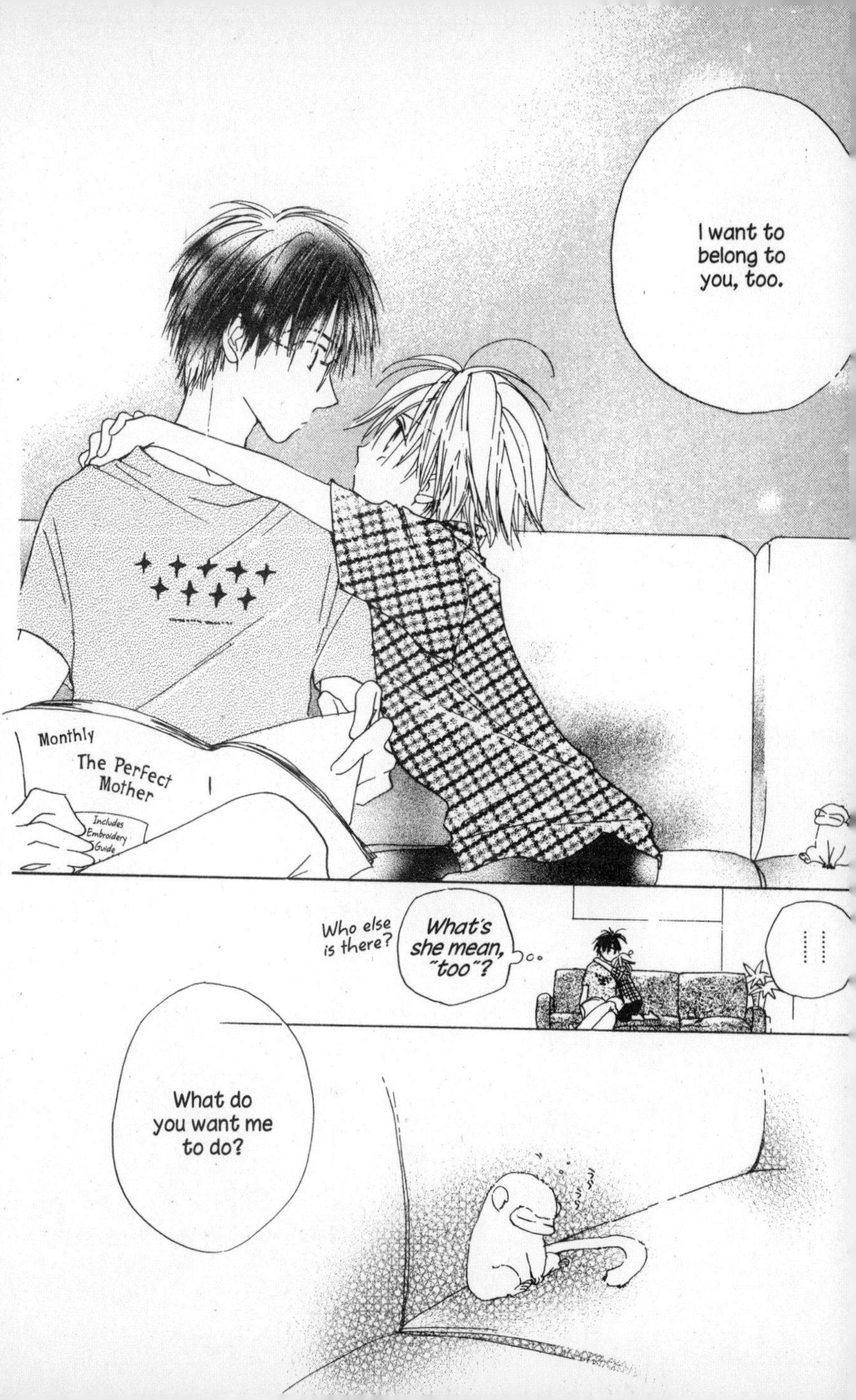
I want to belong to you, too.
Monthly
The Perfect Mother
Includes Embroidery Guide
......
What's she mean, "too"?
Who else is there?
What do you want me to do?

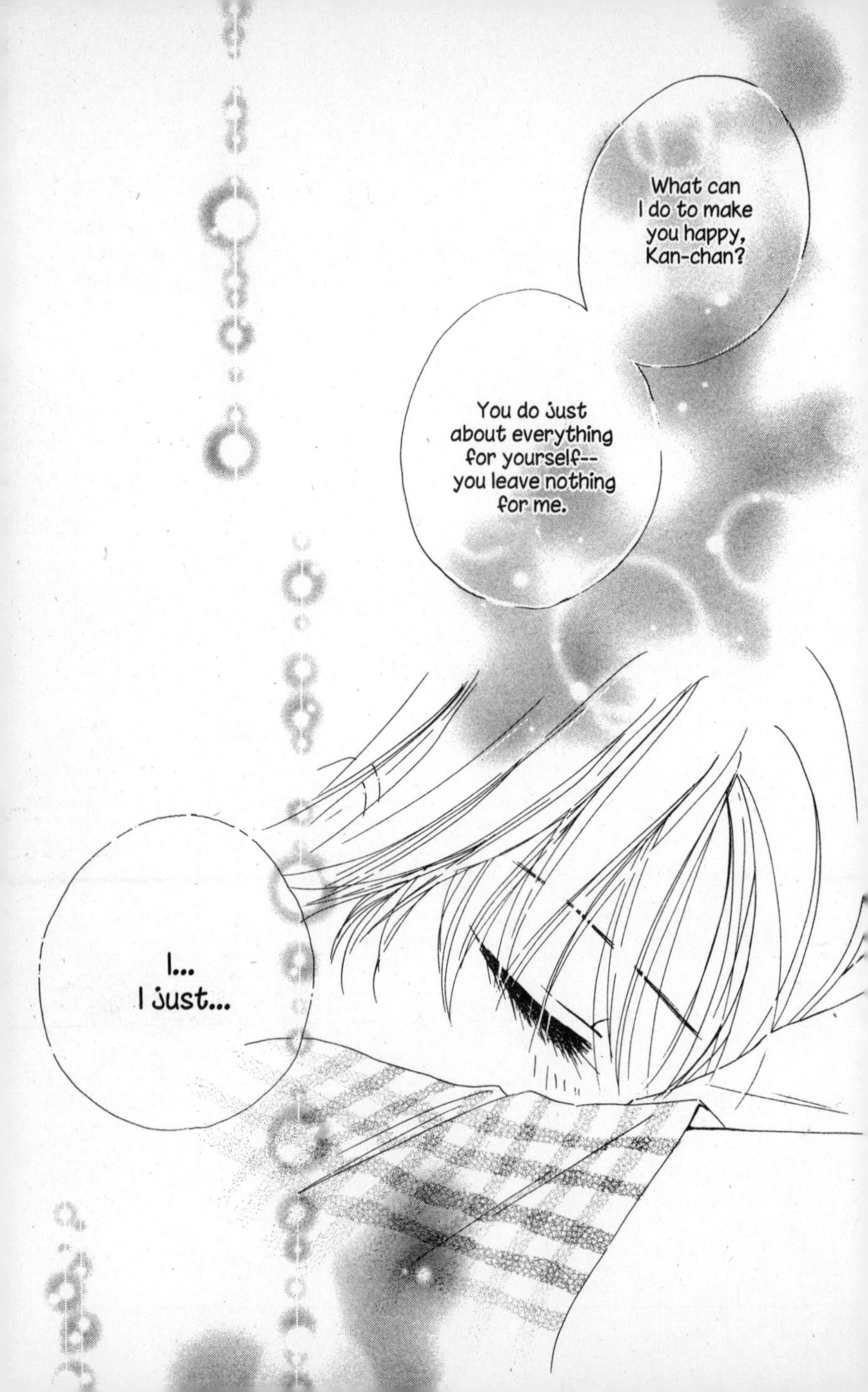
What can I do to make you happy, Kan-chan?
You do just about everything for yourself-- you leave nothing for me.
I... I just...

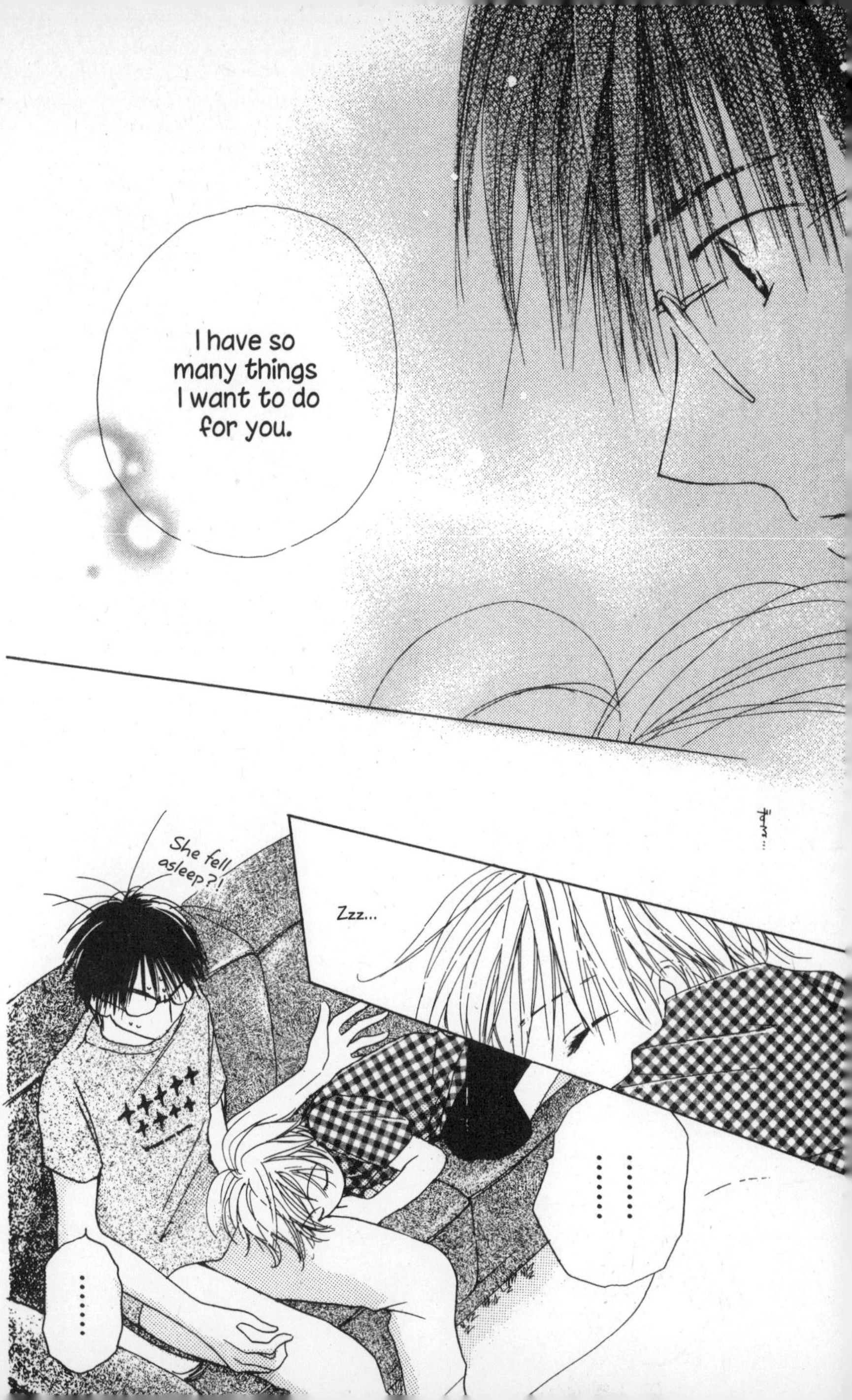
I have so many things I want to do for you.
Zzz...
......
She fell asleep?!
......

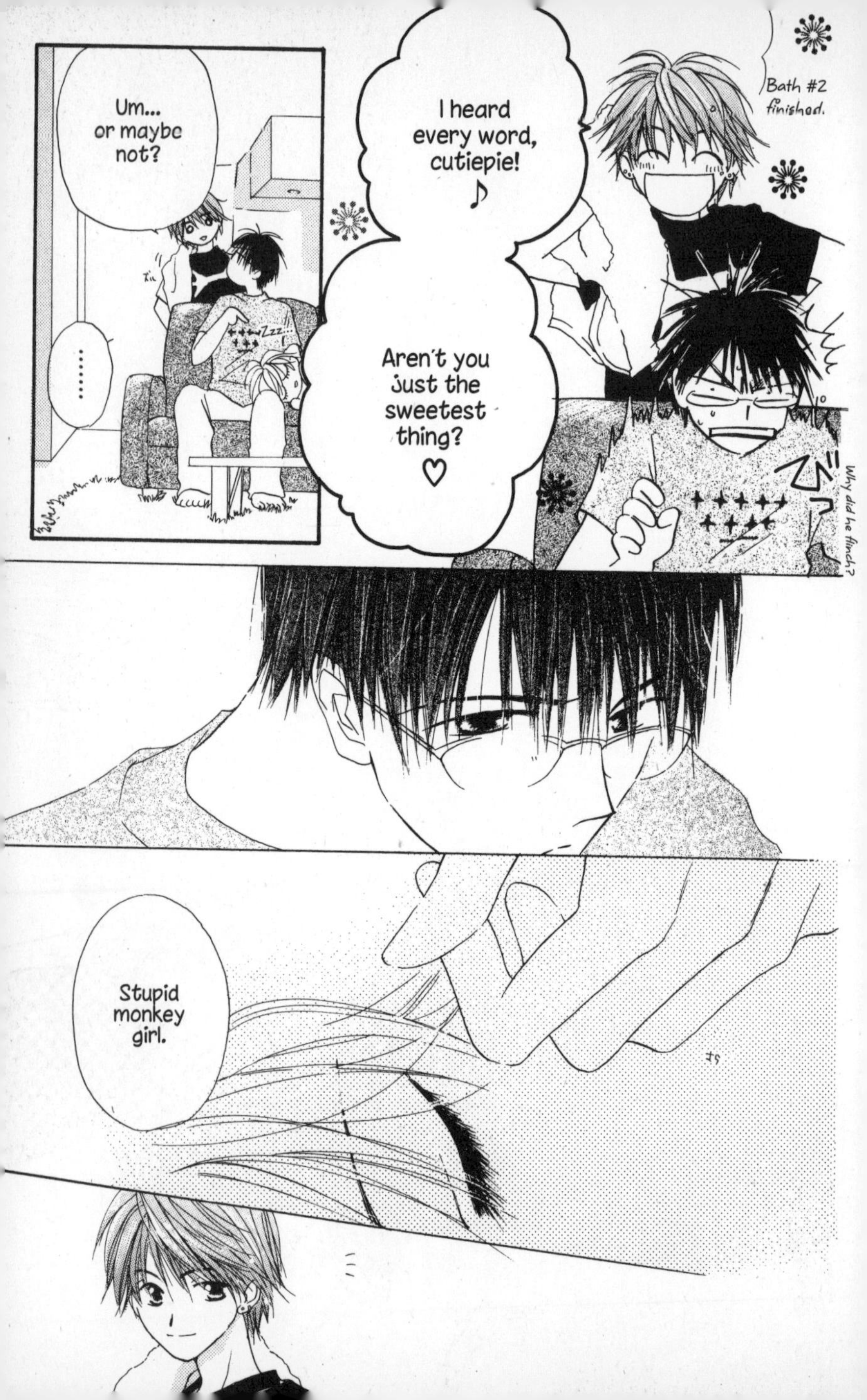
Bath #2 finished.
I heard every word, cutiepie! ♪
Aren't you just the sweetest thing? ♡
Why did he flinch?
Um... or maybe not?
......
Stupid monkey girl.

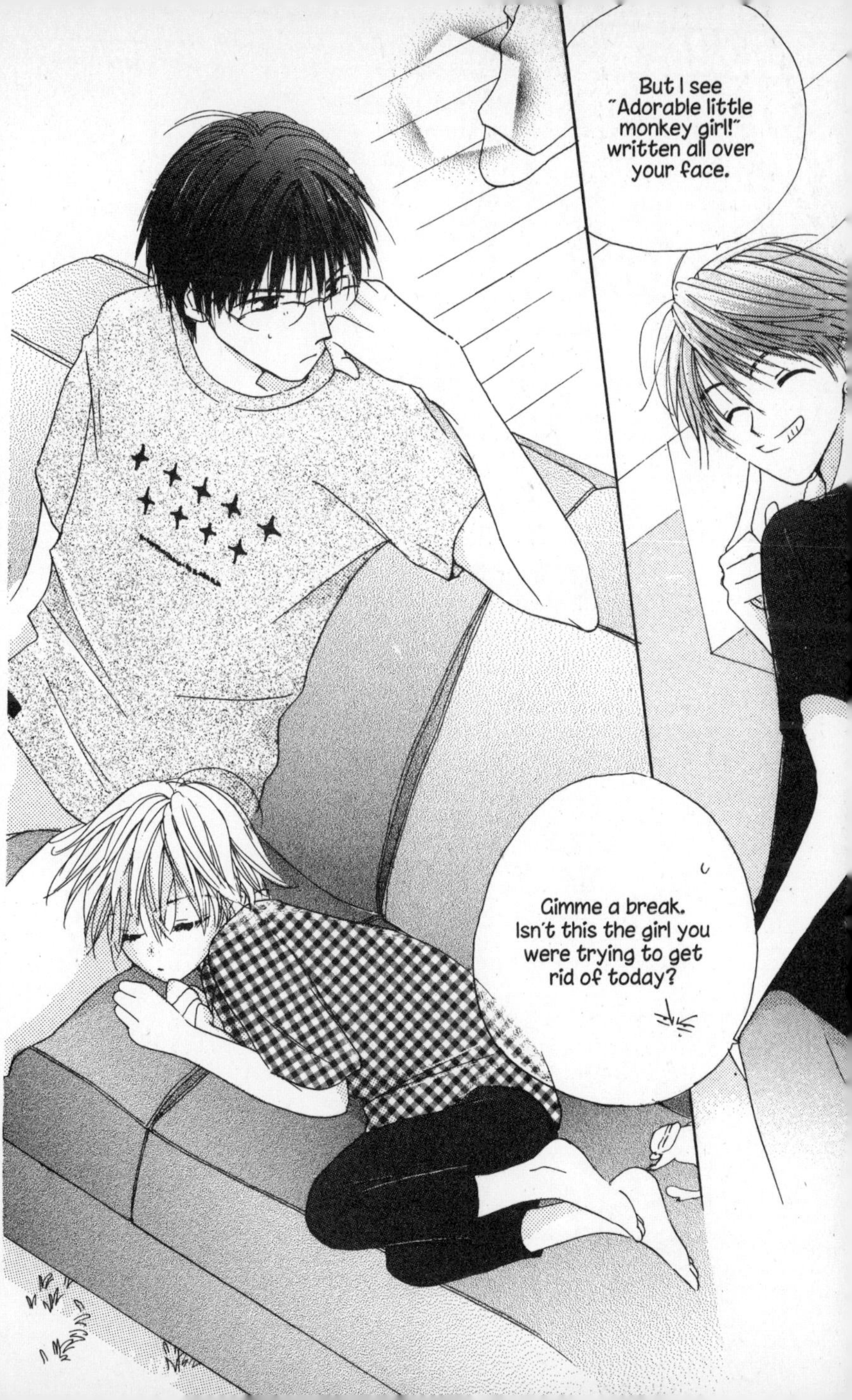
But I see "Adorable little monkey girl!" written all over your face.
Gimme a break. Isn't this the girl you were trying to get rid of today?

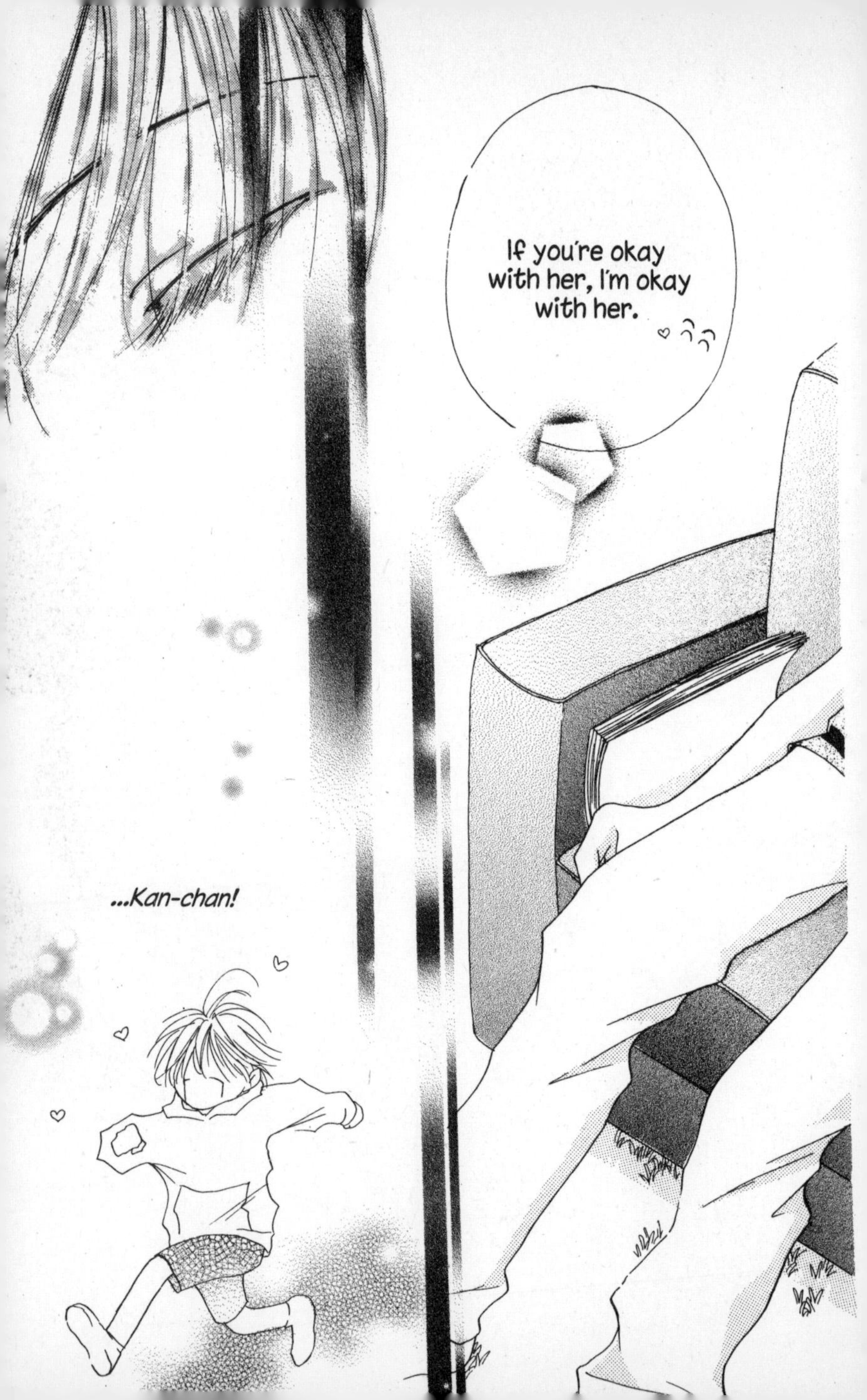
If you're okay with her, I'm okay with her.
...Kan-chan!

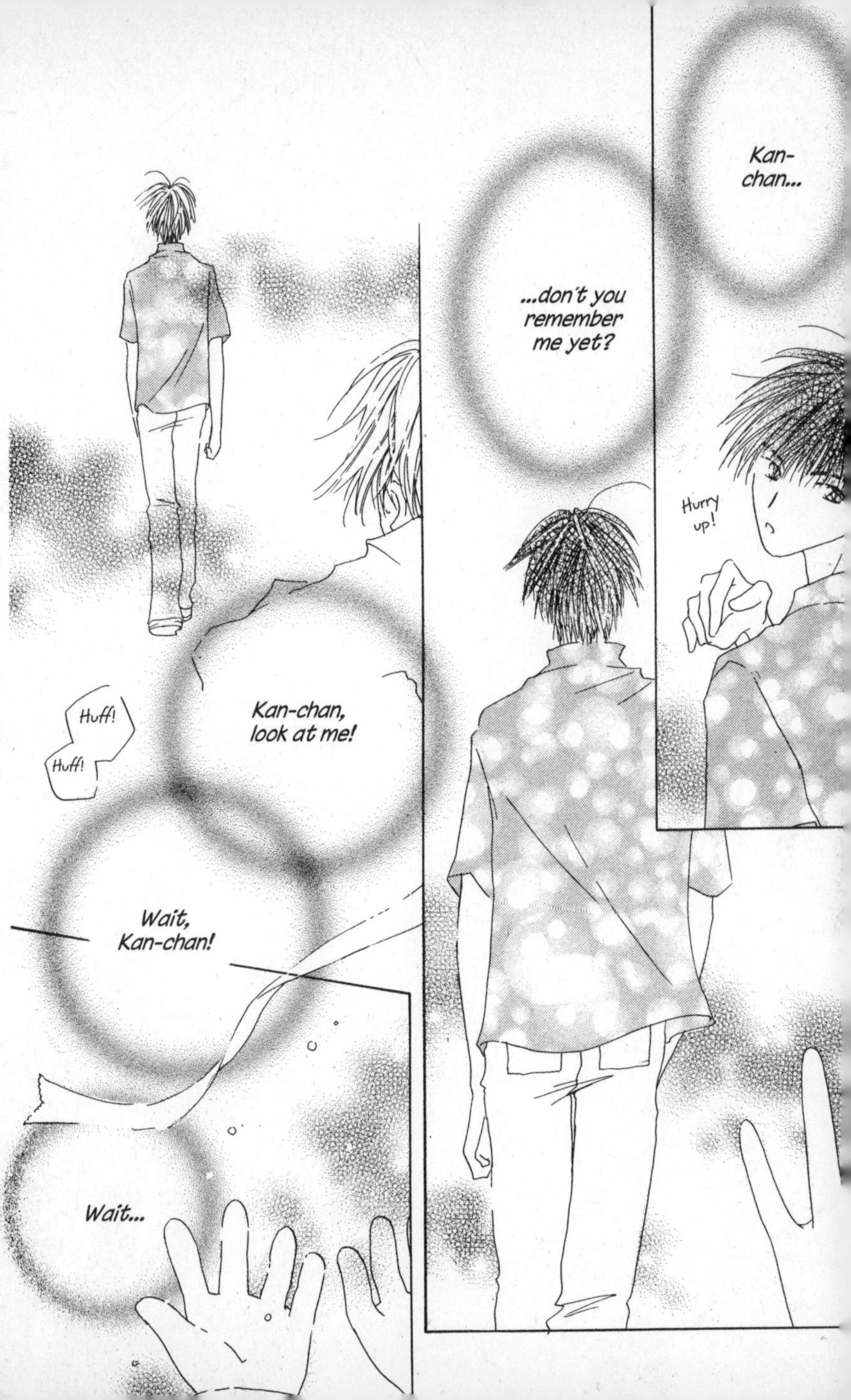
Kan-chan...
Hurry up!
...don't you remember me yet?
Kan-chan, look at me!
Huff! Huff!
Wait, Kan-chan!
Wait...

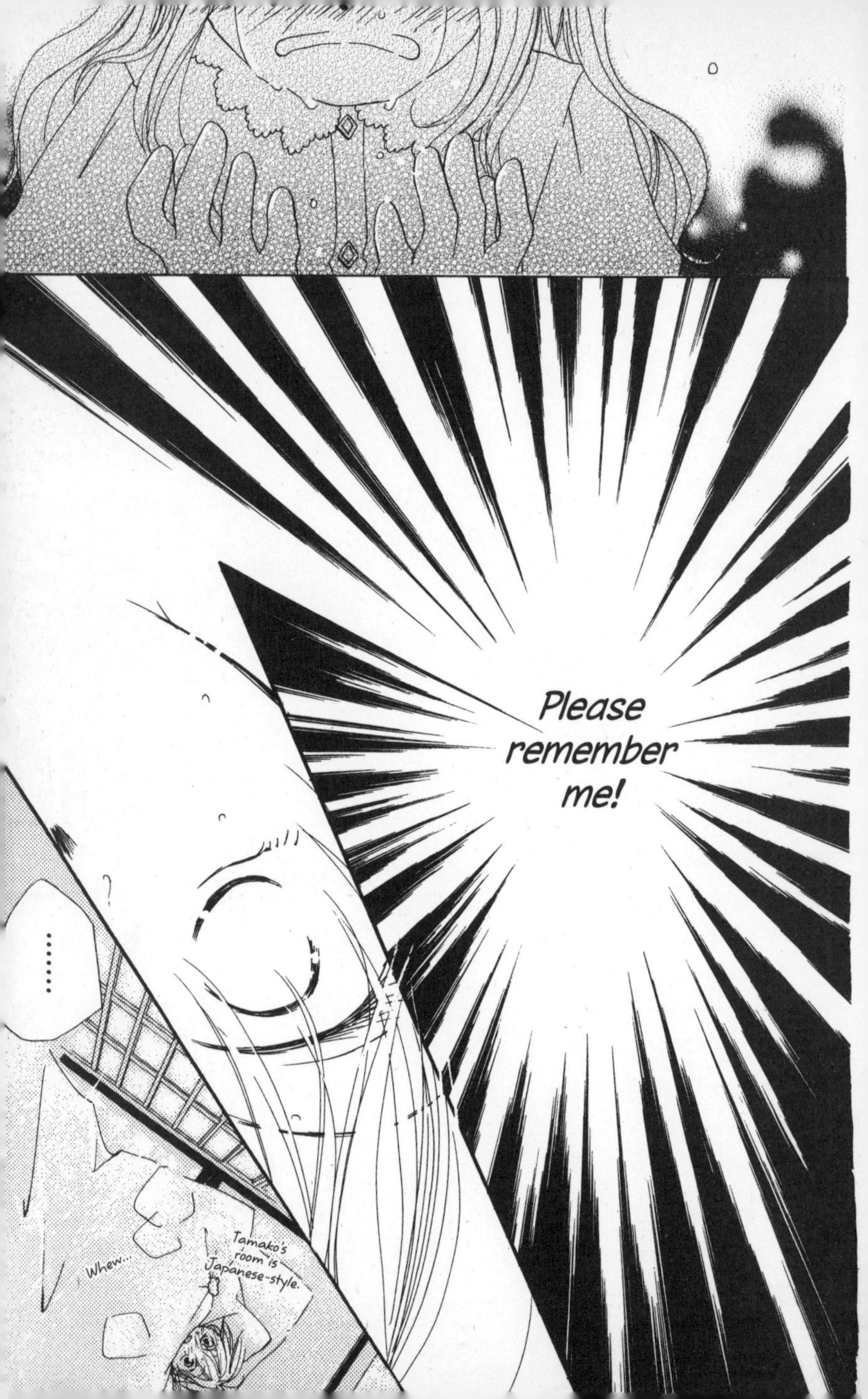
Please remember me!
......
Tamako's room is Japanese-style.
Whew...

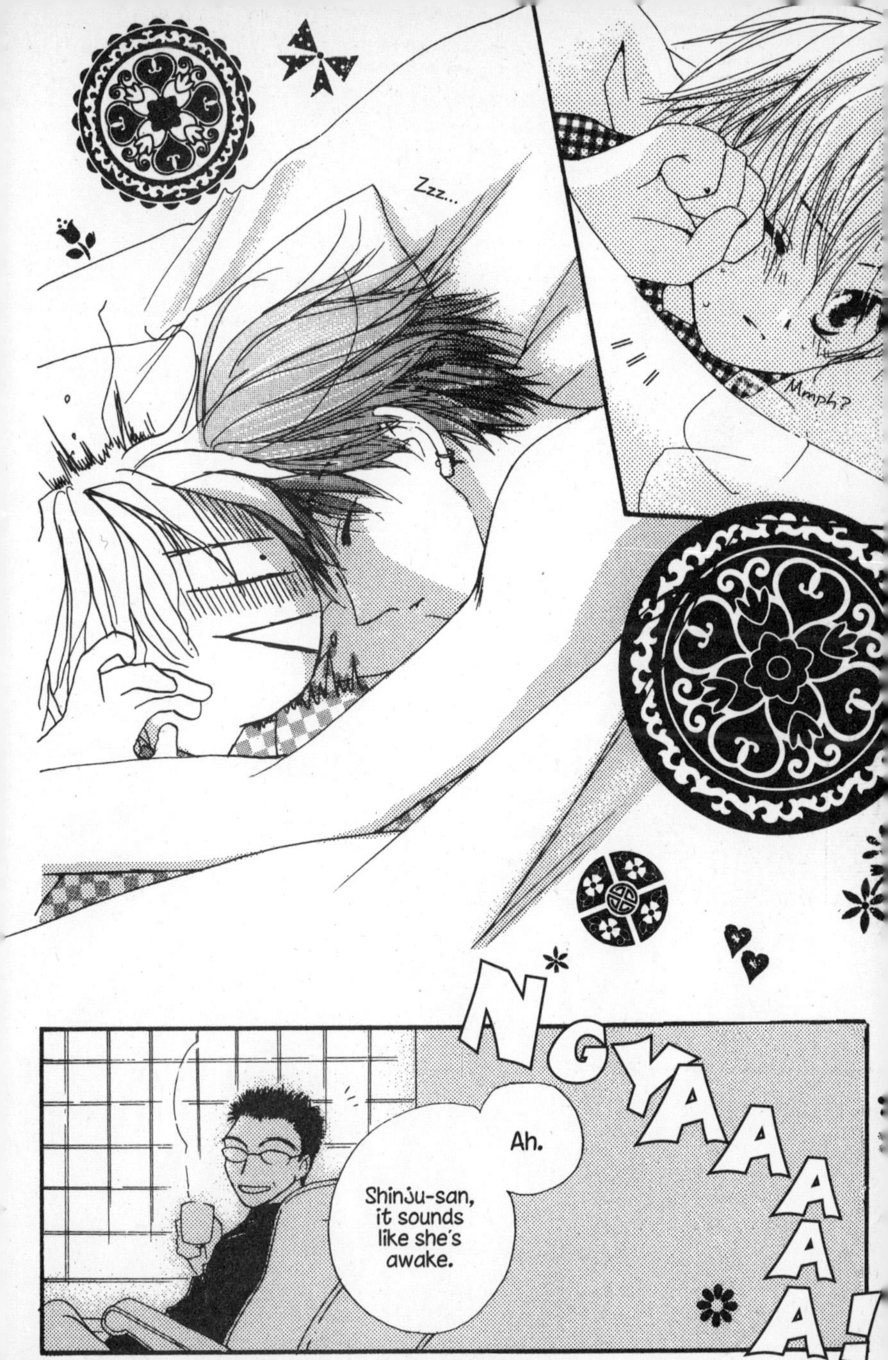
Mmph?
Zzz...
NGYAAAAAAA!
Ah.
Shinju-san, it sounds like she's awake.

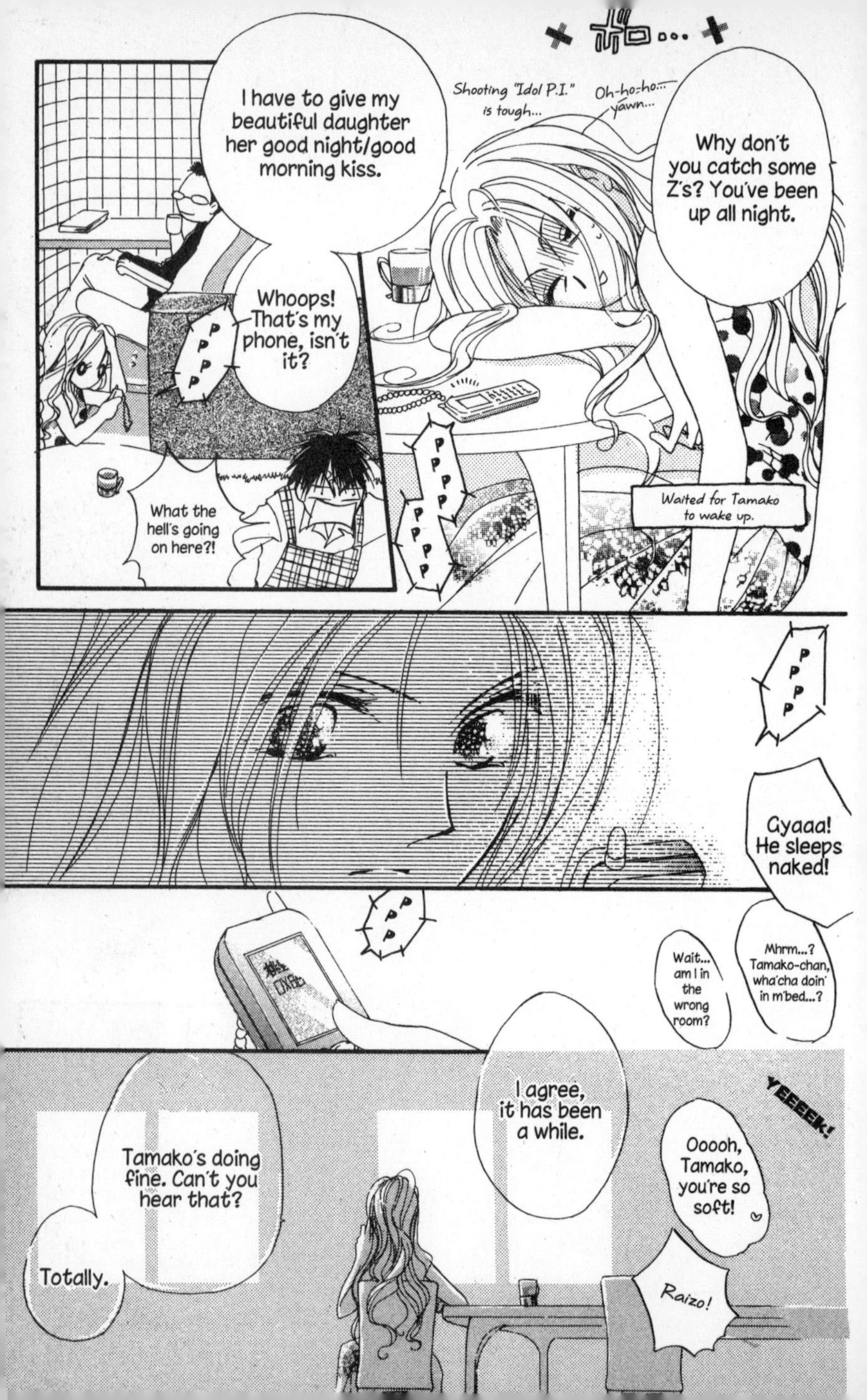

Why don't you catch some Z's? You've been up all night.
Oh-ho-ho... yawn...
Shooting "Idol P.I." is tough...
Waited for Tamako to wake up.
PPPPPPP
I have to give my beautiful daughter her good night/good morning kiss.
Whoops! That's my phone, isn't it?
PPPP
What the hell's going on here?!
PPPP
Gyaaa! He sleeps naked!
Mhrm...? Tamako-chan, wha'cha doin' in m'bed...?
Wait... am I in the wrong room?
PPP
YEEEEK!
Ooooh, Tamako, you're so soft!
Raizo!
I agree, it has been a while.
Tamako's doing fine. Can't you hear that?
Totally.

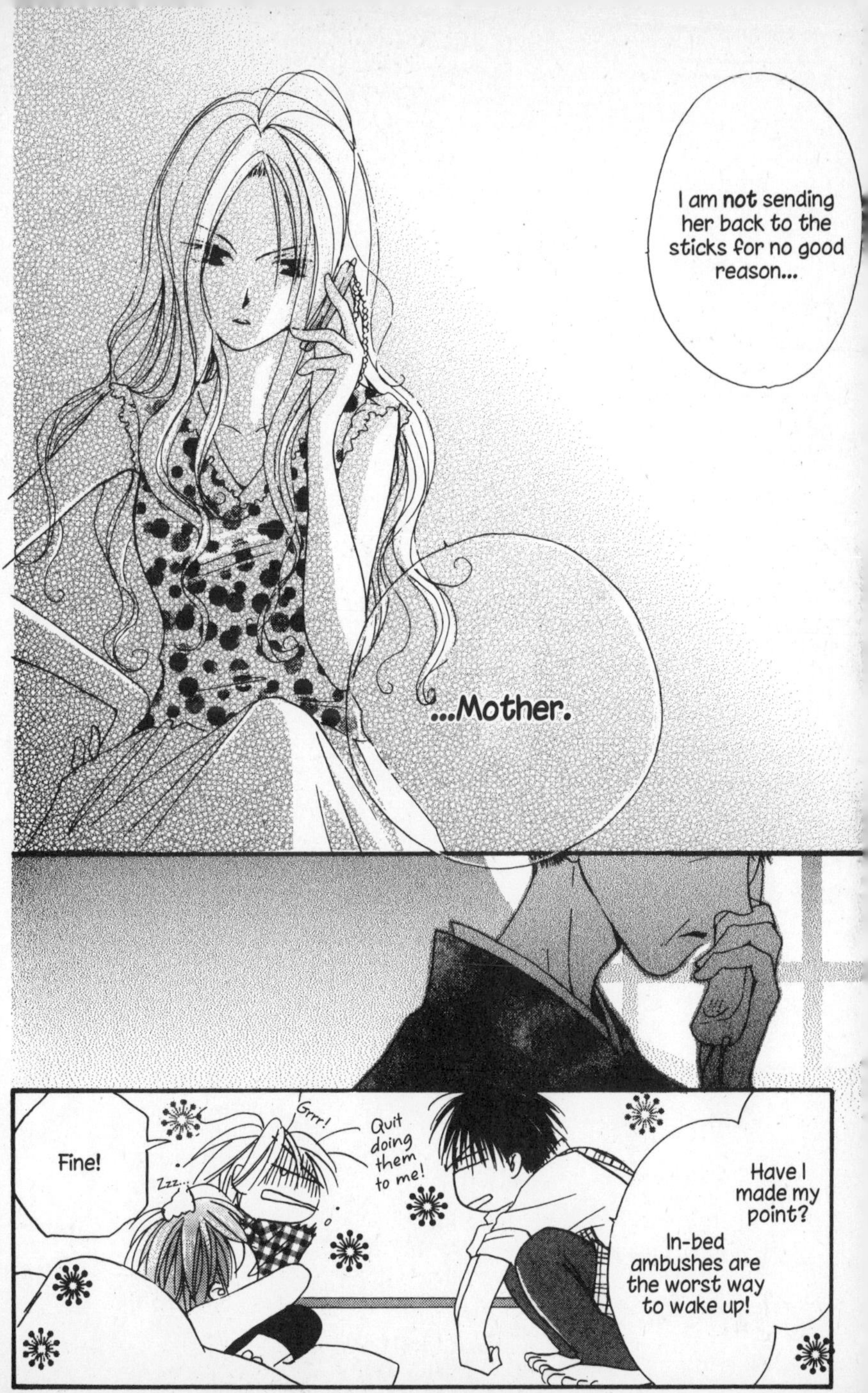
I am **not** sending her back to the sticks for no good reason...
...Mother.
Have I made my point?
In-bed ambushes are the worst way to wake up!
Quit doing them to me!
Grrr!
Zzz...
Fine!

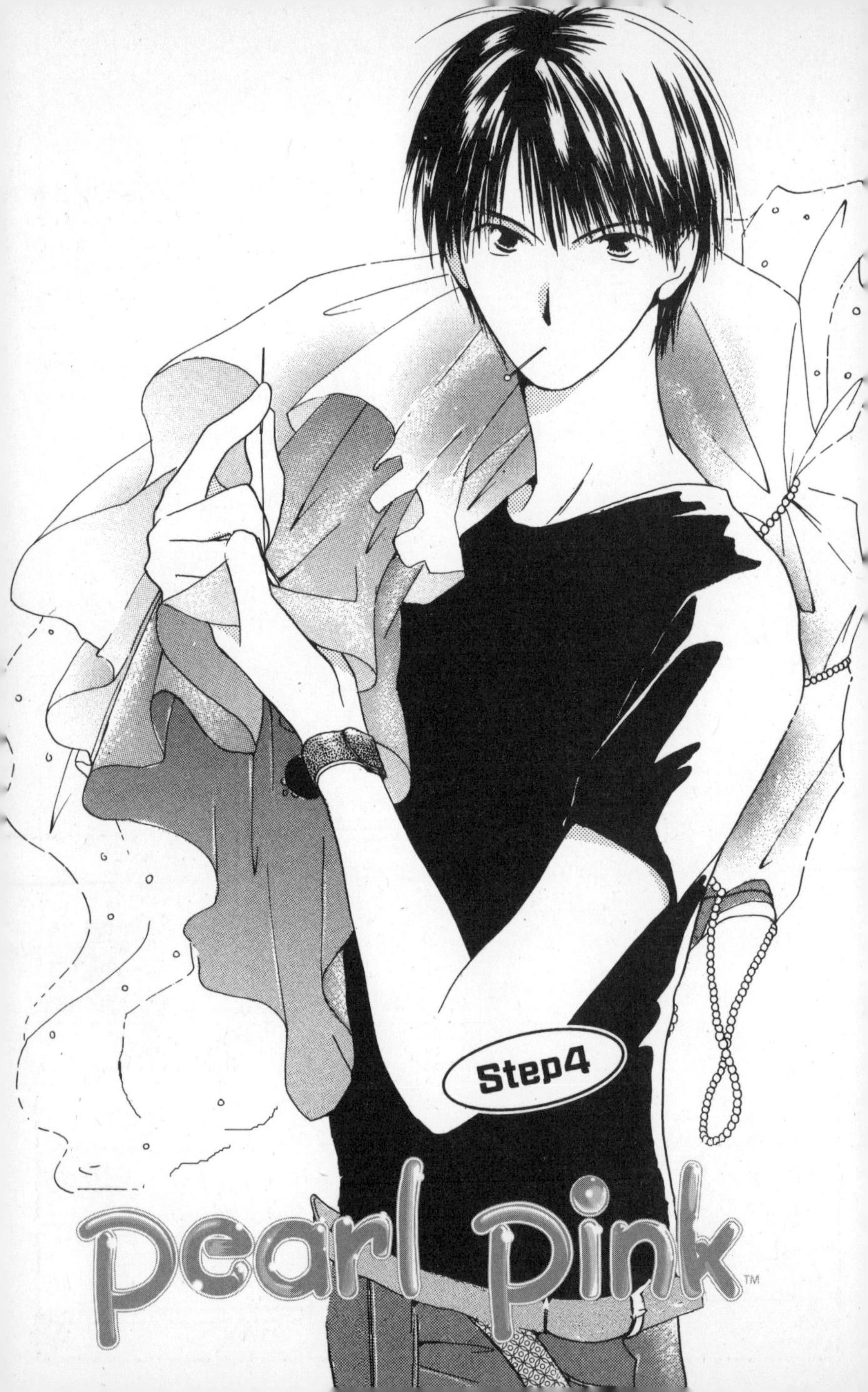
Step4
Pearl Pink™

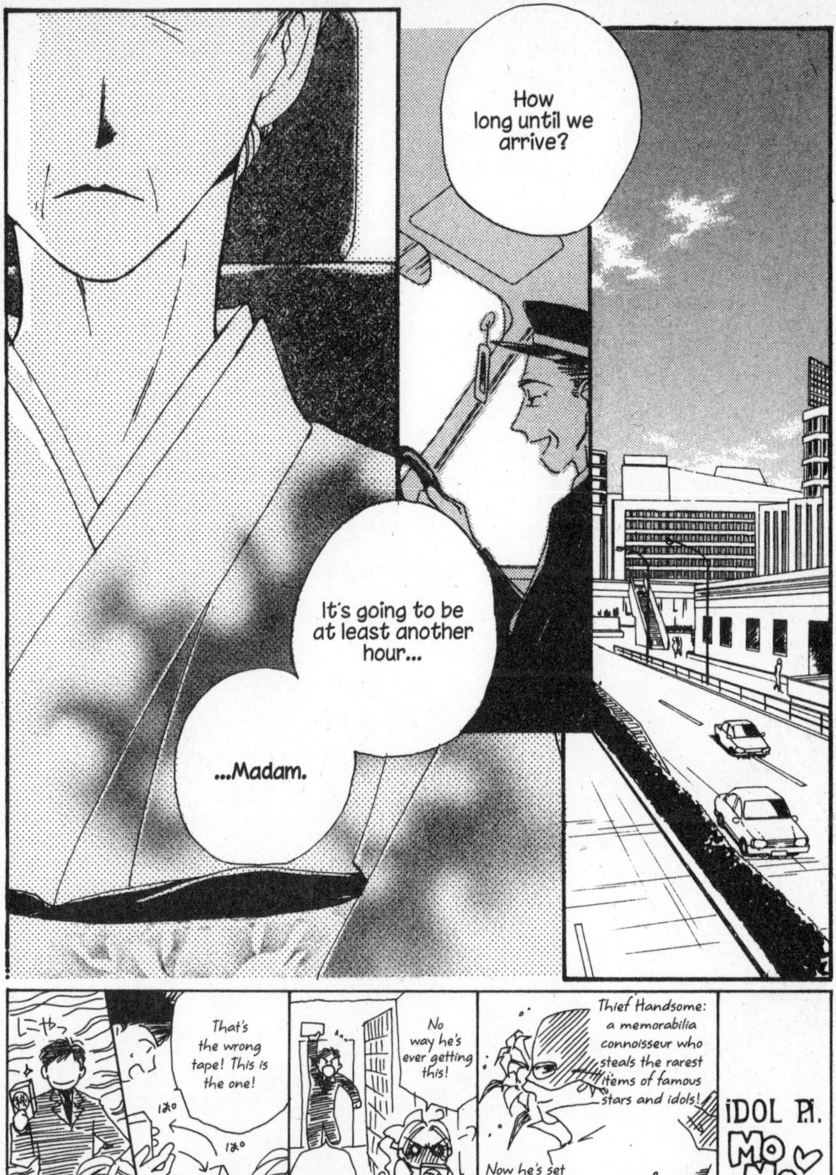
How long until we arrive?
It's going to be at least another hour...
...Madam.
iDOL P.I. MOMOKO 3.
Thief Handsome: a memorabilia connoisseur who steals the rarest items of famous stars and idols!
Now he's set his sights on Momoko's debut film!
TV
No way he's ever getting this!
Momoko-san!
Storage Room
That's the wrong tape! This is the one!
Really? Close call! Thanks!
Huh?
TBC...

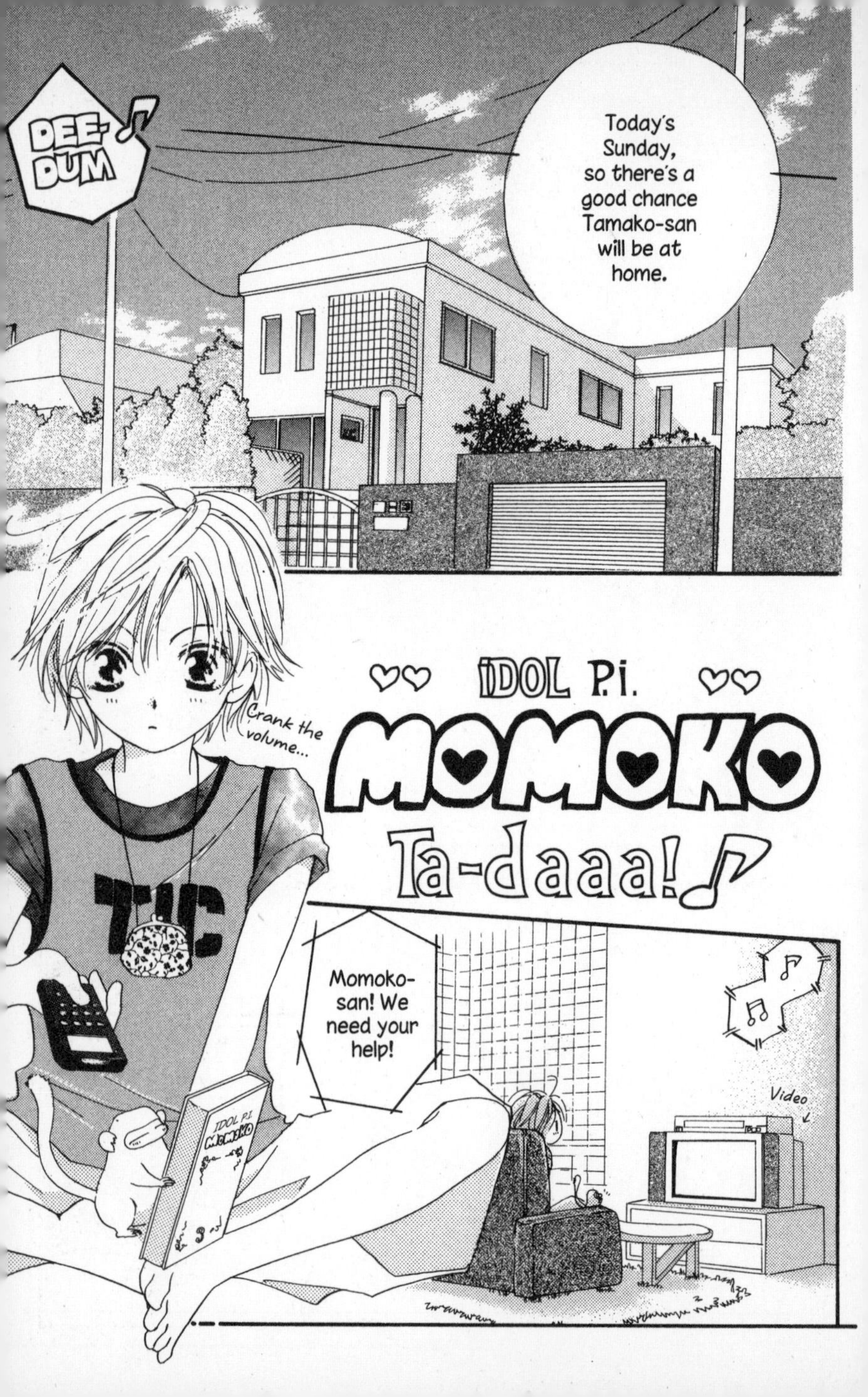
Today's Sunday, so there's a good chance Tamako-san will be at home.
DEE-DUM
IDOL P.I.
MOMOKO
Ta-daaa!
Crank the volume...
Video
Momoko-san! We need your help!
IDOL P.I.
MOMOKO

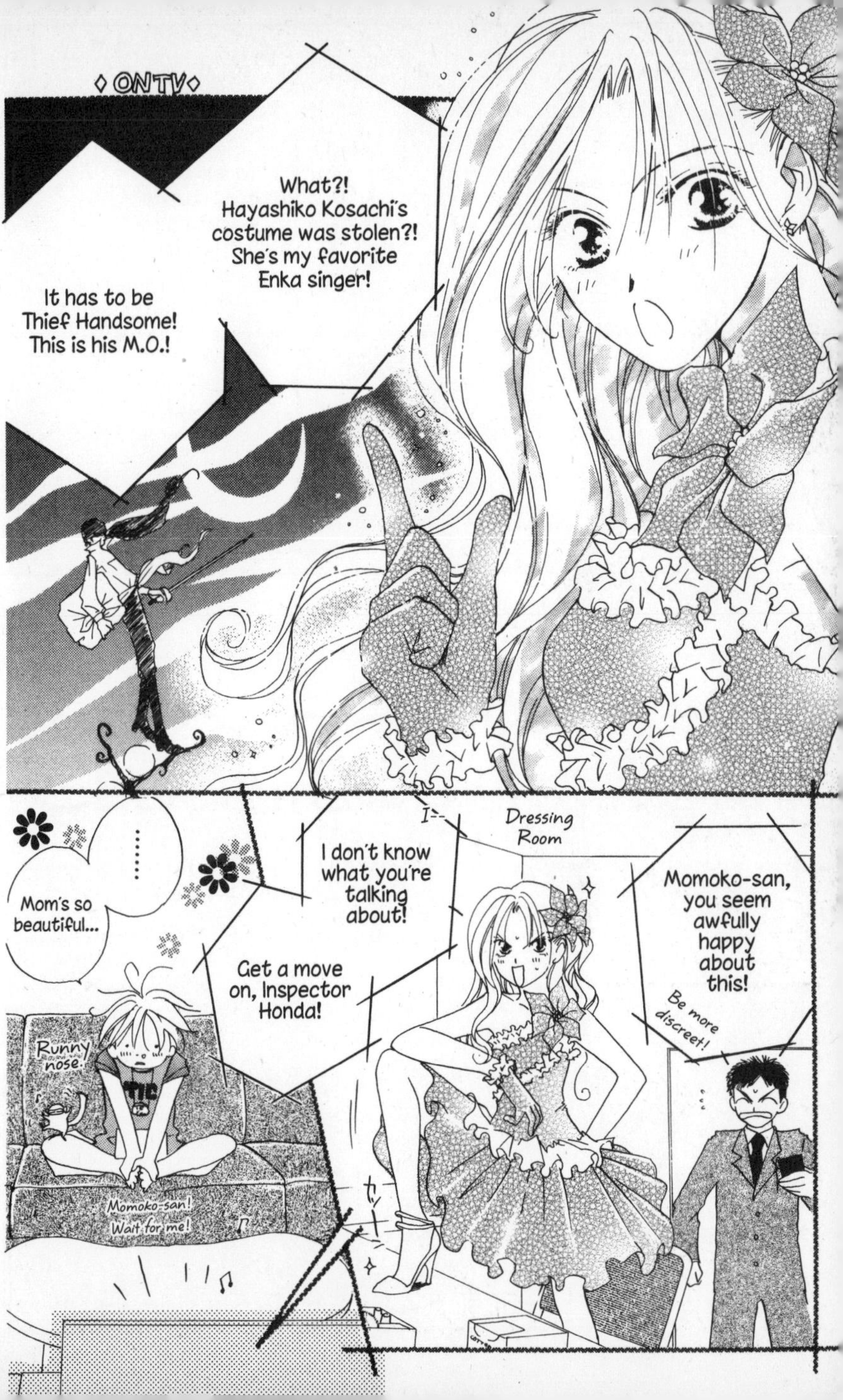
◇ ON TV ◇
What?! Hayashiko Kosachi's costume was stolen?! She's my favorite Enka singer!
It has to be Thief Handsome! This is his M.O.!
Dressing Room
Momoko-san, you seem awfully happy about this!
Be more discreet!
I--
I don't know what you're talking about!
Get a move on, Inspector Honda!
......
Mom's so beautiful...
Runny nose.
Momoko-san! Wait for me!

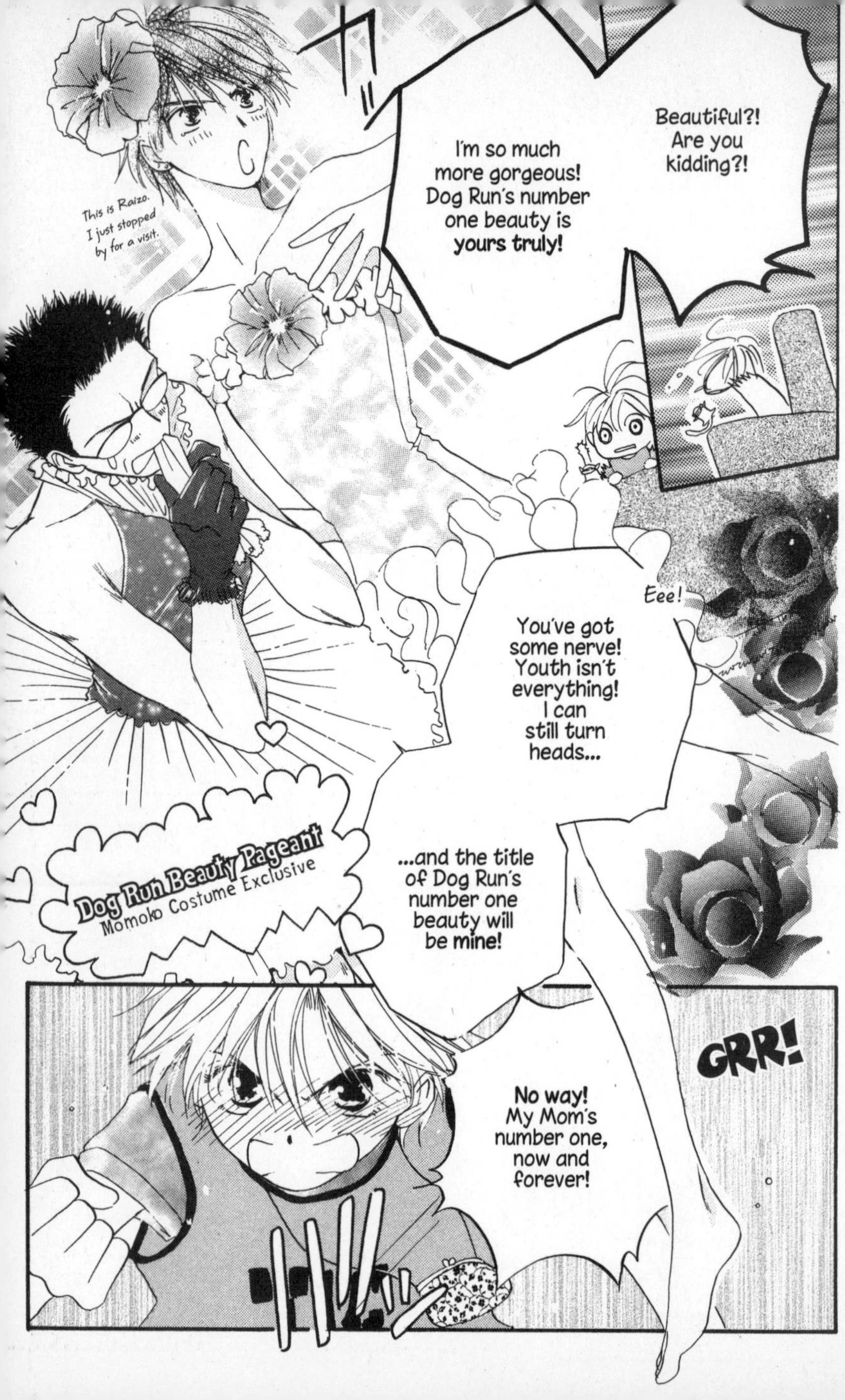
Beautiful?! Are you kidding?!
I'm so much more gorgeous! Dog Run's number one beauty is **yours truly!**
This is Raizo. I just stopped by for a visit.
Eee!
You've got some nerve! Youth isn't everything! I can still turn heads...
...and the title of Dog Run's number one beauty will be **mine!**
Dog Run Beauty Pageant
Momoko Costume Exclusive
GRR!
No way! My Mom's number one, now and forever!

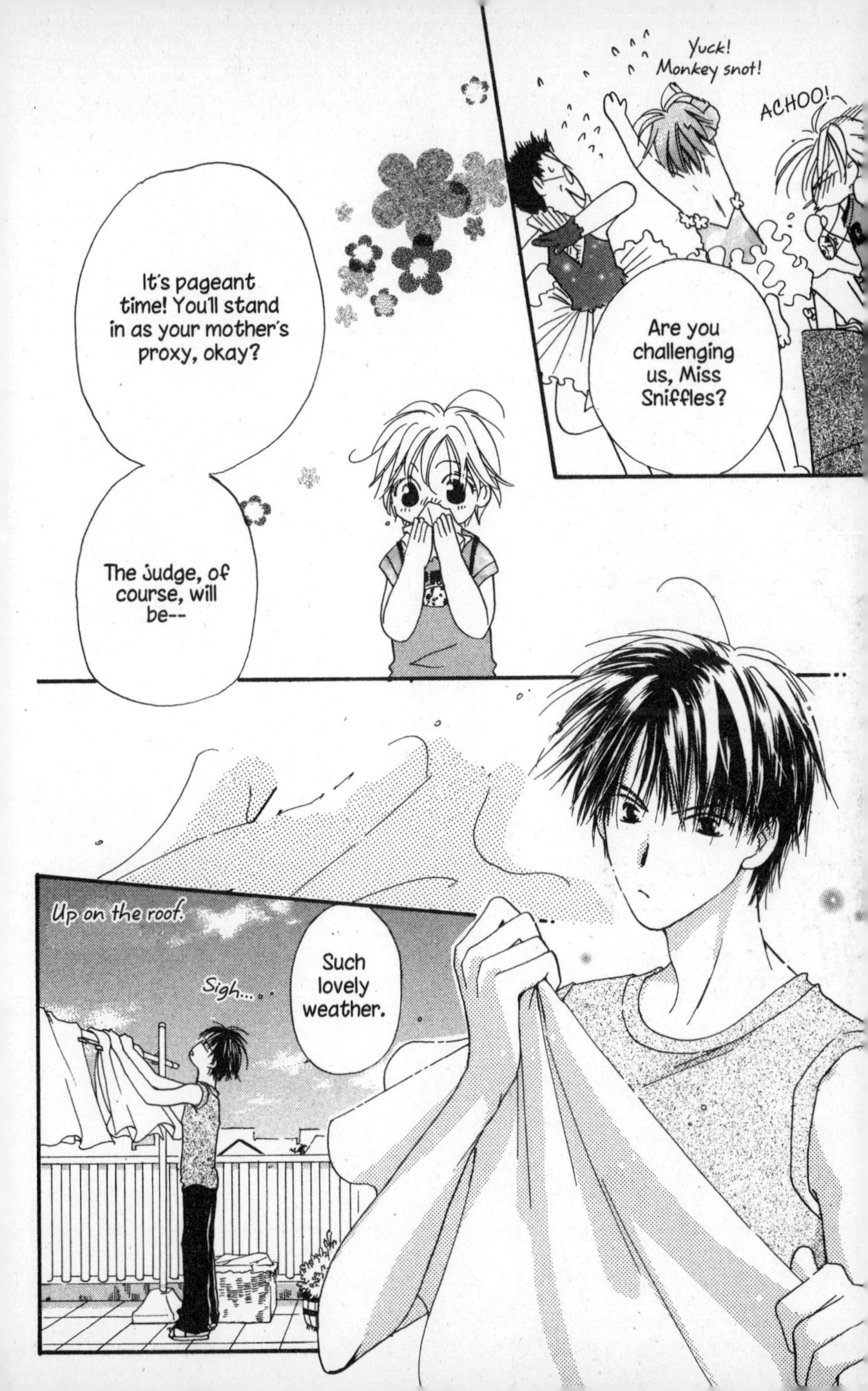
ACHOO!
Yuck! Monkey snot!
Are you challenging us, Miss Sniffles?
It's pageant time! You'll stand in as your mother's proxy, okay?
The judge, of course, will be--
Up on the roof.
Sigh...
Such lovely weather.

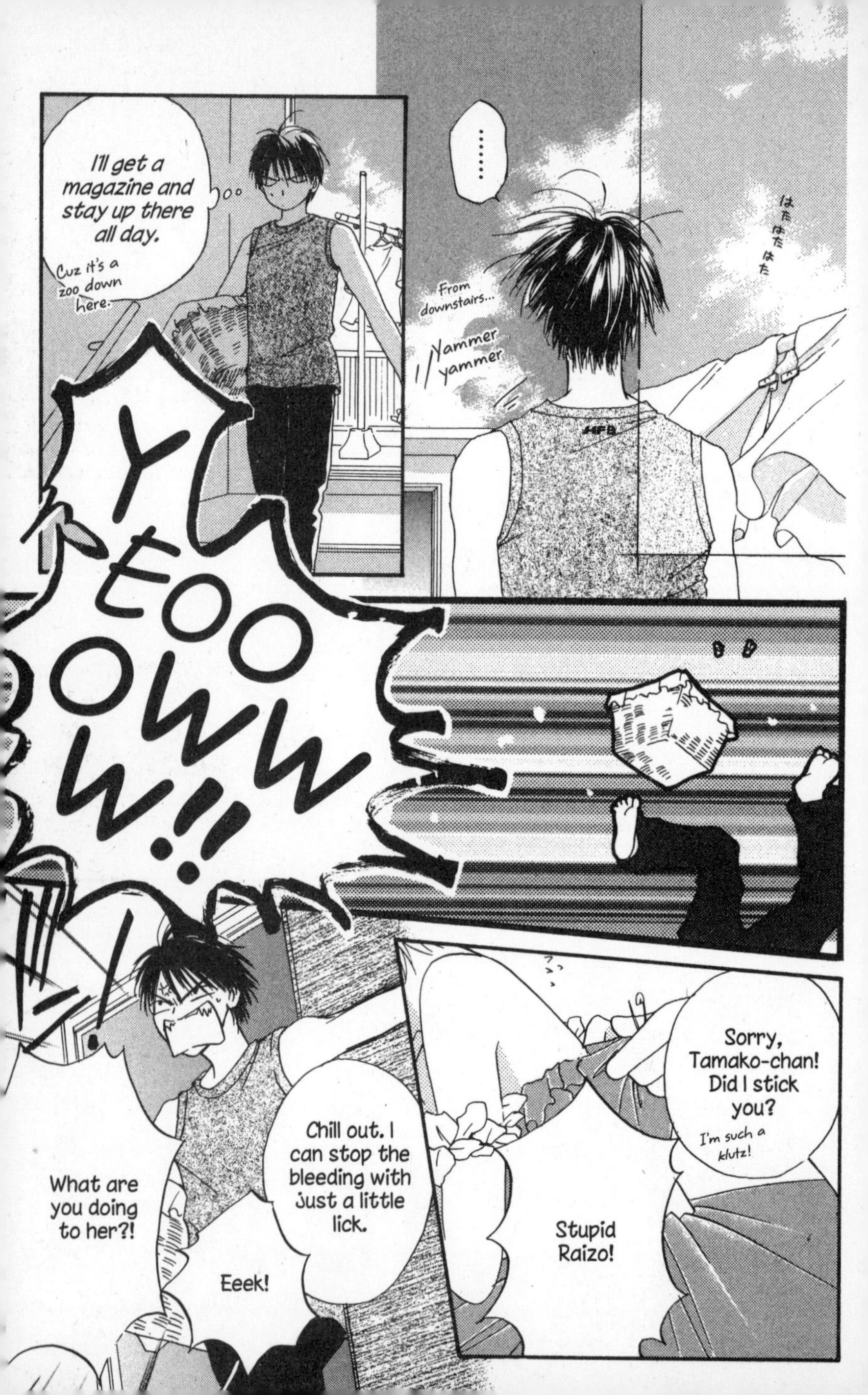
......
はたはたはた
From downstairs...
Yammer yammer
I'll get a magazine and stay up there all day.
Cuz it's a zoo down here.
YEOOOWWW!!
Sorry, Tamako-chan! Did I stick you?
I'm such a klutz!
Stupid Raizo!
Chill out. I can stop the bleeding with just a little lick.
What are you doing to her?!
Eeek!

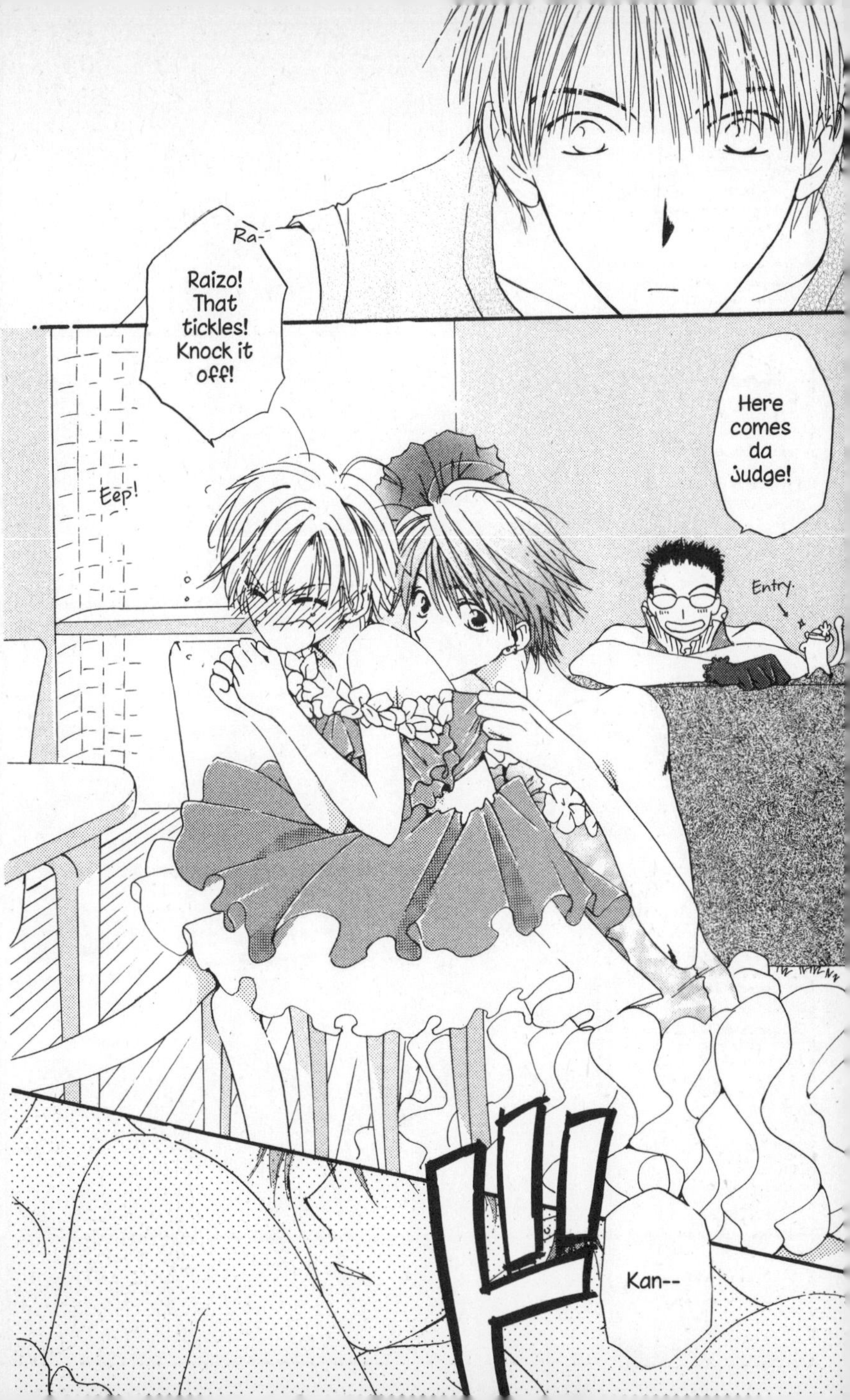
Ra-
Raizo! That tickles! Knock it off!
Here comes da Judge!
Entry.
Eep!
Kan--

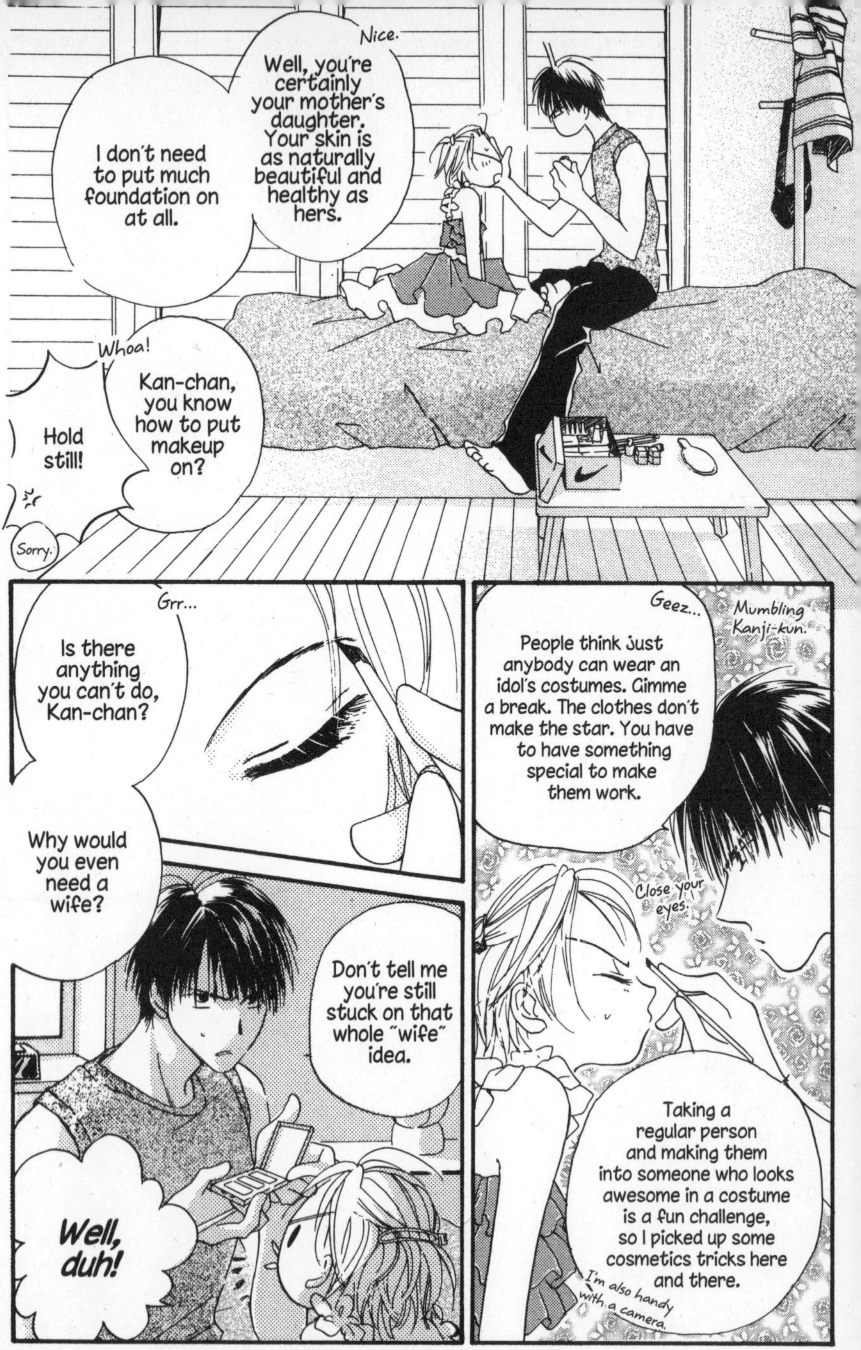

Nice.
Well, you're certainly your mother's daughter. Your skin is as naturally beautiful and healthy as hers.
I don't need to put much foundation on at all.
Whoa!
Kan-chan, you know how to put makeup on?
Hold still!
Sorry.
Mumbling Kanji-kun.
Geez...
People think just anybody can wear an idol's costumes. Gimme a break. The clothes don't make the star. You have to have something special to make them work.
Close your eyes.
Taking a regular person and making them into someone who looks awesome in a costume is a fun challenge, so I picked up some cosmetics tricks here and there.
I'm also handy with a camera.
Grr...
Is there anything you can't do, Kan-chan?
Why would you even need a wife?
Don't tell me you're still stuck on that whole "wife" idea.
Well, duh!

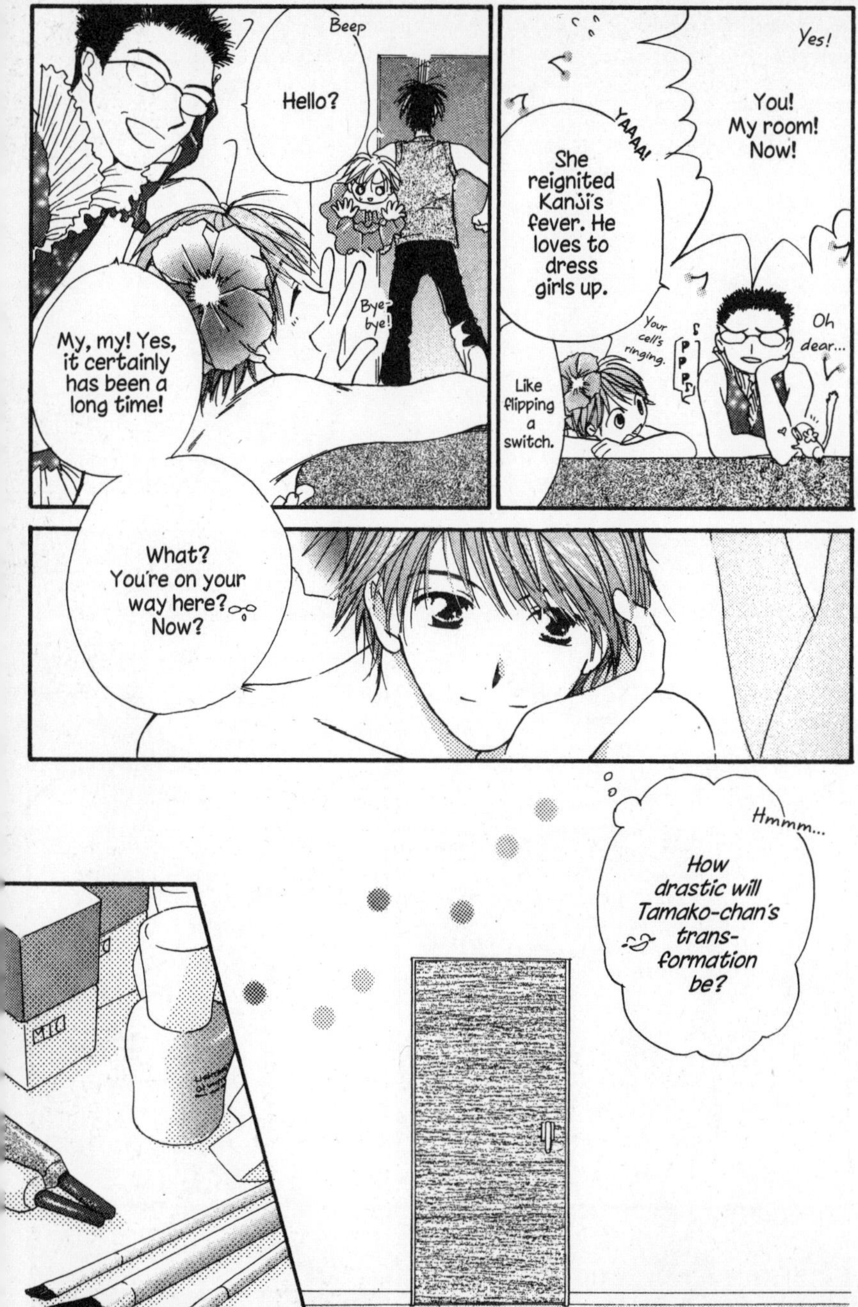
Yes!
You! My room! Now!
YAAAA!
She reignited Kanji's fever. He loves to dress girls up.
Oh dear...
Your cell's ringing.
PPP
Like flipping a switch.
Beep
Hello?
Bye-bye!
My, my! Yes, it certainly has been a long time!
What? You're on your way here? Now?
Hmmm...
How drastic will Tamako-chan's trans-formation be?

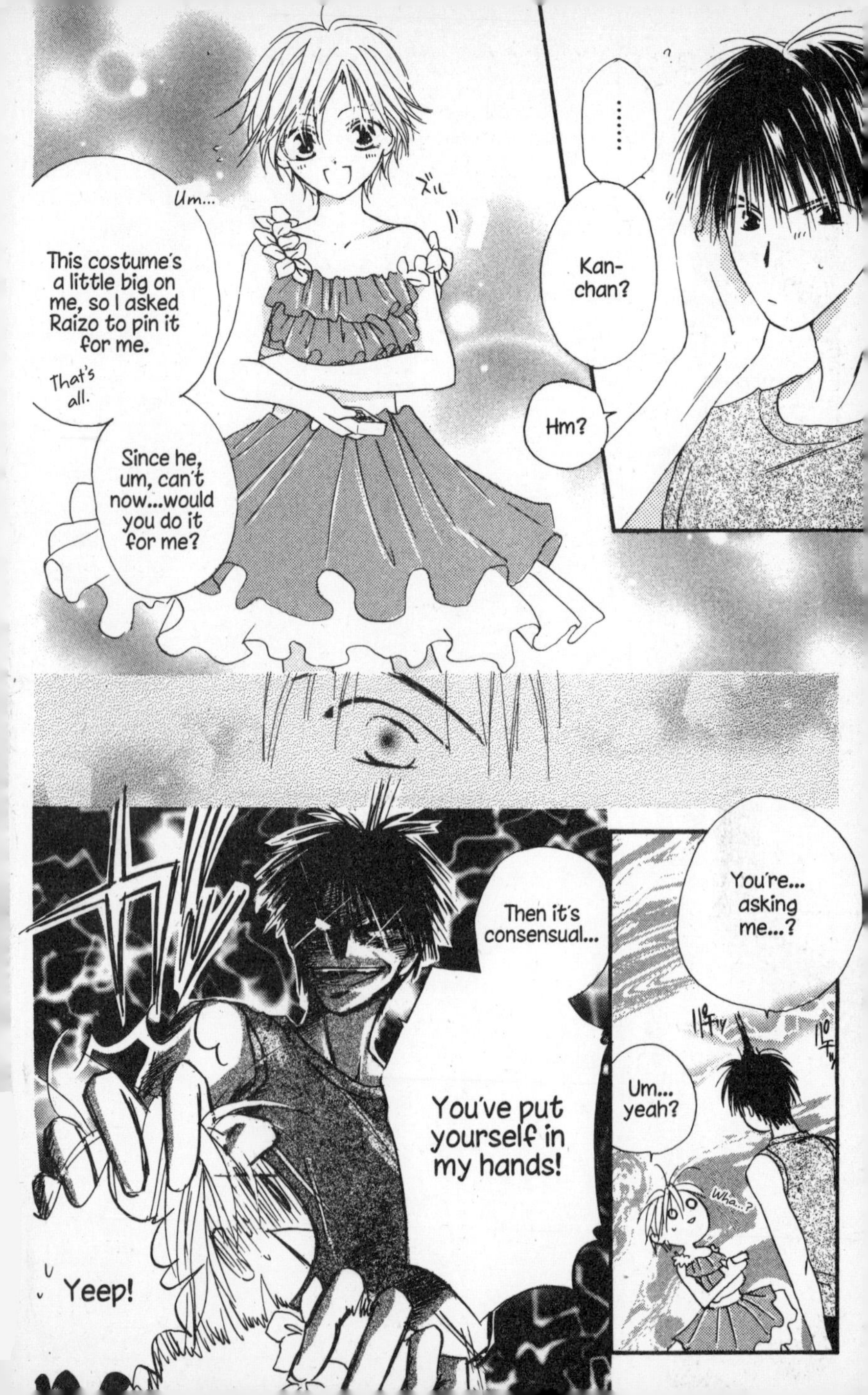

......
Kan-chan?
Hm?
Um...
This costume's a little big on me, so I asked Raizo to pin it for me.
That's all.
ズル
Since he, um, can't now...would you do it for me?
You're... asking me...?
Um... yeah?
Wha...?
Then it's consensual...
You've put yourself in my hands!
Yeep!

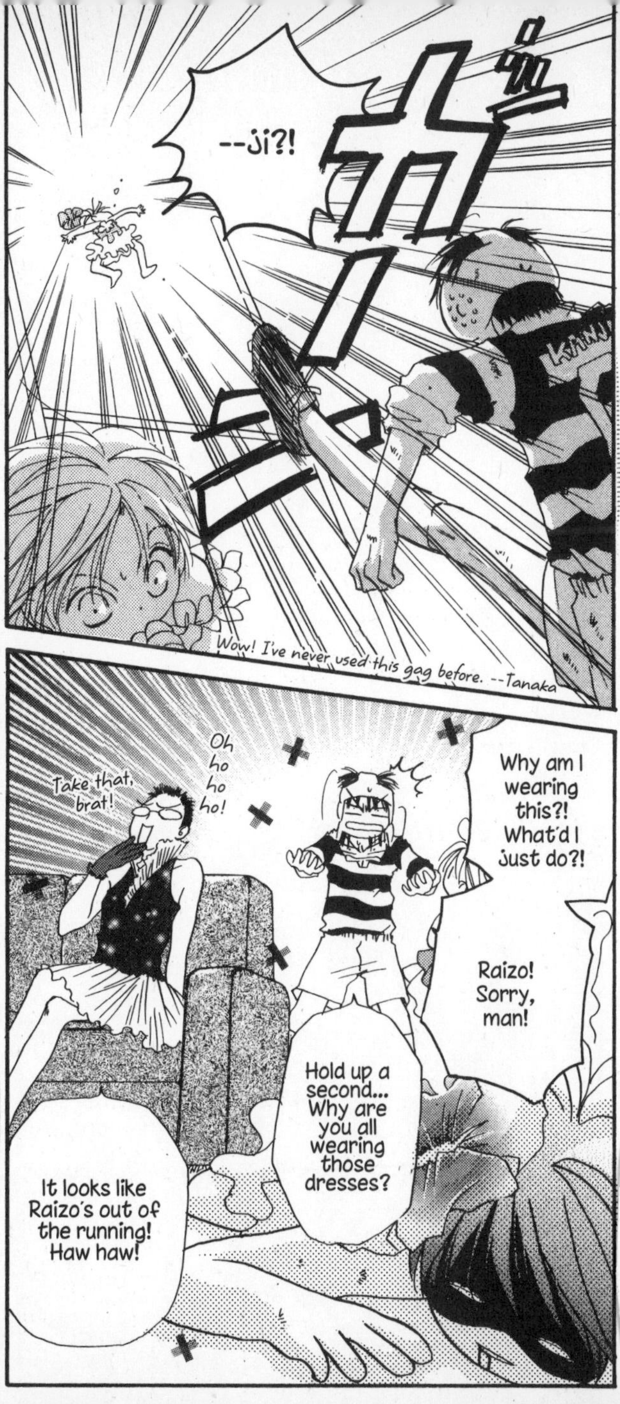
--Ji?!
Wow! I've never used this gag before. --Tanaka
Why am I wearing this?! What'd I just do?!
Raizo! Sorry, man!
Oh ho ho ho!
Take that, brat!
Hold up a second... Why are you all wearing those dresses?
It looks like Raizo's out of the running! Haw haw!

Since i was bored...

I went home to visit my family a little while ago. I was feeling a little bored, so I decided to tag along when my little nephew, Ryuunosuke, went for his vaccinations. We got to the hospital, and the waiting room was all serene and peaceful...

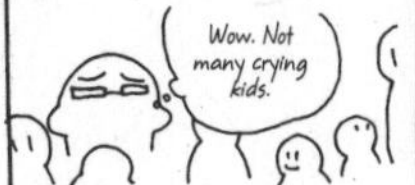
Wow. Not many crying kids.

...or so I thought. But then, when we got to the room where they actually give the shots...

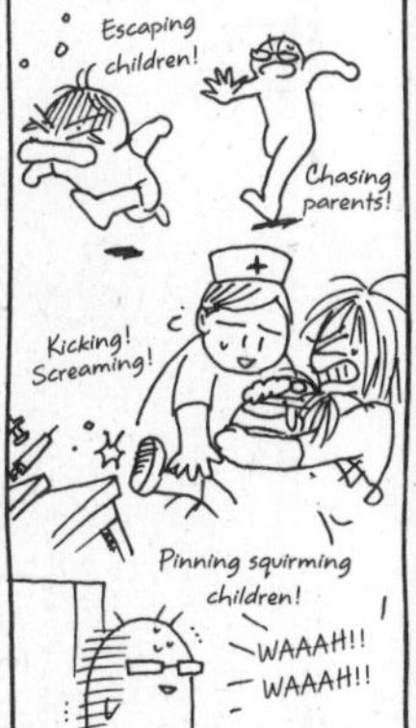
Escaping children!
Chasing parents!
Kicking! Screaming!
Pinning squirming children!
WAAAH!!
WAAAH!!

BATTLEFIELD

Mothers and fathers of Japan, I have a newfound respect for your job.

Oh, one other thing I noticed: the doctor who came in to give the shots to the kicking, screaming, and squirming children...

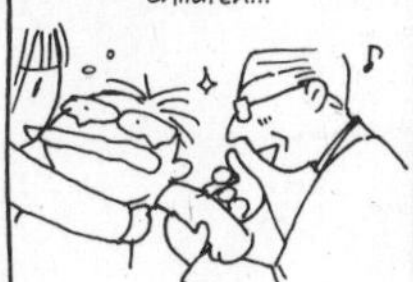

...looked like he was having fun...!

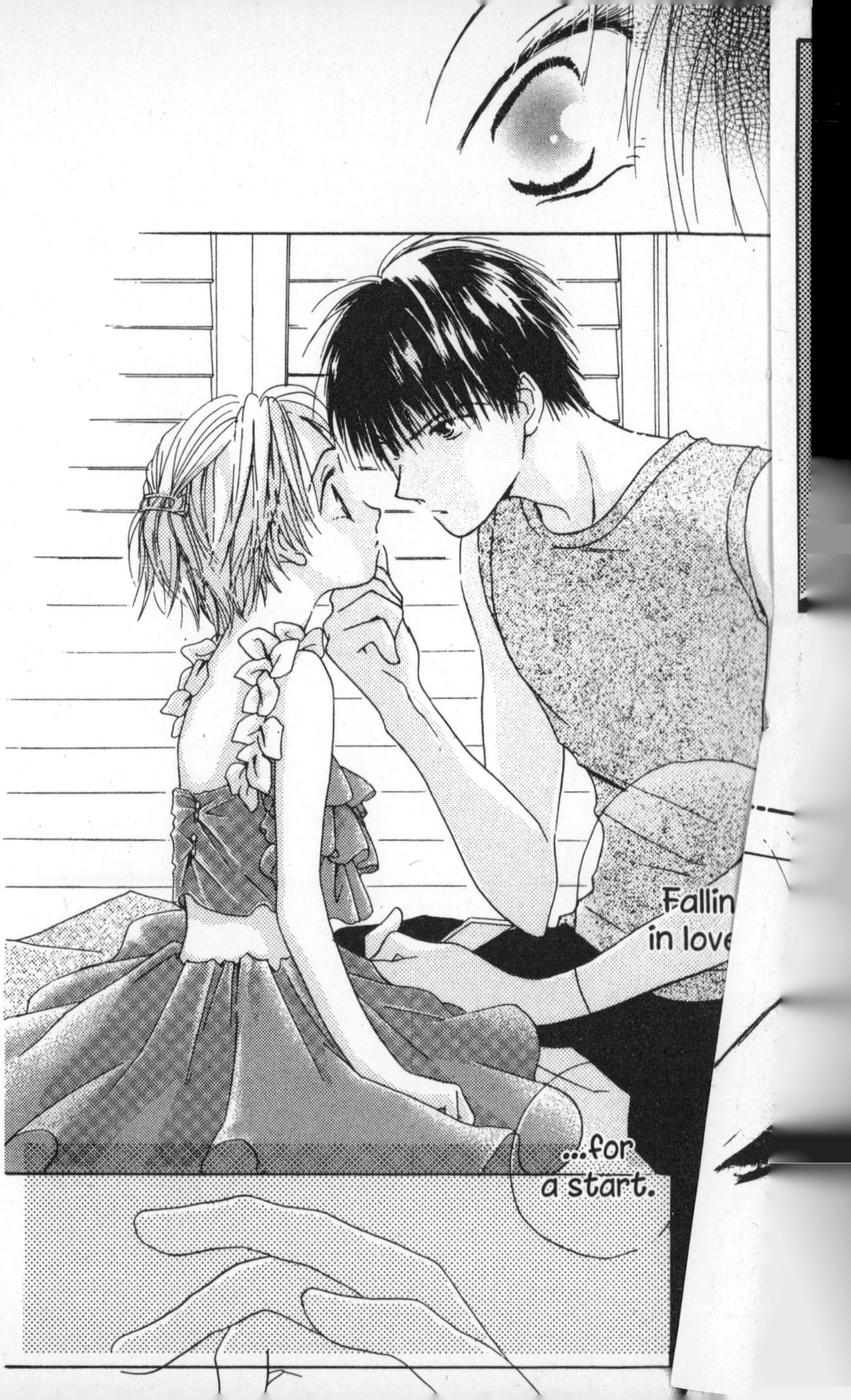
Fallin
in love
...for
a start.

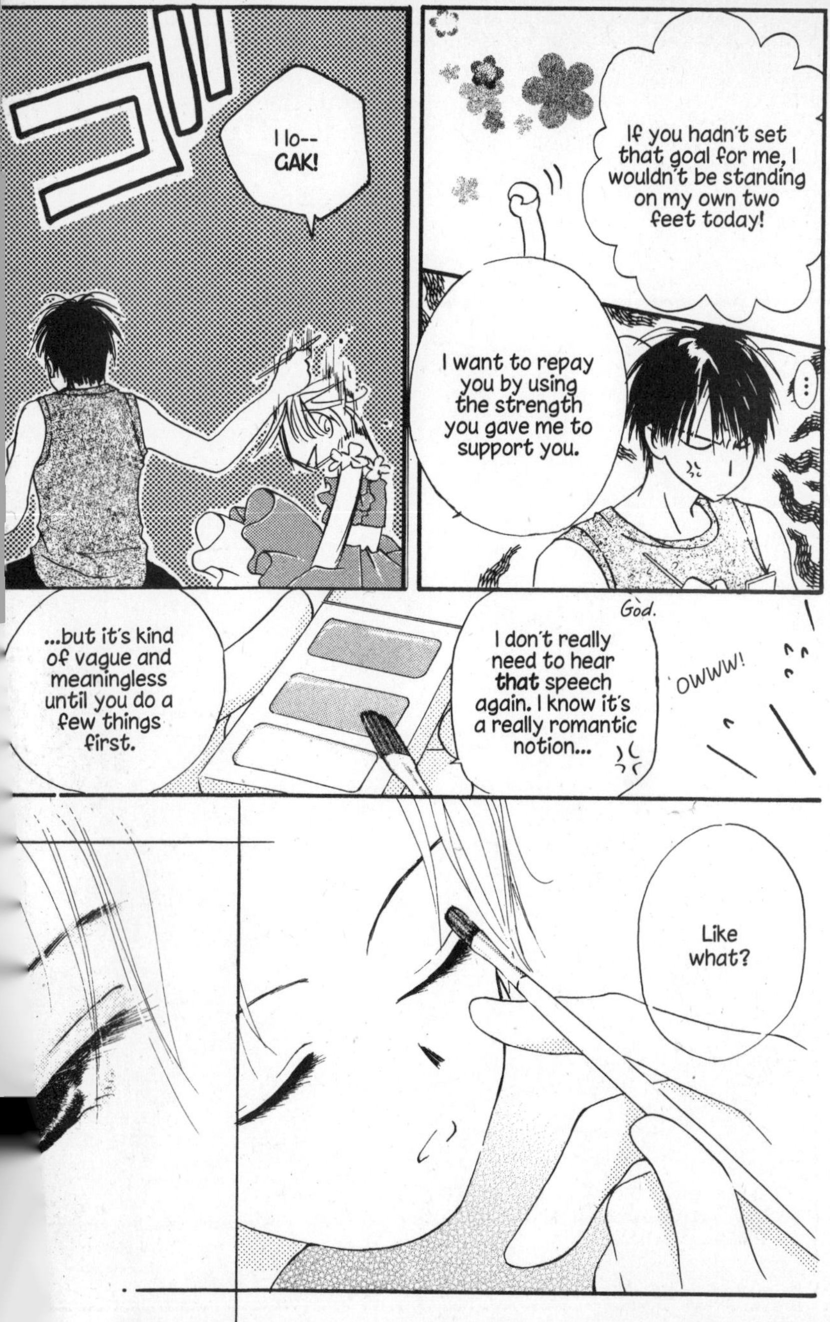
If you hadn't set that goal for me, I wouldn't be standing on my own two feet today!
I want to repay you by using the strength you gave me to support you.
...
I lo-- GAK!
OWWW!
God.
I don't really need to hear **that** speech again. I know it's a really romantic notion...
...but it's kind of vague and meaningless until you do a few things first.
Like what?

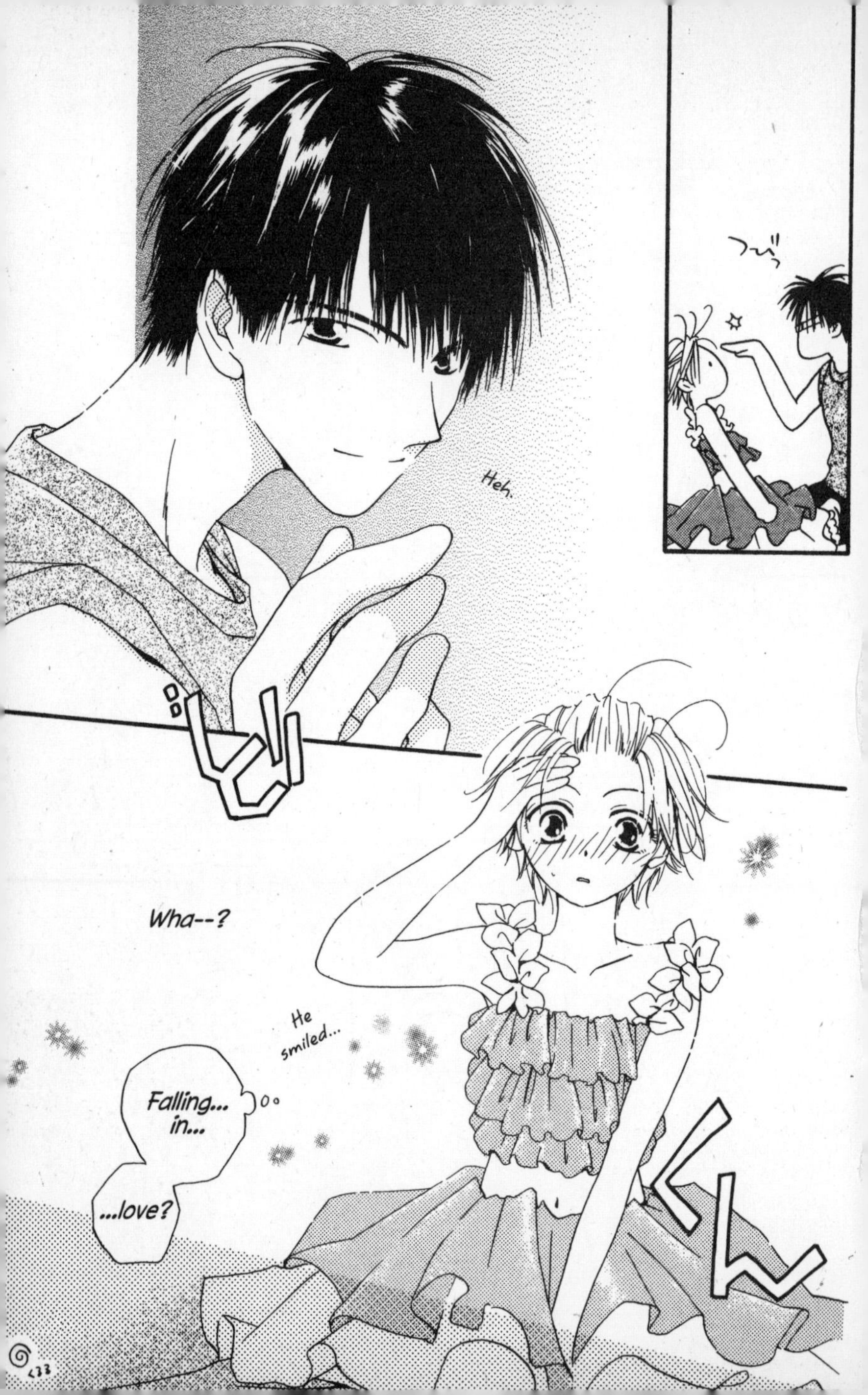
Heh.
Wha--?
He smiled...
Falling... in...
...love?

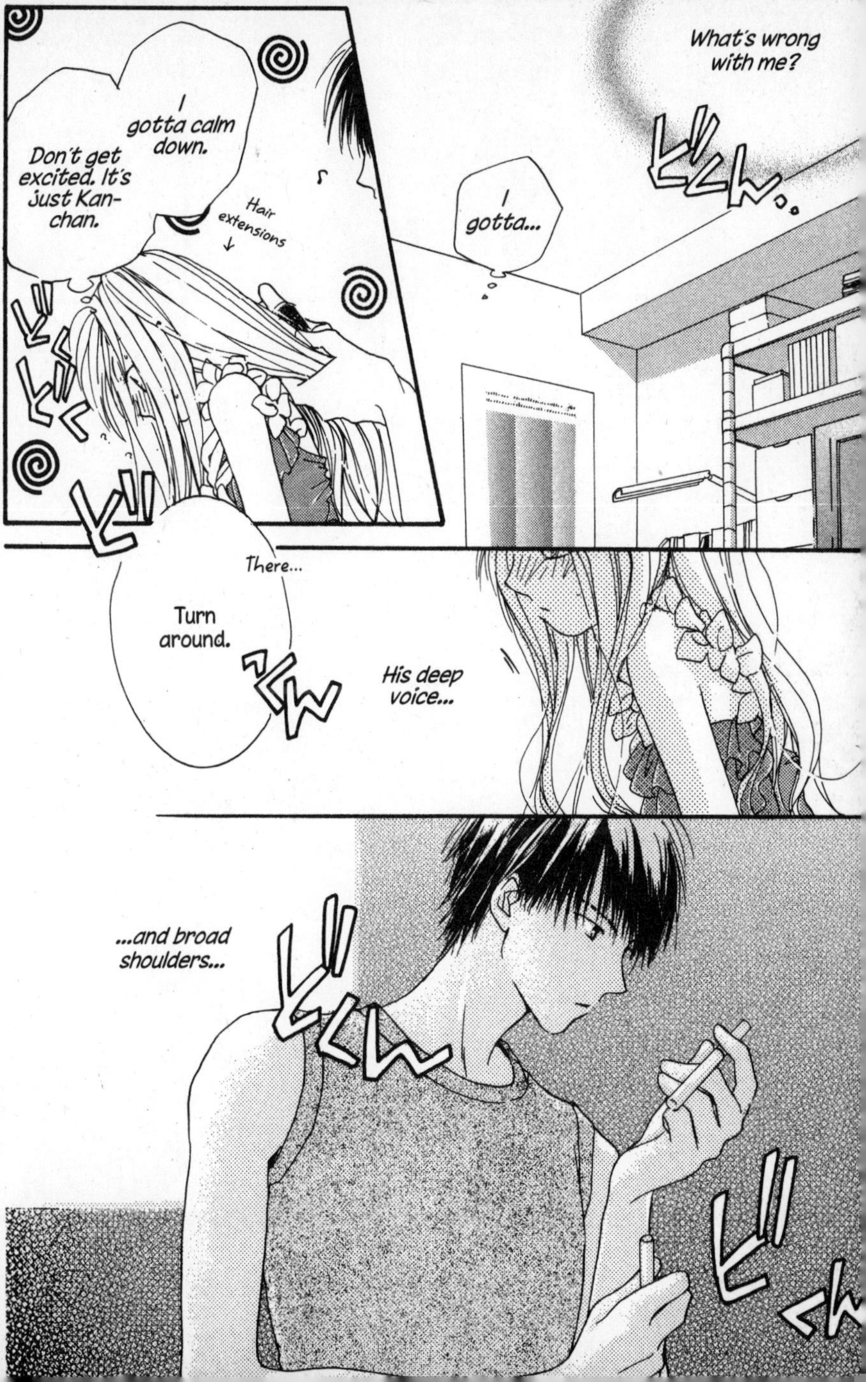
What's wrong with me?
I gotta...
I gotta calm down.
Don't get excited. It's just Kan-chan.
Hair extensions ↓
His deep voice...
There...
Turn around.
...and broad shoulders...

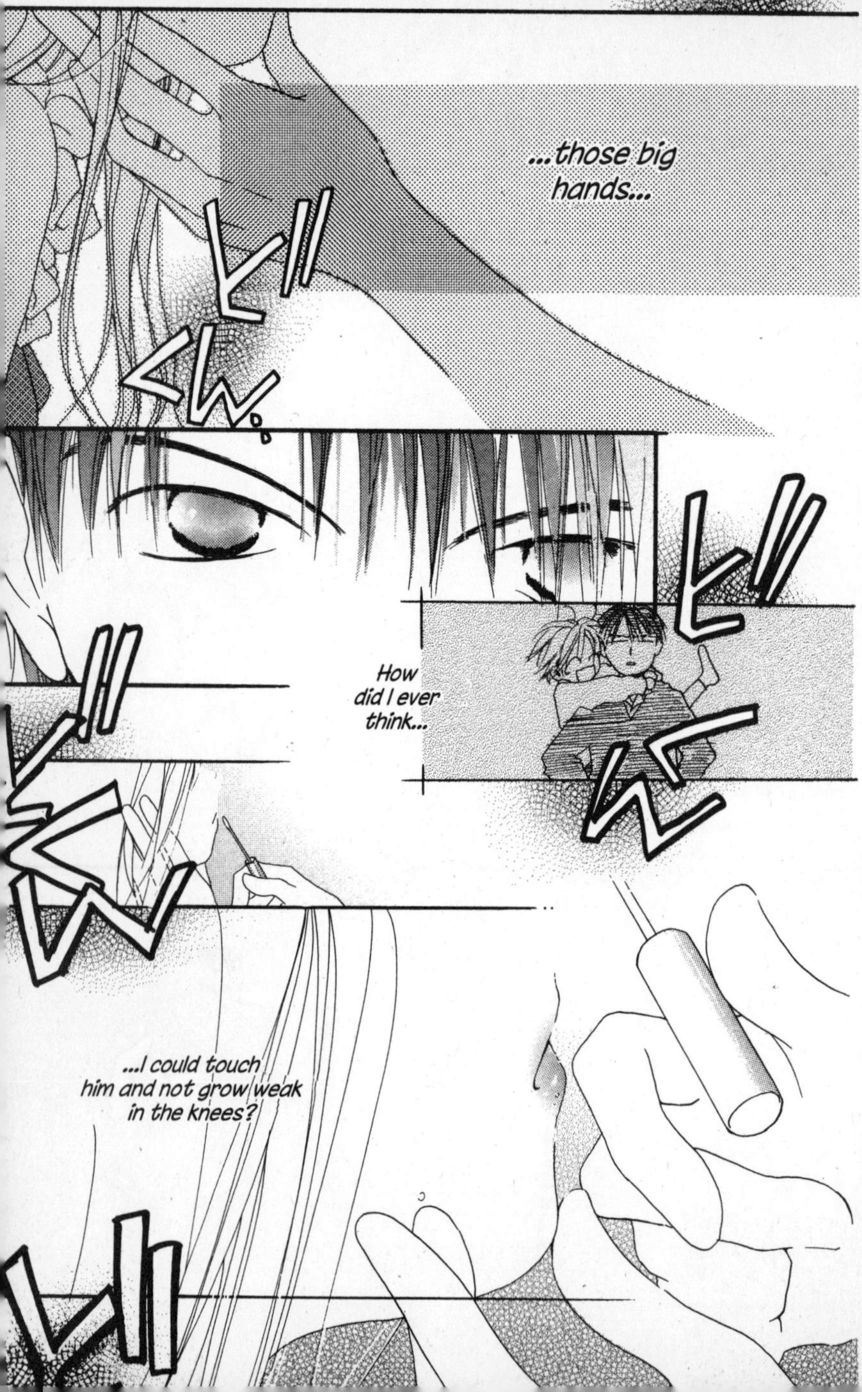
...those big hands...
How did I ever think...
...I could touch him and not grow weak in the knees?

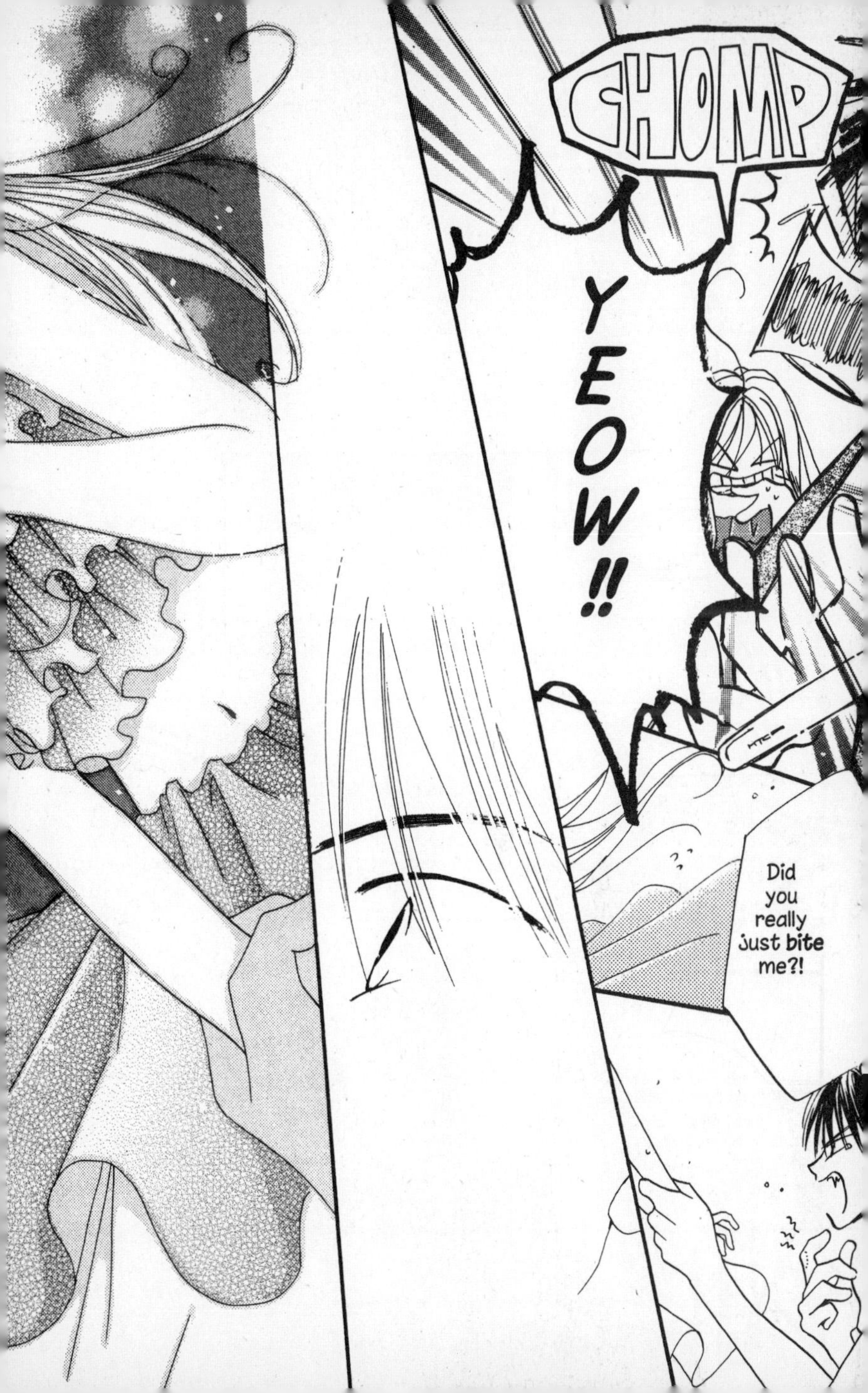
CHOMP
YEOW!!
Did you really just bite me?!

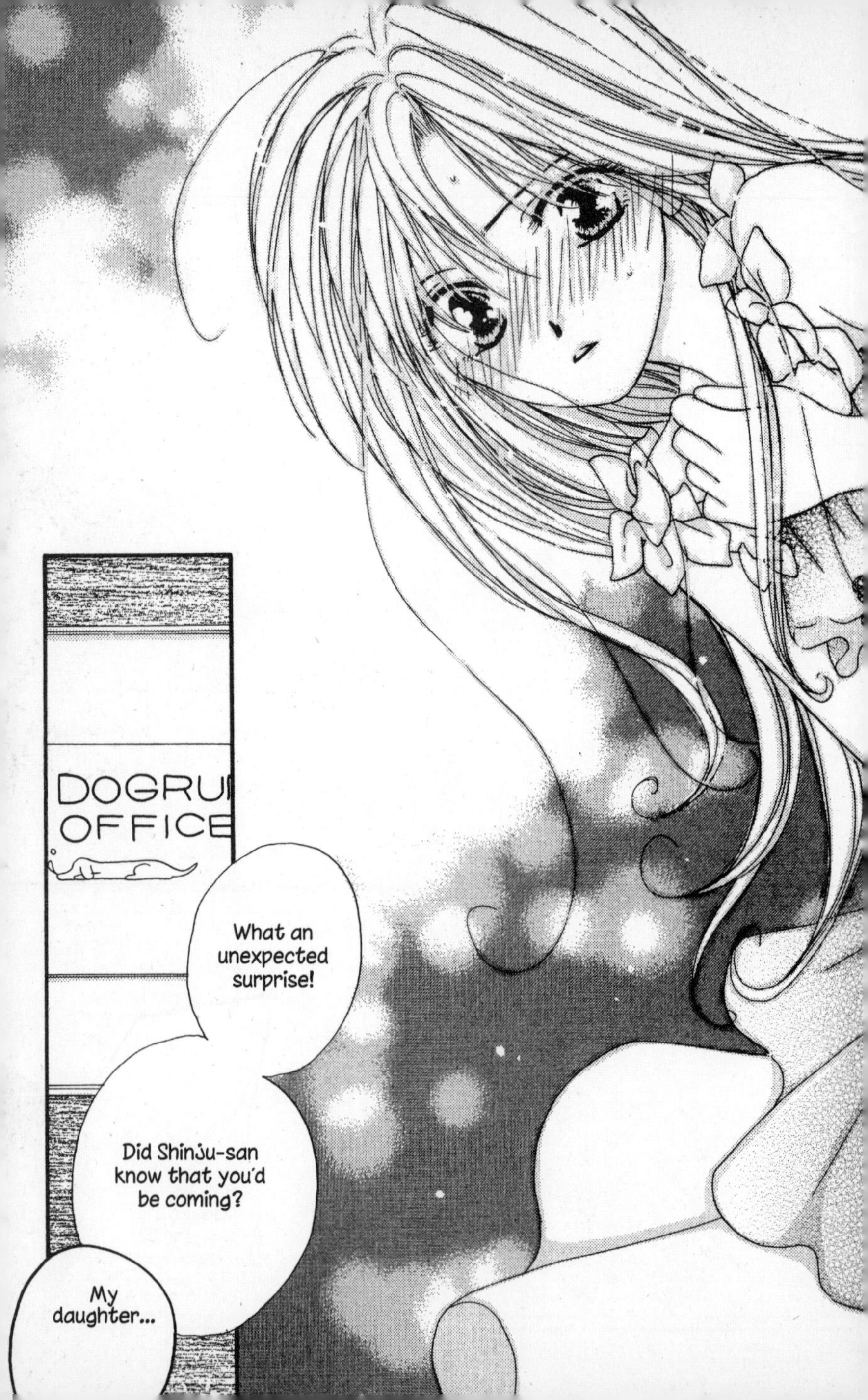
DOGRU
OFFICE
What an unexpected surprise!
Did Shinju-san know that you'd be coming?
My daughter...

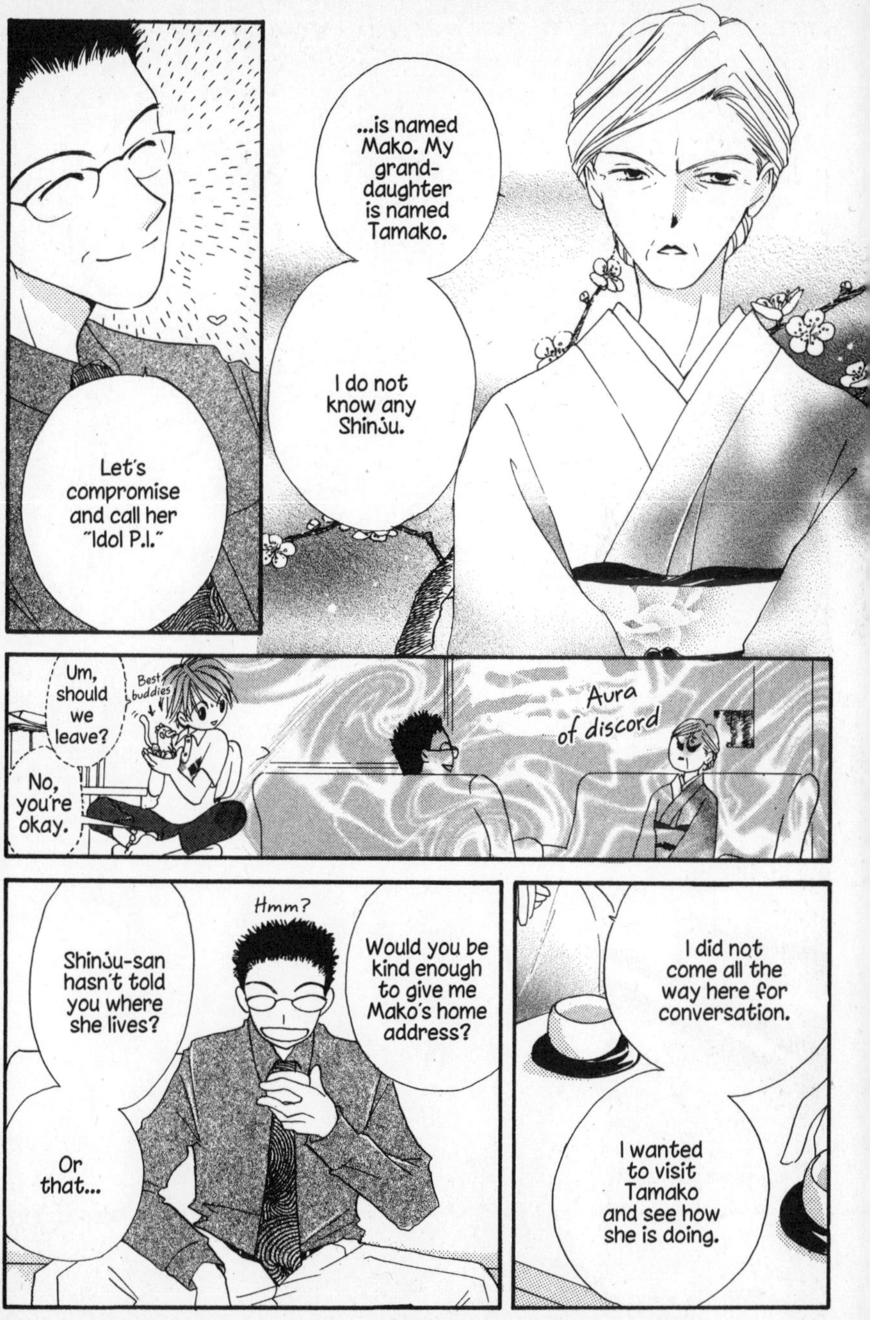
...is named Mako. My granddaughter is named Tamako.
I do not know any Shinju.
Let's compromise and call her "Idol P.I."
Aura of discord
Um, should we leave?
Best buddies
No, you're okay.
I did not come all the way here for conversation.
I wanted to visit Tamako and see how she is doing.
Hmm?
Would you be kind enough to give me Mako's home address?
Shinju-san hasn't told you where she lives?
Or that...

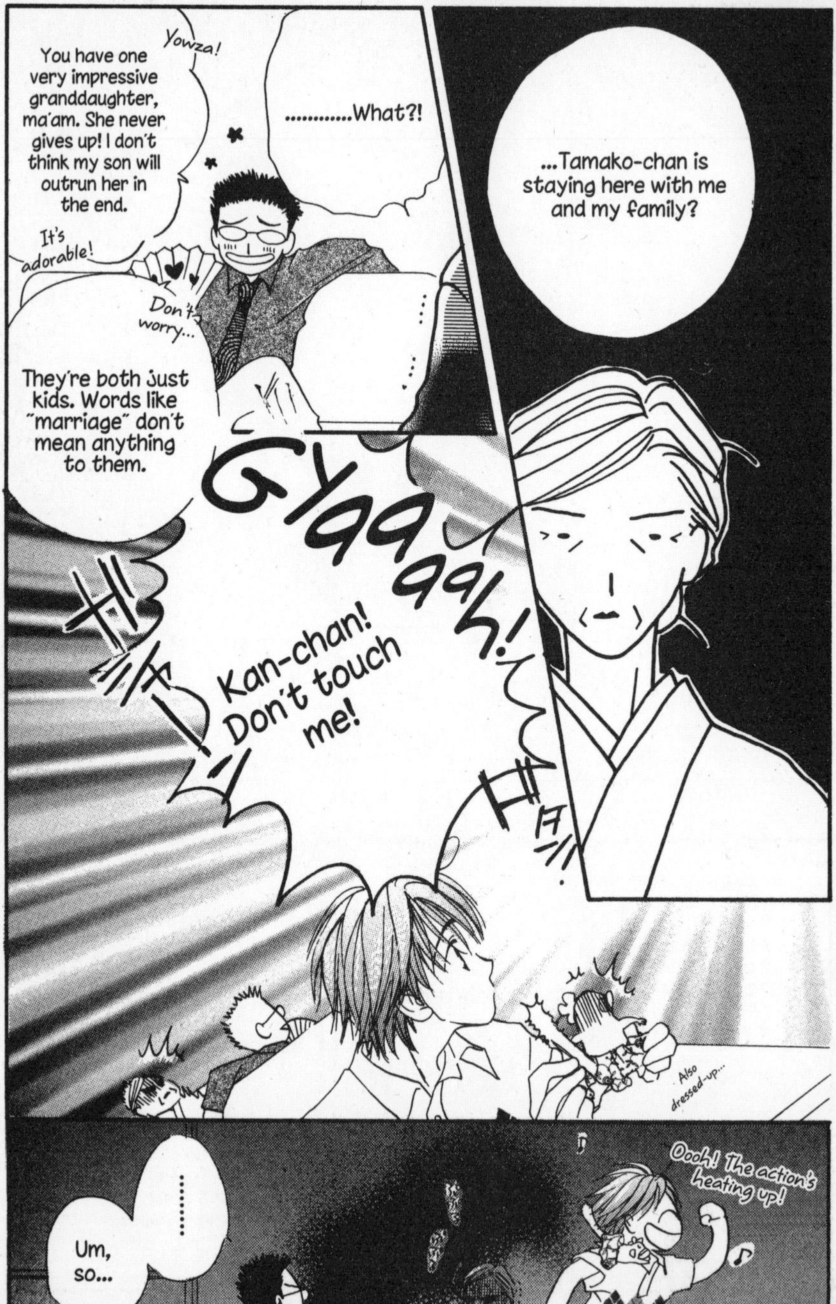
...Tamako-chan is staying here with me and my family?
............What?!
You have one very impressive granddaughter, ma'am. She never gives up! I don't think my son will outrun her in the end.
Yowza!
It's adorable!
Don't worry...
They're both just kids. Words like "marriage" don't mean anything to them.
GYaaaah!
Kan-chan! Don't touch me!
Also dressed-up...
Oooh! The action's heating up!
......
Um, so...

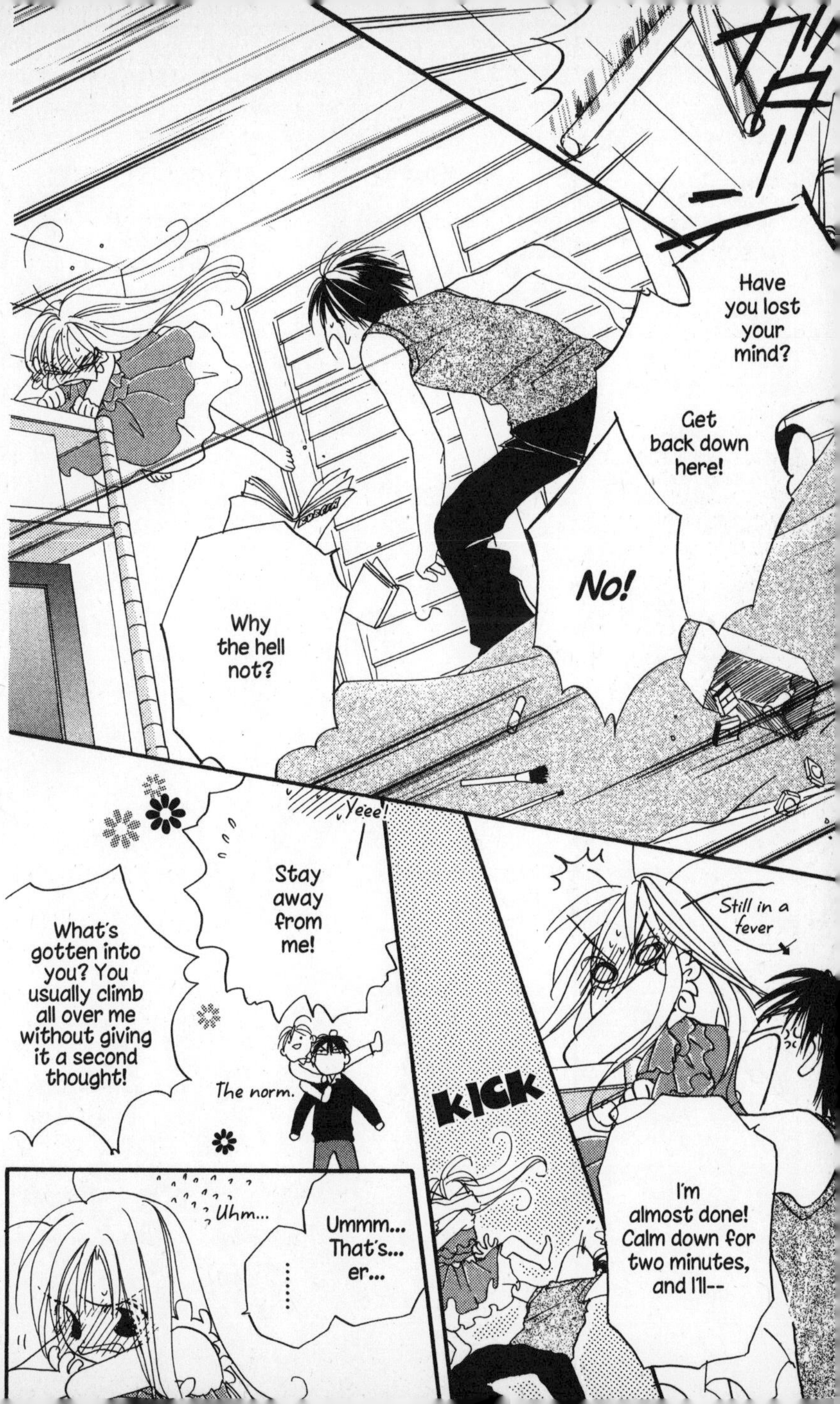
Have you lost your mind?
Get back down here!
No!
Why the hell not?
Still in a fever
I'm almost done! Calm down for two minutes, and I'll--
KICK
Yeee!
Stay away from me!
What's gotten into you? You usually climb all over me without giving it a second thought!
The norm.
Uhm...
Ummm... That's... er...
......

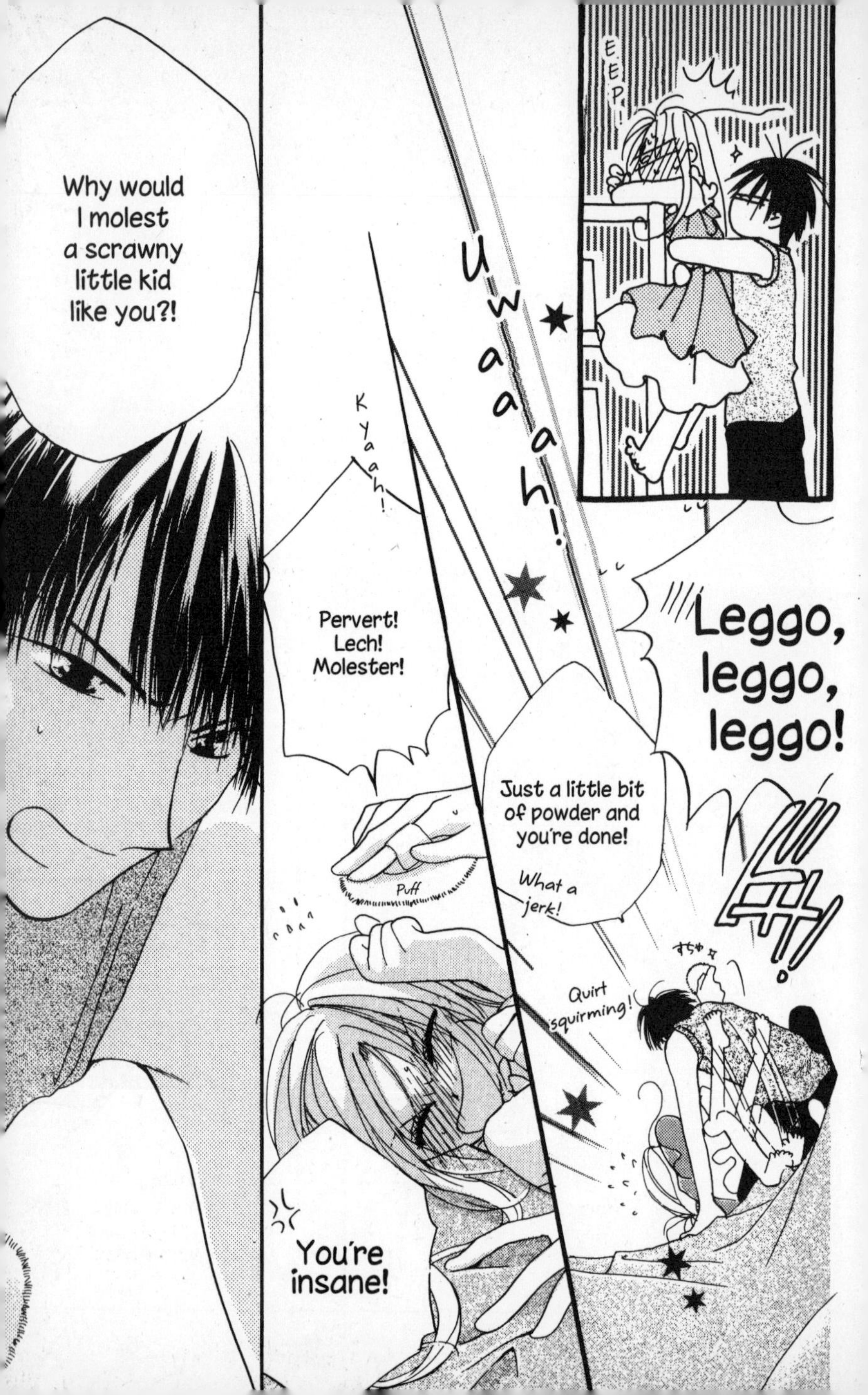
EEP!!
Uwaaaah!!
Leggo, leggo, leggo!
Just a little bit of powder and you're done!
What a jerk!
すちゃ☆
Quirt squirming!
Kyaaah!
Pervert! Lech! Molester!
Puff
You're insane!
Why would I molest a scrawny little kid like you?!

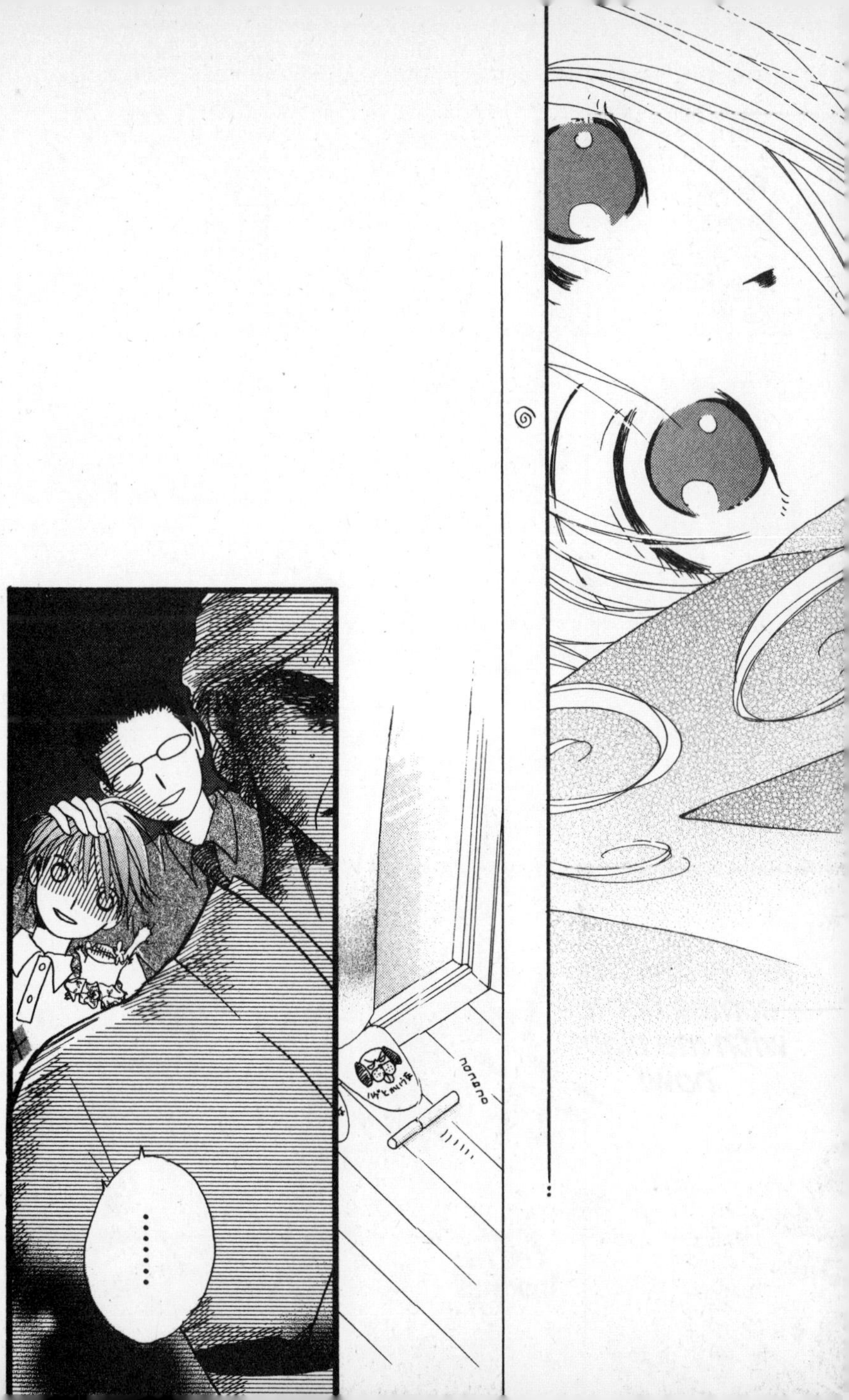
nonono
......

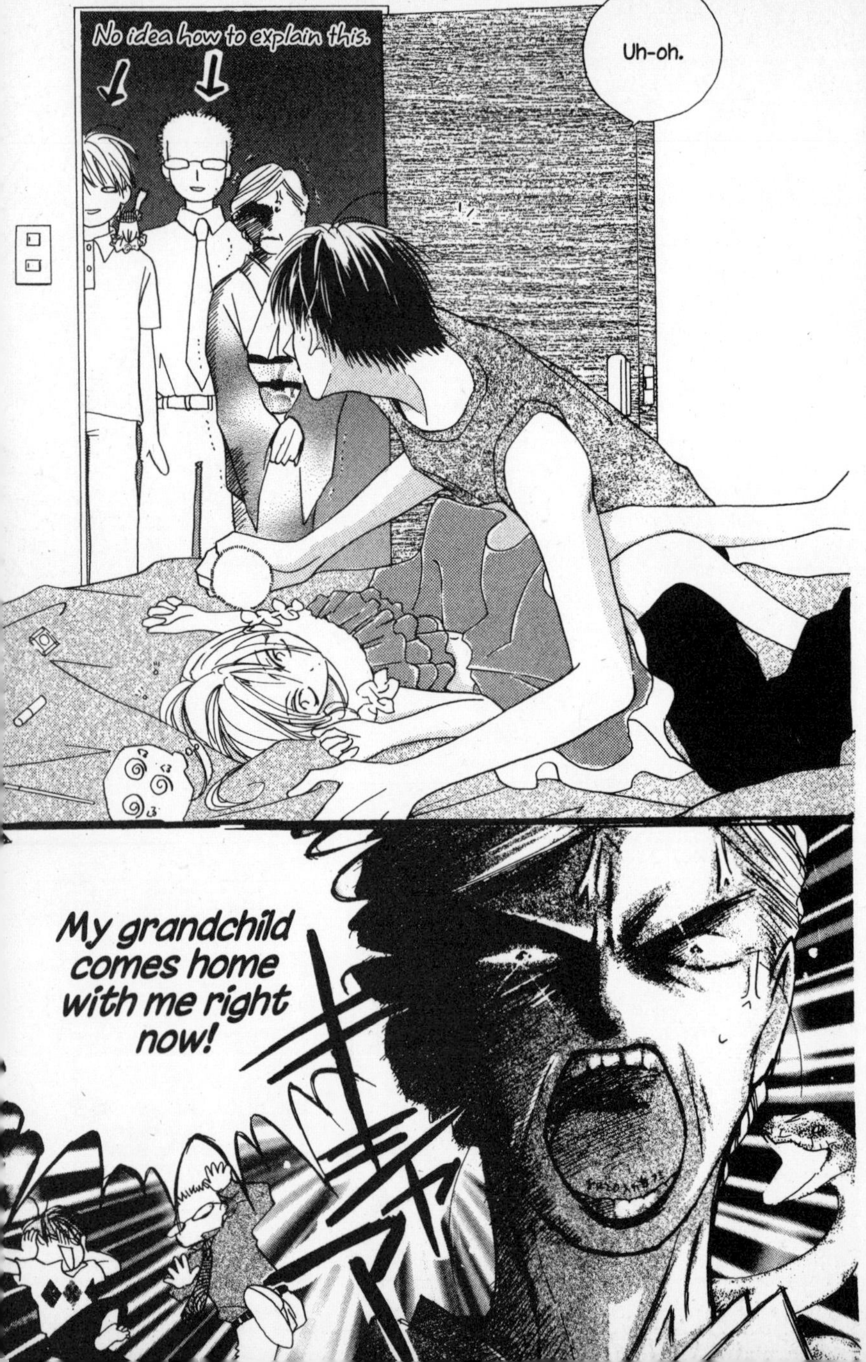
Uh-oh.
No idea how to explain this.
My grandchild comes home with me right now!

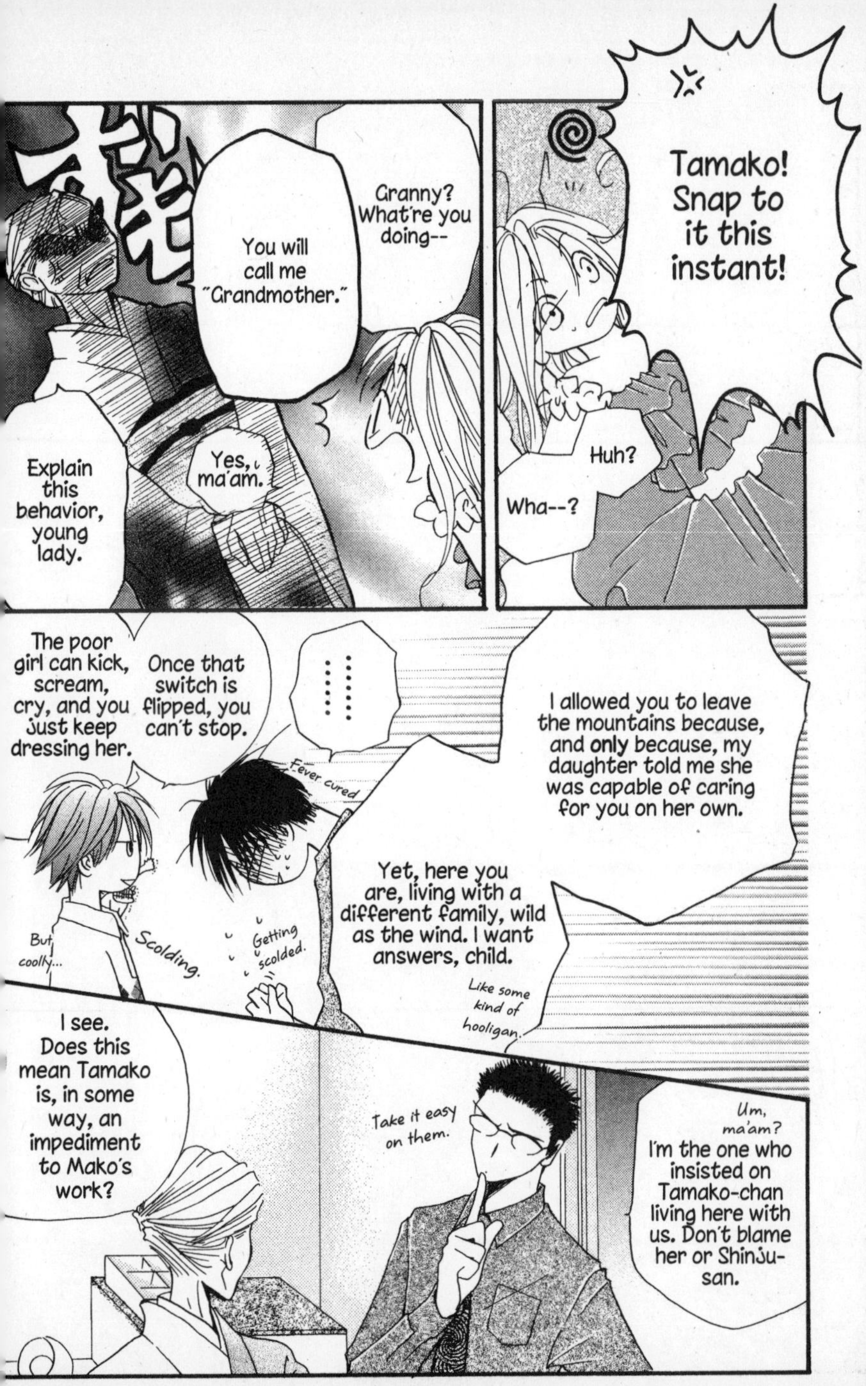
Tamako! Snap to it this instant!
Huh?
Wha--?
Granny? What're you doing--
You will call me "Grandmother."
Yes, ma'am.
Explain this behavior, young lady.
I allowed you to leave the mountains because, and **only** because, my daughter told me she was capable of caring for you on her own.
......
Once that switch is flipped, you can't stop.
The poor girl can kick, scream, cry, and you just keep dressing her.
Fever cured
Yet, here you are, living with a different family, wild as the wind. I want answers, child.
Like some kind of hooligan.
Getting scolded.
Scolding.
But coolly...
Um, ma'am?
I'm the one who insisted on Tamako-chan living here with us. Don't blame her or Shinju-san.
Take it easy on them.
I see. Does this mean Tamako is, in some way, an impediment to Mako's work?

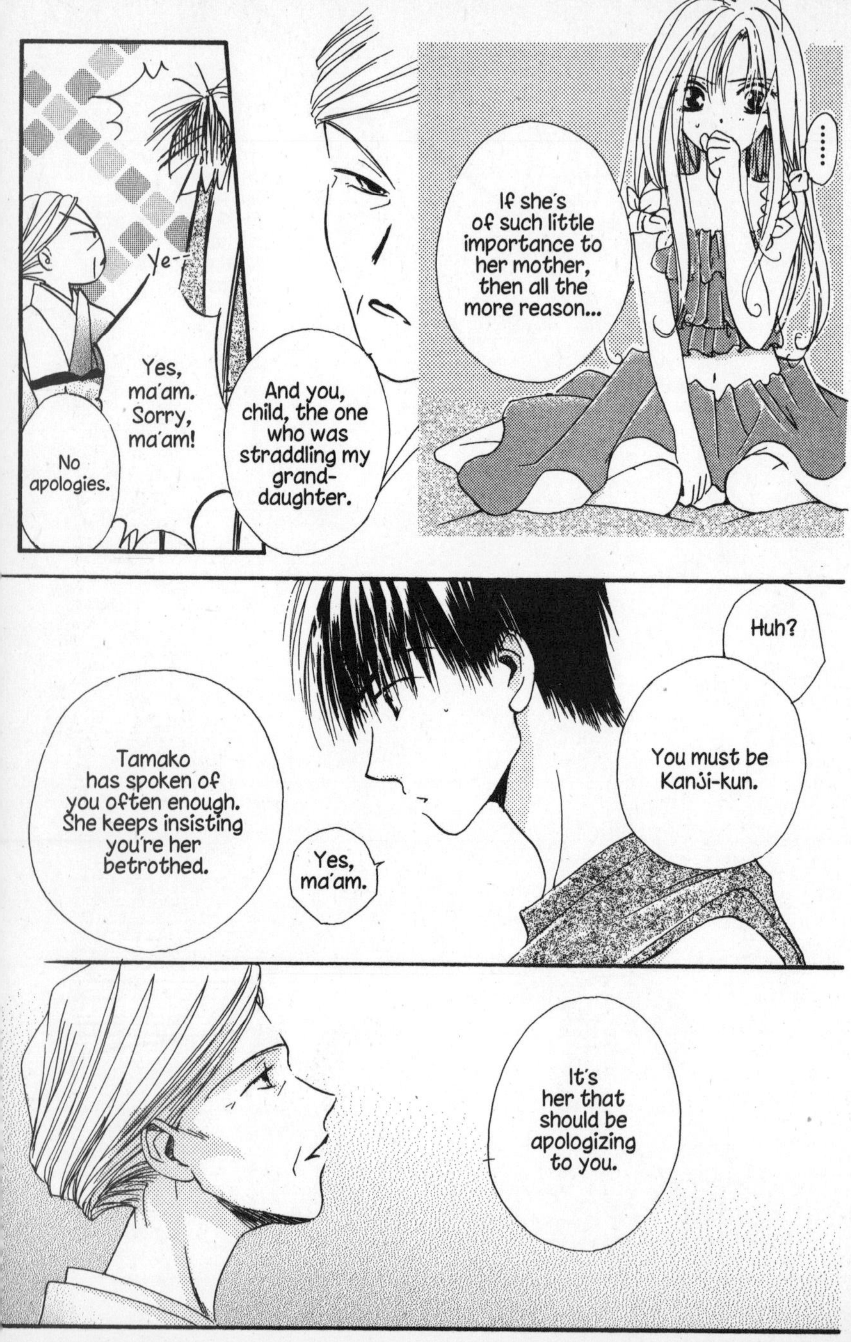
......
If she's of such little importance to her mother, then all the more reason...
And you, child, the one who was straddling my grand-daughter.
Ye-
Yes, ma'am. Sorry, ma'am!
No apologies.
Huh?
You must be Kanji-kun.
Yes, ma'am.
Tamako has spoken of you often enough. She keeps insisting you're her betrothed.
It's her that should be apologizing to you.

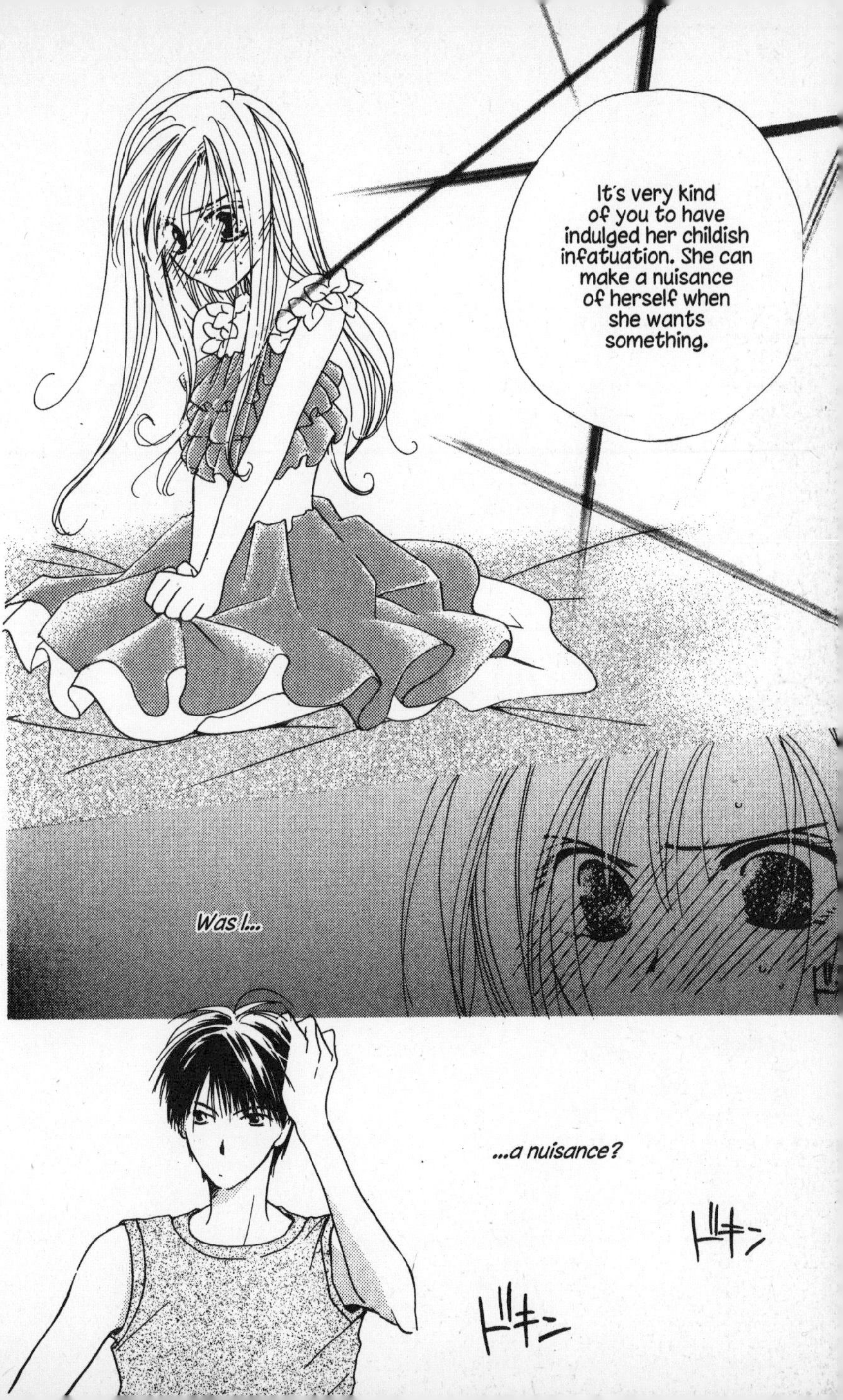
It's very kind of you to have indulged her childish infatuation. She can make a nuisance of herself when she wants something.
Was I...
...a nuisance?
ドキン
ドキン

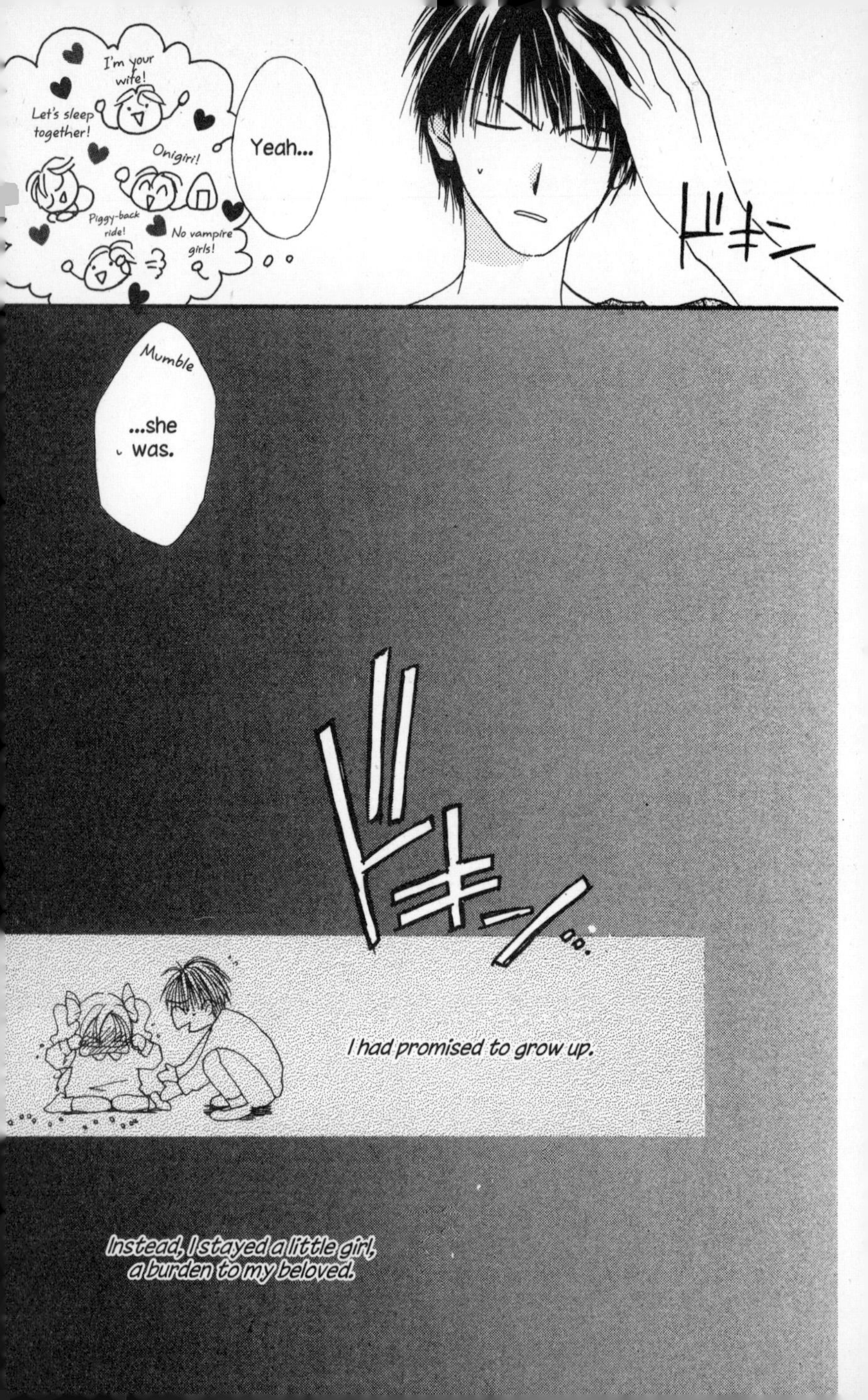

ドキン
Yeah...
I'm your wife!
Let's sleep together!
Onigiri!
Piggy-back ride!
No vampire girls!
Mumble
...she was.
ドキーン
I had promised to grow up.
Instead, I stayed a little girl, a burden to my beloved.

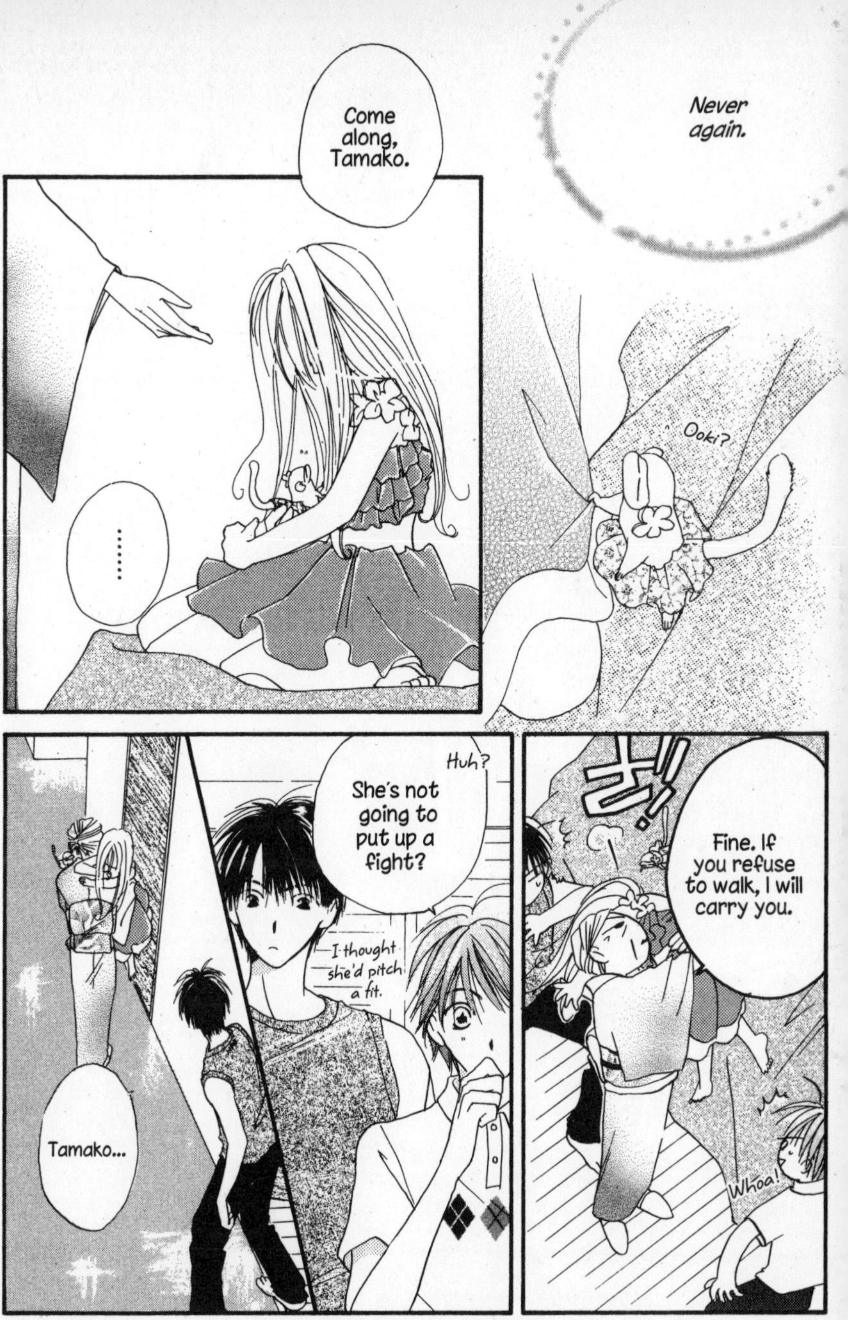
Never again.
Ooki?
Come along, Tamako.
......
Fine. If you refuse to walk, I will carry you.
Whoa!
Huh?
She's not going to put up a fight?
I thought she'd pitch a fit.
Tamako...

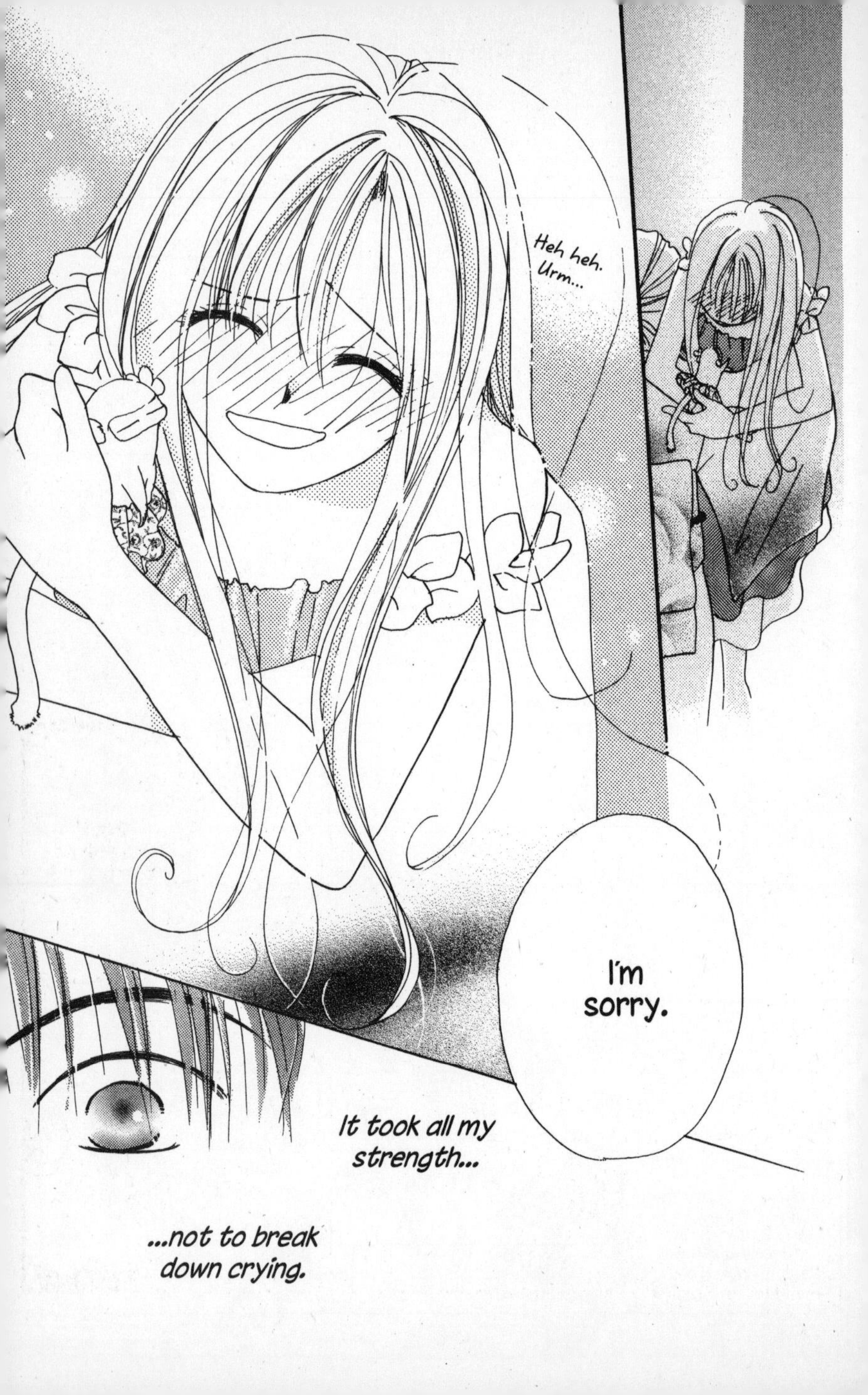
Heh heh. Urm...
I'm sorry.
It took all my strength...
...not to break down crying.

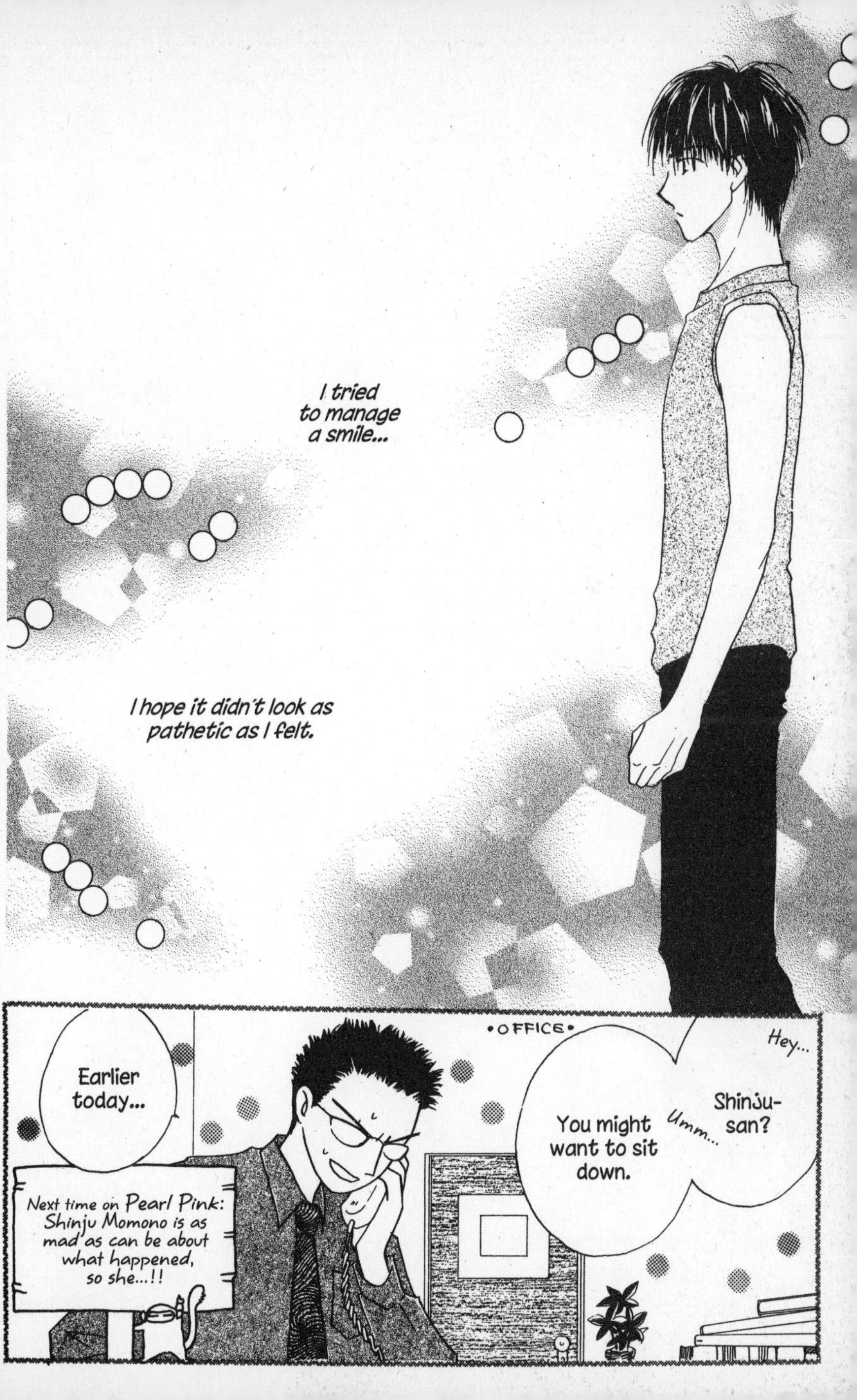
I tried to manage a smile...
I hope it didn't look as pathetic as I felt.
•OFFICE•
Hey...
Shinju-san?
Umm...
You might want to sit down.
Earlier today...
Next time on Pearl Pink: Shinju Momono is as mad as can be about what happened, so she...!!

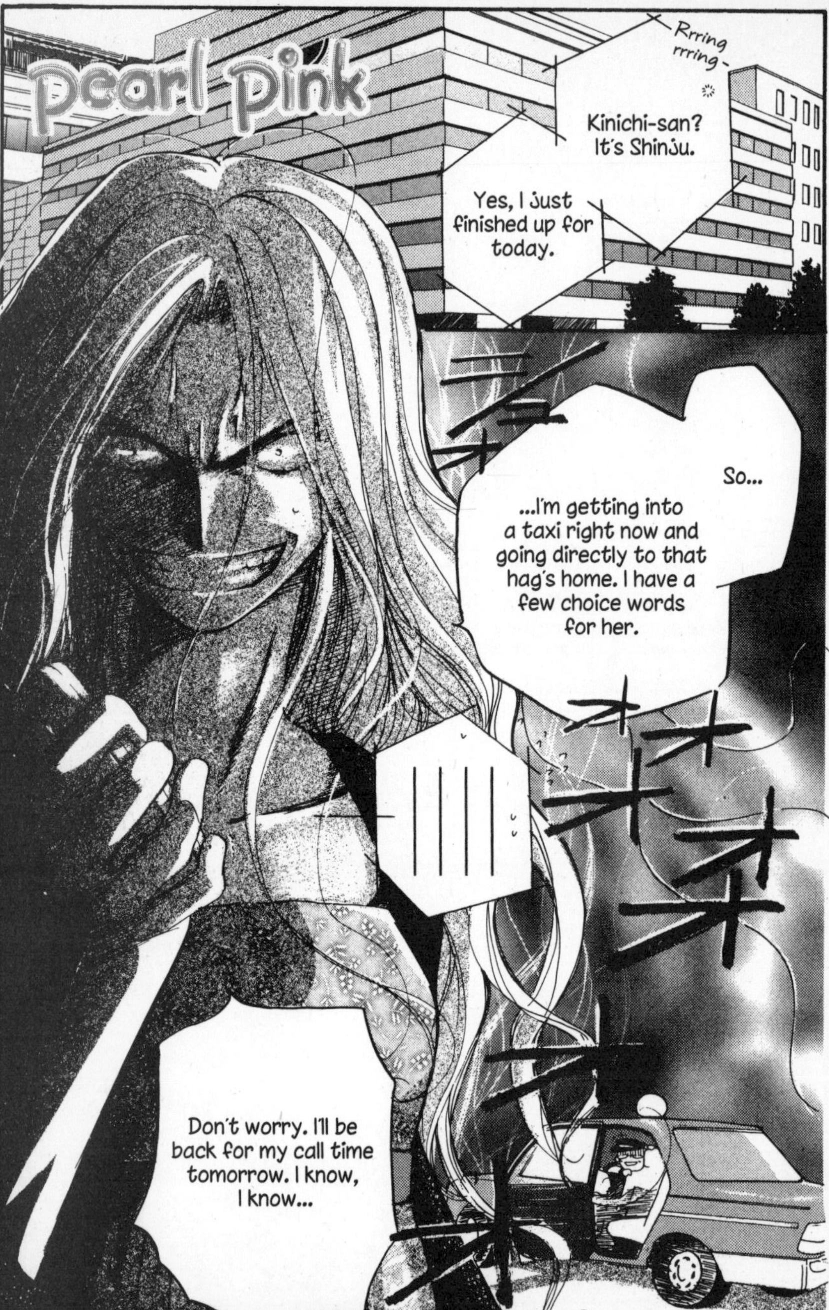
pearl pink
Rrring rrring-
Kinichi-san? It's Shinju.
Yes, I just finished up for today.
So...
...I'm getting into a taxi right now and going directly to that hag's home. I have a few choice words for her.
Don't worry. I'll be back for my call time tomorrow. I know, I know...

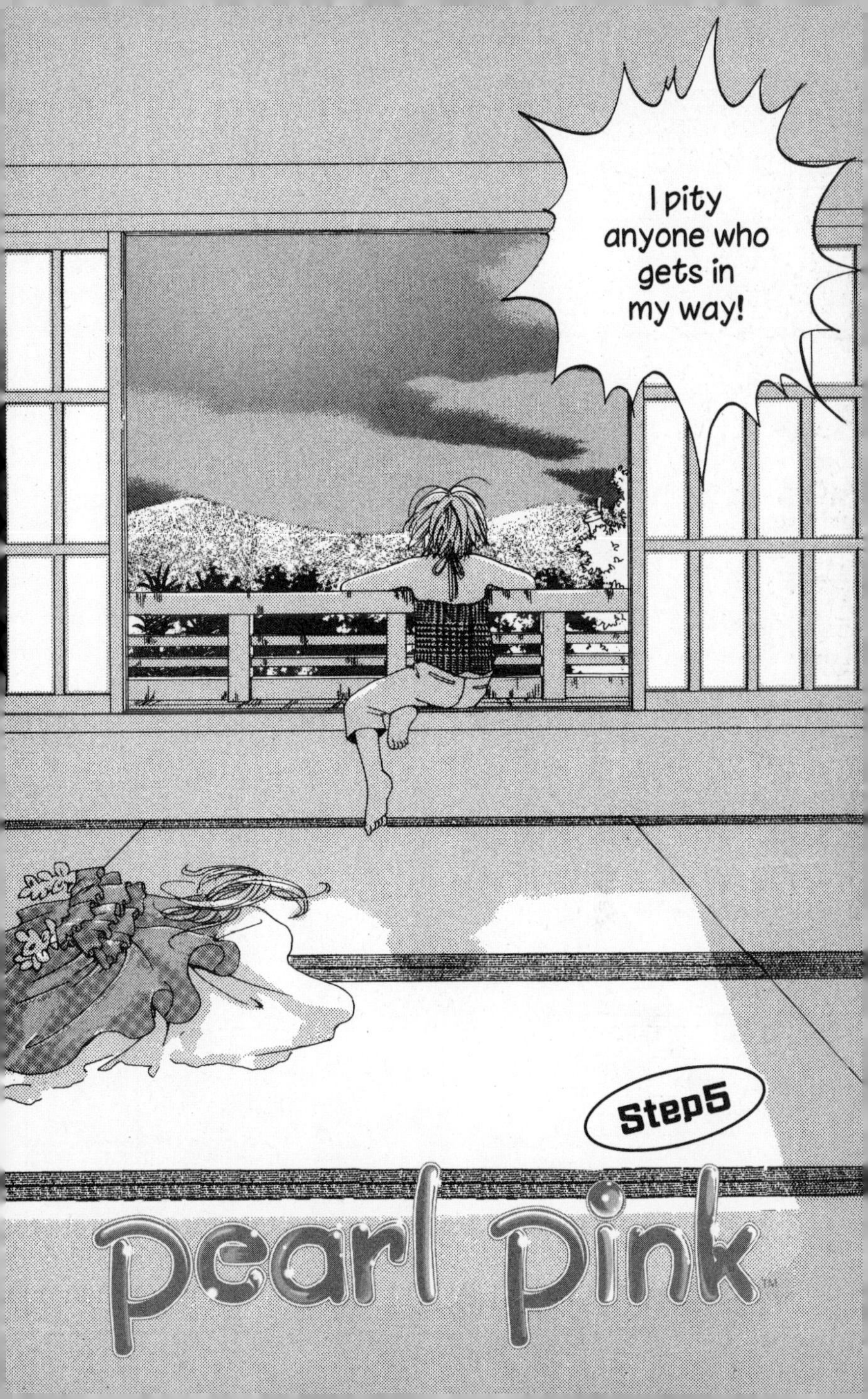
I pity anyone who gets in my way!
Step5
Pearl Pink™

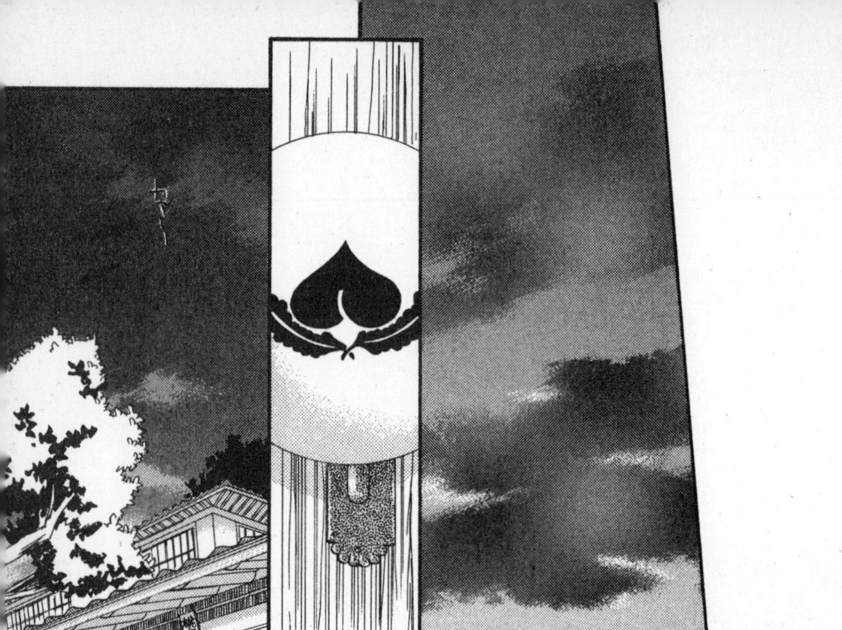

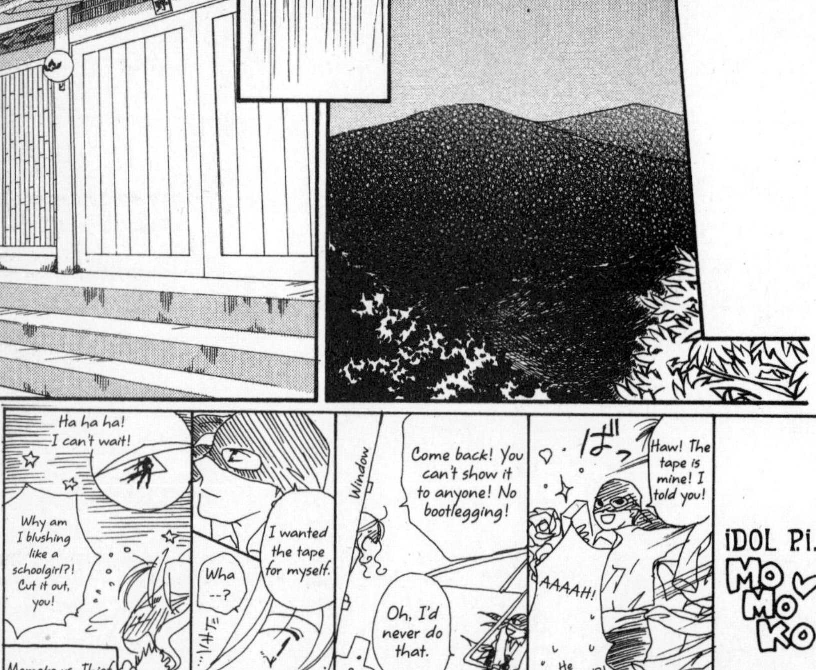

iDOL P.i. MOMOKO 4.
Momoko vs. Thief Handsome! The battle continues...
Ha ha ha! I can't wait!
Why am I blushing like a schoolgirl?! Cut it out, you!
Wha --?
I wanted the tape for myself.
Window
Come back! You can't show it to anyone! No bootlegging!
Oh, I'd never do that.
Haw! The tape is mine! I told you!
AAAAH!
He transformed?!

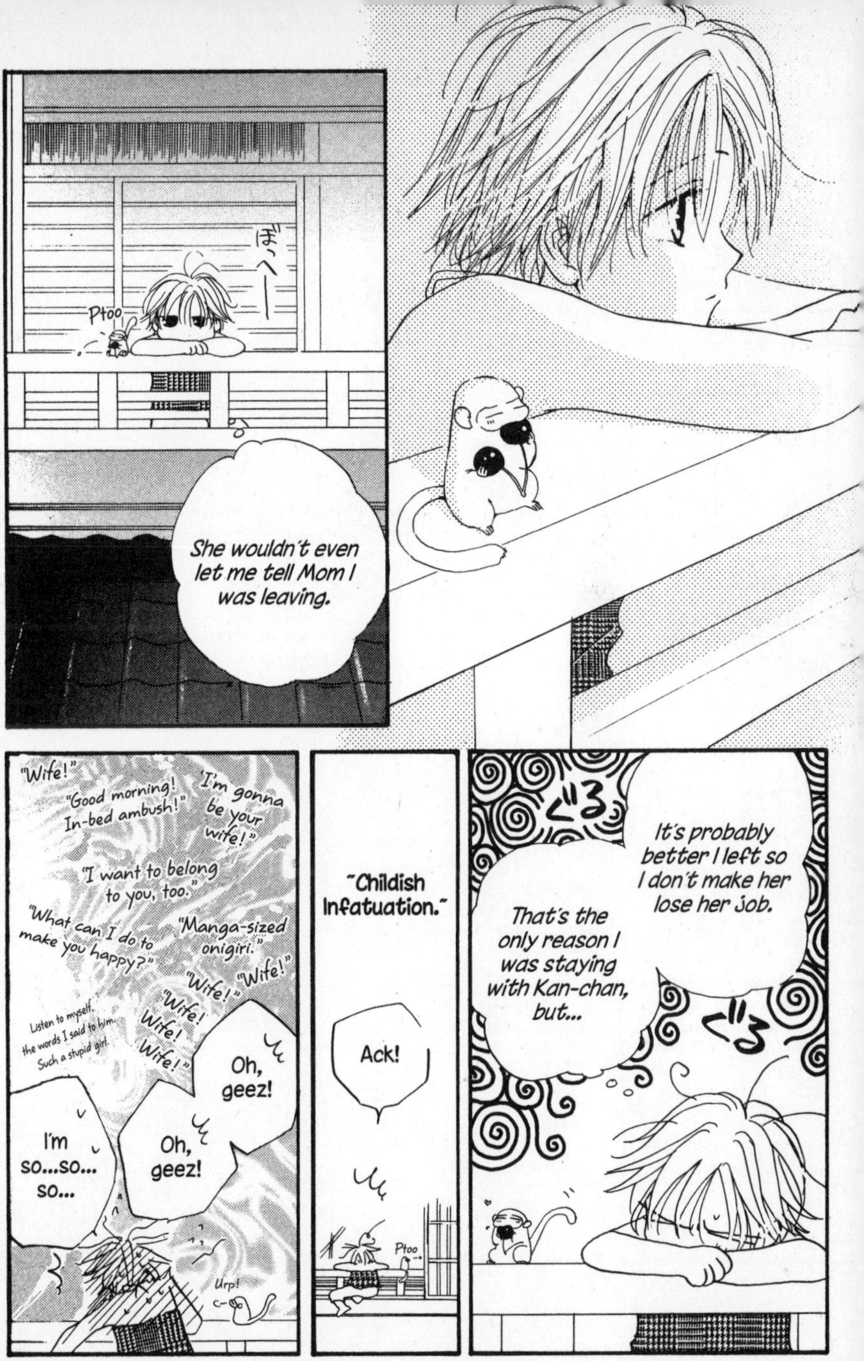
ぼへー
Ptoo
She wouldn't even let me tell Mom I was leaving.
ぐる
It's probably better I left so I don't make her lose her job.
That's the only reason I was staying with Kan-chan, but...
ぐる
"Childish Infatuation."
Ack!
Ptoo
"Wife!"
"Good morning! In-bed ambush!"
"I'm gonna be your wife!"
"I want to belong to you, too."
"What can I do to make you happy?"
"Manga-sized onigiri."
"Wife!" "Wife!"
"Wife! Wife! Wife!"
Listen to myself, the words I said to him. Such a stupid girl.
Oh, geez!
Oh, geez!
I'm so...so... so...
Urp!

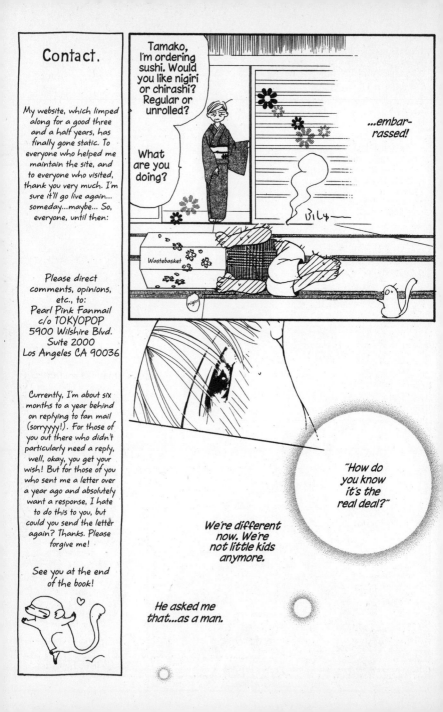

Contact.

My website, which limped along for a good three and a half years, has finally gone static. To everyone who helped me maintain the site, and to everyone who visited, thank you very much. I'm sure it'll live again... someday...maybe... So, everyone, until then:

Please direct comments, opinions, etc., to:
Pearl Pink Fanmail
c/o TOKYOPOP
5900 Wilshire Blvd.
Suite 2000
Los Angeles CA 90036

Currently, I'm about six months to a year behind on replying to fan mail (sorryyyy!). For those of you out there who didn't particularly need a reply, well, okay, you get your wish! But for those of you who sent me a letter over a year ago and absolutely want a response, I hate to do this to you, but could you send the letter again? Thanks. Please forgive me!

See you at the end of the book!

Tamako, I'm ordering sushi. Would you like nigiri or chirashi? Regular or unrolled?

What are you doing?

...embarrassed!

Wastebasket

nigiri

"How do you know it's the real deal?"

We're different now. We're not little kids anymore.

He asked me that...as a man.

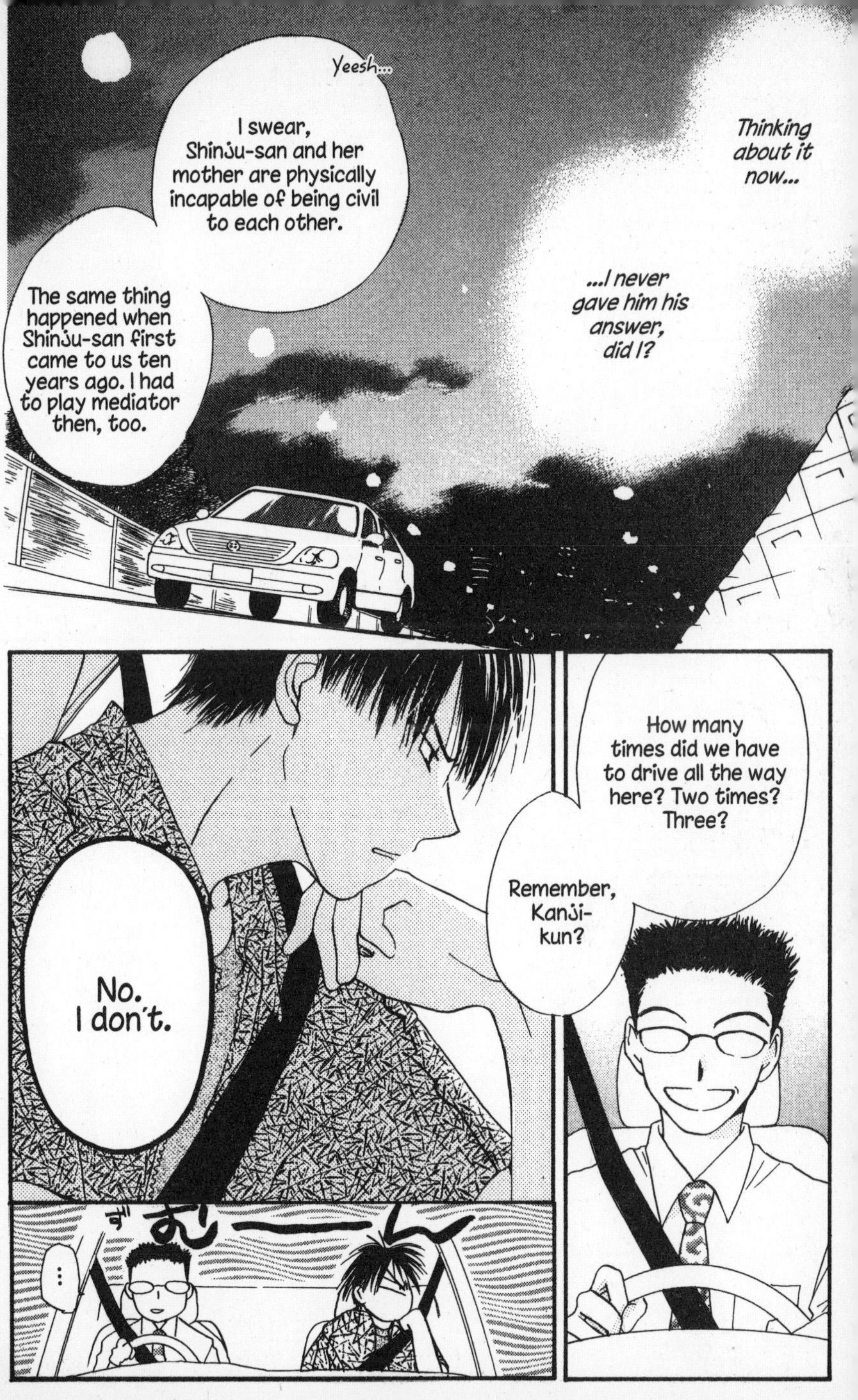
Thinking about it now...
...I never gave him his answer, did I?
Yeesh...
I swear, Shinju-san and her mother are physically incapable of being civil to each other.
The same thing happened when Shinju-san first came to us ten years ago. I had to play mediator then, too.
How many times did we have to drive all the way here? Two times? Three?
Remember, Kanji-kun?
No. I don't.
ずむーーん
...

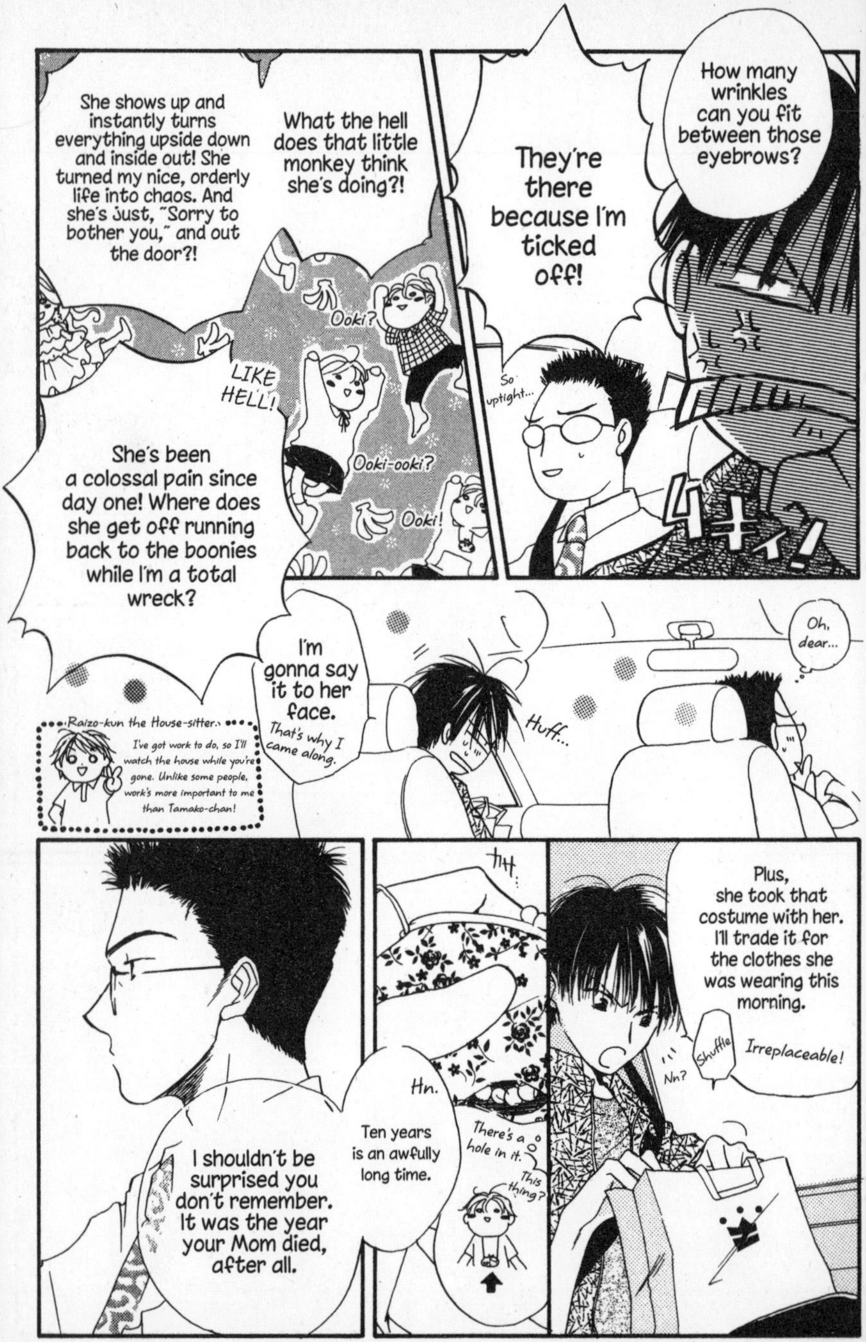
How many wrinkles can you fit between those eyebrows?
They're there because I'm ticked off!
So uptight...
What the hell does that little monkey think she's doing?!
She shows up and instantly turns everything upside down and inside out! She turned my nice, orderly life into chaos. And she's just, "Sorry to bother you," and out the door?!
Ooki?
Ooki-ooki?
Ooki!
LIKE HELL!
She's been a colossal pain since day one! Where does she get off running back to the boonies while I'm a total wreck?
Oh, dear...
Huff...
I'm gonna say it to her face.
That's why I came along.
Raizo-kun the House-sitter.
I've got work to do, so I'll watch the house while you're gone. Unlike some people, work's more important to me than Tamako-chan!
Plus, she took that costume with her. I'll trade it for the clothes she was wearing this morning.
Irreplaceable!
Shuffle
Nn?
Hn.
Ten years is an awfully long time.
There's a hole in it.
This thing?
I shouldn't be surprised you don't remember. It was the year your Mom died, after all.

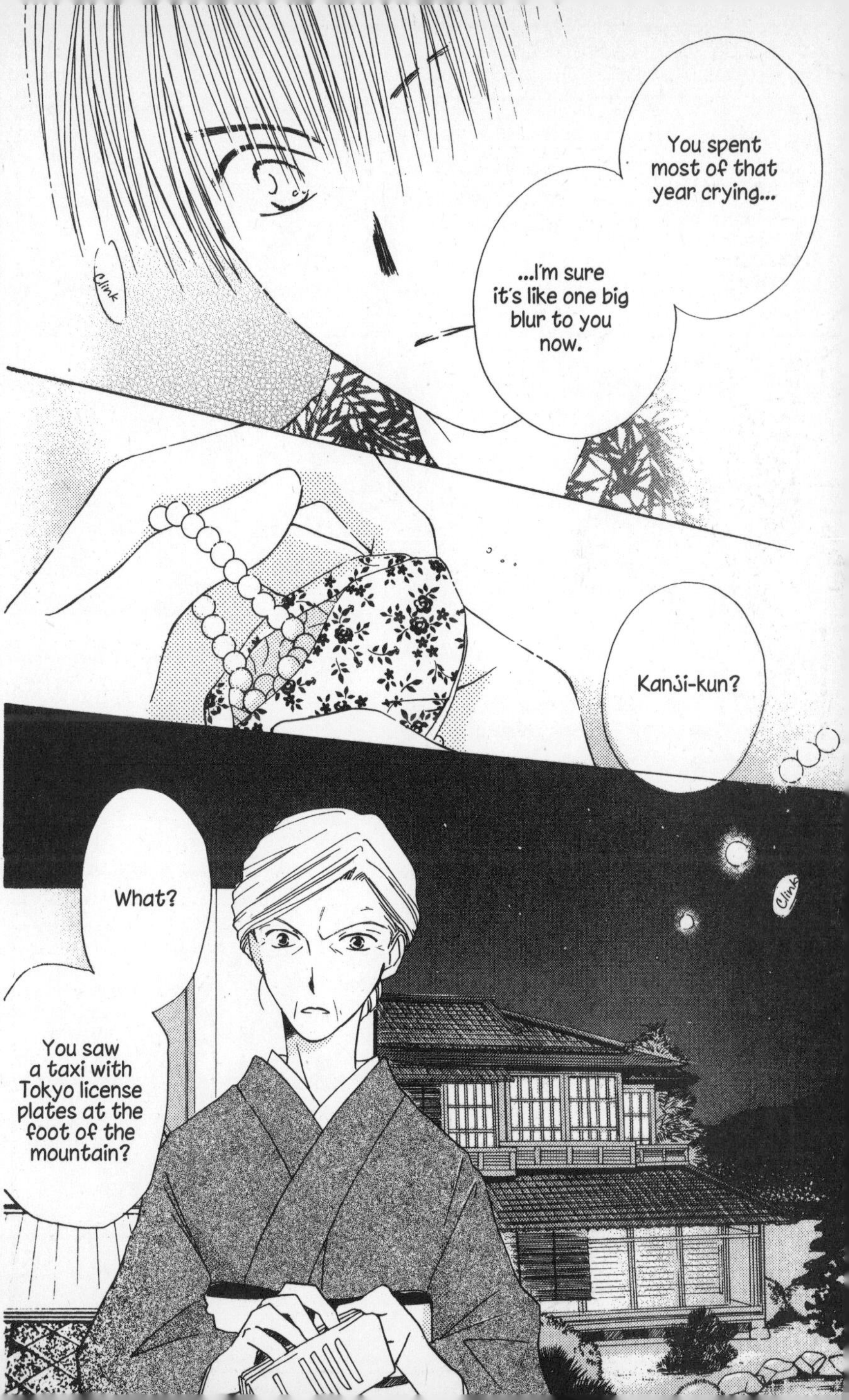
You spent most of that year crying...
...I'm sure it's like one big blur to you now.
Clink
Kanji-kun?
Clink
What?
You saw a taxi with Tokyo license plates at the foot of the mountain?

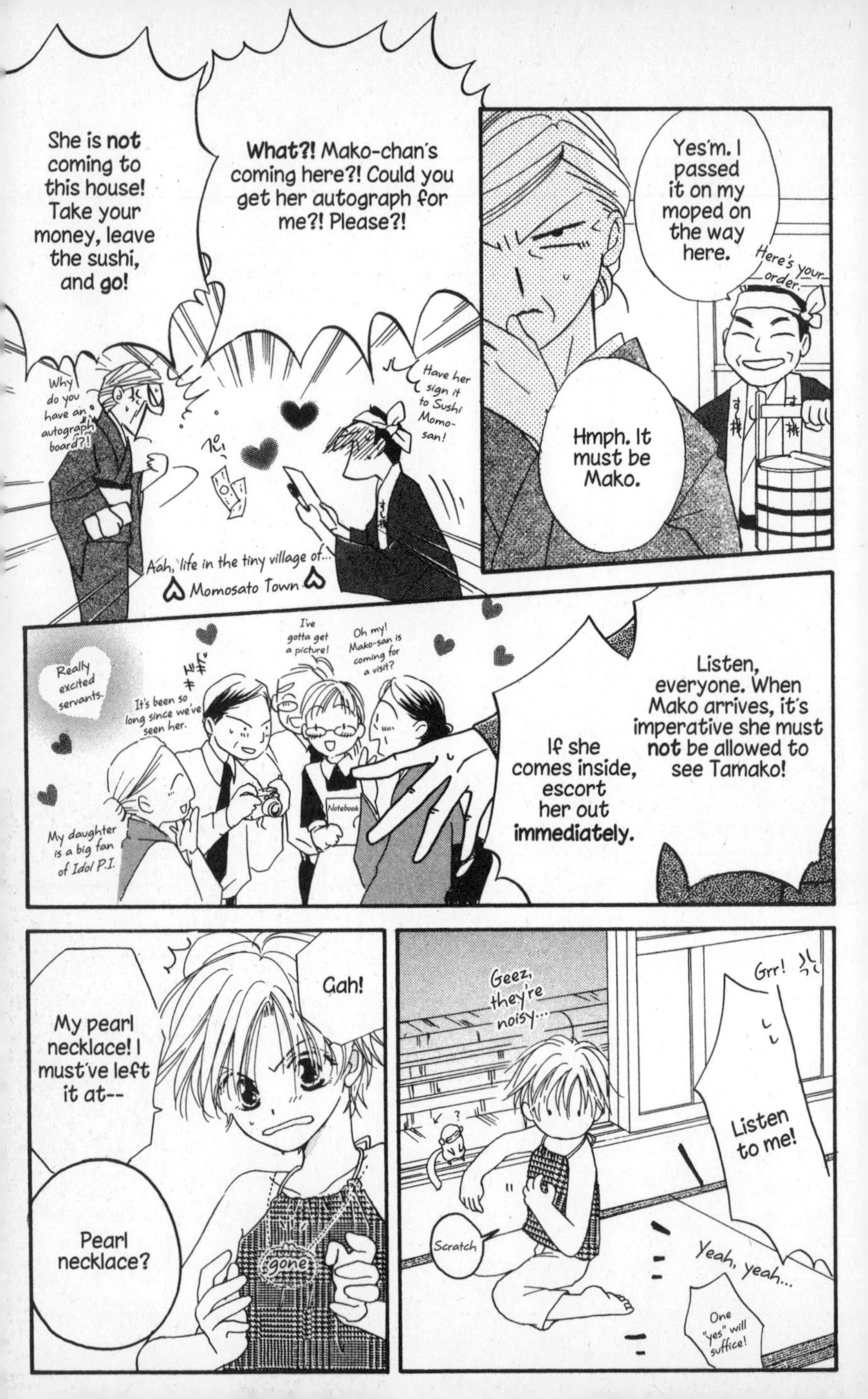
Yes'm. I passed it on my moped on the way here.
Here's your order.
Hmph. It must be Mako.
What?! Mako-chan's coming here?! Could you get her autograph for me?! Please?!
She is not coming to this house! Take your money, leave the sushi, and go!
Have her sign it to Sushi Momo-san!
Why do you have an autograph board?!
Aah, life in the tiny village of... Momosato Town
Listen, everyone. When Mako arrives, it's imperative she must not be allowed to see Tamako!
If she comes inside, escort her out immediately.
Oh my! Mako-san is coming for a visit?
I've gotta get a picture!
It's been so long since we've seen her.
Really excited servants.
Notebook
My daughter is a big fan of Idol P.I.
Grr!
Listen to me!
Geez, they're noisy...
Yeah, yeah...
Scratch
One "yes" will suffice!
Gah!
My pearl necklace! I must've left it at--
gone
Pearl necklace?

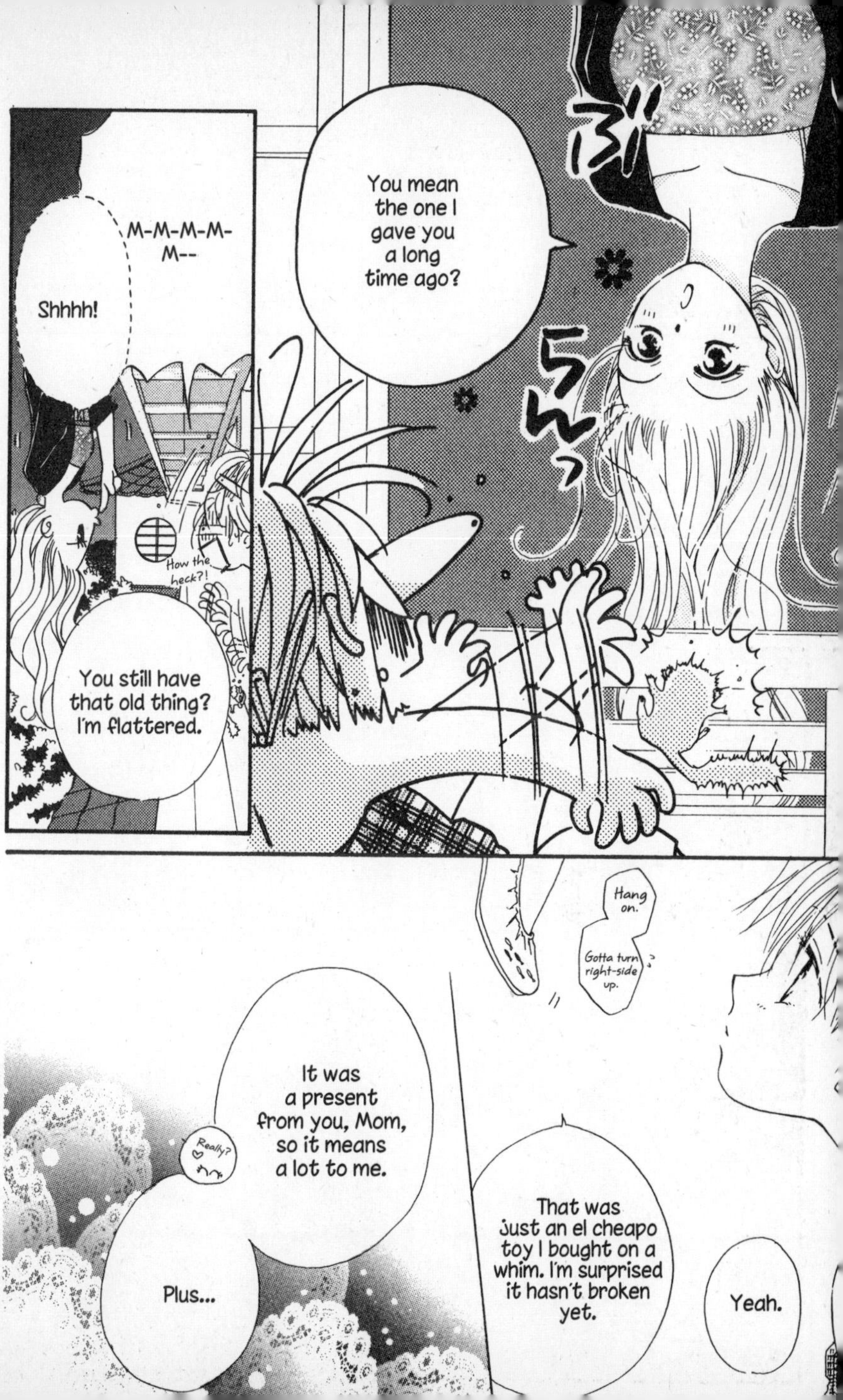
You mean the one I gave you a long time ago?
M-M-M-M-M--
Shhhh!
How the heck?!
You still have that old thing? I'm flattered.
Hang on.
Gotta turn right-side up.
Yeah.
That was just an el cheapo toy I bought on a whim. I'm surprised it hasn't broken yet.
It was a present from you, Mom, so it means a lot to me.
Really?
Plus...

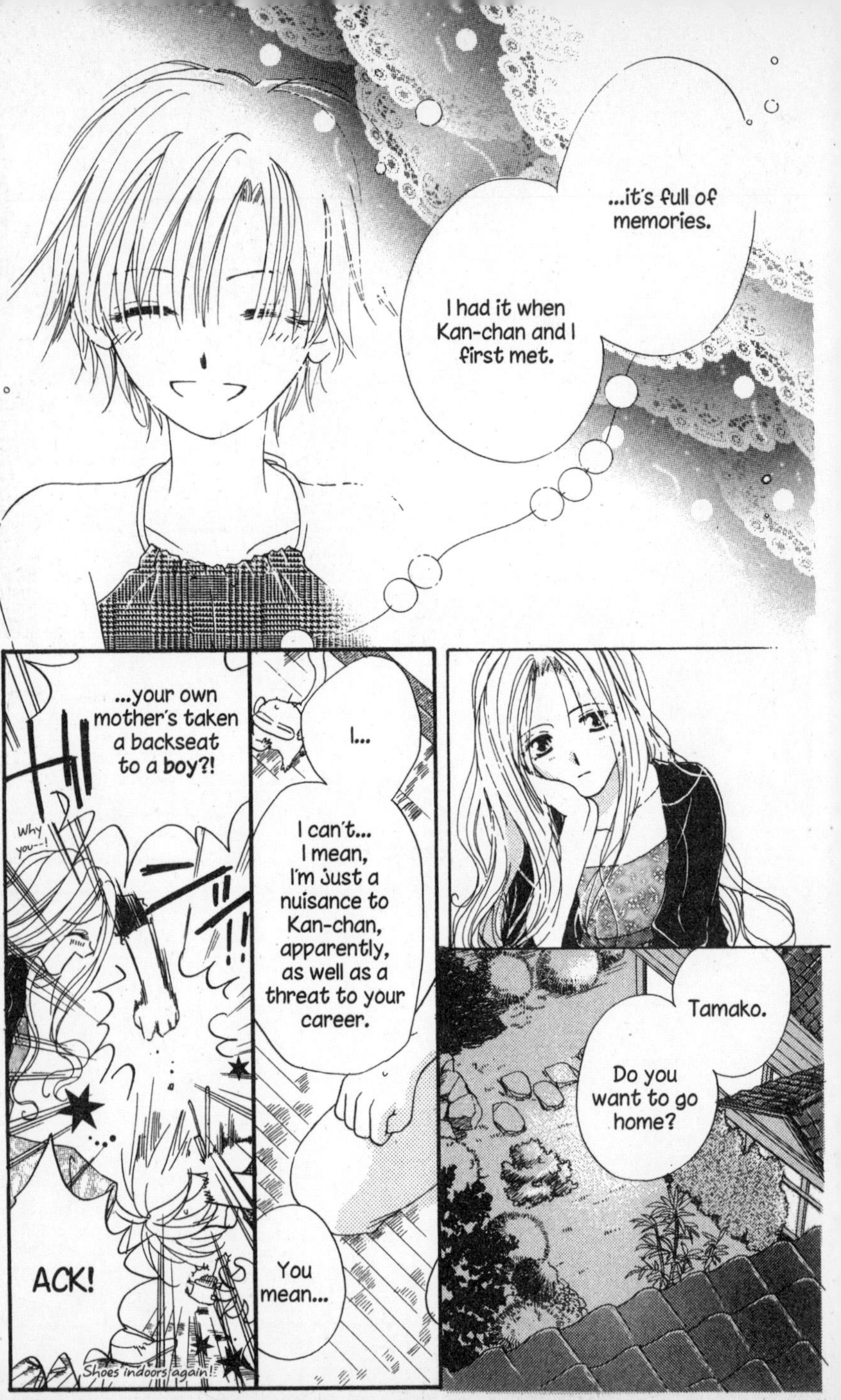
...it's full of memories.
I had it when Kan-chan and I first met.
Tamako.
Do you want to go home?
I...
I can't... I mean, I'm just a nuisance to Kan-chan, apparently, as well as a threat to your career.
You mean...
...your own mother's taken a backseat to a boy?!
Why you--!
ACK!
Shoes indoors again!

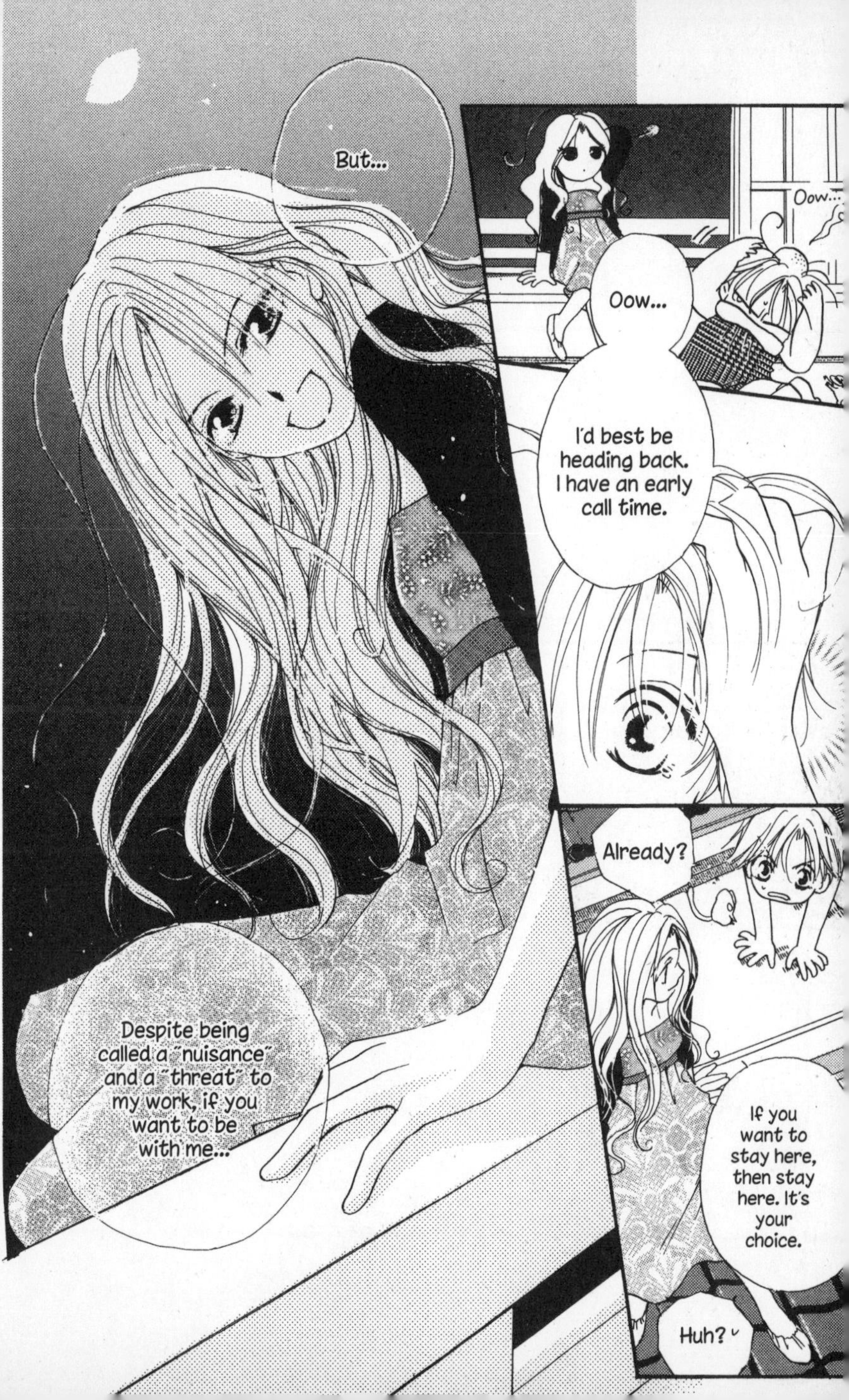

Oow...
Oow...
I'd best be heading back. I have an early call time.
Already?
If you want to stay here, then stay here. It's your choice.
Huh?
But...
Despite being called a "nuisance" and a "threat" to my work, if you want to be with me...

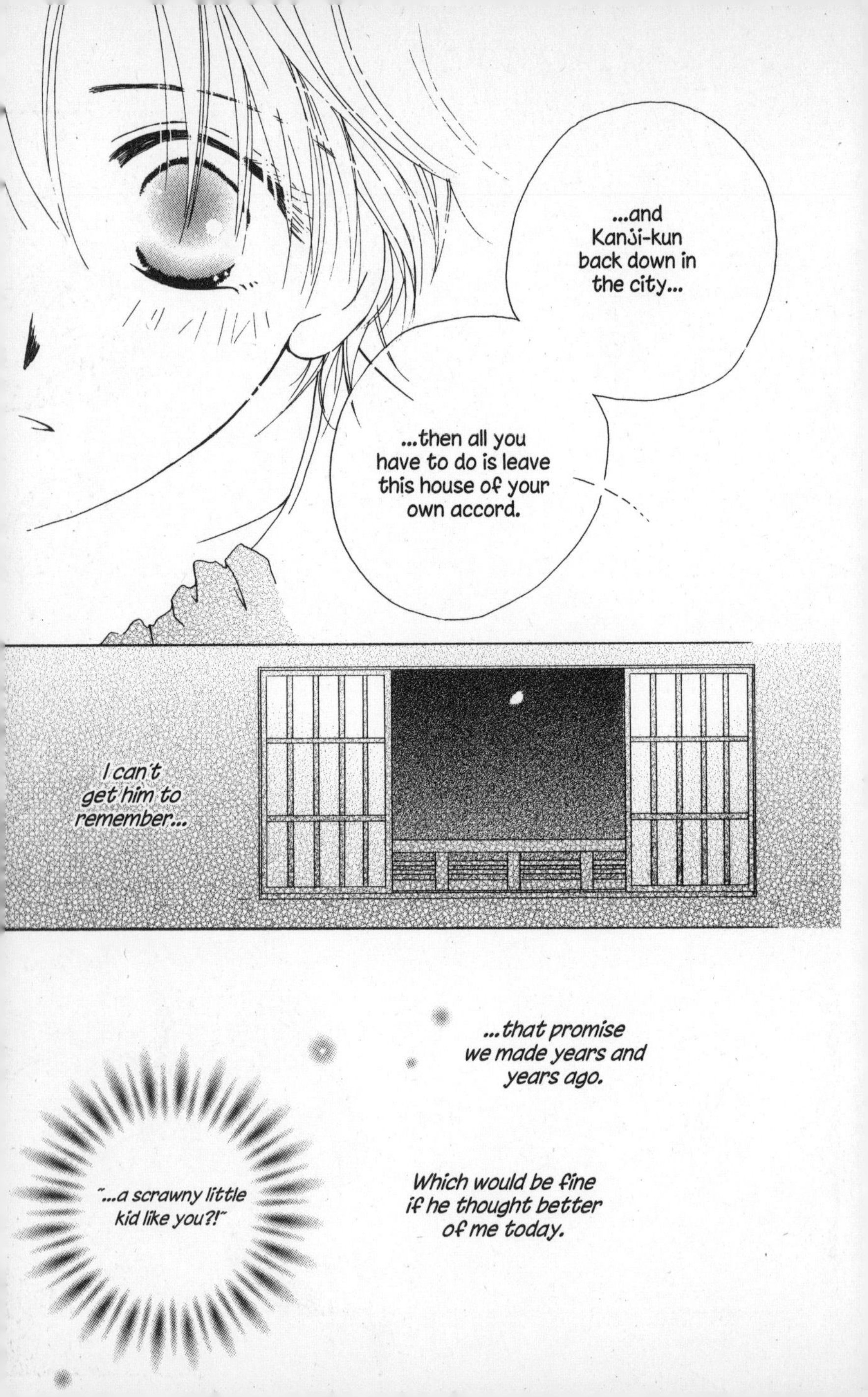
...and Kanji-kun back down in the city...
...then all you have to do is leave this house of your own accord.
I can't get him to remember...
...that promise we made years and years ago.
Which would be fine if he thought better of me today.
"...a scrawny little kid like you?!"

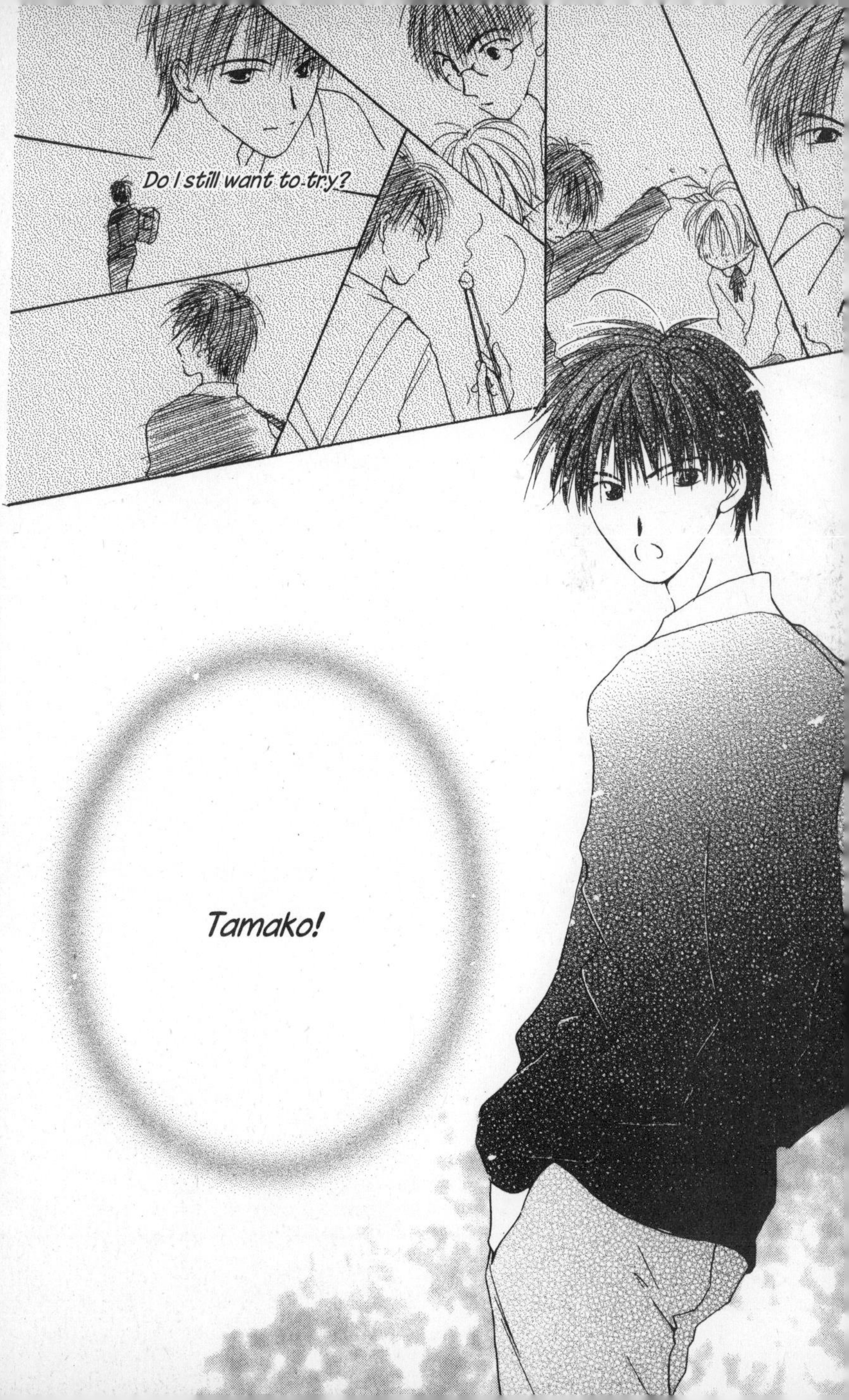
Do I still want to try?
Tamako!

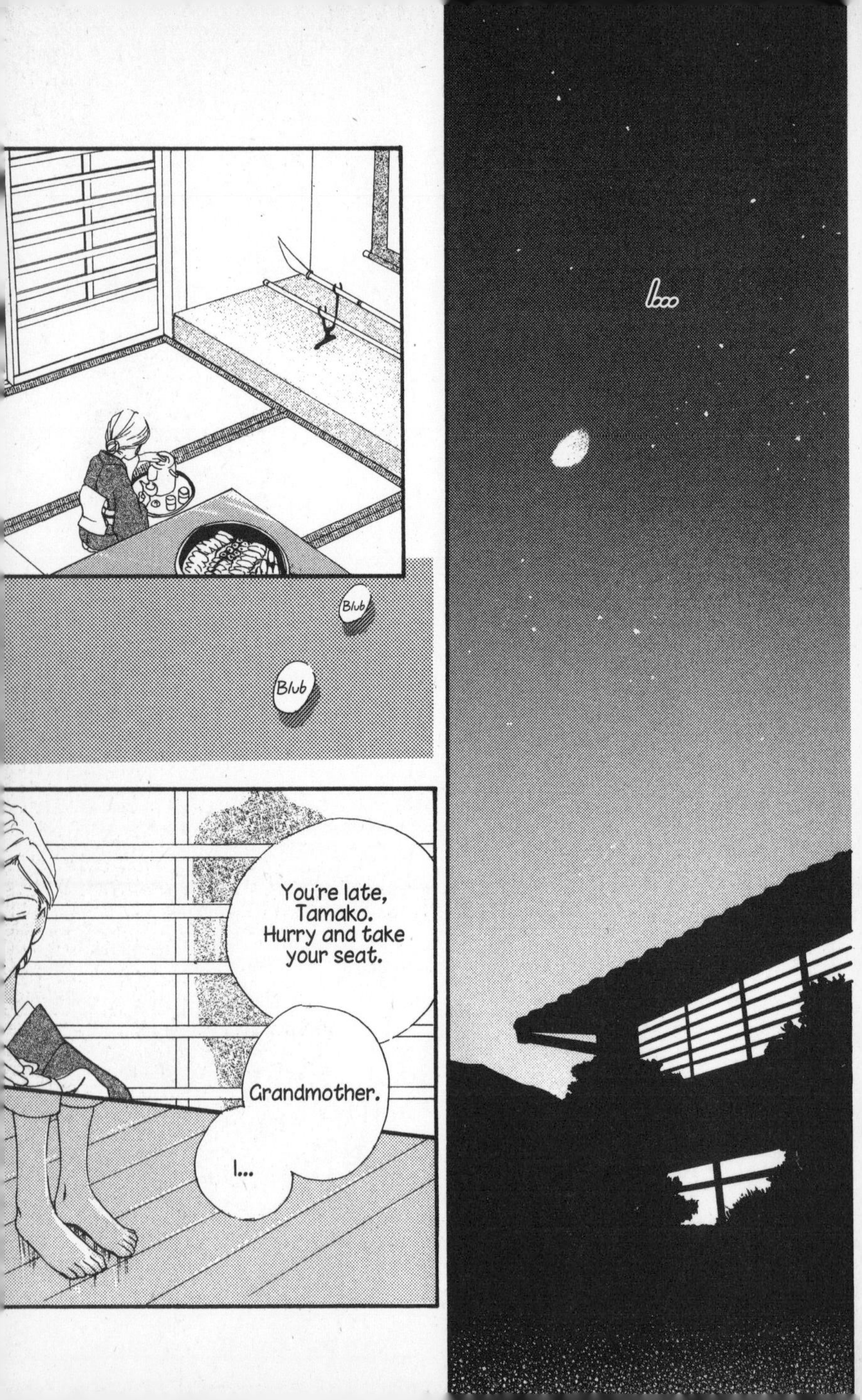
I...
Blub
Blub
You're late, Tamako. Hurry and take your seat.
Grandmother.
I...

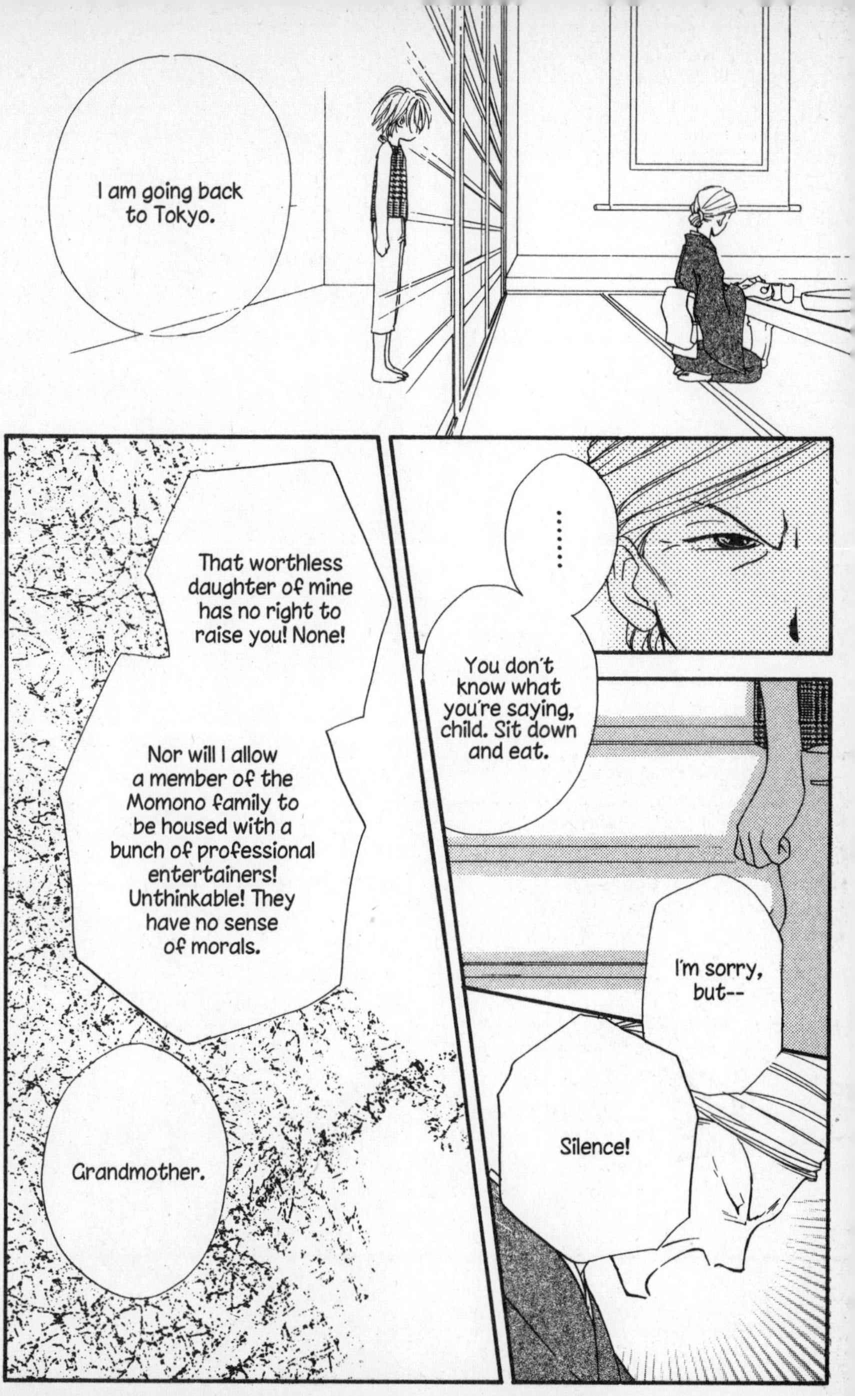
I am going back to Tokyo.
......
You don't know what you're saying, child. Sit down and eat.
I'm sorry, but--
Silence!
That worthless daughter of mine has no right to raise you! None!
Nor will I allow a member of the Momono family to be housed with a bunch of professional entertainers! Unthinkable! They have no sense of morals.
Grandmother.

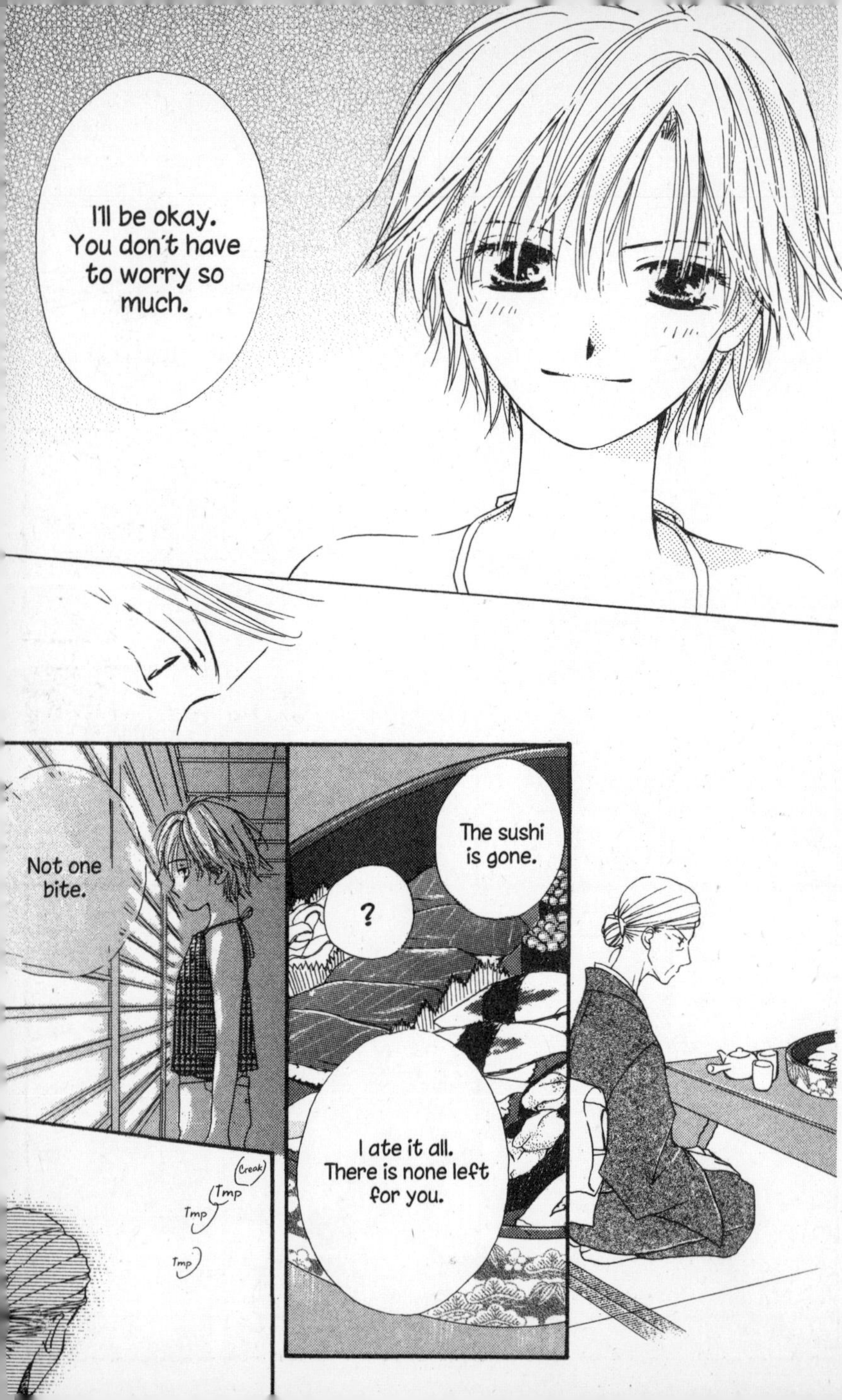
I'll be okay. You don't have to worry so much.
The sushi is gone.
?
I ate it all. There is none left for you.
Not one bite.
Creak
Tmp
Tmp
Tmp

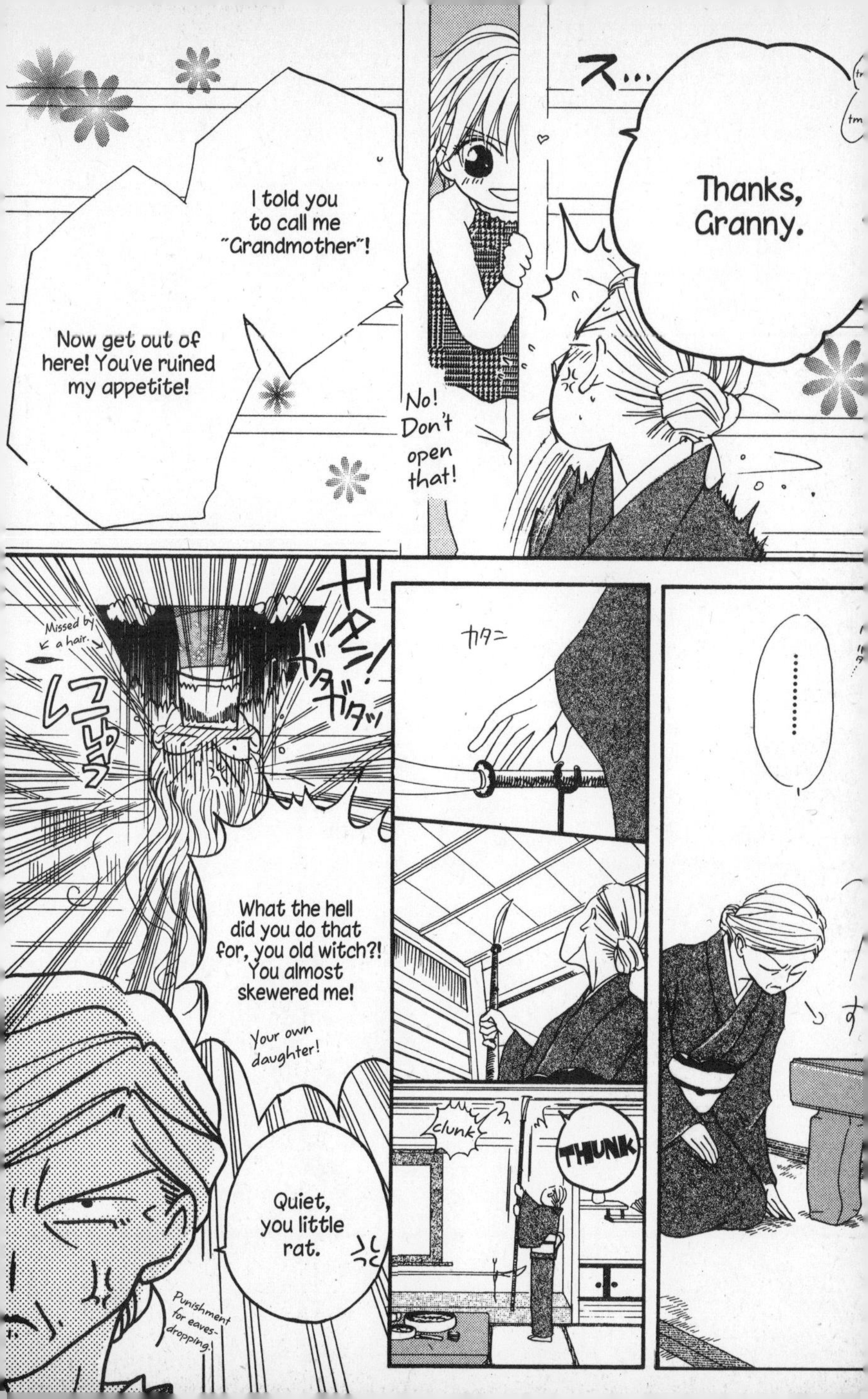
ス…
Thanks, Granny.
I told you to call me "Grandmother"!
Now get out of here! You've ruined my appetite!
No! Don't open that!
……
カタン
clunk
THUNK
ガタン!
ガタガタッ
Missed by a hair.
What the hell did you do that for, you old witch?! You almost skewered me!
Your own daughter!
Quiet, you little rat.
Punishment for eaves-dropping.

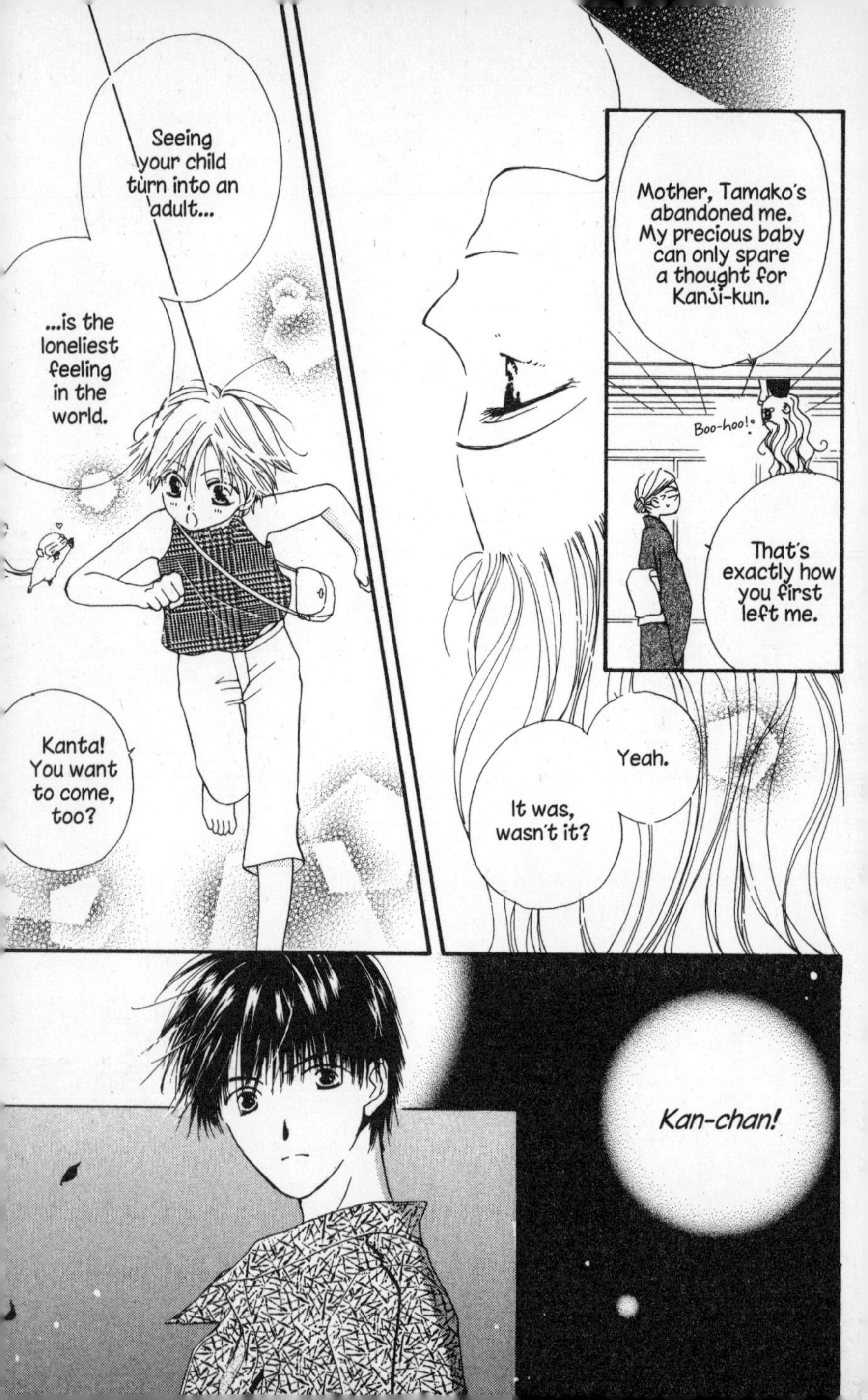
Mother, Tamako's abandoned me. My precious baby can only spare a thought for Kanji-kun.
Boo-hoo!
That's exactly how you first left me.
Yeah.
It was, wasn't it?
Seeing your child turn into an adult...
...is the loneliest feeling in the world.
Kanta! You want to come, too?
Kan-chan!

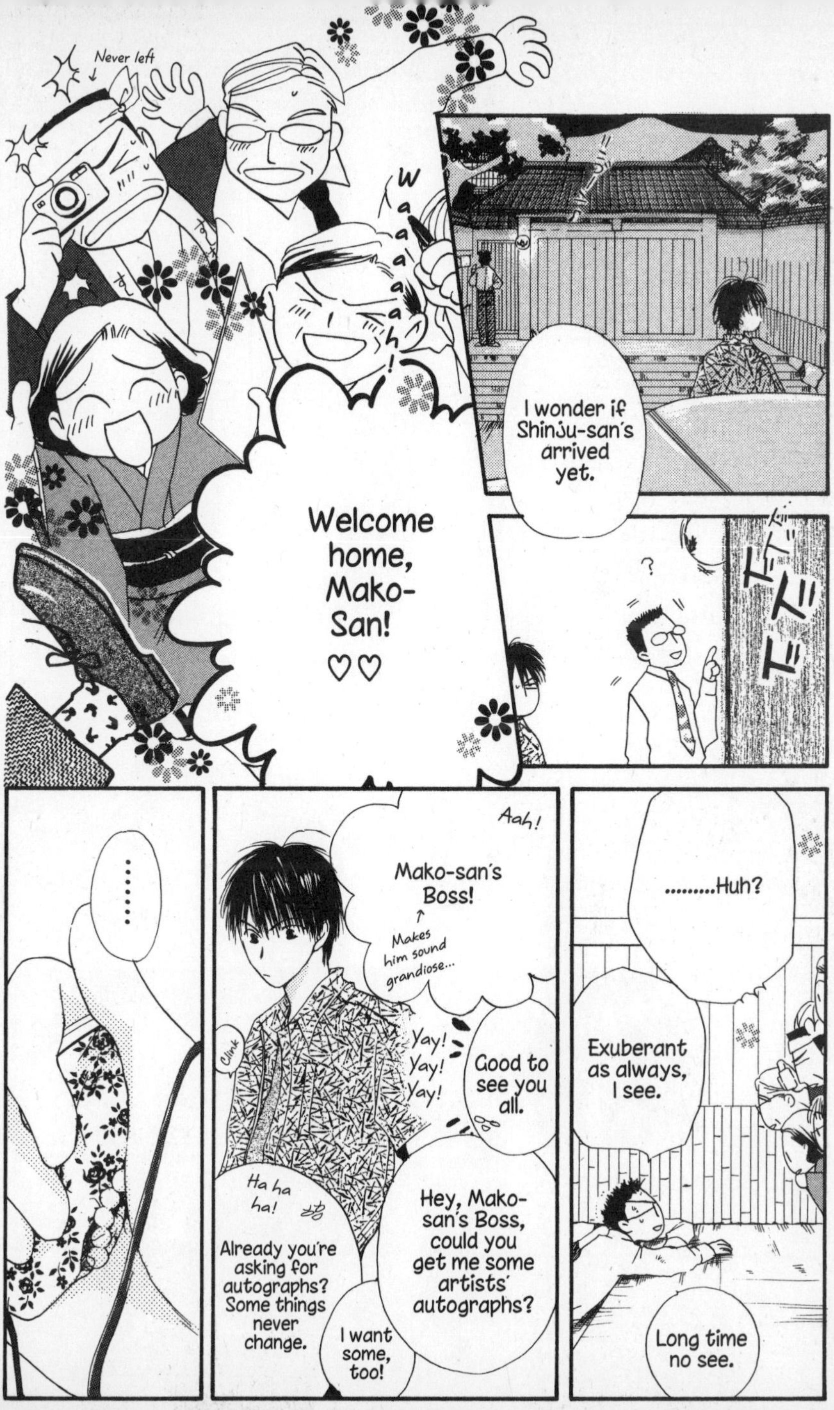

I wonder if Shinju-san's arrived yet.
?
Never left
Waaaaaah!
Welcome home, Mako-San! ♡♡
.........Huh?
Exuberant as always, I see.
Long time no see.
Aah!
Mako-san's Boss!
Makes him sound grandiose...
Good to see you all.
Yay! Yay! Yay!
Clink
Hey, Mako-san's Boss, could you get me some artists' autographs?
Ha ha ha!
Already you're asking for autographs? Some things never change.
I want some, too!
....

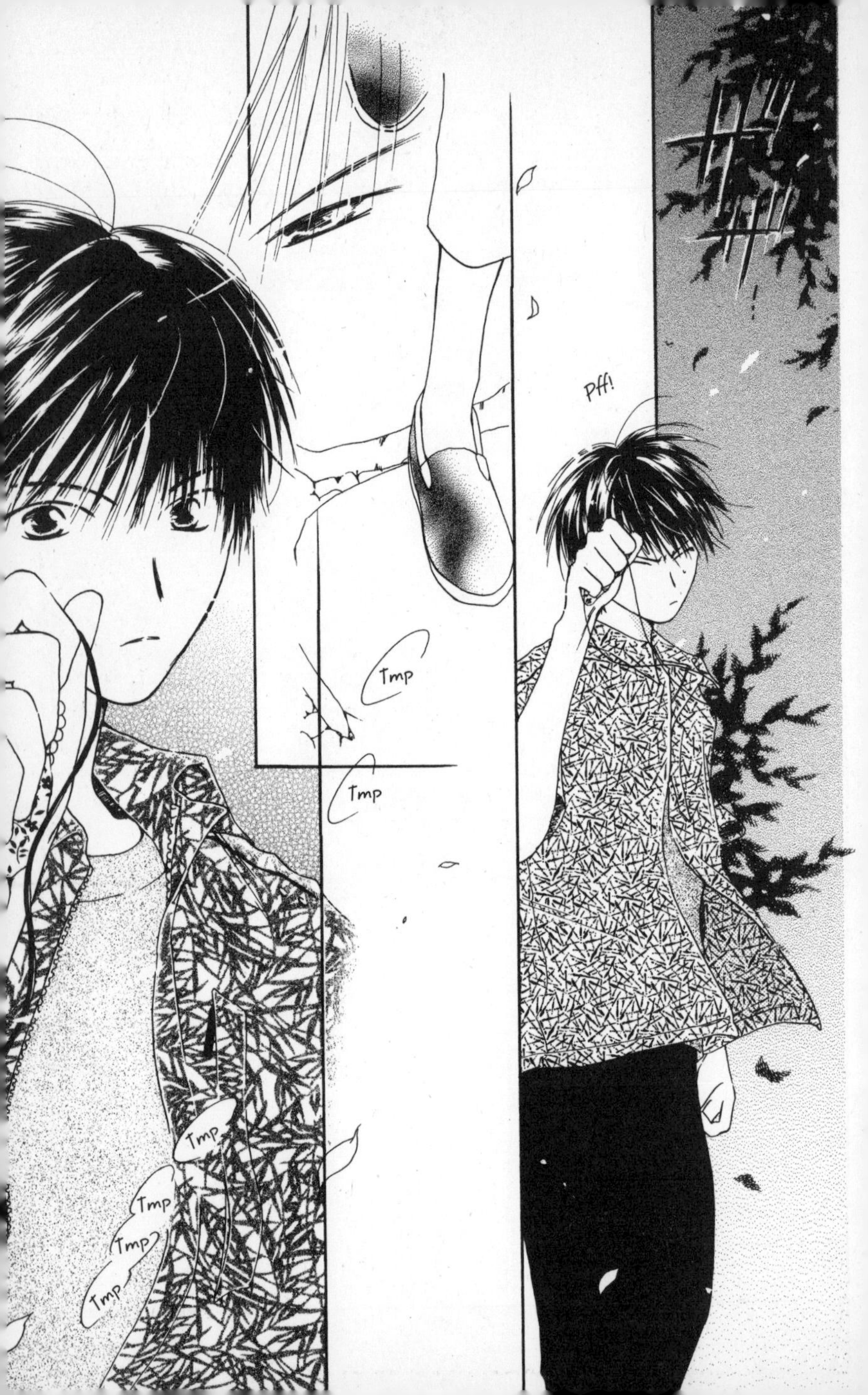
Pff!
Tmp
Tmp
Tmp
Tmp
Tmp
Tmp

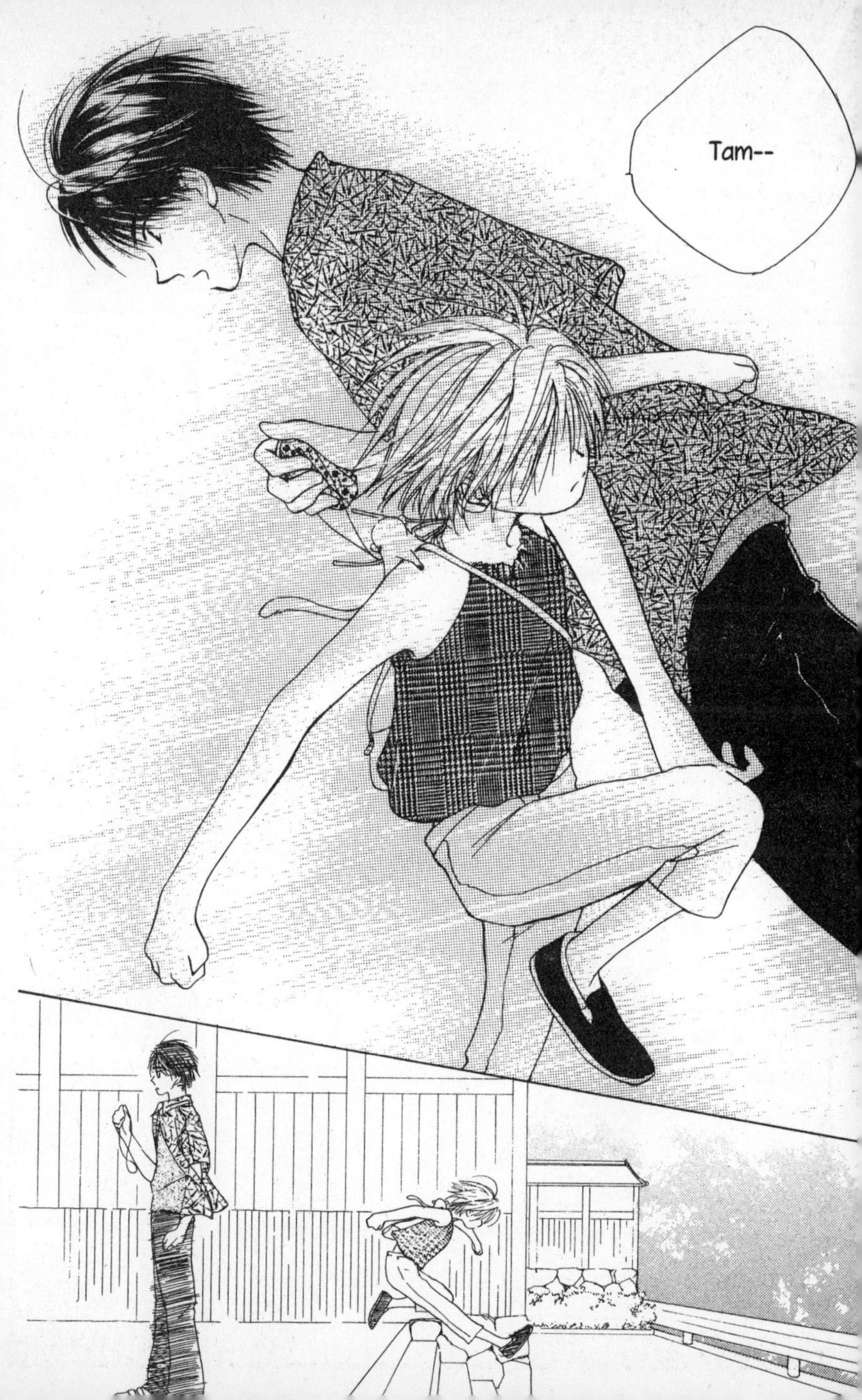
Tam--

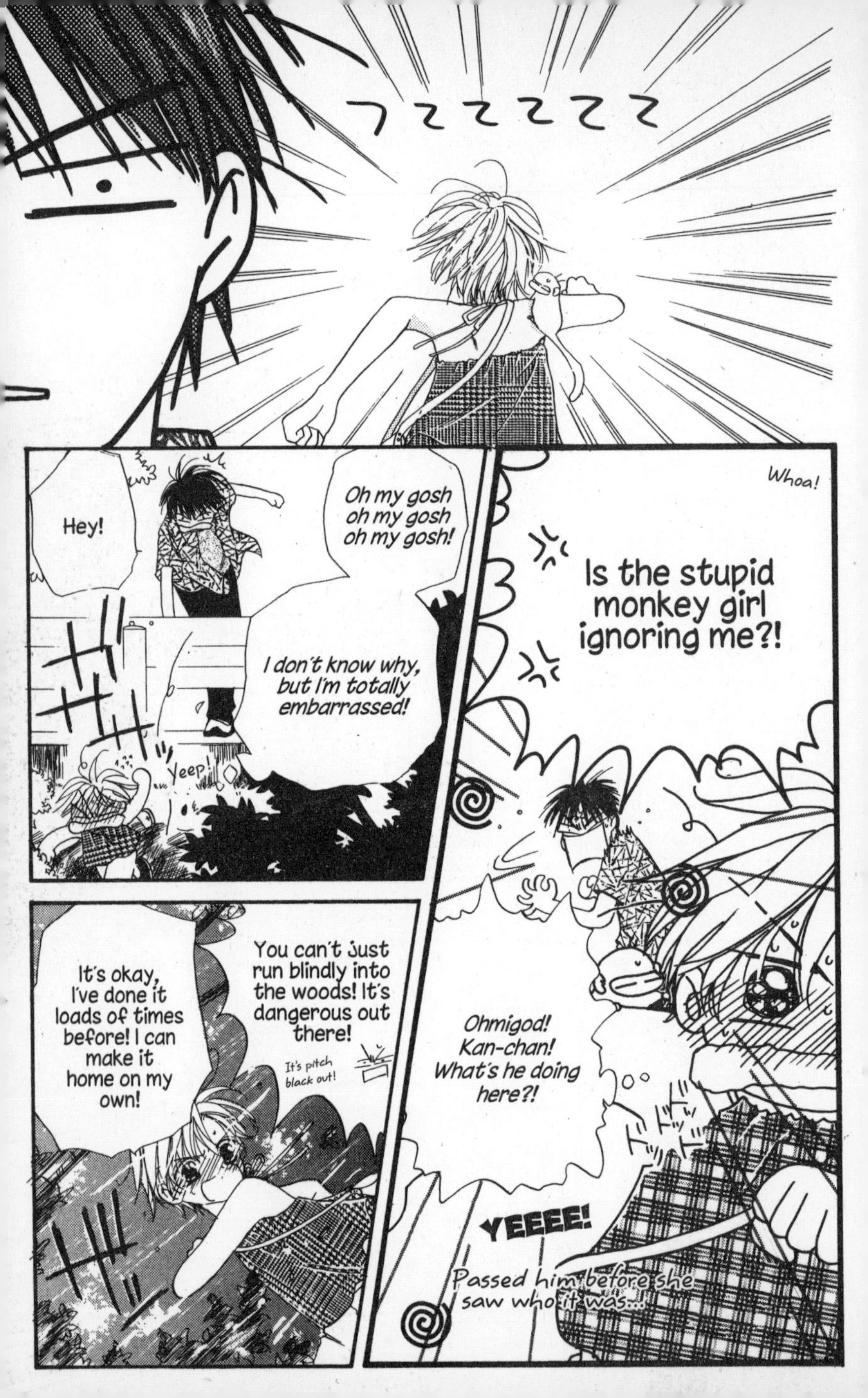
Whoa!
Is the stupid monkey girl ignoring me?!
Ohmigod! Kan-chan! What's he doing here?!
YEEEE!
Passed him before she saw who it was...
Oh my gosh oh my gosh oh my gosh!
Hey!
I don't know why, but I'm totally embarrassed!
Yeep!
You can't just run blindly into the woods! It's dangerous out there!
It's pitch black out!
It's okay, I've done it loads of times before! I can make it home on my own!

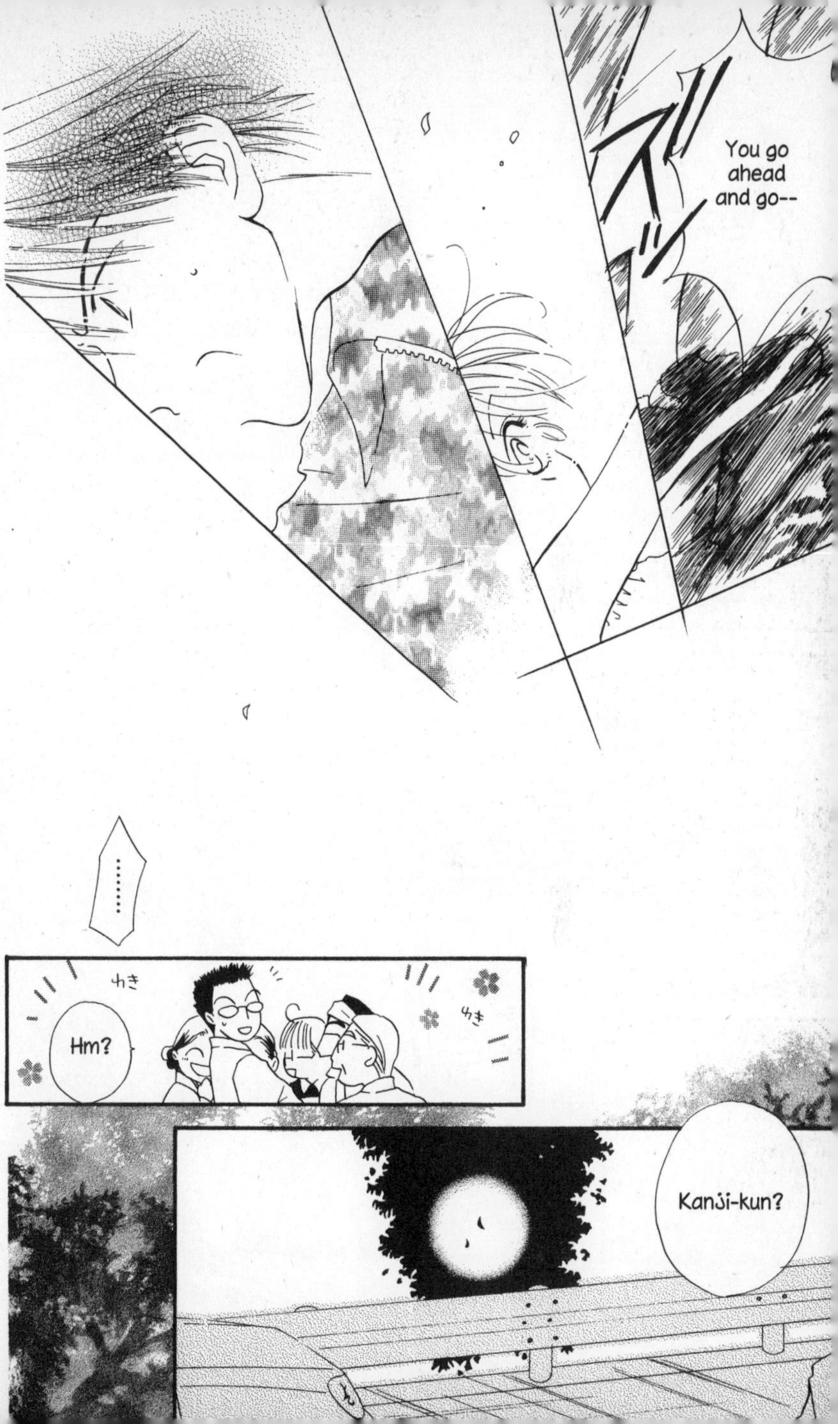
You go ahead and go--
....
Hm?
Kanji-kun?

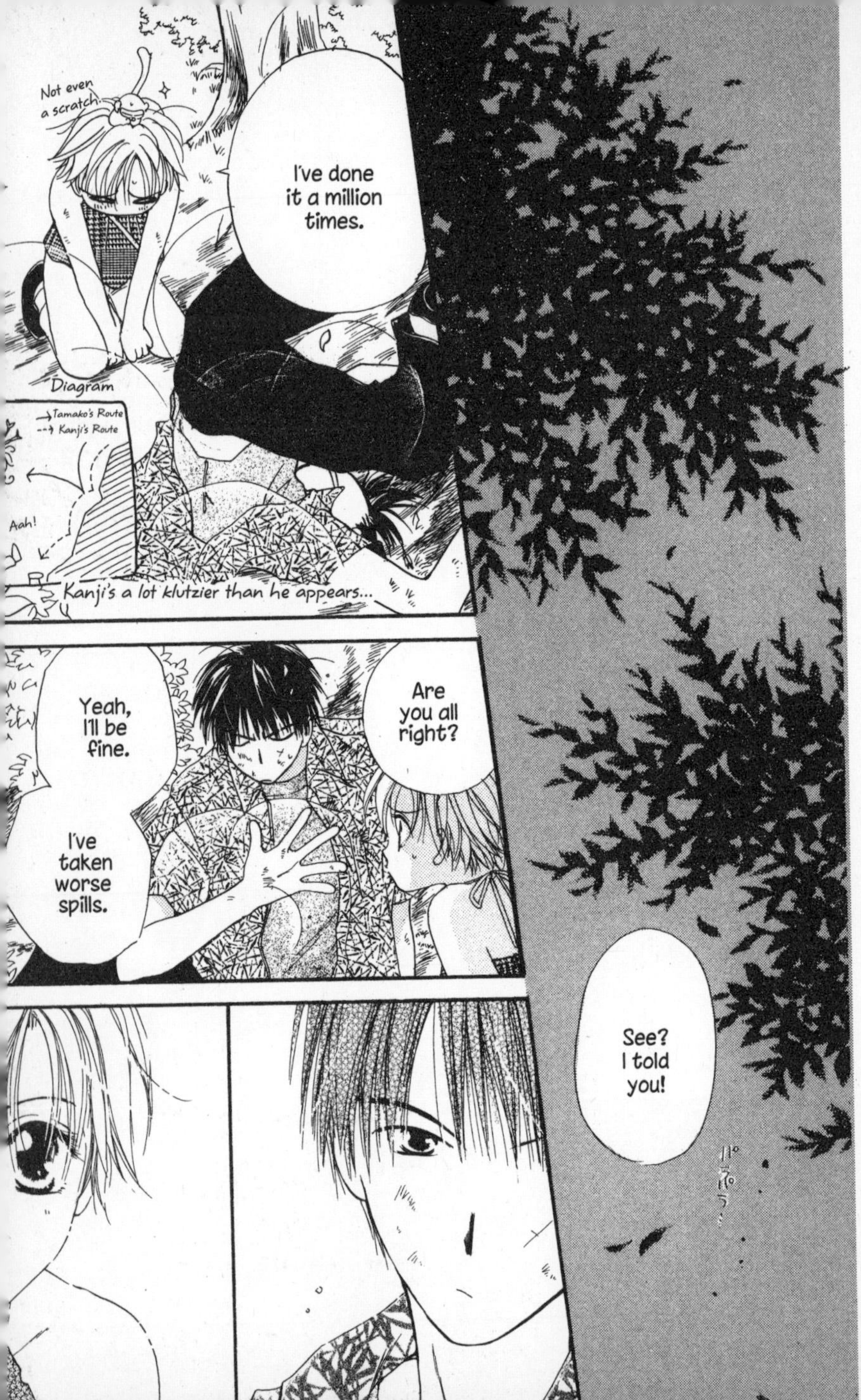
See? I told you!
I've done it a million times.
Not even a scratch.
Diagram
Tamako's Route
Kanji's Route
Aah!
Kanji's a lot klutzier than he appears...
Are you all right?
Yeah, I'll be fine.
I've taken worse spills.

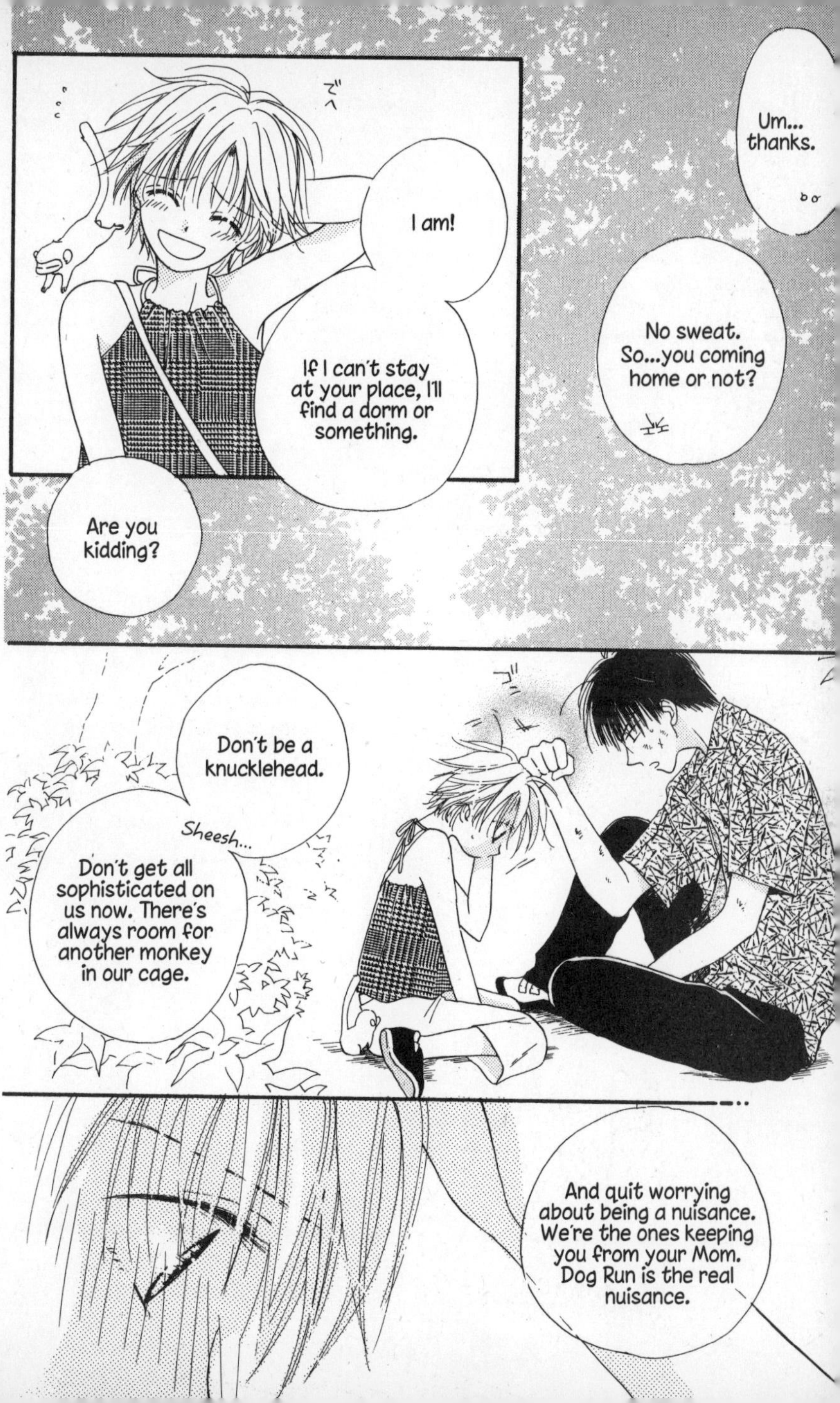
Um... thanks.
No sweat. So...you coming home or not?
I am!
If I can't stay at your place, I'll find a dorm or something.
Are you kidding?
Don't be a knucklehead.
Sheesh...
Don't get all sophisticated on us now. There's always room for another monkey in our cage.
And quit worrying about being a nuisance. We're the ones keeping you from your Mom. Dog Run is the real nuisance.

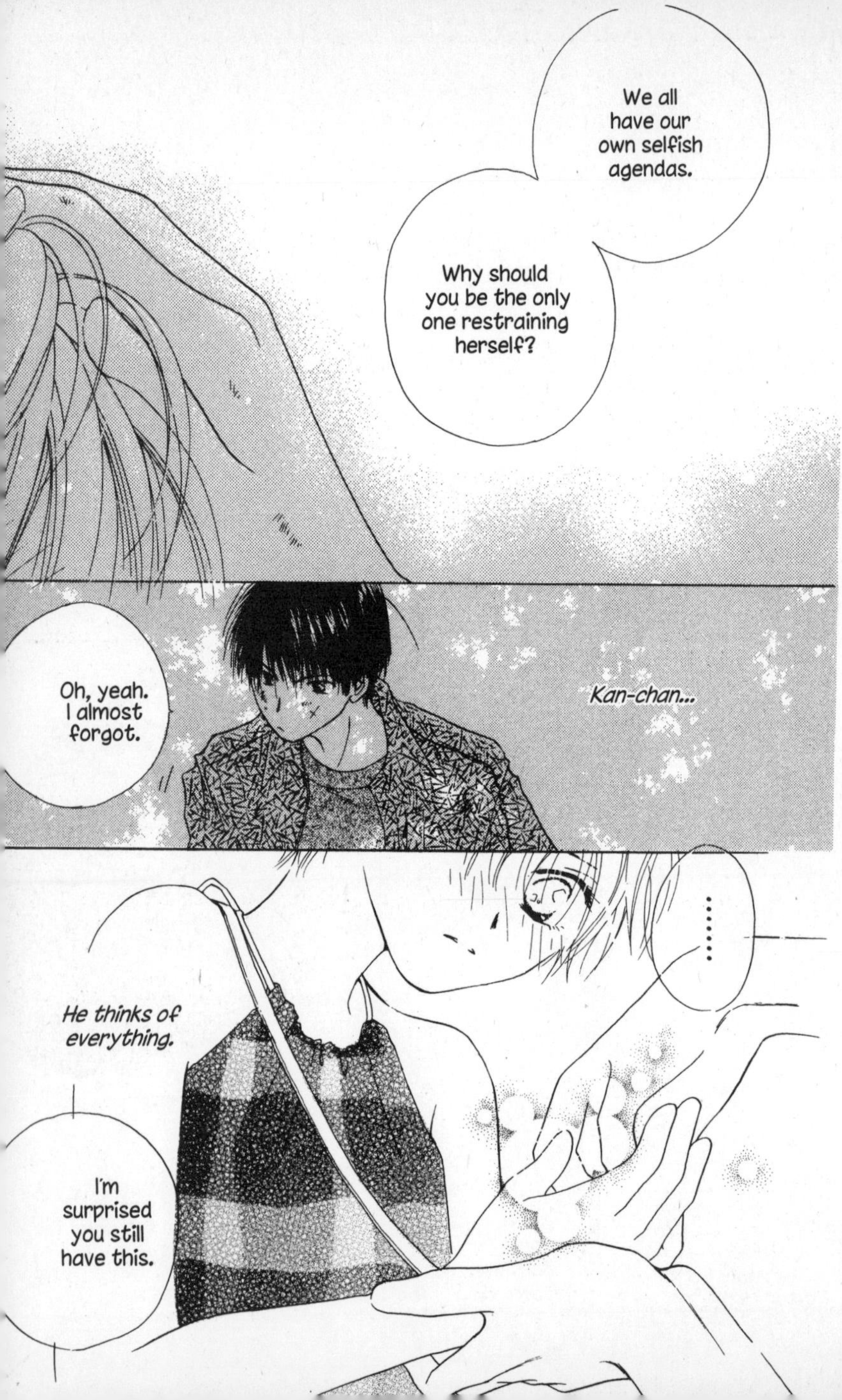
We all have our own selfish agendas.
Why should you be the only one restraining herself?
Kan-chan...
Oh, yeah. I almost forgot.
......
He thinks of everything.
I'm surprised you still have this.

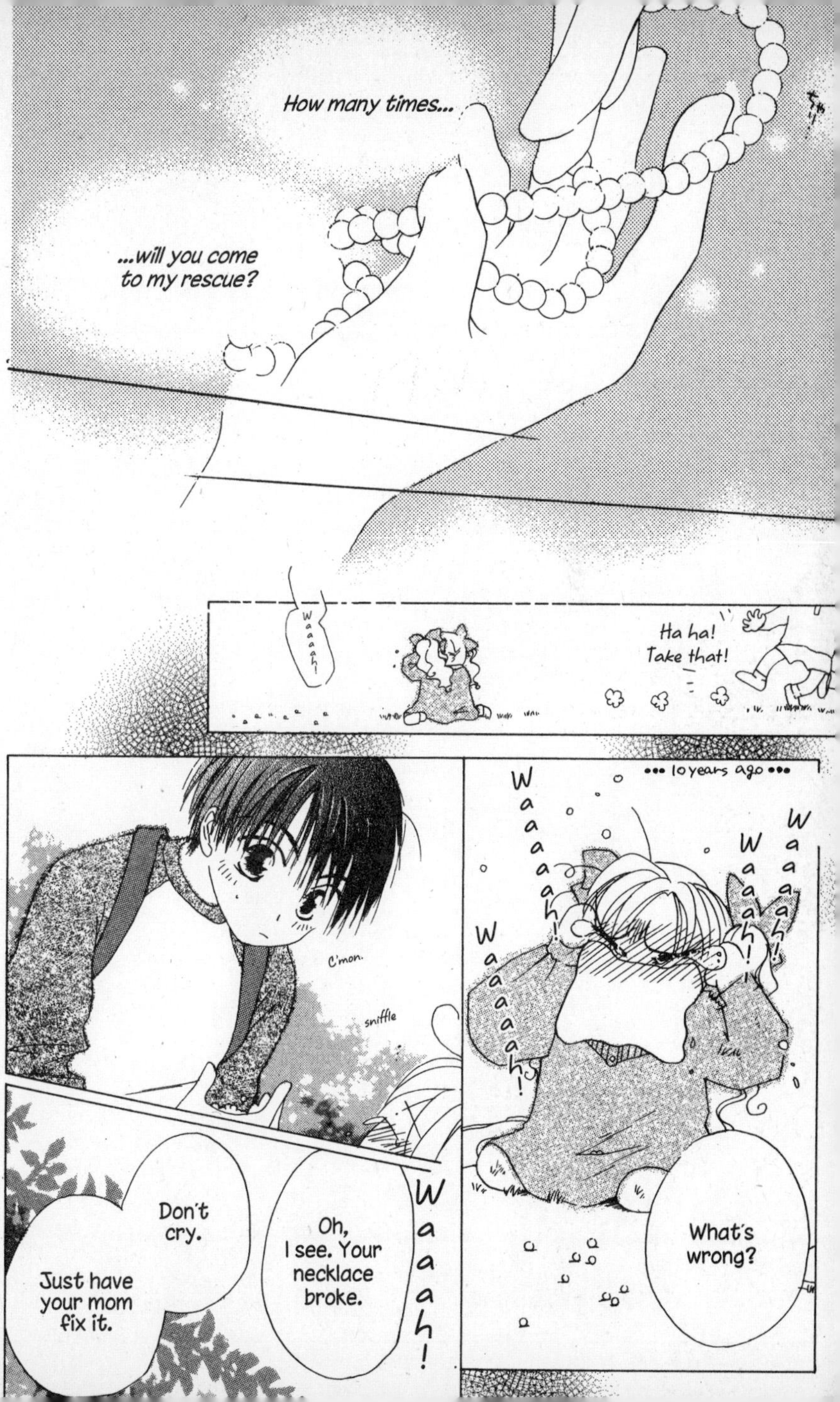

How many times...
...will you come to my rescue?
Ha ha! Take that!
Waaaah!
••• 10 years ago •••
Waaaah!
Waaaah!
Waaaah!
Waaaaaah!
What's wrong?
C'mon.
sniffle
Waaah!
Oh, I see. Your necklace broke.
Don't cry.
Just have your mom fix it.

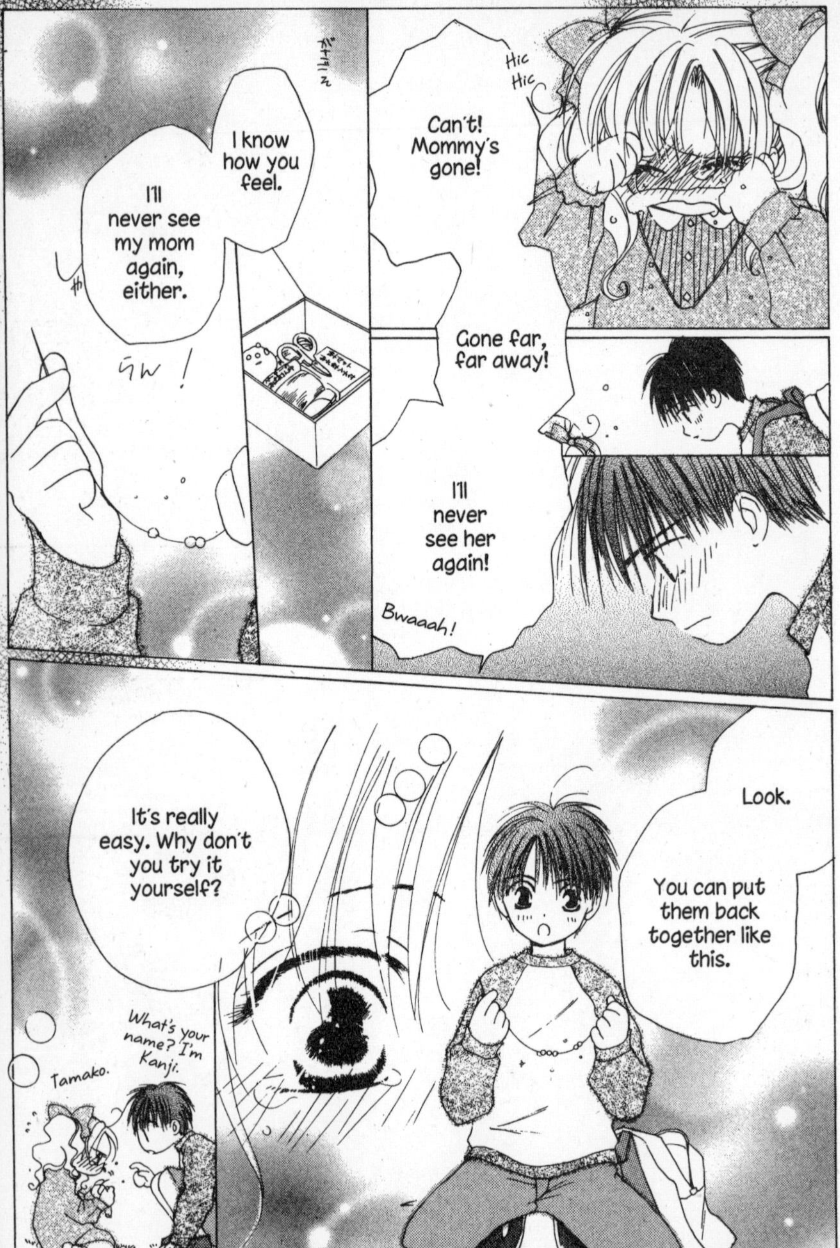
Hic
Hic
Can't! Mommy's gone!
Gone far, far away!
I'll never see her again!
Bwaaah!
I know how you feel.
I'll never see my mom again, either.
Look.
You can put them back together like this.
It's really easy. Why don't you try it yourself?
What's your name? I'm Kanji.
Tamako.

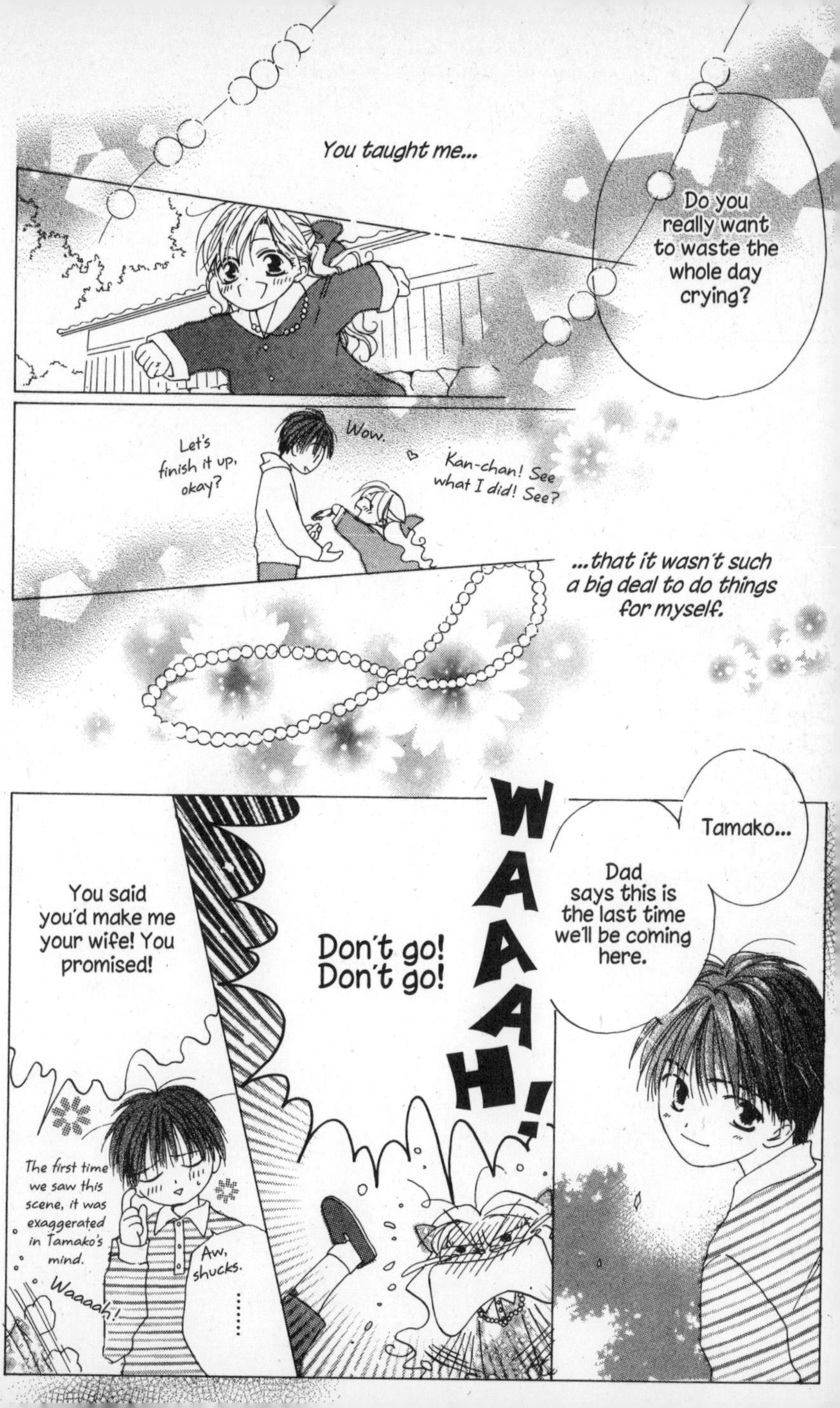
You taught me...
Do you really want to waste the whole day crying?
Kan-chan! See what I did! See?
Wow.
Let's finish it up, okay?
...that it wasn't such a big deal to do things for myself.
Tamako...
Dad says this is the last time we'll be coming here.
WAAAH!
Don't go! Don't go!
You said you'd make me your wife! You promised!
Aw, shucks.
......
The first time we saw this scene, it was exaggerated in Tamako's mind.
Waaaah!

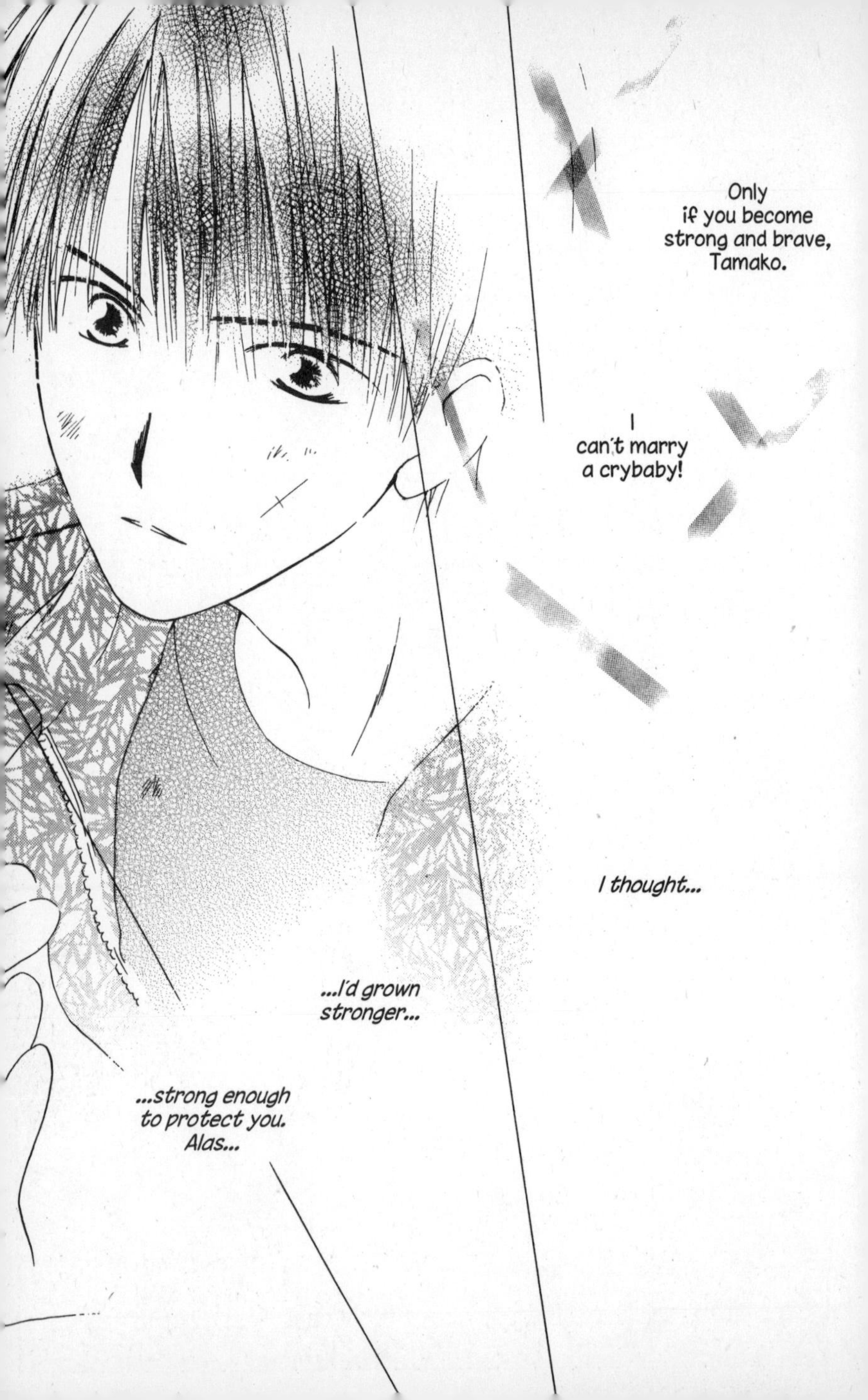
Only if you become strong and brave, Tamako.
I can't marry a crybaby!
I thought...
...I'd grown stronger...
...strong enough to protect you. Alas...

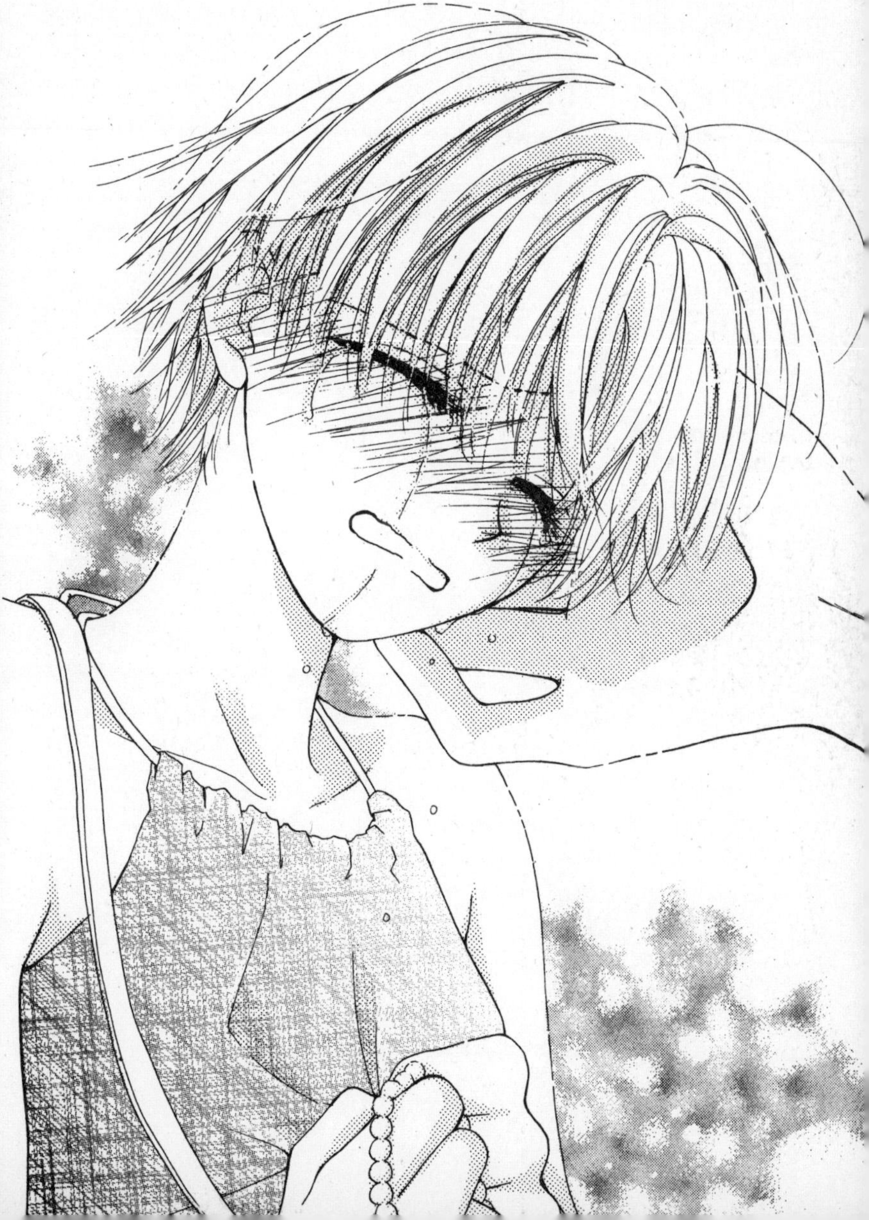

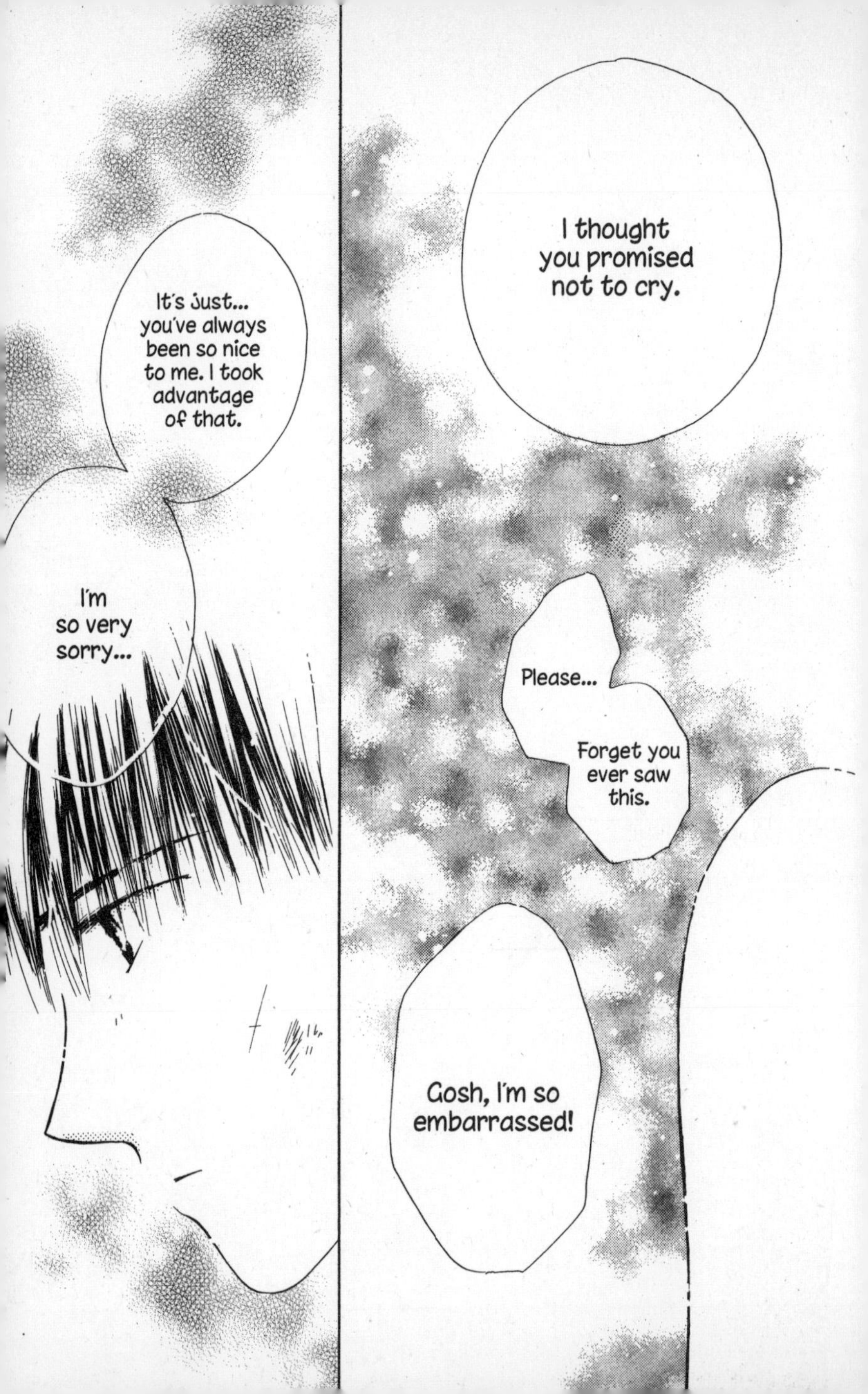
I thought you promised not to cry.
Please...
Forget you ever saw this.
Gosh, I'm so embarrassed!
It's just... you've always been so nice to me. I took advantage of that.
I'm so very sorry...

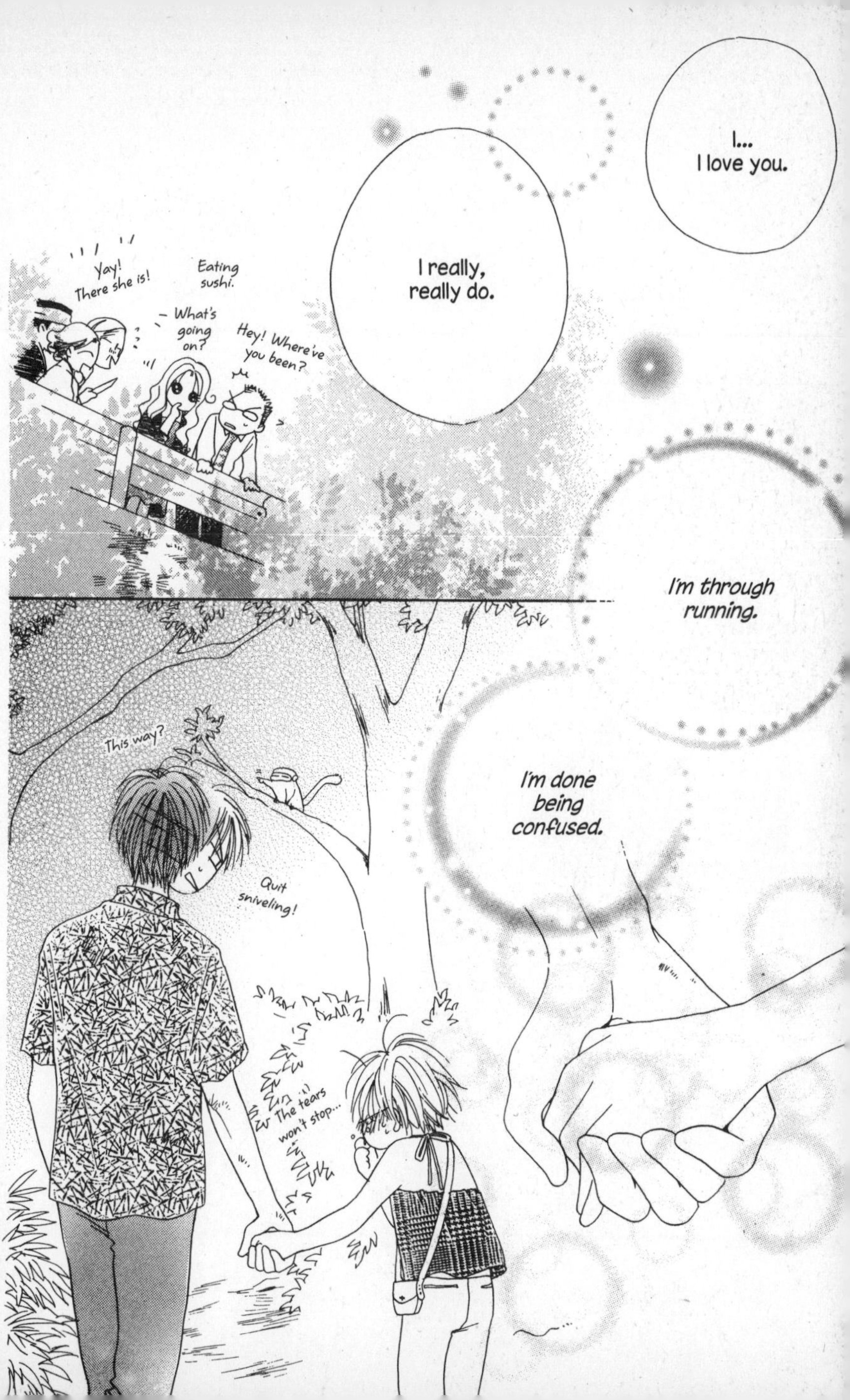
I... I love you.
I really, really do.
I'm through running.
I'm done being confused.
Yay! There she is!
Eating sushi.
What's going on?
Hey! Where've you been?
This way?
Quit sniveling!
The tears won't stop...

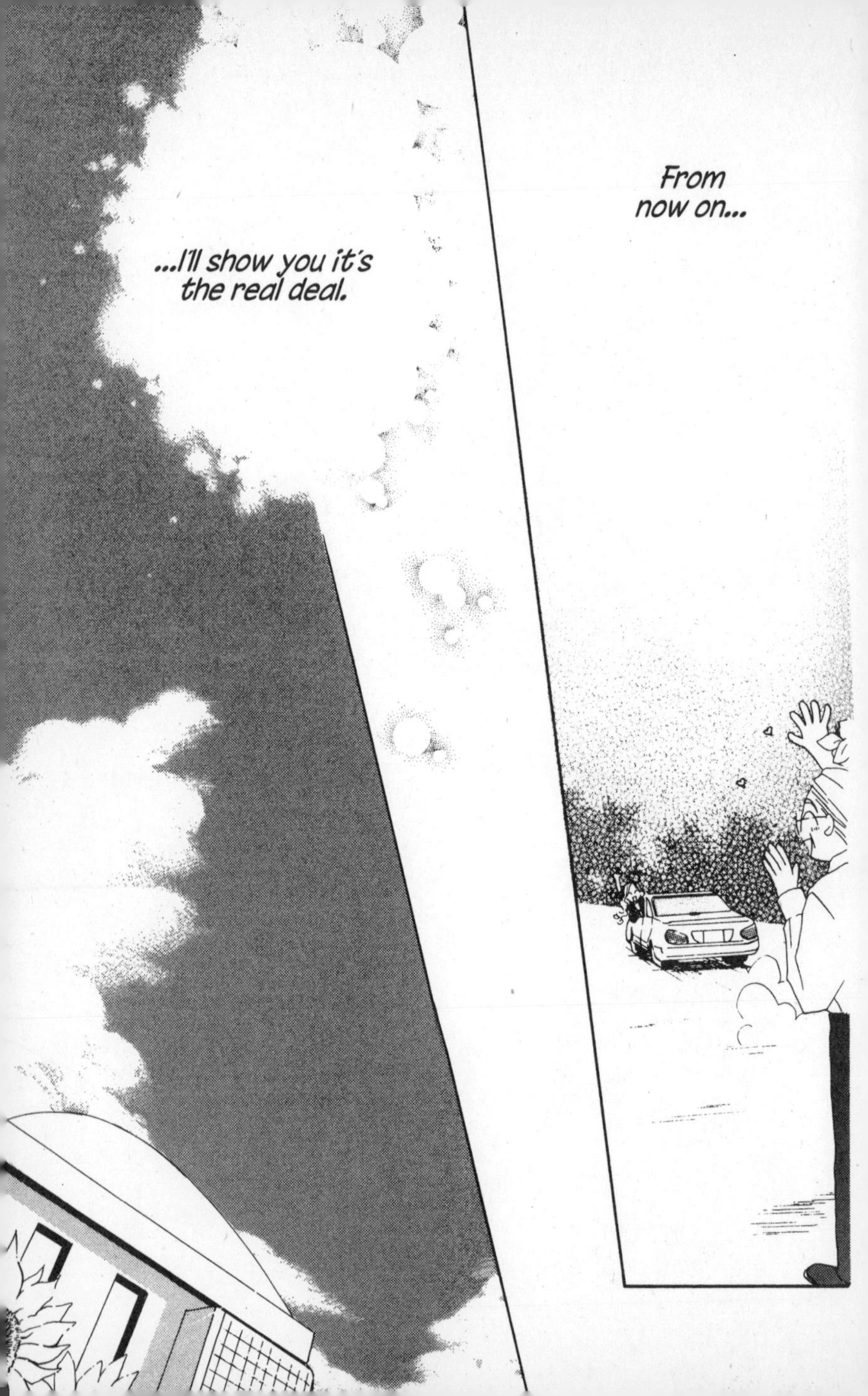
From now on...
...I'll show you it's the real deal.

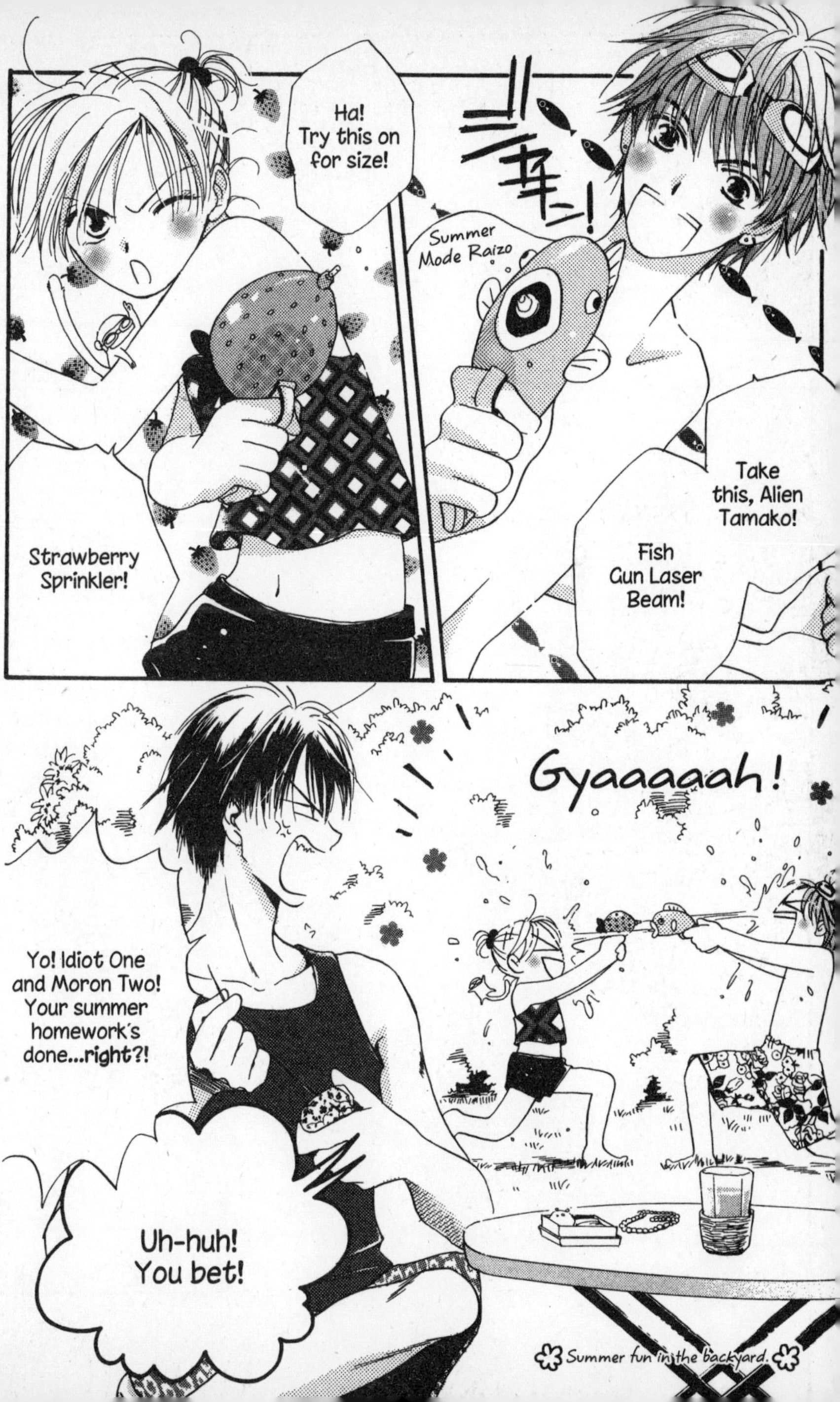
Summer Mode Raizo
Take this, Alien Tamako!
Fish Gun Laser Beam!
Ha! Try this on for size!
Strawberry Sprinkler!
Gyaaaaah!
Yo! Idiot One and Moron Two! Your summer homework's done...right?!
Uh-huh! You bet!
Summer fun in the backyard.

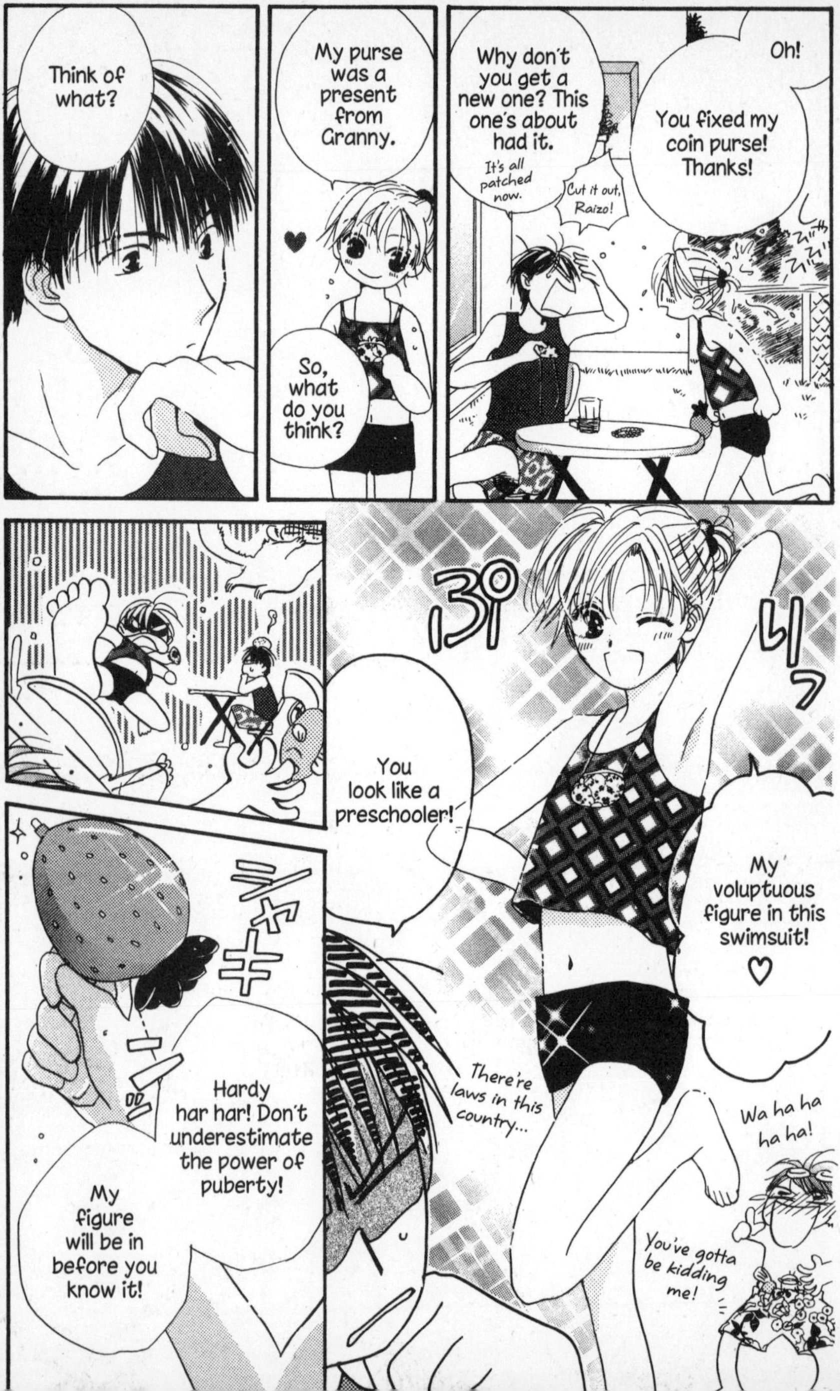
Oh!
You fixed my coin purse! Thanks!
Why don't you get a new one? This one's about had it.
It's all patched now.
Cut it out, Raizo!
My purse was a present from Granny.
So, what do you think?
Think of what?
My voluptuous figure in this swimsuit! ♡
You look like a preschooler!
Wa ha ha ha ha!
There're laws in this country...
You've gotta be kidding me!
Hardy har har! Don't underestimate the power of puberty!
My figure will be in before you know it!

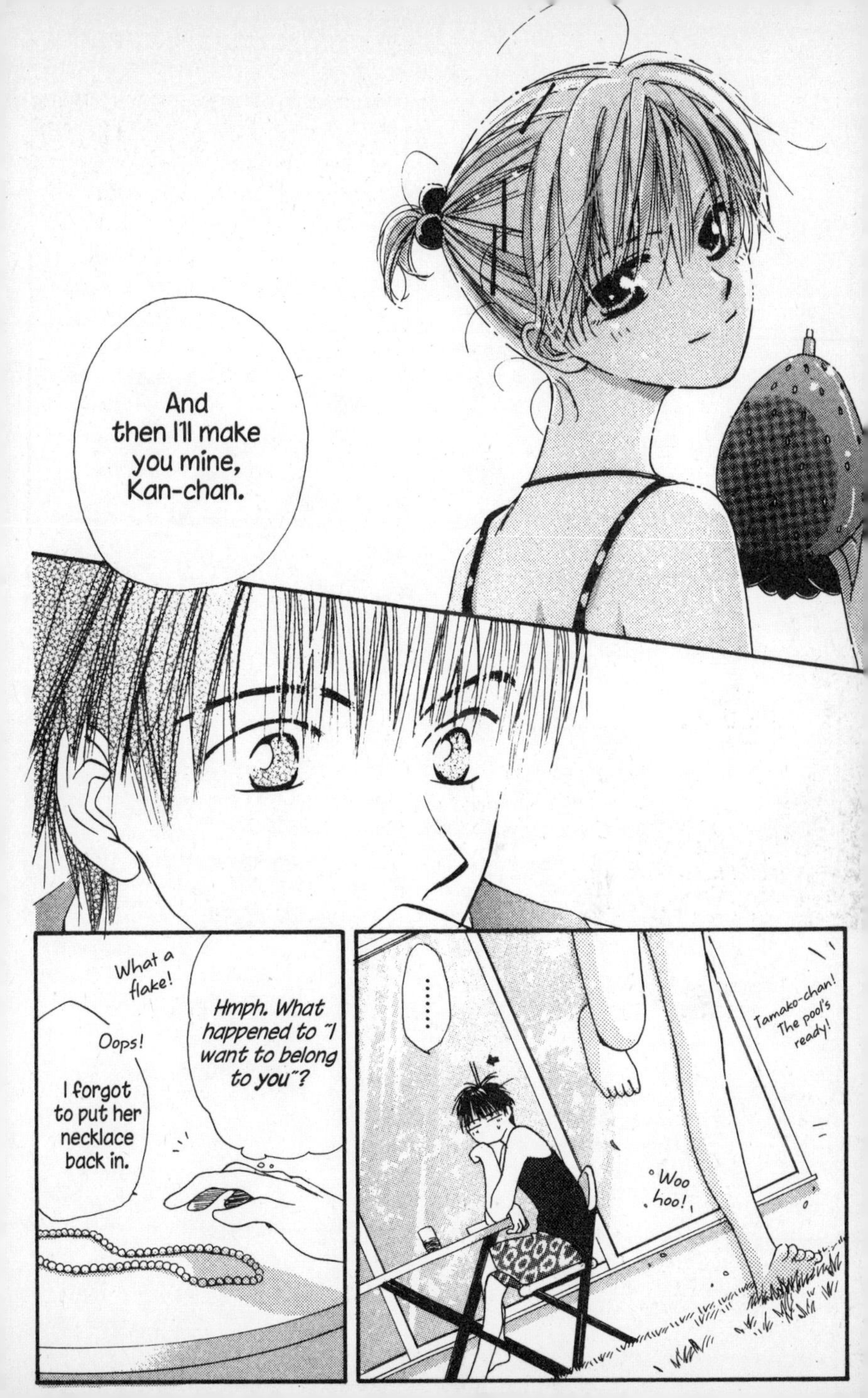
And then I'll make you mine, Kan-chan.
Tamako-chan! The pool's ready!
......
Woo hoo!
Hmph. What happened to "I want to belong to you"?
What a flake!
Oops!
I forgot to put her necklace back in.

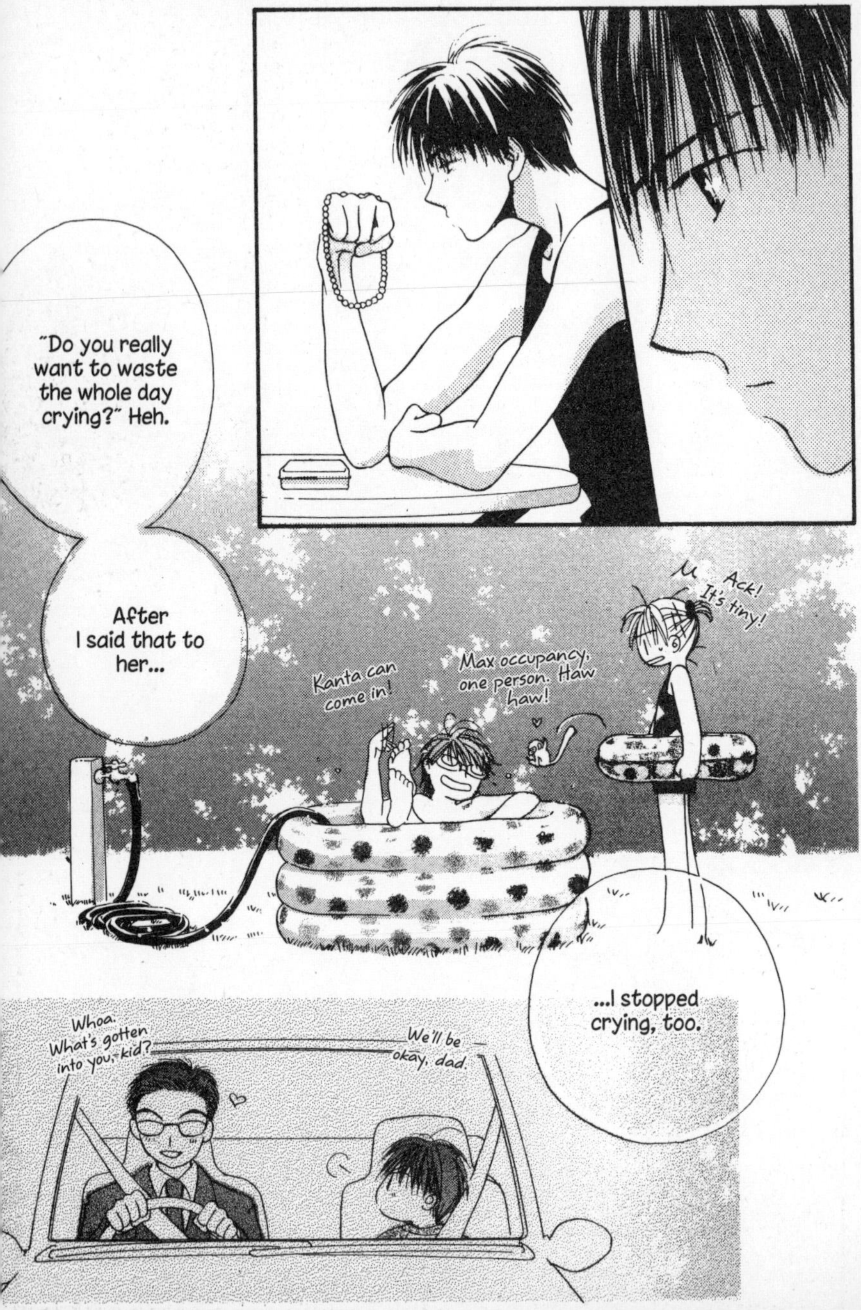
"Do you really want to waste the whole day crying?" Heh.
After I said that to her...
Ack! It's tiny!
Max occupancy, one person. Haw haw!
Kanta can come in!
...I stopped crying, too.
We'll be okay, dad.
Whoa. What's gotten into you, kid?

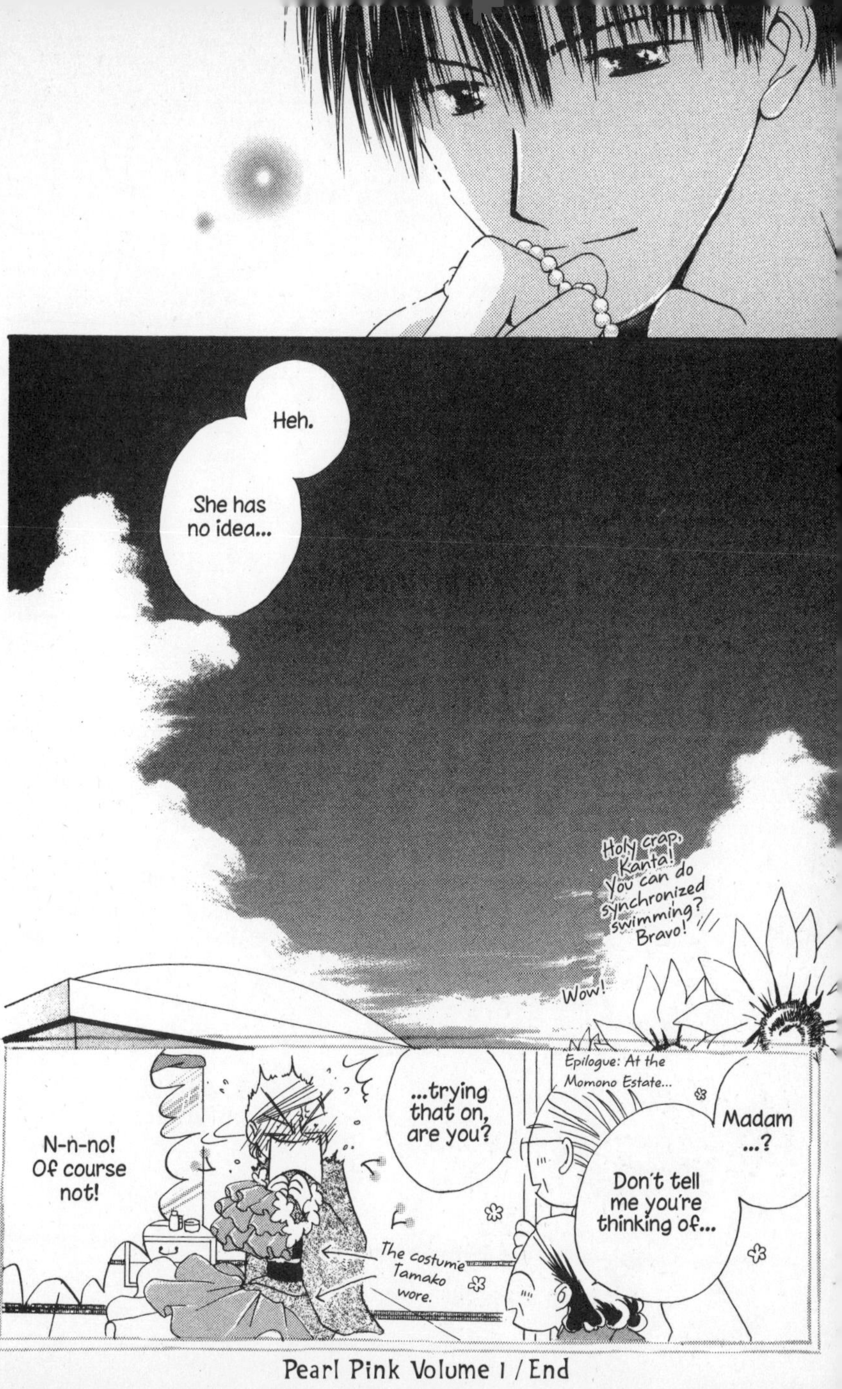
Heh.
She has no idea...
Holy crap, Kanta! You can do synchronized swimming? Bravo!
Wow!
Epilogue: At the Momono Estate...
Madam ...?
Don't tell me you're thinking of...
...trying that on, are you?
The costume Tamako wore.
N-n-no! Of course not!

Pearl Pink Volume 1 / End

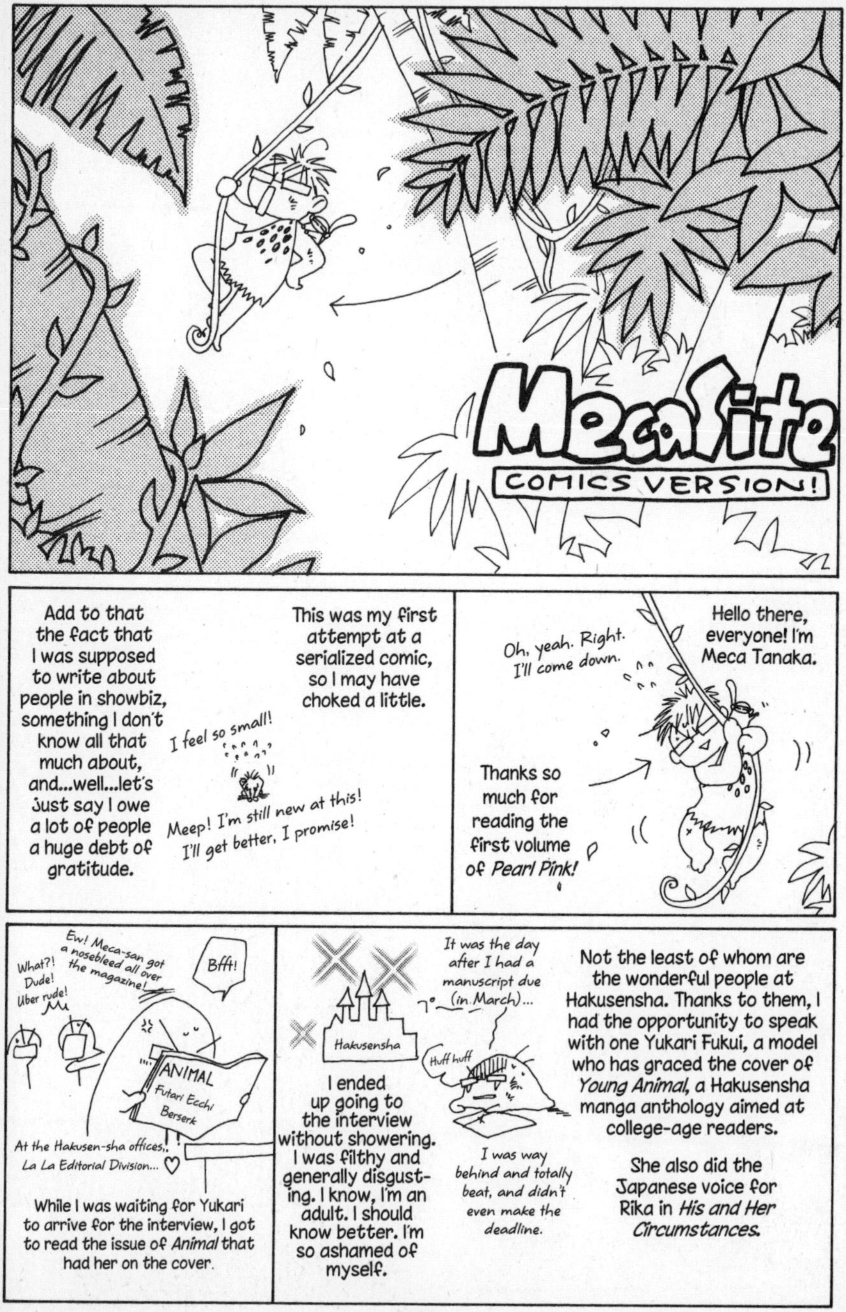

MecaSite
COMICS VERSION!
Hello there, everyone! I'm Meca Tanaka.
Oh, yeah. Right. I'll come down.
Thanks so much for reading the first volume of *Pearl Pink!*
This was my first attempt at a serialized comic, so I may have choked a little.
I feel so small!
Meep! I'm still new at this! I'll get better, I promise!
Add to that the fact that I was supposed to write about people in showbiz, something I don't know all that much about, and...well...let's just say I owe a lot of people a huge debt of gratitude.
Not the least of whom are the wonderful people at Hakusensha. Thanks to them, I had the opportunity to speak with one Yukari Fukui, a model who has graced the cover of *Young Animal,* a Hakusensha manga anthology aimed at college-age readers.
She also did the Japanese voice for Rika in *His and Her Circumstances.*
It was the day after I had a manuscript due (in March)...
Hakusensha
Huff huff
I was way behind and totally beat, and didn't even make the deadline.
I ended up going to the interview without showering. I was filthy and generally disgusting. I know, I'm an adult. I should know better. I'm so ashamed of myself.
Bfft!
Ew! Meca-san got a nosebleed all over the magazine!
What?! Dude! Uber rude!
ANIMAL
Futari Ecchi
Berserk
At the Hakusen-sha offices.. La La Editorial Division... ♡
While I was waiting for Yukari to arrive for the interview, I got to read the issue of *Animal* that had her on the cover.

Mecasite COMICS VERSION!

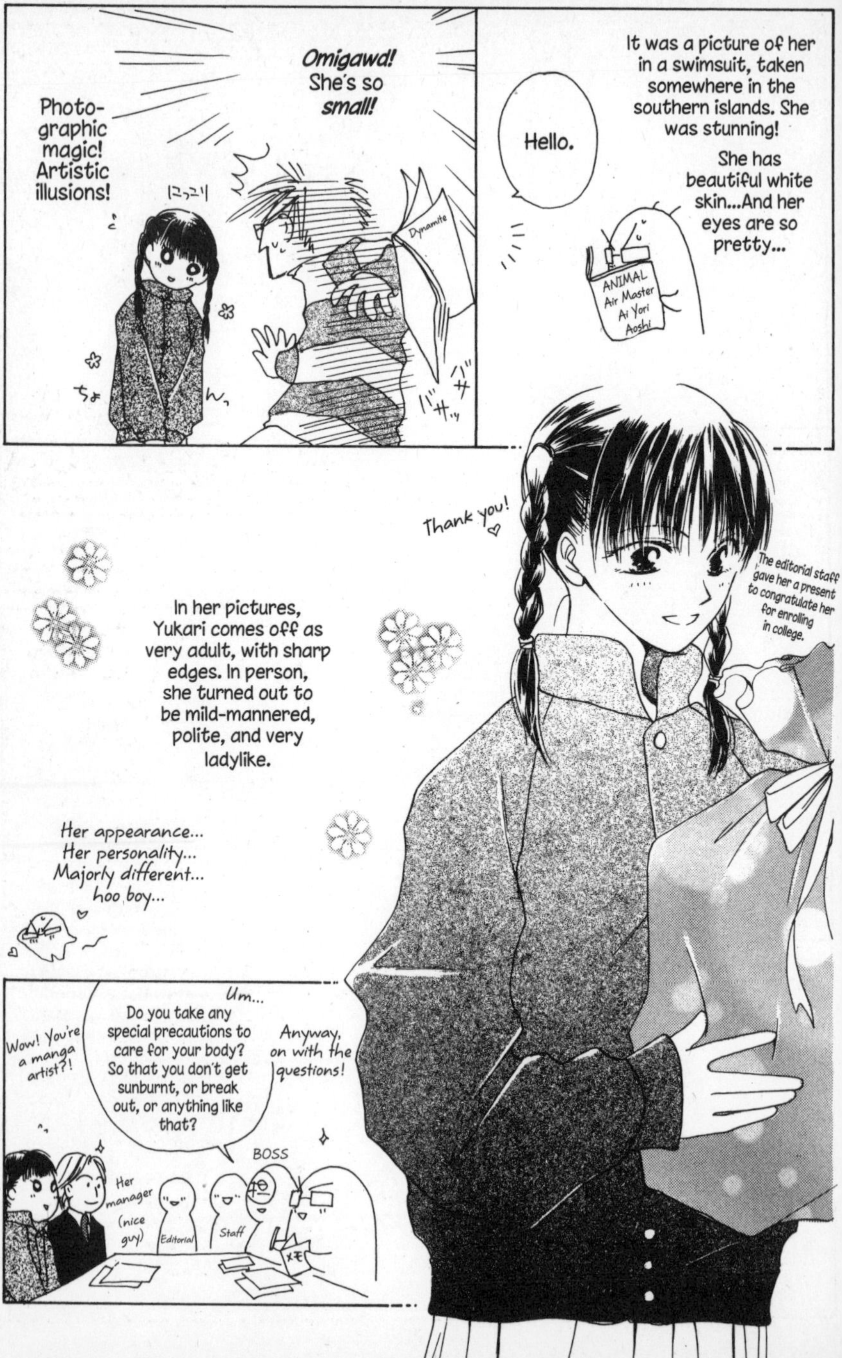

It was a picture of her in a swimsuit, taken somewhere in the southern islands. She was stunning!
She has beautiful white skin...And her eyes are so pretty...
Hello.
ANIMAL Air Master Ai Yori Aoshi
Omigawd! She's so small!
Dynamite
Photo-graphic magic! Artistic illusions!
The editorial staff gave her a present to congratulate her for enrolling in college.
Thank you!
In her pictures, Yukari comes off as very adult, with sharp edges. In person, she turned out to be mild-mannered, polite, and very ladylike.
Her appearance... Her personality... Majorly different... hoo boy...
Anyway, on with the questions!
Um...
Do you take any special precautions to care for your body? So that you don't get sunburnt, or break out, or anything like that?
Wow! You're a manga artist?!
BOSS
Staff
Editorial
Her manager (nice guy)
She is such a sweet girl!

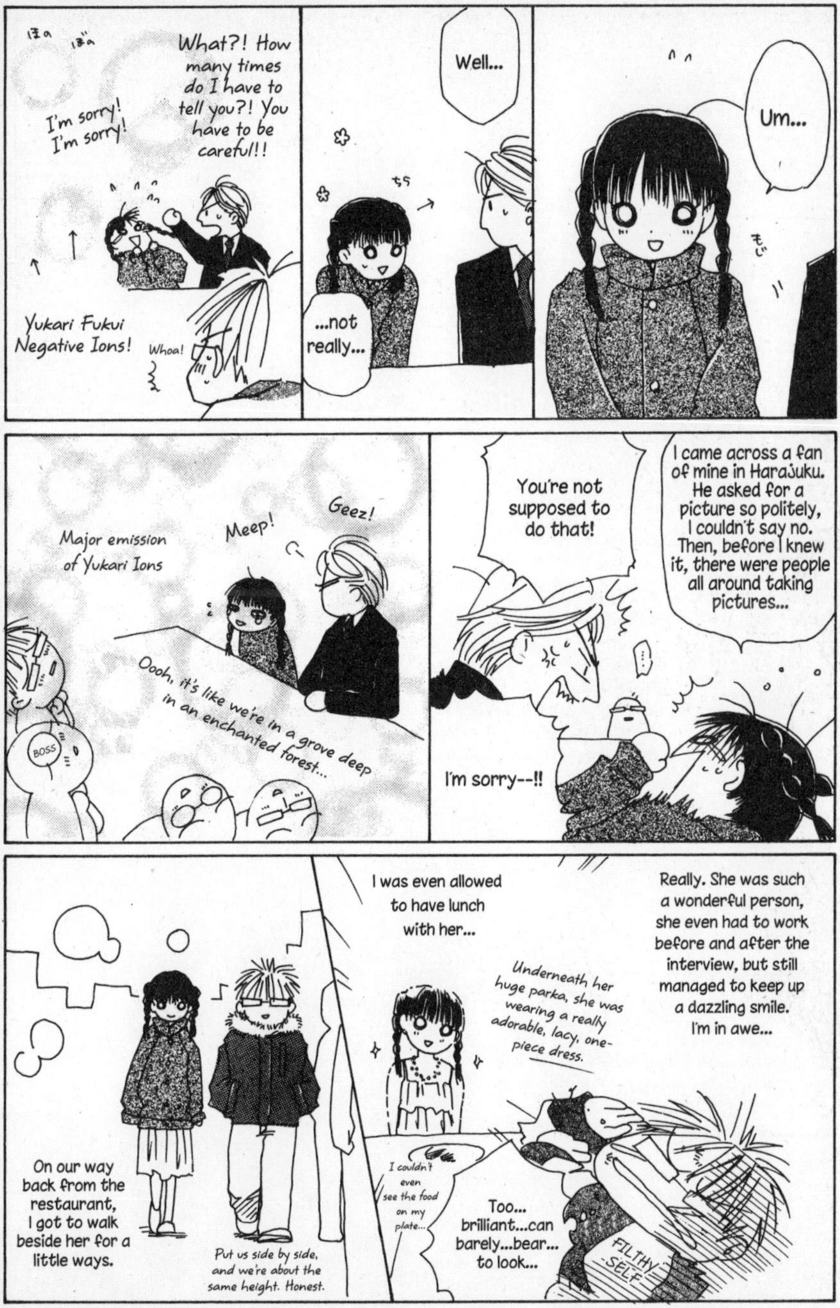
Um...
Well...
...not really...
What?! How many times do I have to tell you?! You have to be careful!!
I'm sorry! I'm sorry!
Yukari Fukui Negative Ions!
Whoa!
I came across a fan of mine in Harajuku. He asked for a picture so politely, I couldn't say no. Then, before I knew it, there were people all around taking pictures...
You're not supposed to do that!
I'm sorry--!!
Geez!
Meep!
Major emission of Yukari Ions
BOSS
Oooh, it's like we're in a grove deep in an enchanted forest...
Really. She was such a wonderful person, she even had to work before and after the interview, but still managed to keep up a dazzling smile. I'm in awe...
I was even allowed to have lunch with her...
Underneath her huge parka, she was wearing a really adorable, lacy, one-piece dress.
I couldn't even see the food on my plate...
Too... brilliant...can barely...bear... to look...
FILTHY SELF
On our way back from the restaurant, I got to walk beside her for a little ways.
Put us side by side, and we're about the same height. Honest.

Mecasite COMICS VERSION!

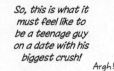

So, this is what it must feel like to be a teenage guy on a date with his biggest crush!

Argh!

Oh man oh man oh man...I want to ask if I can hold her hand! But I'm afraid that if I touch her, she'll vanish!

In the end, I couldn't even scrape up the guts to talk to her. I'm so pathetic...!

She did shake my hand at the close of the interview, though! Woo-hoo!

I was brain dead and dead tired from my deadline crunch, but she was still so nice to me... Every time I looked at her, I could almost see angel's wings sprouting out of her back. Thank you so much, Yukari!

Yukari Fukui is an actress, model, and voice actor for TV shows and magazines of all kinds. If you ever see her around, please join me in cheering her on!

Alrighty! On with the character bios!

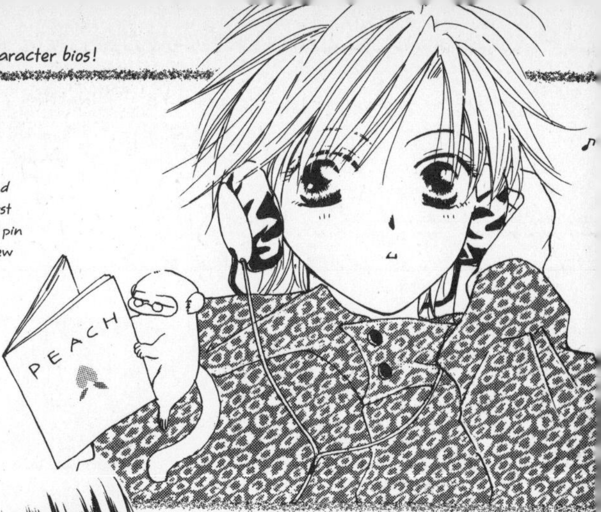
PEACH

Tamako Momono
Born in: January
Blood type: O

The heroine of the story. In the panic and general mass confusion of starting my first serial manga, I never really managed to pin down her personality. (This is nothing new when it comes to my heroines.)

Both her body and her personality will grow and mature across the series. Perhaps the genes she got from her mother will lead her towards a career in acting?
Kanta the monkey got added on thanks to a play on words from an old proverb.

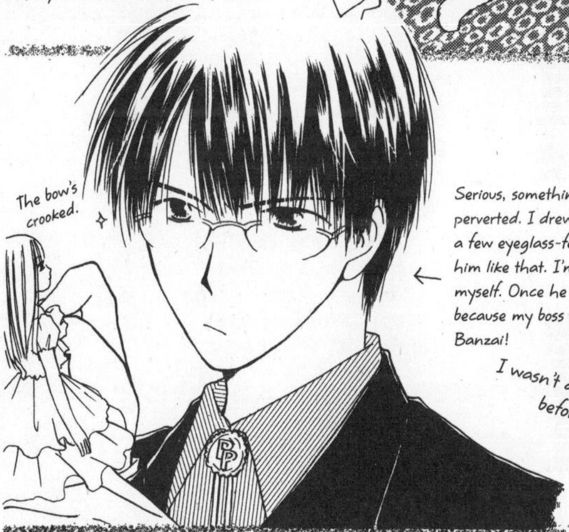
The bow's crooked.

Kanji Inui
Born in: April
Blood type: A

Serious, something of a busybody, and secretly a little perverted. I drew him with glasses on because there are a few eyeglass-fetishists out there who absolutely love him like that. I'm pretty fond of glasses-wearing Kanji myself. Once he takes them off, he's pretty masculine, because my boss finally lifted the No-Macho Rule! Banzai!

I wasn't allowed to before.

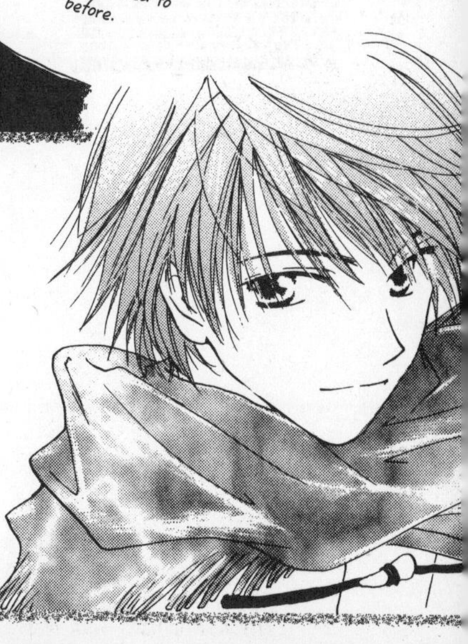

Raizo Hishikawa
Born in: September
Blood type: B

At first, I set him up to be a lot more of a self-centered, high-and-mighty type. But he was too hard to write like that (...) so I changed him into the somewhat selfish kind of guy that easily gets carried away with things. The result: I ended up liking him more than the two "main" characters... (Hey! That's not right!) Next time you see him take center stage, that's just me playing favorites.

Shinju (Mako) Momono & Kinichi Inui
Crazy parents are so much fun to draw.
Aaah...and I miss you...like the deserts miss the rain...

THANKS!

Mr. Yamamoto
Child Planet
Naoko Umeda
Kojima Uchida
Hitomi Yasudachi
Kaori Hayashi
Yukari Fukui
Versatile Entertainment
My Boss
Everyone else who helped and supported me along the way
...and last, but not least, you, who deigned to read the finished product. THANK YOU!!

Read in this order.

Onigiri Girl

Can I help you with dinner?
Okay...
Give everybody a helping of rice.
Done!
Well...I guess that's okay...Give everybody a helping of this next.
Steamed potatoes and vegetables.
Okay!
You stuffed it in the middle of the onigiri?!
30% bigger

That's all for now.
See you around!

Meca Tanaka

Mecasite COMICS VERSION!/End

NEXT iSSUE:

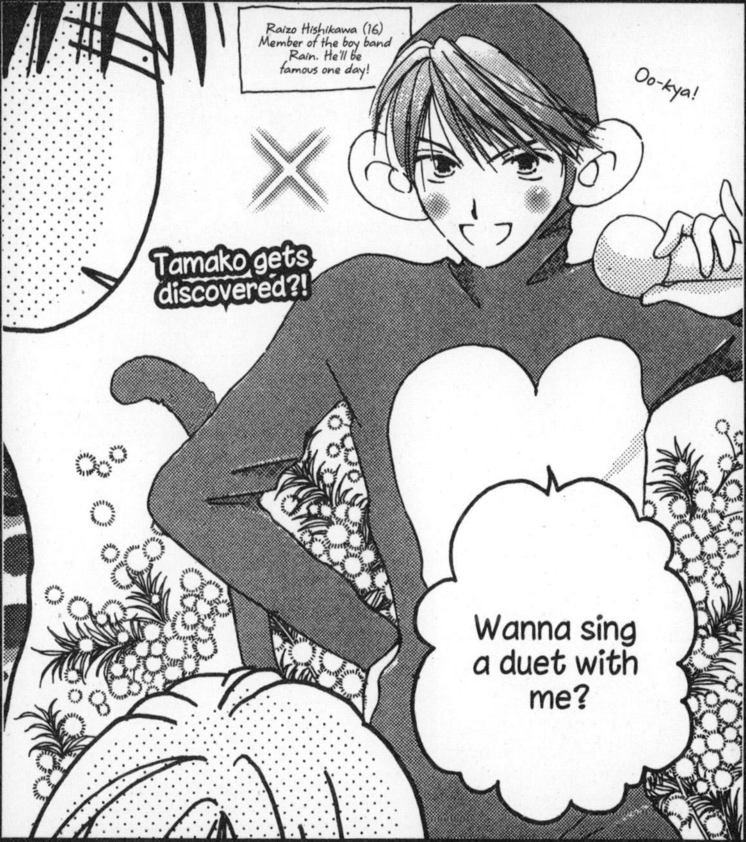
Oo-kya!
Raizo Hishikawa (16) Member of the boy band Rain. He'll be famous one day!
Wanna sing a duet with me?
Tamako gets discovered?!

NOTE: Raizo is an idol.

Loads of Fun is coming your way in volume two of

pearl pink

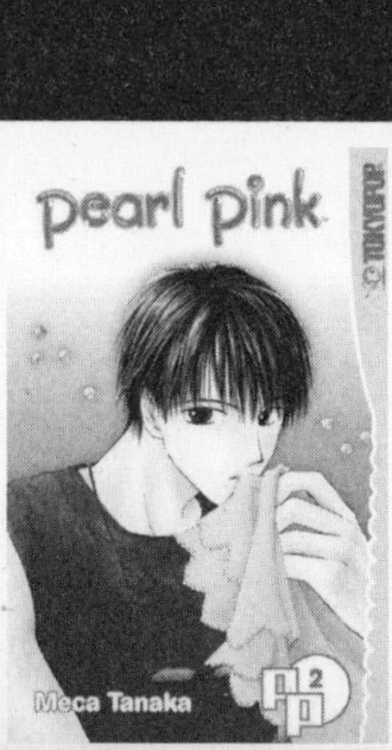
pearl pink
Meca Tanaka

With Tamako back at the Inui home, you'd think things would fall back into place. It couldn't be further from the truth! A Christmas Eve party falls apart before Tamako's very eyes. The two remaining members of Rain make their well-timed debut. And an innocent performance in the park makes Tamako realize...she may be destined for stardom!

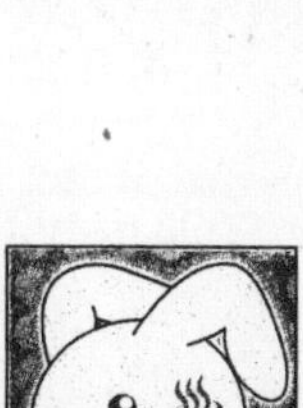

STOP!

This is the back of the book.
You wouldn't want to spoil a great ending!

This book is printed "manga-style," in the authentic Japanese right-to-left format. Since none of the artwork has been flipped or altered, readers get to experience the story just as the creator intended. You've been asking for it, so TOKYOPOP® delivered: authentic, hot-off-the-press, and far more fun!

DIRECTIONS

If this is your first time reading manga-style, here's a quick guide to help you understand how it works.

It's easy... just start in the top right panel and follow the numbers. Have fun, and look for more 100% authentic manga from TOKYOPOP®!

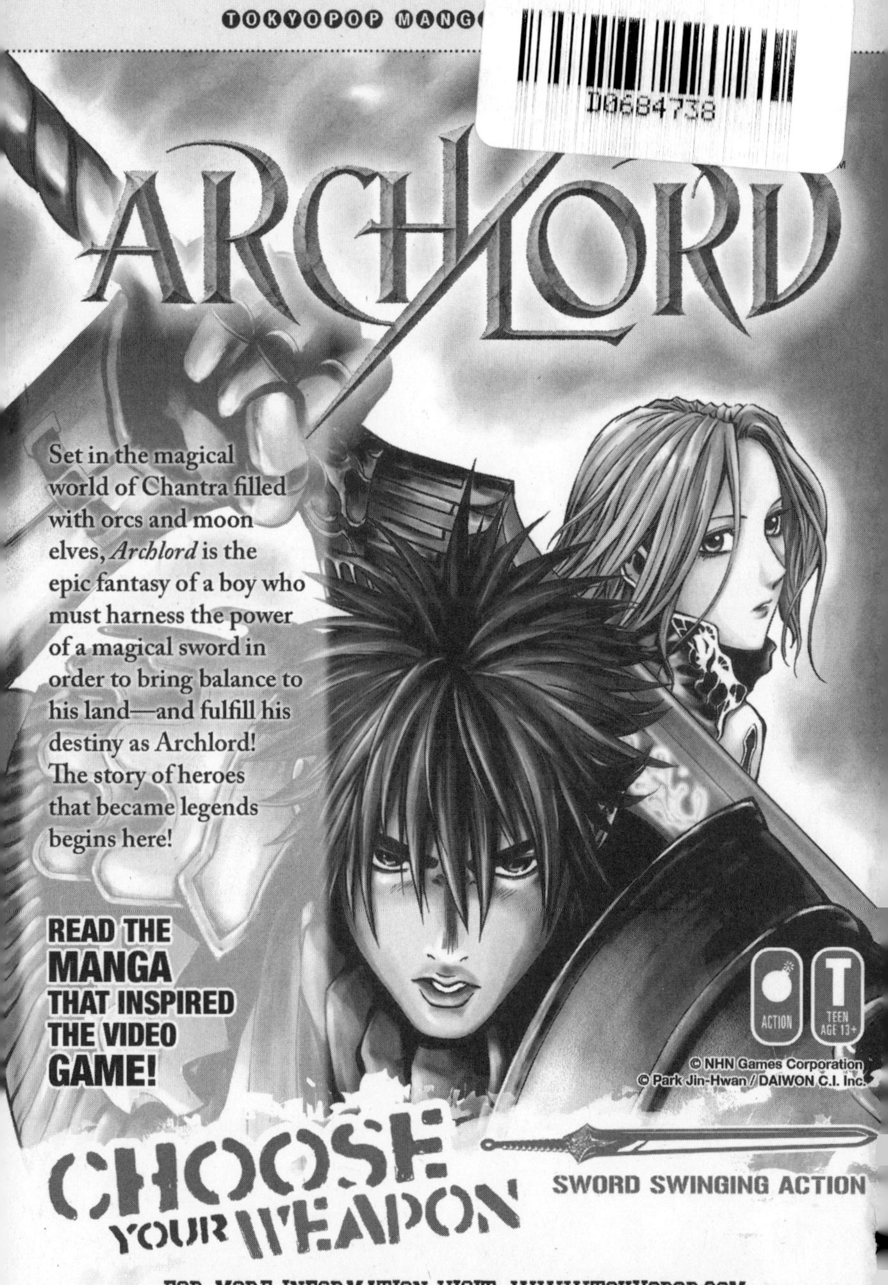
TOKYOPOP MANGA
ARCHLORD
Set in the magical world of Chantra filled with orcs and moon elves, *Archlord* is the epic fantasy of a boy who must harness the power of a magical sword in order to bring balance to his land—and fulfill his destiny as Archlord! The story of heroes that became legends begins here!
READ THE MANGA THAT INSPIRED THE VIDEO GAME!
ACTION
T TEEN AGE 13+
© NHN Games Corporation
© Park Jin-Hwan / DAIWON C.I. Inc.
CHOOSE YOUR WEAPON
SWORD SWINGING ACTION
FOR MORE INFORMATION VISIT: WWW.TOKYOPOP.COM